Degree Gradation of Verbs

Jens Fleischhauer

d|u|p

Hana Filip, Peter Indefrey, Laura Kallmeyer,
Sebastian Löbner, Gerhard Schurz & Robert D. Van Valin, Jr.
(eds.)

Dissertations in Language and Cognition

2

Jens Fleischhauer

2016

Degree Gradation of Verbs

d|u|p

**Bibliografische Information
der Deutschen Nationalbibliothek**
Die Deutsche Nationalbibliothek verzeichnet diese Publikation in der Deutschen Nationalbibliografie; detaillierte bibliografische Daten sind im Internet über http://dnb.dnb.de abrufbar.

D 61

© düsseldorf university press, Düsseldorf 2016
http://www.dupress.de
Einbandgestaltung: Doris Gerland, Christian Horn, Albert Ortmann
Satz: Jens Fleischhauer, LaTeX
Herstellung: docupoint GmbH, Barleben

Gesetzt aus der Linux Libertine
ISBN 978-3-95758-025-2

Für Angela und Jannes

Contents

1	**Introduction**	**1**
2	**Gradation and degree expressions**	**11**
	2.1 Gradation	12
	2.2 Scales	25
	2.3 Degree expressions	36
	2.4 Cross-categorical distribution of degree expressions	45
	2.4.1 Degree expression continuum	45
	2.4.2 Cross-linguistic distribution of degree expressions	50
	2.5 Conclusion	59
3	**Verb classification**	**61**
	3.1 Semantic verb classes	62
	3.2 Event structure	66
	3.2.1 Aktionsart	67
	3.2.2 Predicate decomposition	77
	3.3 Manner/result complementarity	83
	3.4 Degree verbs	92
	3.4.1 Tenny (2000) on 'measure adverbs'	93
	3.4.2 Tsujimura's (2001) analysis of Japanese degree verbs	96
	3.5 Conclusion	101
4	**Syntax of verb gradation**	**103**
	4.1 Syntactic analysis of adverbial *beaucoup*	104
	4.1.1 Doetjes (1997)	105
	4.1.2 Vecchiato (1997)	108
	4.1.3 Preliminary observations of the syntactic ambiguity of *beaucoup*	112
	4.2 Role & Reference Grammar	115

	4.3	Scope relationships	123
		4.3.1 Grammatical aspect in German, French, and Russian	124
		4.3.2 Grammatical aspect and verb gradation	129
	4.4	Syntactic analysis of degree expressions	133
		4.4.1 Syntactic analysis of verb gradation	133
		4.4.2 Syntax of adnominal degree expressions	137
	4.5	Conclusion	143
5	**Gradable predicates and intensifiers**		**145**
	5.1	Gradable adjectives	145
		5.1.1 Kennedy & McNally (2005a)	146
		5.1.2 Löbner (1990)	151
	5.2	Semantic type of degree expressions	155
		5.2.1 Quantification vs. modification	156
		5.2.2 Classification of degree expressions	160
	5.3	Semantics of intensifiers	164
	5.4	Degrees, scales, and verbs	170
	5.5	Conclusion	178
6	**Change of state verbs**		**179**
	6.1	Change of state verbs – a general perspective	179
	6.2	Argument realization	186
	6.3	Scalar changes and the lexicalization of scales	192
	6.4	Scalar analysis of telicity	200
	6.5	Degree gradation of change of state verbs	207
		6.5.1 Degree gradation of degree achievements	207
		6.5.2 Degree gradation of accomplishments	214
	6.6	Degree gradation and telicity	219
	6.7	Conclusion	225
7	**Verbs of emission**		**227**
	7.1	Emission verbs – a general perspective	227
	7.2	Degree gradation of verbs of smell emission	235
	7.3	Degree gradation of verbs of light emission	242
	7.4	Degree gradation of verbs of sound emission	245
	7.5	Degree gradation of verbs of substance emission	251
	7.6	Conclusion	261

8	**Experiencer verbs**		**263**
	8.1	Experiencer verbs – a general overview	264
	8.2	Types of experiencer verbs	267
		8.2.1 Subject-experiencer verbs	268
		8.2.2 Object-experiencer verbs	271
	8.3	Degree gradation of experiencer verbs	276
		8.3.1 Degree gradation of subject-experiencer verbs . . .	277
		8.3.2 Degree gradation of object-experiencer verbs . . .	280
	8.4	Conclusion	285
9	**Gradation, aspect, and telicity**		**287**
	9.1	Compositional patterns	287
		9.1.1 Changes, emissions, and experiences	287
		9.1.2 Verbs expressing divergence & similarity	289
		9.1.3 Erratic verbs	293
		9.1.4 Gradable action verbs	296
		9.1.5 Similarities in the compositional patterns	297
	9.2	Subcompositionality of verbal degree gradation	299
	9.3	Event-dependent degree gradation	304
	9.4	Conclusion	313
10	**General conclusions**		**315**

Appendix: Language data   **325**

References   **345**

Index   **372**

List of Figures

1	Scale partitioning by degree expressions	43
2	Partial classification of adverbs	44
3	Constituent and operator structure in RRG	116
4	Aspect typology	124
5	Syntactic representation of degree gradation in German	135
6	Syntactic representation of extent gradation in German	135
7	Syntactic representation of degree gradation in French	136
8	Syntactic representation of extent gradation in French	137
9	Syntactic representation of complex NP	142
10	Representation of phase quantifiers	153
11	Types of degree expressions	161
12	Scale partitioning by *sehr*	165
13	Relationship between unfolding events and increasing degrees	306

List of Tables

1	Classification of degree expressions	41
2	Degree expression continuum for French and German	49
3	Degree expression continuum for Persian	50
4	Possible distribution of adverbial degree expressions	51
5	Cross-linguistic distribution of degree expressions used for verb gradation	52
6	Cross-categorical distribution of 'd'- and 'e'-adverbials	54
7	Cross-categorical distribution of 'd/e'-adverbials	55
8	Cross-categorical distribution of degree expressions in 'Swahili-type' languages	58
9	Feature matrix of aktionsart properties	68
10	Scale type and verb class relationship	91
11	Adjective declension in German	140
12	Deadjectival degree achievements and their corresponding adjectival bases	185
13	Typology of scalar (under)specification	196
14	Extended typology of scalar (under)specification	198
15	Types of predicates and their associated types of telos	224
16	Classes of verbs and their associated types of scales	288

List of Abbreviations

ABL	Ablative	NEG	Negation
ABS	Absolutive	NOM	Nominative
ACC	Accusative	NPST	Non-past
ADD	Additive connective	NSUB	Non-subject
ADE	Adessive	OBJ	Object
ADJ	Adjective	PAR	Partitive
AM	Assertive marker	PARC	Participle
ASP	Aspect	PART	Particle
AUX	Auxiliary	PF	Perfective
AV	Actor voice	PL	Plural
CAU	Causative	PREP	Preposition
CL	Clitic	PROC	Process
CLA	Classifier	PROG	Progressive
COM	Completive	PRS	Present
COMP	Comparative	PST	Past
CON	Converb	REAL	Realis
DAT	Dative	REFL	Reflexive
DEC	Declarative	REMPST	Remote past
DEF	Definiteness	RES	Result
DISTR	Distributive	SG	Singular
DPST	Distant past	SJ	Subject case
DS	Different subject	SUB	Subject
E	Exclusive	SUP	Superlative
ERG	Ergative	TNS	Default tense
GEN	Genitive	TOP	Topic
ILL	Illative	UV	Undergoer voice
INCEP	Inceptive	=	Clitization
INE	Inessive		
INTS	Intensifier		
IPS	Impersonal		
LNK	Linker		
LOC	Locative		
NC	Noun class		

1 Introduction

Gradation is usually considered to be a property of adjectives. Gradable adjectives such as *tall* can be used in comparative constructions such as (1a) and license degree expressions such as, for example, *very* (1c), while ungradable ones like *dead* neither allow comparison (1b) nor license degree expressions (1d) without coercing the graded predicate.

(1) English (Germanic < Indo-European)
 a. Peter is taller than Mary.
 b. #Peter is deader than Mary.
 c. Peter is very tall.
 d. #Peter is very dead.

Gradation is often taken to be a prototypical property of adjectives. But it is not limited to adjectives and even if a language does not have a distinct class of adjectives, gradation can be expressed. This can be seen in Choctaw (2), which uses verbs for what other languages express by means of adjectives.

(2) Choctaw (Muskogean; Broadwell 2006, 317)
 Alta chito-fûhna-h-o ikbi-ttook.
 altar big-very-TNS-PARC.DS make-DPST
 'He made a very big altar.'

Gradation of verbs is not restricted to languages that do not have a distinct lexical class of adjectives but is also possible in English (3a) and German (3b). Examples such as (3a) and (b) have received considerably less attention in the linguistic literature than cases like those in (1).

(3) a. He loves his mother very much.
 b. Sie bewundert Thomas Mann sehr.
   she admires   Thomas Mann very
   'She admires Thomas Mann very much.'

1 Introduction

The aim of my thesis is to discuss the notion of verbal degree gradation in more detail. Verbal degree gradation is of particular interest as it interacts on the one hand with the grammatical as well as the lexical aspect, especially telicity, and on the other hand, it raises questions regarding the notion of 'compositionality' and the lexical semantics vs. conceptual knowledge distinction. Two central claims of the thesis are: (i) verbal degree gradation is a subcompositional phenomenon (following Löbner 2012b) and (ii) most gradable verbs are not lexically scalar but the gradation scale is retrieved from the conceptual knowledge associated with the gradable verb.

Subcompositionality means that the interpretation of a single morphosyntactic construction like 'intensifier + verb' cannot be accounted for by a single compositional rule. Rather each semantic class of gradable verbs displays an irreducible compositional pattern of verbal degree gradation. The thesis presents a detailed study of subcompositionality by exploring the degree gradation of three semantic classes of verbs (change of state verbs, verbs of emission, and experiencer verbs) in detail.

Related to subcompositionality is the fact that neither verbs of emission nor experiencer verbs are lexically scalar, i.e., they do not express a scalar predication. A gradation scale can be activated in a degree context by retrieving a suitable attribute like INTENSITY or QUANTITY from the conceptual knowledge associated with the verb. This process is not unconstrained but depends on the meaning components lexically specified by the verb.

The structure of the thesis is as follows: chapter 2 is concerned with the notion of 'gradation.' It starts with a general discussion of the notion of 'gradation' and defines it as any linguistic process comparing two or more degrees. Verb gradation is introduced as a subtype of gradation that is concerned with verbs. Grading verbs can either express the specification of a degree 'inherent' to the verb (degree gradation) or specify a gradable property of the event such as its duration or frequency (extent gradation). This is shown in (4) for English. In (a) *a lot* indicates the intensity of the feeling of the subject referent, whereas in (b) *a lot* merely reflects the frequency of the subject referent's going to the cinema.

(4)   a.   *He misses her a lot.*
       b.   *He went to the cinema a lot.*

Both German and Russian use different degree expressions for extent and degree gradation, whereas French uses one and the same adverbial[1] for both subtypes of verb gradation. In German *sehr*, as shown in (3b), is used for degree gradation but *viel* 'much' for extent gradation (5).

(5) Er geht viel ins   Kino.
     he goes much in.the cinema
     'He goes to the cinema a lot.'

Extent intensifiers are also used as adnominal quantity expressions like in the German examples in (6).

(6) a. *viel   Wasser*
         much water
         'much water'
     b. *viele Bücher*
         many books
         'many books'

The contrast between the examples discussed above prompts an investigation of both the cross-categorical and the cross-linguistic distribution of degree expressions at the end of the chapter. The limited typological study will reveal that we only find a small set of distributional patterns which do not seem to be random but rather require a further explanation. Before turning to this limited typological study, the very basic notion of a 'scale' is introduced. A scale is a linearly ordered set of values of a measurement dimension and gradation involves establishing a relation between two or more degrees on such a scale. One of these degrees is a comparison degree introduced by degree expressions like English *very* or German *sehr*. Even though the chapter focuses on gradation and especially verb gradation from a general perspective, the research topic of the thesis is limited to verbal degree gradation as it is more closely related to the lexical semantics of the graded verbs than verbal extent gradation is.

Degree expressions are merely one side of verb gradation, the other one is verbs. Chapter 3 deals with verbs from a general perspective and pro-

---

[1] I am analyzing degree expressions such as German *sehr* and *viel* as adverbials rather than adverbs. The reason is that these are adverbially used adjectives, as I argue in chapter 2.

vides some background for the later chapters. Several classifications of verb are discussed, starting with Levin's (1993) semantic verb classes. Later on, an event structural classification and also the manner/result dichotomy are discussed. The chapter leads to the question whether degree gradability of verbs is dependent on one of these classifications. It will turn out that gradability is independent from the semantic features that are used in the abovementioned verb classifications.

Chapter 4 puts the focus on the syntactic realization of verb gradation. The chapter is concerned with the cross-categorical and cross-linguistic distribution of degree expressions and starts with the question of how the difference between extent and degree gradation arises in languages such as French which uses one and the same degree expression for both types of verb gradation (7).

(7) French (Romance < Indo-European)
    a. *Il aime beaucoup cette langue.*
        he loves a lot   this language
        'He loves this language very much.'
    b. *Il va beaucoup au cinema.*
        he goes a lot   to.the cinema
        'He goes to the movies a lot.'

After discussing previous accounts on French *beaucoup* 'a lot,' it is shown that *beaucoup* exhibits syntactic differences depending on whether it is used for extent or degree gradation. The interpretation of beaucoup is constrained by its syntactic position. The grammatical framework for the syntactic analysis is Role & Reference Grammar (RRG; Van Valin & LaPolla 1997, Van Valin 2005). Essential for the syntactic analysis of verb gradation are scope relationships between adverbial degree expressions and grammatical operators, especially grammatical aspect. Grammatical aspect affects the interpretation of some classes of gradable verbs (8). In (a) the intensifier specifies the total amount of change, as the sentence licenses a perfective reading. Sentence (b) has a progressive interpretation and *sehr* indicates the amount at a certain stage of the event.

(8)   a. *Der Riss hat sich sehr verbreitert.*
          the crack has REFL very widened
          'The crack has widened a lot.'

b. *Der Riss ist sich sehr am Verbreitern.*
　　the crack is REFL very at.the widening
　　'The crack is widening a lot.'

Examples like those in (8) allow determining the syntactical realization of extent and degree intensifiers in relation to aspectual operators. Hence, a discussion of verbal aspect, basically from its morphosyntactic side, will be part of that chapter. The discussion will show that both types of verb gradation are related to different syntactic layers. Degree intensifiers are related to the nucleus layer and modify the predicate, whereas extent intensifiers are realized at the core layer at which the event is syntactically expressed. Furthermore, the analysis will show that degree gradation is uniformly expressed across languages, irrespective of whether they use different adverbials for degree and extent gradation, like German and Russian, or not – as in the case of French. Finally, the chapter provides a syntactic explanation for the distributional patterns of degree expressions that emerged from the typological investigation in chapter 2.

After discussing the syntax of verb gradation, the relevant semantic background is discussed in chapter 5. The literature on gradable expressions mostly focuses on gradable adjectives; therefore gradable adjectives provide the starting point of the discussion. After discussing gradable adjectives and the basis of degree-based analyses, degree expressions are put in focus. Based on the work of Kennedy & McNally (2005b) it will be shown that degree expressions are heterogeneous and are of various semantic types. Intensifiers, which are the relevant class of degree expressions for the thesis, are adjectival as well as adverbial modifiers. The semantics of these degree expressions is discussed thereafter. A central topic will be the differences between adjectival and verbal degree gradation. First, whereas a strictly compositional analysis for adjectival degree gradation is possible, it is not for verbal degree gradation. Rather, verbal degree gradation is a subcompositional phenomenon Löbner (2012b) that requires different compositional rules for different semantic classes of verbs. Second, adjectives lexically encode scales, whereas most gradable verbs do not. Examples include verbs of emission like *stinken* 'stink,' *bellen* 'bark' or *bluten* 'bleed' as well as experiencer verbs such as *ängstigen* 'frighten,' *fürchten* 'fear' and *amüsieren* 'amuse.' For these verbs I assume that a suitable gradation scale has to be retrieved from the conceptual knowledge associated

1 Introduction

with the verb. It will be shown that this is not an arbitrary process but that only attributes of lexically specified meaning components can be activated.

Chapters 6 to 8 present case studies on change of state verbs (chapter 6), verbs of emission (chapter 7) and experiencer verbs (chapter 8). Each chapter starts with a general discussion of the respective class of verbs. The discussions include the event structural properties of the verbs, their argument realization and also the lexical semantics of the verbs. In the second part, degree gradation of verbs of the respective classes is discussed. For each verb class, the focus is on interaction with certain semantic properties: telicity for change of state verbs, punctuality/iterativity for verbs of emission and agentivity for experiencer verbs. Special focus is put on the notion of 'telicity' in chapter 6, since different degree-based analyses of telicity have been presented in the literature. The discussion will reveal that a telos cannot necessarily be equated with a maximal degree on a scale since telic change of state verbs such as *stabilisieren* 'stabilize' admit degree gradation. Rather, different types of telos need to be distinguished: a maximum telos which is identical to the maximal degree on a scale and a standard telos that marks the onset of an extended result state. Telic change of state verbs that are related to a standard telos admit degree gradation, whereas those related to a maximum telos do not.

Chapter 9 starts with a summary of the compositional patterns identified in chapters 6 to 8 and a discussion of further compositional patterns that show up with other classes of verbs such as action verbs or erratic verbs. A central topic of this chapter is the notion of 'subcompositionality' introduced by Löbner (2012b). After summarizing the various compositional patterns identified for gradable verbs, it can be demonstrated that verbal degree gradation is subcompositional. The reason for subcompositionality is that each semantic verb class shows an irreducible pattern of verbal degree gradation. Hence, even if we have a uniform syntactic construction, we require different rules of semantic composition. The notion of subcompositionality contradicts one of the major assumptions of formal semantics, namely that semantic composition is regular, meaning that for each syntactic construction there is a single rule of interpretation. The central theoretical result of the current dissertation consists in providing further emprirical support for Löbner's notion of subcompositionality and by exploring why verbal degree gradation is a subcompositional phenomenon.

The second part of chapter 9 is concerned with the notion of 'event-dependent degree gradation.' Degree gradation is event-dependent if grammatical aspect, i.e., the view on the event, affects the interpretation of degree gradation. This holds for change of state verbs as well as verbs of substance emission. The semantic feature underlying event-dependent degree gradation is 'incremental change.' Incremental changes are described in terms of a homomorphic mapping between the part structure of the event and the degree of the scale. This homomorphism explains why grammatical aspect affects degree gradation in the case of change of state verbs and verbs of substance emission and it explains why degree gradation leads to a telic interpretation of atelic change of state verbs. An open question at the end will be why degree gradation does not affect the telicity of verbs of substance emission.

Chapter 10 summarizes the relevant findings of the thesis and presents the results of the analysis. It is followed by an appendix to chapter 2.4 that lists data on the cross-linguistic and cross-categorical distribution of degree expressions in different languages.

Finally, a note on the data used in the thesis is required. All data taken from published sources – including the Internet – are indicated as such. I made use of corpora and databases for Russian and German. For Russian, I used the open access Russian National Corpus[2], whereas for German I was able to rely on a database assembled as part of the project 'Verb gradation' (DFG grand LO 454/1) headed by Sebastian Löbner. Russian examples taken from the Russian National Corpus are marked by $^{'R'}$ at the end of the translation, whereas German examples taken from Löbner's database are marked by $^{'G'}$ All examples which are taken neither from a published source nor from a corpus were collected from informants. The list of informants is presented below; I do not again indicate the informants in the main body of the thesis. Also, the German examples which were made up by me have been checked by native speakers, since the data are very subtle. This holds for grammaticality as well as semantic judgments, and if there is huge disagreement, I indicate this in the discussion of the respective examples. Due to the subtlety of the judgments, I decided not to include language data, if it was not possible to check them with more than one native speaker. Exceptions are the distributional data cited in

---

[2] http://www.ruscorpora.ru/en/

chapter 2.4 and the appendix, which in many cases are collected by using one native speaker.

I would like to end this short introduction with some acknowledgements. First, I would like to thank Sebastian Löbner for many things but especially for our many discussions on the topic and for reading and commenting the first draft of the thesis. He has had a major impact on my work and I hope that he finds his ideas, suggestions and criticisms reflected in the thesis. He helped me not to get lost in the data and to find my way through the analysis and I am very thankful for everything he has done for me throughout all the years I have known him.

I also would like to thank my second supervisor Robert D. Van Valin Jr. who helped me with the syntactic analysis of verbal degree gradation and also gave comments on various other aspects of the topic. He made the essential suggestion to do a comparative analysis from which the whole thesis greatly benefited.

Thomas Gamerschlag has been my post-doc mentor since I started working on the topic. He was always open for discussion and also read the first full draft of the thesis. I appreciated his comments and questions very much and it was always fun sharing my ideas and problems with him during the process of writing up and especially finishing the thesis.

Hana Filip and Adrian Czardybon were also very important in the process of writing the thesis. Hana's comments always helped me to make progress and I much appreciated our discussions. Adrian's comments regarding the thesis were much more helpful than he probably might expect. He was always open for discussion or reading a chapter and I was always able to count on his help. I would also like to thank Adrian Czardybon, Koen Van Hooste and especially Nick Quanitmere for proofreading which improved the thesis a lot. Finally, I like to thank Timm Lichte and Friedhelm Sowa for helping me to solve the problems I had with LaTeX. All remaining errors are my own!

I would also like to express my deepest thanks to all the colleagues, whether they are from Düsseldorf or outside of Düsseldorf, who discussed various aspects of the thesis with me: Anja Latrouite, Rainer Osswald, Albert Ortmann, Wiebke Petersen, Willi Geuder, Doris Gerland, Christian Horn, Daniel Schulzek, Lei Li, Tanja Osswald, Katina Bontcheva, Julia Zinova, Younes Samih, Ivo-Pavao Jazbek, Jean-Pierre Koenig, Louise McNally, Berit Gehrke, Andrew Koontz-Garboden, Bernhard Wälchli, Sergej Tatevosov, Pierre Bourreau and Ryan Dux. Also I would like to thank the audiences of the various conferences or colloquia at which I gave presentations related to the thesis topic. Finally, I would like to thank all my informants and colleagues, especially those on Russian and French without whom the comparative part of this thesis would never have been finished: Adrian Czardybon (Polish), Lei Li (Mandarin Chinese), Syuzan Sachliyan (Bulgarian), Sergei Tatevosov (Russian, Tatar), Nikolai Skorolupov (Russian, Estonian), Julia Zinova (Russian), Pavel Sirotkin (Russian), Ekatarina Auer (Russian), Aurelian Jarry (French), Anselm Ter Halle (French), Patrice Soom (French), Alexandra Fischoeder (French), Bernhard Wälchli (Swedish), Liane Ströbele (French, Spanish, Italian), Mine Güven (Turkish), XuPing Li (Wu Chinese), Koen Van Hooste (Dutch), Pia van de Kerkhof (Dutch), Mats Exter (Finnish), Nansalmaa Tsagaan (Khalka Mongolian), Parinaz Maghferat (Persian), Thomas Brochhagen (Spanish), Robert Van Valin Jr. (English), Ryan Dux (English), Ivo-Pavao Jazbec (Croation), Sir Shushan Rana, jr. (Nepali), Yuka Höfler (Japanese), Hideharu Umehara (Japanese), Fumiko Arakawa-Brock (Japanese), Sebastian Löbner (Japanese), Myeong-Hi Min (Korean), Jeruen Dery (Tagalog), Dafna Graf (Hebrew), Oana Costache (Romanian), Souhail Bouricha (Morrocian Arabic), C. Patrick Kihara (Swahili, Kikuyu).

At the end I would like to thank Angela for everything!

The thesis has been written in the project "Verb Frames at the Syntax-Semantic Interface" which has been part of the Collaborative Research Center "The Structure of Representations in Language, Cognition, and Science" ('CRC 991') supported by the German Science Foundation (DFG).

2 Gradation and degree expressions

This chapter of the thesis aims at providing the relevant background by discussing the notions of 'gradation' and 'degree expressions.' Section 2.1 starts with a discussion of gradation in general and of verb gradation in particular. Generally, gradation will be defined as a linguistic process of comparing degrees. Degree expressions are considered to be linguistic devices that are used to introduce a degree of comparison. Although gradation is not limited to a single syntactic class such as adjectives, it shows differences with regard to the syntactic class the graded element belongs to. In particular, verb gradation differs from grading elements of other syntactic classes since verbs are eventive. A subclassification of types of verb gradation will be discussed at the end of section 2.1.

In section 2.2, the central notion of a 'scale' is discussed in detail. Section 2.3 goes back to the notion of 'degree expressions' and starts with a short overview of different linguistic realization patterns of gradation devices. Different classifications of degree expressions will be discussed, before I turn to a deeper discussion of the cross-categorical distribution of degree expressions in section 2.4. This section starts with a discussion of Doetjes' (1997) 'degree expression continuum' which is a hypothesis about restrictions in the distribution of degree expressions. After rejecting the continuum hypothesis, a cross-linguistic comparison of the distribution of degree expression is presented. This comparison leads to the identification of different types of languages with regard to the expression of verb gradation and allows some tentative generalizations regarding the cross-linguistic distribution of degree expressions.

2 Gradation and degree expressions

2.1 Gradation

The aim of this first section is to clarify the notion of gradation and to indicate which phenomena are covered by this term. 'Gradation' is frequently used synonymously with 'intensification' and throughout the thesis I will use both terms interchangeably. Gradability is often considered a prototypical property of adjectives. Bhat & Pustet (2000) state that all languages that have a distinct category of adjectives also make use of specific constructions for grading them. Bierwisch (1989, 71), in his discussion of gradable adjectives, uses the notion of 'gradation' as a cover term for "a range of phenomena which, for the time being, I shall call quantitative evaluations regarding dimensions of features." The phenomena Bierwisch wants to cover by his notion of 'gradation' are exemplified in (1). (1a) is a comparative construction, (b) an equative construction[1], (c) exemplifies the superlative construction, in (d) we have a measure construction and in (e) a vague degree expression is used for gradation.

(1)   a.   *John is taller than his brother.*
         b.   *John is as tall as his brother.*
         c.   *John is the tallest boy in his class.*
         d.   *John is 180 cm tall.*
         e.   *John is very tall.*

All constructions in (1) compare the degree of John's tallness with some other degree like the degree of his brother's tallness in (a) and (b) or the degree of all boys in his class in (c). The comparative says that John's tallness exceeds the tallness of his brother, whereas the equative indicates that both – John and his brother – have the same degree of tallness. The superlative expresses that among the boys in his class, John's tallness exceeds the tallness of all others. In (d) it is the measure phrase *180 cm* that introduces the degree to which John's height is compared. It expresses that his height is 180 cm. In the last case, the vague degree expression *very* introduces an imprecise degree to which John's height is compared. The sentence in (e) states that John's height is 'high' compared to 'normally tall,' i.e. not very tall but still quite or reasonably tall people. Such a com-

---

[1]   See Rett (2013) and the literature cited therein for a more extensive discussion of equative constructions.

parison, as expressed by the examples in (1), either predicates equality or inequality of degrees. The examples in (1) do not cover all types of gradation and therefore do not provide an exhaustive listing of instances that fall under the notion of 'gradation.'[2] Two examples are illustrated in (2), in which the comparative is combined with a measure construction (a) and a vague degree expression (b). The examples in (2) show that the different constructions in (1) can also be combined (cf. Bierwisch 1989, 155ff. and Löbner 1990, 143ff. for a discussion of such cases in German).

(2) a. *John is 10 cm taller than his brother.*
     b. *John is much taller than his brother.*

Gradability is a semantically relevant property of adjectives as it distinguishes between adjectives such as *tall* which admit degree morphemes (3a) and such adjectives as *dead* which do not allow them (3b). As the examples show, the gradable adjective *tall* takes the comparative morpheme *-er* as well as the superlative morpheme *-est* in English. Nongradable adjectives normally reject degree morphemes and only admit them after some process of coercion.[3] This definition is only suitable for languages that have adjectival degree morphology – which many languages lack. A more general definition of nongradable adjectives is: adjectives that cannot be used in gradation constructions without any need to coerce their meaning.

(3) a. *tall, taller, tallest*
     b. *dead, #deader, #deadest*

Such a general definition of nongradable adjectives can be based on the observation of Bolinger (1967, 3) that if an adjective admits degree adverbials such as English *very* it also licenses the comparative construction (cf. (4)).

(4) a. *very tall*
     b. *#very dead*

---

[2] Löbner (1990), for example, also accounts for constructions as *zu groß* 'too tall' and *groß genug* 'tall enough' as basic patterns of adjectival gradation. See Morzycki (2013, 169) for a formal analysis of corresponding English examples.

[3] In English, only monosyllabic and some bisyllabic adjectives take degree morphemes, whereas most polysyllabic ones use *more* for expressing the comparative. Hence, ungradable polysyllabic adjectives reject *more* without a process of coercion.

2 Gradation and degree expressions

Therefore, when I am speaking of a gradable expression throughout this thesis, I am always referring to an expression, irrespective whether it is an adjective or belongs to some other lexical category, that can be used in a gradation construction without coercing its meaning.

For adjectives, the positive form can be considered to be the basic form since it is morphologically less marked than the comparative and superlative in languages such as English, French (5) or Polish (5). In French the comparative is marked by the particle *plus* 'more,' whereas the adjective is uninflected for degree. The superlative also requires the definite article. Polish marks the comparative morphologically and the superlative is morphologically derived from the comparative, unlike in English where both the comparative and the superlative of monosyllabic adjectives are derived from the positive form of the adjective.

(5) French
    a. *grand*
       'tall'
    b. *plus grand*
       more tall
       'taller'
    c. *le plus grand*
       the more tall
       '(the) tallest'

(6) Polish (Slavic < Indo-European)
    a. *grub-y*
       thick-MASC.SG.NOM
       'fat'
    b. *grub-sz-y*
       thick-COMP-MASC.SG.NOM
       'fatter'
    c. *naj-grub-sz-y*
       SUP-thick-COMP-MASC.SG.NOM
       '(the) fattest'

But there are also languages – like Mandarin Chinese (7) – in which the positive is marked compared to a comparative interpretation of gradable adjectives. A plain (gradable) adjective receives a comparative reading in

Mandarin Chinese (7a) and the comparandum is inferred from the context (cf. Liu 2010, Grano 2012, Grano & Kennedy 2012, Zhang 2015).[4] The adjective only acquires a positive interpretation by the addition of a degree expression (7b). Li & Thompson (1989, 143f.) state that sentences such as (7b) are ambiguous between two readings: (i) Zhangsan is tall, (ii) Zhangsan is very tall. The ambiguity arises if *hěn* 'very' is not heavily stressed.[5]

(7) Mandarin Chinese (Sinitic < Sino-Tibetian; Sybesma 1999, 27, slightly modified)
 a. *Zhāngsān gāo.*
 Zhangsan tall
 'Zhangsan is taller (than someone known from context).'
 b. *Zhāngsān hěn gāo.*
 Zhangsan very tall
 'Zhangsan is tall.'

The contrast between Mandarin Chinese on the one hand and the Indo-European languages English, French and Polish on the other hand indicates that the positive form is cross-linguistically not always the unmarked one.[6] Semantically, many authors assume a similarity between the positive form and the comparative in that both express a relation between two degrees. Stating that someone is *tall* always requires some explicit or implicit comparison class with regard to which the respective individual is judged as *tall*. Taking (8) as an example, John's height has to be of quite different degree depending on the actual comparison class. If he is tall for a three-year old child, he does not – at the same time – qualify as tall for a basketball player. Thus, in the positive form, the degree of the argument of the adjec-

---

[4] For a typological overview of the expression of comparison constructions see Stassen (1984, 1985) and Bobaljik (2012) for an extensive discussion of adjectival degree morphology.

[5] See Chui (2000) for the claim that *hěn* turns into a bound morpheme in Mandarin Chinese.

[6] Mauwake (New Guinea) makes use of an intensifier, in one of its comparative constructions, as a marker of a comparative rather than positive construction:
 i. *Poka fain maala, ne oko maala akena.*
 stilt this long ADD other long very
 'This stilt is long but the other one is longer (lit. very long).'
 (Berghäll, 2010, 272)

tive is compared to some other degree contributed by a possibly implicit comparison class.

(8)   *John is tall (for a basketball player/for a three-year old child)*.

Authors differ as to whether they analyze the positive form as a relational expression, as Cresswell (1976) and Bierwisch (1989) do. In this case, the positive form would take two arguments, of which only one is a syntactic argument. Others, such as Löbner (1990), take the positive form as an inherently contrastive but nevertheless nonrelational construction (I will come back to this discussion in chapter 5). Irrespective of the exact analysis of the positive form, I take the positive of gradable adjectives as an instance of adjectival gradation because it expresses a relation between two degrees. The relational aspect also provides the basis for an explication of the notion of 'gradation,' for which I propose the following definition in (9):

(9)   Gradation is the linguistic process of comparing two (or possibly more) degrees.

The definition of gradation is based on the notion of 'comparison,' which all the gradation constructions discussed above have in common. Since (9) is a semantic definition, I consider all constructions in which two (or more) degrees are compared as instances of gradation. This is independent of the syntactic realization of these constructions but it is also independent from the distinction between explicit comparisons (e.g. the comparative construction in English) and implicit ones (as, for example, the positive form of adjectives in English). The definition is essentially based on the notion of 'comparison' for which Bolinger (1967, 4) states that "comparability is a semantic feature coextensive with 'having different degrees' or 'susceptible of being laid out on a scale.'" A detailed discussion of the notion of a 'scale' will be provided in chapter 2.2; for the moment it is enough to say that a scale is formed by a linearly ordered set of degrees. Something like Bolinger's characterization of 'comparability' forms the heart of current theories of gradable adjectives (Bierwisch 1989, Löbner 1990, Kennedy 1999b,a, Kennedy & McNally 2005a among others). Gradable adjectives map their individual argument onto a scale or as Kennedy (1999b, xiii) writes: "Semantically, gradable adjectives can be informally defined as predicative expressions whose domains can be partly ordered according to some property that permits grading." Gradable and nongradable adjectives both induce a partial order of the objects in their domain but they do not induce the same kind of ordering (Kennedy, 1999b, xiii). An ungradable adjective as *dead* induces a distinction between those objects which are dead and those which are not. But there is no ranking of objects with respect to their degree of being dead. It is simply a binary contrast between 'alive' and 'dead' and it is not possible to distinguish different degrees of being dead. Gradable adjectives like *tall* order the objects in their domain according to a measure such as 'height' and the objects in the domain are ordered with respect to their degree of height. One can say that nongradable as well as gradable objects specify some property that functions as a basis for ordering the objects in the respective domains but they differ in that only the latter express gradable properties.[7]

To distinguish between gradable and nongradable adjectives, the notion of a 'gradable property' is essential. Often the notion of 'gradable property' is used without an explicit definition, as for example in Tsujimura (2001). I am aware of only two explicit definitions of this notion (Moltmann 1997; Koenig & Chief 2008), which are both very similar. Koenig & Chief (2008, 251) write: "[a] gradable property is a relation between an entity and a degree d that obeys the following entailment pattern: For all eventualities e, entities o, and degrees d, if e is such that the property holds of o to degree d, it also holds of o to non-zero degrees d' inferior to d." Moltmann bases her explication of 'gradable property' on the notion of 'scalar inclusion,' which is defined as in (10).

(10) For any scalar property P, if an object x is P to a degree d, then x is P to the degree d', for any d'<d.
(Moltmann, 1997, 185)

Both explications focus on the assumption that if a gradable property holds to some degree, it is entailed that it also holds to a lesser degree. This is a scalar implicature as mentioned by Koenig & Chief and only captures a certain characteristic of gradable properties but does not define what a gradable property is. Departing from the abovementioned authors,

---

[7] This does not mean that the objects in the domain of *dead* cannot be ordered with regard to some gradable property like 'weight' but only that *dead* itself does not express such a gradable property.

2 Gradation and degree expressions

I take the fact that gradable properties can hold of two individuals at the same time but allow that these individuals differ with respect to the degree of the property as their defining characteristic. An informal definition is given in (11).

(11)   A property P is gradable if the property holds of two distinct entities A and B and it can truthfully be said that A's degree of P is higher than B's degree of P.

Based on the definition in (11) it can be said that an adjective is gradable, if it is possible that two individuals possess the property denoted by the adjective but differ in degree. This holds for *tall* as two boys can be tall but do not need to be of the same height. But it cannot be said that the degree to which Mozart is dead is higher than the degree to which Bach is dead.[8]

So far, the discussion has focused on gradation of adjectives but gradation is not limited to adjectives, as was mentioned quite early by Sapir (1944) and extensively discussed by Bolinger (1972). (12) shows a German example of a graded adverb:

(12)   *Der Junge lief sehr schnell.*
         the boy ran very fast
         'The boy ran very fast.'

Gnutzmann (1975, 421) argues that only adjectives and adverbs can be graded and states that "[i]n the case of nouns and verbs it is only the adjectives and adverbs associated with them which can undergo grading, not the nouns and verbs themselves." In his analysis, a grading construction such as '*what a* noun' is derived from a construction as '*what an* adjective noun.' In his view, it is not the noun but "some predicated quality or associated adjectival modifier" (Gnutzmann, 1975, 422) that is graded. I will not follow such a derivational approach but rather assume that nouns and verbs can be graded as such.

One reason to assume that nouns and verbs as such can be graded and that gradation does not merely affect an associate adjective is that in some languages adjectives and nouns require different degree expressions. One

---

[8]   I do not want to exclude coercion, which allows us to shift a normally ungradable property to a gradable property interpretation. All I want to say is that a property like 'being dead' is normally conceived as being ungradable and requires coercion for a gradable property interpretation.

example is French, which uses *très* 'very' for grading adjectives (13a) and *beaucoup* for nouns (b). Such a difference in the choice of degree expressions would be unexpected if it were really the adjective that is graded in (b) and not the noun itself.

(13) a. *Jean est très grand.*
Jean is very tall
'Jean is very tall.'
b. *Jean a beaucoup faim.*
Jean has a lot hunger
'Jean is very hungry (lit. Jean has a lot hunger).'

In (13b) the noun *faim* 'hunger' is used predicatively, following Doetjes (2008, 127), and graded by the degree expression *beaucoup*. *Beaucoup* also combines with nonpredicatively used nouns as shown in (14). Such examples are often referred to as 'adnominal quantification.' The difference between the predicatively used noun in (13b) and the nonpredicatively used nouns in (14) is that in the latter case the partitive article *de* is required.

(14) a. *J'ai mangé beaucoup de soupe.*
I=have eaten a lot of.the soup
'I ate a lot of soup.'
b. *Je possède beaucoup de libres.*
I own a lot of.the books
'I own many books.'

Examples such as (14) seem therefore to indicate that there is no clear-cut distinction between gradation on the one hand and quantification on the other hand. I come back to this point at the end of this section, turning first to verbs and the question of how they differ regarding gradation from adjectives and nouns. With respect to verbs, two subtypes of gradation can be distinguished: extent and degree gradation.[9] Extent gradation is exemplified by the English examples in (15). It is the frequency of the event that is specified by *a lot* in (15a), whereas *a lot* specifies the temporal duration of the event in (b). Both these sentences require different paraphrases. The

---

[9] The distinction originally goes back to Bolinger (1972), but I use the terminology by Löbner (2012b) rather than Bolinger's original terms of 'extent' and 'inherent' intensification.

2 Gradation and degree expressions

one in (a) can be paraphrased by a sentence containing the frequency adverb *often* (16a), whereas sentence (b) can be paraphrased by a sentence containing an expression such as *for a long time* (16b).

(15)   a.   *He goes to the cinema a lot.*
          b.   *Last night, he slept a lot.*

(16)   a.   *He often goes to the cinema.*
          b.   *Last night, he slept for a long time.*

In the case of degree gradation, the degree expression *a lot* neither specifies the frequency nor the temporal duration of the eventuality. Rather, as it is the case with the stative verb in (17), *a lot* specifies the degree of the intensity of the feeling. An appropriate paraphrase for (17) is (18).

(17)   *The boy hates his teacher a lot.*

(18)   *The boy feels a lot of hate for his teacher.*

The different paraphrases for extent and degree gradation indicate that both cannot be reduced to a single type; rather, they instantiate different subtypes of verb gradation. In fact, one could argue that we have three subtypes of verb gradation: degree gradation, durative gradation and frequentative gradation. I subsume durative and frequentative gradation under the notion of 'extent gradation' and put it in opposition to degree gradation. The reason is that the split between extent and degree gradation is due to the eventivity of verbs. It is a real property of the event, i.e., its frequency or temporal duration, that is specified in the process of extent gradation, and, furthermore, non-eventive adjectives and nouns do not license an extent gradation.[10] There are two further reasons to subsume durative and frequentative gradation under the label of 'extent gradation.' First, extent and degree gradation are realized in two different syntactic configurations (which will be shown in chapter 4). The two subtypes of extent gradation, on the other hand, are uniform regarding their syntactic realization (also shown in chapter 4). Second, some languages, such as German, use different degree expressions for extent and degree gradation (cf. (19) and (20))

---

[10] A question which I do not raise is whether eventive nouns license extent gradation, although some clearly allow for a combination with frequency adjectives, e.g., *frequent visits, a frequent update*.

but the same degree expression for both subtypes of extent gradation.[11]

(19) a. *Er geht viel ins Kino.*
       he goes much in.the cinema
       'He goes to the cinema a lot.'
    b. *Letzte Nacht hat er viel geschlafen.*
       last night has he much slept
       'Last night, he slept a lot.'

(20) *Der Junge hasst seinen Lehrer sehr.*
     the boy hates his teacher very
     'The boy hates his teacher a lot.'

Third, extent and degree gradation differ with regard to the source that contributes the respective gradable property. In the case of both subtypes of extent gradation, the gradable property is contributed by the eventuality, since it is a property of the event that is specified. It is either the frequency or the temporal duration of the event as such. In the case of degree gradation, it is a property of the predicate that is specified by the degree expression. 'Intensity' as the relevant gradable property in (17) and (20) is not a property of the event but of the emotion felt by the experiencer. Bosque & Masullo (1998) argue for further subtypes of what they call 'verbal quantification.' On the one hand they distinguish between 'eventive quantification,' 'durative quantification' and 'inherent quantification'; the first two correspond to Bolinger's extent gradation and the last one to degree gradation. On the other hand, Bosque & Masullo mention 'argument quantification' and 'unselective binder' as two further types of verbal quantification. Neither of them are covered by Bolinger's discussion of verb gradation. 'Argument quantification' is exemplified by the Spanish example in (21) in which *mucho* 'a lot' quantifies over an implicit or unexpressed argument of the verb.[12] They mention that in case of argument quantification disagreement exists as to whether *mucho* functions as an adverbial or as a quantificational pronoun that features as the direct object of the verb.

---

[11] The cross-categorical distribution of degree expression will be discussed in more detail in section 2.3
[12] Cf. Bhatt & Pancheva (2006) for an overview of different types and analyses of non-overt expressed and implicit arguments.

(21) Spanish (Romance < Indo-European; Gallego & Irurtzun 2010, 6)
    a. *Comí mucho (chocolate).*
       ate   a lot   chocolate
       'I ate a lot (of chocolate).'
    b. *María leyó pocos (libros).*
       Maria read few   books
       'Maria read few (books).'

The German sentence in (22a) is similar to the Spanish one in (21a). It is stated that we ate a lot of food, without an overt realization of an argument referring to the consumed food. As (22b) shows, the sentence can also be passivized with *viel* figuring as the subject of the passive sentence.

(22) a. *Wir haben viel gegessen.*
       we   have   much eaten
       'We ate a lot.'
    b. *Viel wurde (von uns) gegessen.*
       much was   by   us   eaten
       'A lot was eaten by us.'

The German example in (22b) can be taken as argument against an adverbial analysis of *viel* in constructions like those in (22a). Since *viel* functions as an argument of *essen*, I do not include cases similar to (21) and (22) in the discussion of adverbial degree gradation.

In (23), *mucho* is used in an unselective binder construction. The notion of 'unselective binder' goes back to Lewis (1975) and Bosque & Masullo (1998, 30) mention that in such constructions *mucho* acts as a generic operator that binds a variable provided by indefinite noun phrases and type-denoting nominals.

(23) *La gente ha leído mucho este libro.*
    the people have read a lot   this book
    'People have read this book quite a lot.'
    (Bosque & Masullo, 1998, 29)

Unselective binder constructions can probably be taken as an instance of extent gradation but nevertheless are a topic of their own which would require a discussion of genericity and how the generic reading of these examples arises. As the focus of the thesis is on degree gradation and only partly on how it is distinguished from extent gradation, I leave the topic of genericity and therefore the unselective binder construction aside.

As already mentioned above, Bosque & Masullo consider 'degree' to be a subtype of quantification. This is also reflected in their choice of terminology, speaking of 'verbal quantification' rather than 'gradation' or 'intensification.' The authors neither explicate their notion of 'quantification' nor argue for this position. Probably the notion of 'quantification' is motivated by the fact that *mucho* is not only found in gradational contexts but is also used for indicating an adnominal quantity as in (24). It seems that Bosque & Masullo extend a quantificational analysis of adnominal *mucho* to its adverbial use and analyze it as a quantifier in all instances.

(24)   a.   *mucha leche*
               a lot   milk
               'a lot of milk'
      b.   *muchos amigos*
               a lot   friends
               'many friends'

Drawing the line between gradation and quantification is not simple, as indicated by the examples above. Several authors propose an explicit relationship between gradation and quantification. Bosque & Masullo (1998, 22) subsume gradation under the notion of 'quantification' and write: "we crucially take degree to be a subtype of quantification." Sapir (1944, 93) claims that grading precedes counting and measurement. He writes (1944: 93f.) "judgments of quantity in terms of units of measure or in terms of number always presuppose, explicitly or implicitly, preliminary judgments of grading. [...] all quantifiables (terms that may be quantified) and all quantificates (terms to which notions of quantity have been applied) involve the concept of grading." Hence, grading provides the basis for quantification. Gary (1979) argues instead that 'degree' and 'quantity' are manifestations of the same category which he calls 'extent.'

Whether gradation and quantification are related depends on the notion of 'quantification.' There are two senses of quantification. In a narrow view, quantification is the expression of a relation between two predicates, a nucleus and a domain of quantification. In a broader sense, quantification merely means the specification of a quantity. The narrow sense of quantification is usually employed in formal semantics and represented by an approach such as Generalized Quantifier Theory (GQT, Barwise & Cooper 1981). In the broader use of quantification, 'quantity' can be set in opposition to 'quality' and covers such dimensions as AMOUNT, NUMBER or VOLUME (cf. Eschenbach 1995, 241). Such a notion of 'quantity' does not allow distinguishing between gradation on the one hand and quantification on the other hand. This is indicated by the example in (25).

(25) *Der Junge hat sehr geblutet.*
      the boy   has very bled
      'The boy bled a lot.'

In (25) *sehr* indicates that the boy emitted a large quantity of blood. An appropriate paraphrase for (25) is (26), in which an explicit adnominal construction is used to specify the emitted quantity of blood. As these examples indicate, the notion of 'quantity' shows up in constructions which are often treated as quantificational but also in typical gradation constructions.

(26) *Der Junge hat viel   Blut   verloren.*
      the boy   has much blood lost
      'The boy has lost a lot of blood.'

There is a clear relationship between gradation and quantification in the broad sense, as specification of a quantity is nothing more than indicating a degree on a quantity scale. Quantification in the broad sense is an instance of gradation, but not the other way round, as gradation does not always consists in specifying a degree on a quantity scale. Example (27) illustrates this point, as *very much* cannot be interpreted as specifying the quantity but rather the intensity of love.

(27) *The boy loves his girlfriend very much.*

In chapter 5.2.1, I show that gradation is not related to quantification in the narrow sense, meaning that degree expressions are not generalized quantifiers. In the following, I will refer to expressions such as German *viel*, French *beaucoup* or Spanish *mucho* as 'degree expressions' irrespective whether they specify a degree on a quantity scale or rather grade some quality, i.e., intensity. To focus on the adnominal use of these expressions, I will use the term 'adnominal quantity expression.' It will be shown in chapter 4 that, syntactically speaking, adnominal quantity expressions have to be conceived as quantity adjectives and I will argue in chapter 5 that they figure semantically as modifiers rather than quantifiers (in the sense of GQT).

In this section, I have shown that gradation is a phenomenon which is not restricted to a single syntactic class but can be found with adjectives, adverbs, nouns as well as verbs. I have argued for a uniform definition of gradation as a linguistic process of comparing degrees. A central component of such an analysis of gradation is the notion of a 'scale,' which is the topic of the next section.

2.2 Scales

In the last section, gradation was described as the process of comparing two or more degrees on a scale. Several constructions were mentioned as instances of gradation, some repeated in (28). The sentences in (28b) to (d) differ from the one in (a) in that gradation is explicitly expressed by some operator. This is the case with the comparative morpheme *-er* in (b), the equative *as ... as* in (c) and *very* in (d).

(28) a. *Tom is tall.*
      b. *Tom is taller than Angela.*
      c. *Tom is as tall as Angela.*
      d. *Tom is very tall.*

There is no explicit operator in (a) – the positive construction – used for expressing gradation. Kennedy & McNally (2005a) argue for a morphological null positive morpheme in languages like English and German, whereas the Sinitic languages, like Mandarin and Cantonese, show an overt realization of such a morpheme. Hence, if Kennedy & McNally are right, each gradational construction has some operator, either morphological null or explicit, expressing gradation. I will call such operators 'degree operators.'

The degree operators differ in their semantics as well as their syntax, which can be seen by the fact that the comparative licenses a comparison phrase (*than Angela* in (28b)), whereas the positive does not (29).

2 Gradation and degree expressions

(29) *Tom is tall than Angela.

The last section also revealed that degree operators can take different operands. The degree operators in (28) take adjectives as operants but in the last section, we also saw examples of verbs and nouns being operants in gradational constructions. A central question is how the set of operants is restricted. Clearly, in order to be an operant in a gradational construction, a predicate needs to be gradable. Keeping the possibility of coercion in mind, the question is what it means for a predicate to be gradable. Adjectives are gradable if they denote a gradable property; but most verbs differ from adjectives in not being simple property denoting concepts. The common core for all gradable expressions is that they somehow allow access to a gradable property. Gradable properties can formally be analyzed as 'measure functions.'

Measure functions are a central ingredient in the analysis of gradable expressions, as they provide the mapping of invidivuals onto scales and thereby return the degree of the individual on that scale (see below for a discussion of the notion of 'scale'). The domain of the measure function comprises individuals, whereas its range consists of degrees (Kennedy, 2007, 32). Krifka (1990, 494) has a somewhat more differentiated view on measure functions and writes: "[a] measure function is a function from concrete entities to abstract entities such that certain structures of the concrete entities, the empirical relations, are preserved in certain structures of the abstract entities, normally arithmetical relations. That is, measure functions are homomorphisms which preserve an empirical relation in an arithmetical relation." A measure function like 'degrees Celsius' is a mapping such that the empirical relation 'x is cooler than y' is represented by numerical values, in this case temperature values. The structure is preserved in such a way that if x is cooler than y, the numerical value of x is lower than the value of y. In addition, differences are also preserved but not proportions. Krifka argues for the existence of two different types of measure functions, which he terms 'extensive' and 'non-extensive measure functions.' Extensive measure functions, like 'weight,' allow the addition of values. If x weighs 6 kilograms and y weighs 3 kilograms, together they weigh 9 kilograms. Such an addition of values is not possible in case of non-extensive measure functions like 'temperature.' This is a non-extensive measure function, since if the water in a bucket has a temperature of 30 degrees and one fills in water that has a temperature of 40 degrees, the overall temperature of the water in the bucket does not become 70 degrees. Temperature degrees of different individuals cannot simply be added or summed-up.

The distinction between 'extensive' and 'non-extensive measure functions' is not of primary relevance in the context of verb gradation and therefore I simply use the term 'measure function' to denote any function from individuals onto degrees. Gradable adjectives and gradable verbs differ with respect to the encoding of the individual argument of their measure functions. With regard to adjectives, the argument of the measure function is the syntactic argument of the adjective. In (30a) the argument of the predicatively used adjective *tall* is *the man*, while it is also *the man* in case of the attributively used adjective in (b).

(30) a. *The man is tall.*
 b. *The tall man enters the room.*

In the case of verb gradation, the argument of the measure function does not necessarily coincide with one of the syntactic arguments of the verb. Take, for example, the German verb *bluten* 'bleed' in (31). The sentence has the interpretation that the boy is emitting a large quantity of blood. The gradable property is QUANTITY and the argument of the encoded measure function is *blood* not *the boy* since it is the quantity of blood that is measured and not the quantity of the boy.

(31) *Der Junge blutet sehr.*
 the boy bleeds very
 'The boy is bleeding a lot.'

The contrast between (30) and (31) consists in the encoding of the argument that is mapped on the gradation scale. The notion of a 'scale' is crucial in the analysis of gradation and in linguistics different notions of 'scale' are used, as discussed by Westney (1986). I follow the particular approach to scales presented in Kennedy (1999b) and Kennedy & McNally (2005a). Kennedy and Kennedy & McNally propose a definition of 'scales' as consisting of three parameters: a set of degrees (D), a linear ordering relation (R) – 'less than' or 'more than' – and a dimension (Δ). They write that dimensions represent the kind of measurement that is represented by the scale. Kennedy (1999b) equates dimensions with gradable properties but does not provide a definition of what a dimension actually is. The same holds for Schwarzschild (2006, 72), who writes that "A dimension is a kind of property like weight, volume or temperature, which can be had in varying degrees." A definition of the notion of 'dimension' is provided by Gamerschlag (2014, 277), based on the work of Löbner (1979, 173). Gamerschlag considers dimensions to represent "a space of variation which is given for a specific object property" and defines them as "a set of mutually exclusive properties of which an individual has exactly one at each point in time." A dimension, such as AGE, is a property of an object and allows for different instantiations. Different objects can be of different ages, and the age of a single objects does not need to be constant but can vary over time. A crucial fact of dimensions, in the sense of Löbner, is that they are functional and provide a unique mapping of an object onto a specific degree. This means that if AGE is a property of an object, it has some value for this dimension and also only one value at the same time.

'Dimensions' are independent from scalarity and Gamerschlag straightforwardly distinguishes between 'scalar' and 'non-scalar dimensions.' The value range of scalar dimensions is inherently linearly ordered; examples are PRICE or SIZE. An example of a non-scalar dimension is COLOR which assigns an entity a color value, but the different values, i.e., 'blue,' 'red,' 'green' and so on, are not linearly ordered (see Gärdenfors 2000). If the value range of a dimension is linearly ordered, I use the term 'degrees' to denote these values. In this view, the defining characteristic of a dimension is functionality rather than scalarity.

Kennedy & McNally assume that all three scale parameters are explanatorily relevant. Parameter R, the ordering relation, is used in Kennedy and Kennedy & McNally's account to distinguish between antonymous adjectives like *warm* and *cold*. These adjectives operate in the same dimension, but induce a different linear order of the temperature values (cf. Kennedy 1999b, Kennedy & McNally 2005a). Parameter Δ, the measurement dimension, is used to explain incommensurability phenomena, as indicated by the sentence in (32). The example is odd since it expresses a comparison of degrees in two different dimensions.

(32)   #*The girl is taller than the boy is old.*

2.2 Scales

Sebastian Löbner (p.c.) mentions that it is not dimensions but scales that have to be compatible – as indicated by examples like (33a) which express a comparison in two different dimensions HEIGHT and WIDTH. Kennedy & McNally (2005a, 352) account for examples such as (33b) by assuming that "*wide* and *tall* [...] involve orderings along a dimension of linear extent". Kennedy & McNally lump different spatial dimensions together under the notion of 'linear extent' but Lang (1990) presents arguments for a distinct representation of the different spatial dimension encoded in language. I agree with Löbner's comment and do not assume that the incommensurability can be reduced to a fit of dimension. But I do not discuss this topic further as it is not central to my topic.

(33) a. The chair is higher than the table is broad.
 b. They call him 'The Bus' because he's kind of as wide as he is tall.
 (Kennedy & McNally, 2005a, 352)

The parameter D – the set of degrees – specifies whether a minimal and/or maximal scale value exists (e.g. Kennedy & McNally 2005a, Kennedy 2007, 32). A maximal scale value is the highest degree, so that no higher degree exists. The reverse holds for minimal scale values. The presence vs. absence of minimal and maximal scale values determines one of the formal characteristics of scales, namely whether they are (partially) closed or open. With respect to the presence vs. absence of maximal/minimal scale values four types of scales are distinguished: (i) a scale can have a minimal and a maximal scale value, then it is closed; (ii) a scale can have a minimal but no maximal scale value, then it is closed at the lower end, (iii) a scale can have a maximal but no minimal scale value, then it is an upper closed scale, and (iv) a scale can have neither a minimal nor a maximal scale value. In this case it is an open scale. These distinctions result in the scale typology summarized in (34).

(34) a. $\langle D_{[0,1]}, R, \Delta \rangle$ = (totally) closed scale
 b. $\langle D_{[0,1)}, R, \Delta \rangle$ = lower closed scale
 c. $\langle D_{(0,1]}, R, \Delta \rangle$ = upper closed scale
 d. $\langle D_{(0,1)}, R, \Delta \rangle$ = open scale
 (Kennedy & McNally, 2005a, 354)

2 Gradation and degree expressions

Kennedy and Kennedy & McNally assume that degrees can be considered as isomorphic to the real numbers between 0 and 1. The interval of real numbers is marked as a subscript to parameter D. Round and square brackets are used to indicate whether the interval includes 0 and 1 (in this case, the scale is closed at the respective end) or only approximates 0 and 1. As there is "no smallest non-zero between 0 and 1, and no largest non-one number either" (Morzycki 2013, 126) the scale is an open interval. Kennedy & McNally do not assume that degrees actually are real numbers or that all dimensions are associated with numerical degrees. The assumption that degrees are isomorphic to real numbers is merely a way of formalizing degrees. I will not go on to discuss the question whether this assumption is necessary or probably even too strong since nothing in my analysis hinges on this assumption.

The structure of the scales, whether they are (partially) closed or open, is reflected by different linguistic asymmetries. The endpoint modifier is *completely* oriented toward an endpoint of a scale, irrespective whether it is a minimal or a maximal one. As can be seen in (35), the two antonymous adjectives *empty* and *full* can both be combined with *completely*, which indicates that the scale measuring 'fullness' is closed at both ends. This coincides with the intuition that if something is full or empty it cannot get fuller or emptier. Hence, the compatibility of an expression with *completely* can be taken as evidence for the presence of a maximal, resp. minimal scale value and therefore for a (partially) closed scale.

(35)   a.   *The bucket is completely empty.*
           b.   *The bucket is completely full.*

Proportional modifiers like *half* and *halfway* require totally closed scales, since the determination of a mid-value requires a beginning and an end point (cf. Kennedy & McNally 2005a, Bochnak 2013b). Therefore, the compatibility with *half* indicates a totally closed scale, as is the case with *full* in (36).

(36)   *The bucket is half full.*

Open scale predications reject the combination with endpoint modifiers as well as proportional modifiers. Intuitively, adjectives such as *expensive* and *tall* are related to open scales, since one always can think of an increase in price or some higher 'height.' Linguistically this is reflected by the fact that the combination of *expensive/tall* with *completely/half* results in odd sentences (37). Lexically, there is no upper or lower bound specified by these adjectives.

(37) a. #*The book is completely expensive.*
b. #*The book is half expensive.*
c. #*The tower is completely tall.*
d. #*The tower is half tall.*

Also adjectives that are related to closed-scale predications are gradable. This is shown by the fact that they admit comparative constructions (38), which require some coercion with ungradable adjectives like *nuclear* or *extinct* (39). The difference between *nuclear* and *extinct* on the one hand and *full* and *visible* on the other hand is that the latter denote a gradable property while the former do not. *Full* is related to a scale of 'fullness' and denotes, following the argumentation presented above, the maximal degree on that scale.

(38) a. *The glass isn't as full as I would like it to be.*
b. *The sign for the Main Street exit is less visible than the one for the Spruce Street exit.*
(Kennedy & McNally, 2005a, 356)

(39) a. ??*The energy we use these days is more nuclear than it was before they build that plant down the road.*
b. ??*Dinosaurs are more extinct than spotted owls.*
(Kennedy & McNally, 2005a, 356)

Above, I mentioned that endpoint-oriented adjectives denote the maximal scale value, but that statement is too simplistic. As Ropertz (2001) as well as Kennedy & McNally show, some endpoint-oriented adjectives also have non-endpoint-oriented uses (Kennedy & McNally 2005a, 357 call them 'imprecise uses'). A sentence such as (40a) does not necessarily mean that the glass is completely full and nothing more could be filled in. For example, a drinking glass in a restaurant is normally not filled up to the brim but nevertheless a sentence such as (40a) would be true of the drinking glass, even if more liquid could be filled in. Kennedy & McNally also mention the example in (40b), which shows that something can be described as full, but at the same time is not necessarily completely full.

(40) a. *The glass is full.*
      b. *The gas tank is full, but you can still top it off. It's not completely full yet.*
          (Kennedy & McNally, 2005a, 357)

One closed-scale adjective which does not allow an 'imprecise use,' or at least not as easily as English *full* does, is German *unsichtbar* 'invisible.' *Unsichtbar* expresses a zero degree of 'visibility' and a sentence like (41) is rather odd.

(41) #*Der Mann ist unsichtbar, aber er könnte noch unischtbar-er sein.*
       the man is invisible   but he could still invisible-COMP be
      'The man is invisible but he could be even more invisible.'

'Imprecise uses' of *full* and other closed-scale adjectives can either be seen as an instance of coercion or rather as exemplifying the fact that they do not denote a single value on the scale, i.e., the scale's maximal degree, but rather a range of values. This range of values can be taken as an extended endpoint; it consists of the endpoint and a set of degrees preceding the endpoint. I use the term 'end range,' in opposition to 'endpoint' for such an extended endpoint. An 'end range' has a lower and an upper bound. The upper bound is the maximal scale value, whereas the lower bound is context-dependent. We have different standards for judging a glass as 'full, but not completely full' opposed to judging a theater as 'full, but not completely full.' 'End range'-adjectives, unlike strict endpoint adjectives, are compatible with endpoint expressions like *completely* but also allow for 'imprecise uses.' The notion of an 'end range' will figure crucially in the analysis of gradable telic change of state verbs in chapter 6.

Closed-scale as well as open-scale adjectives require an evaluation standard that is referred to as 'comparison class.' The notion of a 'comparison class' has to be set apart from the notion of a 'standard.' A comparison class specifies a contextually relevant subset of the domain of the gradable predicate. If one says that John is tall for a basketball player, then the comparison class restricts the domain of the adjective to those entities who are basketball players. John's tallness is not compared to the tallness of all individuals in the adjective's domain, which would be all individuals that have some degree of height. As (42) shows, the comparison class can be overtly specified, but it can also be left implicit.

(42)   a.   *This is expensive for a book.*
      b.   *This is expensive for a car.*

A standard can be defined, following Kennedy (1999b, 9), as "a value that provides a means of separating those objects for which the statement x is φ [φ being a gradable predicate] is true from those objects for which x is φ is false, in some context." Morzycki (2013, 108) describes a standard as "the smallest degree on a scale consistent with satisfying the predicate – that is, the cut-off point that divides, say, the tall from the non-tall." The standard is the actual value (it can be rather imprecise and does not need to be a concrete degree) that induces a separation within the comparison class between those individuals for which the respective predication is true and those for which it is not. Clearly, the standard is dependent on the comparison class. If I am saying that someone is tall, the respective standard is different depending on the chosen comparison class. The standard is a higher degree if I compare John's tallness with those of basketball players than if I compare it with three-year-old children. Furthermore, Kennedy & McNally (2005a) propose that a relationship between the type of scale (open vs. closed) and the nature of the evaluation standard exists. They distinguish between two types of standards, which they call 'relative' and 'absolute standard.' A relative standard is context-dependent as in the examples in (42). In (a) the actual price could be 50 euros, which would be expensive for an ordinary book, whereas in (b) the price has to be clearly higher, probably more than 30,000 euros. Whether the price of the referent of *this* is conceived as expensive or not depends on the comparison class. Adjectives related to relative standards are called 'relative adjectives' by Kennedy & McNally (2005a). Absolute standards are not context-dependent but fall together with an endpoint of the scale. An adjective such as *full* in (43) can be evaluated with regard to its absolute standard. This does not require a comparison class, as a sentence like (43) does not mean that the Honda is full compared to a van in general. Rather in the endpoint oriented reading *full* means that nothing more could be put into the Honda independent of any comparison class.

2 Gradation and degree expressions

(43)   The Honda is full.

Absolute standards default to a scale endpoint and, in the case of closed-scale adjectives, they either fall together with the minimal or the maximal scale value. Kennedy & McNally (2005a) call adjectives related to absolute standards 'absolute adjectives.'[13]

Open-scale adjectives cannot be related to absolute standards since they lack such endpoints. As mentioned above, *full* is an 'end range' rather than 'endpoint' adjective and therefore also allows an evaluation with respect to a context-dependent standard which marks the lower bound of the 'end range.' The presence of two standards explains the different reading of *full* discussed above. Standards do not have to be proposed as an additional scale component, but result from the structure of the scale (open vs. closed). A more fine-grained distinction of types of (relative) standards is provided by Leisi (1971). He does not use the term 'standard' but instead speaks of 'norm.' In the following, I will use the terms 'standard' and 'norm' interchangeably. Leisi distinguishes between the following three types of norms: 'species norm,' 'appropriateness norm' and 'individual expectation norm.' A species norm is a standard value determined by a prototypical proponent of a certain species. Example (44) indicates this kind of norm, since the standard value is determined by the height of prototypical basketball players. In this case, the nominal phrase *basketball players* represents a 'species' of individuals.

(44)   The guy is tall for a basketball player.

An appropriateness norm is context-dependent, like the other norms too. Unlike the species norm, it is not a prototypical member of a species that determines the standard but the appropriateness of the referent of the argument with regard to some goal. For example, someone can be judged as *tall* with respect to some species but, at the same time, he can be small with regard to some goal. So he can be described as small if he has to change a bulb and is not able to reach it. The last type of norm – individual expectation norm – is based on the speaker's expectations. If, for example, I have not seen my nephew for a while and expect him to have grown quite a lot

---

[13]   Yoon (1996) and Rotstein & Winter (2004) are speaking of 'partial' and 'total adjectives' rather than absolute and relative ones.

and realize that he hasn't, the sentence in (45) is based on my expectation of his size, resp. change of size. In such a case, I am not comparing him to other children of his age, so the individual expectation norm is not the same than the species norm.

(45)   *He is still small.*

As the examples have shown, species norm, appropriateness norm and individual expectation norm are subtypes of relative standards. Leisi's norms provide a more fine-grained subdivision of what Kennedy & McNally call a relative standard. In the remainder, I will speak only of relative standards and leave open what subtype of relative standard is actually invoked.

Kennedy & McNally's scale typology is only based on the presence vs. absence of maximal/minimal scale values. A different scale typology is proposed in measurement theory and formulated by Stevens (1946). He distinguishes between nominal, ordinal, interval and ratio scales. Nominal scales do not presuppose a linear order, but only allow for determination of equality or inequality. Nominal scales are enough to express a comparison, which is only concerned with a judgment of inequality/equality. But Kennedy & McNally's definition of scales requires a linear order on the set of degrees. Therefore, scales in the sense of Kennedy & McNally cannot be nominal scales. Rather they have to be at least ordinal scales of which school grades are an example. Like interval and ration scales, ordinal scales induce a linear order, but these three types of scales differ in their formal properties. Interval scales, in contrast to ordinal scales, allow the determination of an interval between two distinct degrees. Therefore, a difference between any two arbitrary degrees can be calculated. An example for a scale of such a type is temperature on the Celsius scale. Ratio scales, which have the same properties as interval scales, also allow multiplication and addition of degrees and have a meaningful zero point. Temperature on the Kelvin scale is measured on a ratio scale. Sassoon (2010) argues that the distinction between ordinal, interval and ratio scales is not merely mathematically but also linguistically relevant. But there is very little reflection of that type of scale typology in the semantics literature; exceptions are Wiese (1997) and Sassoon (2010). However, the analysis of verb gradation this scale typology does not seem to be of greater relevance, and therefore it will play no further role in the following analysis.

2.3 Degree expressions

The notion of a 'degree expression' is closely related to the notion of 'gradation' as degree expressions are devices used for gradation. The function of a degree expression is to specify the comparison degree to which the argument of gradable property is compared. As will be made clear during the latter parts of the thesis, specification of a comparison degree can consist either in introducing such a degree, for example, in case of the positive null morpheme, or in, for example, specifying a difference between the two degrees compared. At this stage, I use the term 'degree expression' for devices used for gradation rather than 'intensifiers.' The reason is that intensifiers form a certain subtype of degree expressions which will be formally distinguished from other subtypes of degree expressions in chapter 5. In the current section, I aim at a general discussion of gradation devices and therefore speak of degree expressions in general.

Gradation can be expressed by different morphosyntactic means. Following Bhat & Pustet (2000, 759), we have two different morphosyntactic types of adjectival degree constructions in (46a) to (e), which are repeated from chapter 2.1. The examples in (a) and (c) show a morphological expression of gradation, by suffixing the degree morphemes *-er* and *-est* to the adjective. Examples (b), (d) and (e) are characterized as syntactic ways of expressing gradation. Each non-morphological way of expressing gradation is considered by Bhat & Pustet to be a syntactic construction.[14]

(46) a. *John is taller than his brother.*
      b. *John is as tall as his brother.*
      c. *John is the tallest boy in his class.*
      d. *John is 180 cm tall.*
      e. *John is very tall.*

Languages differ with respect to the morphosyntactic realization of gradation constructions. An extensive discussion of this point can be found in Stassen (1985) with regard to the comparative construction (also cf. Bhat & Pustet 2000, 759). Beside explicit degree morphology, as in the English

---

[14] Bhat & Pustet (2000) do not mention phonological devices for gradation, as for example prosody (cf. Bolinger 1972, chapter 15) or phonological lengthening (cf. Bolinger 1967, 4).

2.3 Degree expressions

cases in (46a) and (c), reduplication is another often used morphological way of expressing gradation. (47) shows an example from Basque, in which an adjective is reduplicated to intensify its meaning. Moravcsik (1978) mentions that reduplication is also used for expressing iterativity (48)/(49), which is similar to verbal extent gradation (also Moravcsik 2013, 129f.).[15]

(47) Basque (Isolate; Bhat & Pustet 2000, 759)
 zopa bero-bero dago
 soup hot-hot is
 'The soup is very hot.'

(48) Tzeltal (Mayan; Moravcsik 1978, 318)
 -pik   -pikpik
 'touch it lightly' 'touch it lightly repeatedly'

(49) Sundanese (Austronesian; Moravcsik 1978, 318)
 guyon guguyon
 'to jest' 'to jest repeatedly'

German does not have productive reduplication, but a repetition of words can be used to express intensification. The example in (50) allows for an interative or durative interpretation and hence represents an instance of extent gradation.

(50) *Er hat gelogen, gelogen, gelogen.*
 he has lied   lied   lied
 'He lied, lied, lied.'
 (van Os 1989, 111)

Degree morphology is not restricted to adjectives and the expression of comparative and superlative constructions.[16] Jalonke, for example, does not have a separate class of adjectives rather what is expressed as adjectives in German or English is realized as a verb in Jalonke. The distributive morpheme *ma-* is used in Jalonke for degree gradation (51) as well as extent gradation (52), expressing iteration. Note that the prefix *ma-* in Jalonke

---

[15] Reduplication is not exclusively used for gradation but serves many other semantic functions as shown in Moravcsik (1978).
[16] See Wellwood et al. (2012) for a discussion of nominal and verbal comparative constructions.

specifies a low degree with adjectival concepts but a high degree if used as specifying the extent.

(51)　　Jalonke (Mande < Niger-Congo; Lüpke 2005, 308)
　　　　a.　*bundaa　ma-bundaa*
　　　　　　'be wet' 'be a little wet'
　　　　b.　*fisa　　ma-fisa*
　　　　　　'be better' 'be a little better'

(52)　　Nxo　ma-giri　　xure-n'　　i.
　　　　1.PL.E DISTR-cross stream-*def* at
　　　　'We crossed the stream a lot.'
　　　　(Lüpke, 2005, 309)

Syntactic devices used for gradation are free morphemes that are used for expressing gradation. In languages such as English or German, such expressions are realized as adjectives or adverbs. (53) shows the gradational function of some adjectives in English; the operants of gradation are nouns (also see the literature mentioned in Morzycki (2013, 245) on nominal gradability).

The adjectives *enormous*, *big* and *huge* function as degree expressions in (53), taken from Morzycki (2009, 176), hence they function as degree operators. Commonly, they are used as operands of gradation, as they are plain gradable adjectives. The difference between use as degree operator and that of being an operant of gradation can be exemplified by (53b). *Big* expresses that some individual is large in seize but in (53b) the sentence does not express that Gladys is big or that she is big and a stamp collector. Rather *big* intensifies *stamp collector* and has the interpretation that Gladys is very 'into' collecting stamps.

(53)　　a.　*George is an enormous idiot.*
　　　　b.　*Gladys is a big stamp collector.*
　　　　c.　*Three huge goat-cheese enthusiasts were arguing in the corner.*

Gary (1979, 46) states that "[a]lmost any adjective or adverb that connotes some sense of extremity can serve a degree modification function."[17]

---

[17] Cf. Edel (1992) for an overview of devices for gradation of nouns in Russian and Bulgarian.

2.3 Degree expressions

Kirschbaum (2002) presents an extensive analysis of adjectival intensification and demonstrates how productively different kinds of expressions can be used as degree expressions. Expressions such as *big* and *huge* on the one hand differ from such expressions as *much, very, viel* or *sehr* in that the latter are restricted to being degree operators whereas the former function as degree operator only in certains uses. A crucial difference between degree expressions like German *sehr* and adjectives such as *laut* 'loud' is that the latter lexically specify a scale, whereas the former do not. In (54), the adverbially used adjective *laut* is combined with a verb of sound emission in (a) and with an action verb in (b). Irrespective of the verb, *laut* indicates a high degree on a LOUDNESS scale. This is different for *sehr*, as the scale is dependent on the semantic class of the graded verb. The examples in (55) can be used for illustration. With respect to *weinen* 'cry,' *sehr* specifies the INTENSITY, i.e., the LOUDNESS, of the emitted sound. But with a verb like *bluten* 'bleed' it is the QUANTITY of the emitted substance and not the INTENSITY that is specified by *sehr*.

(54) a. *Das Kind weint laut.*
   the child cries loud
   'The child is crying loudly.'
   b. *Das Kind hämmert laut.*
   the child hammers loud
   'The child is hammering loudly.'

(55) a. *Das Kind weint sehr.*
   the child cries very
   'The child is crying loudly.'
   b. *Das Kind blutet sehr.*
   the child bleeds very
   'The child is bleeding profusely.'

Sehr and other degree expressions do not lexically encode a scale and are compatible with different types of scales such as INTENSITY and QUANTITY. Hence, the degree expressions require that the graded predicate provides a suitable gradation scale. *Laut* is restricted to the LOUDNESS scale as it lexically encodes this scale. Therefore, the adjective does not require a predicate that provides a loudness scale but only one which is compatible with its own predication. In the remainder, I restrict myself to lexical expressions that only serve as degree expressions and thereby exclude such cases as in (54) which do not show such a restriction.

Bhat & Pustet (2000, 759) note that languages sometimes correlate degree modification with other functions such as plurality marking of nouns. The authors mention the case of Obolo, which uses the verbal affix *mi-* for marking plurality of the subject (56a) if the verb is in the past or completive indicative (Faraclas, 1984, 10). Example (56b) shows that *mi-* is ambiguous between indicating a plurality of the subject and intensifying the predicate.

(56)   Obolo (Niger-Congo; Faraclas 1984, 10f.)

   a.   *Èmâ míbàbíge   íkpá.*
        1PL   MI.write.COMP book
        'They wrote the book (already).'

   b.   *íkpá mîjàán*
        book MI.be.beautiful
        'The books are good.' or 'The book is very good.'

The examples from Obolo raise the question whether plurality can in general be taken as an instance of gradation.[18] This question goes beyond the limits of the current thesis but surely the data indicate that the expression of quantity is deeply connected to gradation. This has already been indicated in section 2.1 and will be shown in more detail in section 2.4.2. As a consequence, I consider expressions used for the specifying quantity, such as English *much* and German *viel* in their adnominal uses, to be degree expressions.

Degree expressions can be classified based on "the region of the scale that they occupy" (Bolinger, 1972, 17). Degree expressions differ with respect to the degree they induce, which means that they lead to different partitions of a scale. Several authors, such as Biedermann (1969), Bolinger (1972) and van Os (1989), assume that a fixed set of regions of a scale can be identified and that each degree expression introduces a degree falling in one of these regions. The authors differ with regard to the exact number of scale regions they distinguish and also with regard to the question whether 'negative' should also be considered as a scale region or not. An affirmative answer to this question implies that negation expressions would also have to be

---

[18]   See Cresswell (1976) for a degree-based analysis of plurality.

2.3 Degree expressions

considered to be degree expressions. Biedermann assumes 'negative' to be a scale region, whereas Van Os argues that English *not* is not a degree expression.[19] Instead he proposes the seven scale regions listed in table 1, which are illustrated with examples from German (following Kirschbaum 2002, 43).

(i)	absolute	*völlig* 'absolutely,' *ganz* 'completely'
(ii)	approximate	*fast* 'almost,' *beinahe* 'nearly'
(iii)	extremely high	*höchst* 'highly,' *furchtbar* 'terribly'
(iv)	high	*sehr* 'very,' *besonders* 'notably'
(v)	moderate	*ziemlich* 'rather,' *relativ* 'relative'
(vi)	weak	*etwas* 'slightly,' *ein bisschen* 'a bit'
(vii)	minimal	*wenig* 'little,' *kaum* 'rarely'

Table 1: Classification of degree expressions.

The classification of degree expressions in table 1 is based on Horn's (1969) suspension test. With respect to degree expressions, the idea of this test is that a degree expression A indicates a higher degree than degree expression B, if it is possible to say *something is B, if not A*. Degree expression B is weaker than degree expression A, if the suspension test does not lead to a contradiction. The test construction leads to a contradiction if A indicates a lower degree than B. Crucial for this test is the notion of 'scalar implicature,' which means that certain lexical expressions entail a lower bound, in case of degree expressions the standard introduced by them, but only conventionally implicate an upper bound (cf. Horn 1989, 1998 on scalar implicatures). The contradiction arises in cases in which A indicates a degree that falls below the entailed lower bound of B. Since the upper bound is merely an implicature, it can be suspended. (57) and (58) illustrate this test for the German degree expressions *etwas* 'slightly,' *sehr* 'very' and *höchst* 'highly.'[20]

---

[19] I do not take a stance on the question whether *not* and similar expressions are degree expressions or not.
[20] Cf. Gary (1979, 9ff., 97ff.) for a classification of English degree expression based on the suspension test.

(57)   a.   *Sein Zustand hat sich etwas verbessert, wenn nicht sogar*
            his condition has REFL slightly improved if not even
            sehr.
            very
            'His condition has improved slightly, if not significantly'.
    b.   #*Sein Zustand hat sich sehr verbessert, wenn nicht sogar*
            his condition has refl very improved if not even
            etwas.
            slightly

(58)   a.   *Er war sehr, wenn nicht sogar höchst erfreut.*
            he was very if not even highly pleased
            'He was very, if not extremely pleased.'
    b.   ??*Er war höchst, wenn nicht sogar sehr erfreut.*
            he was highly if not even very pleased

In the case of endpoint expressions such as German *völlig* and *ganz*, which are classified as 'absolute' by van Os and Kirschbaum, a suspension of the implicated upper bound is not possible. This is due to the fact that in such cases the entailed lower bound and the implicated upper bound fall together. An essential point that has to be kept in mind is that 'absolute' degree expressions and approximaters only apply to closed-scale predicates, and whereas it is assumed for other degree expressions, such as English *very*, that they require an open-scale predicate (cf. Kennedy & McNally 2005a). Due to scale incompatibility, not all degree expressions can be contrasted in the suspension test. Ignoring those degree expressions that require closed scales, the strength of degree expressions can be arranged as illustrated in figure 1. Canonically, open scales are represented by an arrow and degrees increase from left to right. Figure 1 shows the subdivision of a scale into five different regions, which is based on the suspension test. The boundaries of the regions do not correspond to fixed degrees but are context-dependent.

Abeillé et al. (2004) present a classification of different types of adverbs which focuses on those used for the expression of extent and degree gradation. The authors base their classification on previous work by de Swart (1993) and Doetjes (1997) and argue for a distinction between, on the one hand, adverbs of quantification and on the other hand, degree

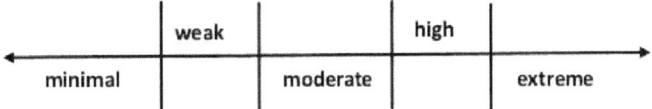

Figure 1: Scale partitioning induced by lexical degree expression.

adverbs. Adverbs of quantification consist of two subclasses: frequency adverbs such as *often* and *seldom* and iterative adverbs like *two times*. The function of these adverbs is counting events.[21] Degree adverbs are subdivided into three classes: degree quantifiers, intensity adverbs and adverbs of completion. Adverbs of completion are expressions like *completely*, which are oriented towards an endpoint of a scale. Intensity adverbs, like German *sehr*, indicate a degree on a scale and are, following Abeille et al., restricted to degree gradation of adjectives and verbs. The last class of degree adverbs is called 'degree quantifiers.' An example of a degree quantifier is French *beaucoup* 'a lot' and such adverbs can have "a quantificational-like interpretation" (Abeillé et al., 2004, 196). The quantificational-like interpretation can be observed in examples like (59b), in which *beaucoup* is near synonymous with *souvent* 'often' (a). But in contrast to *souvent*, *beaucoup* can be used for indicating a degree, therefore it is not classified as an adverb of quantification, rather it seems to be in between intensity adverbs and adverbs of quantification. Abeille et al.'s partial classification of adverbs is summarized in figure 2.

(59)   a.   *Jean va souvent au cinéma.*
              Jean goes often to.the cinema
              'Jean often goes to the movies.'
      b.   *Jean va beaucoup au cinéma.*
              Jean goes a lot to.the cinema
              'Jean goes to the movies a lot.'

There are some problems that show up with the classification in figure 2. First, the term 'degree quantifier' is (at least) confusing, since it seems to indicate that expressions such as *beaucoup* are ambiguous between a quantificational and an intensifying function. Second, the classification

---

[21] I will discuss the question, whether 'adverbs of quantification' are quantifiers, in the sense of 'Generalized Quantifier Theory' in chapter 5.

2 Gradation and degree expressions

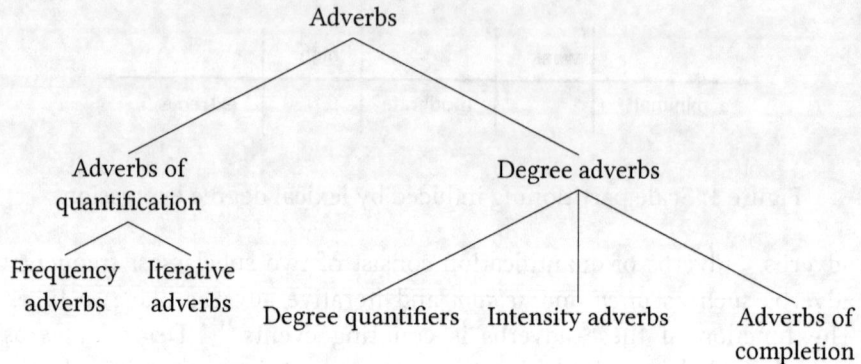

Figure 2: Partial classification of adverbs (Abeillé et al., 2004).

does not really capture degree expressions such as German *viel*, which can be used in sentences like (60), which is the German equivalent of (59b). But unlike *beaucoup*, *viel* is not used for expressing degree gradation of verbs. So it is not clear to me whether Abeille et al. would classify *viel* as a degree quantifier, as an adverb of quantification, or if they would have to make up a fourth category of degree adverbs.

(60) *Peter geht viel ins Kino.*
   Peter goes much in.the cinema
   'Peter goes to the movies a lot.'

Instead of relying on Abeille et al.'s classification of degree adverbs, in the next section I will provide a different classification based on the cross-categorical and cross-linguistic distribution of degree expressions. Before I turn to the cross-categorical disctribution of degree expressions, a note on the use of the notion 'degree adverb' is required. I do not analyse *viel* and *sehr* as adverbs, rather they are adjectives. In the context of verb gradation, these adjectives are used adverbially. Hence, I am speaking of 'degree adverbials' instead of 'degree adverbs' and focus on the function of the expression rather than on its lexical category. One argument in favor of an analysis of *viel* and *sehr* as adjectives is that they have suppletive comparative and superlative forms like other adjctives do. Both *sehr* and *viel* share their comparative and superlative forms which are *mehr* 'more' and *am meisten* 'most' respectively.

2.4 Cross-categorical distribution of degree expressions

In this section, I discuss the cross-categorical distribution of degree expressions. In 2.4.1, I start with Doetjes' 'degree expression continuum,' which is intended to describe the cross-categorical distribution of degree expressions and provides a constraint on their distribution. Section 2.4.2 compares the distribution of degree expressions from a cross-linguistic perspective.

2.4.1 Degree expression continuum

In her work on French, Dutch and English degree expressions, Doetjes (2008) mentions that degree expressions differ with regard to their cross-categorical distribution. Depending on their cross-categorical distribution, she identifies different types of degree expressions. I will not focus on the types of degree expressions she distinguishes, but on her general claim that degree expressions form a continuum and that the continuum constrains their distribution. An essential part of her analysis is the claim that degree expressions can only apply to adjacent contexts in the degree expressions continuum.

Doetjes distinguishes the following six contexts in which degree expressions can be used: (i) gradable adjectives, (ii) gradable nominal predicates, (iii) gradable verbs, (iv) eventive verbs, eventive adjectives, comparatives, (v) mass nouns, and (vi) plural nouns. I illustrate these contexts below by taking French (*très* and *beaucoup*) and German high degree expressions (*sehr* and *viel*) as examples. I will show parallel examples from French in (a) and German in (b).

The first context is the combination of a gradable adjective with a degree expression. This is the only context in French in which *très* is used.[22] German uses *sehr* with gradable adjectives. The other mentioned degree expressions, *beaucoup* in French and *viel* in German, cannot be used in this context.

---

[22] Cf. Doetjes (2008) for a case study of *très* and examples in which it (non-systematically) extends to other degree contexts.

(61) a. *Paul est très grand.*
Paul is   very tall
'Paul is very tall.'
b. *Paul ist sehr groß.*
Paul is   very tall
'Paul is very tall.'

The second context comprises gradable nominal predicates, i.e. predicatively used nominals as in (62). French uses *beaucoup* for grading such nouns and German makes use of *viel*. This is not unexpected since *beaucoup* as well as *viel* also function as adnominal quantity expressions in French and German.

(62) a. *Jean a   beaucoup faim.*
Jean has a lot   hunger
'Jean is very hungry.' (Doetjes, 2008, 127)
b. *Jean hat viel   Hunger.*
Jean has much hunger
'Jean is very hungry.'

Doetjes uses the label 'gradable verbs' for verbal degree gradation. Whereas French uses a different expression for degree gradation of verbs (*beaucoup*) than for grading the positive form of adjectives (*très*), German uses the same expression – *sehr* – in both contexts.

(63) a. *Il aime beaucoup cette langue.*
he loves a lot   this language
'He loves this language very much.'
b. *Er liebt diese Sprache   sehr.*
he loves this language very
'He loves this language very much.'

In the fourth context, Doetjes lumps together several distinct subcontexts. The first subcontext is called 'eventive verbs' by Doetjes and represents what was called 'extent gradation' above. For this case (64), French uses *beaucoup*, whereas German makes use of *viel* rather than *sehr*. German shows a split in marking of verbal extent and degree gradation, whereas such a split does not show up in French. The second subcontext is gradation

2.4 Cross-categorical distribution of degree expressions

of predicatively used adjectives as in (65). Doetjes uses the term 'eventive adjectives' to denote this context. The reason is that in (65a) and (b) the degree expression specifies the frequency of Paul being ill. Doetjes' term 'eventive adjective' is dependent on the fact that *beaucoup*, and similarly *viel* in German, results in a frequency specification. In (65a) and (b) it is the frequency of Paul being ill that is indicated by the degree expression. Using *très* in (c) rather than *beaucoup* and *sehr* instead of *viel* leads to a degree reading specifying the intensity of Paul's illness.

(64) a. *Il va beaucoup au cinema.*
       he goes a lot   to.the cinema
       'He goes to the movies a lot.'
   b. *Er geht viel ins Kino.*
       he goes much in.the cinema
       'He goes to the movies a lot.'

(65) a. *Paul est beaucoup malade.*
       Paul is a lot   ill
       'Paul is ill a lot.'
   b. *Paul ist viel krank.*
       Paul is much ill
       'Paul is ill a lot.'
   c. *Paul est très malade.*
       Paul is very ill.
       'Paul is very ill.'
   d. *Paul ist sehr krank.*
       Paul is very ill
       'Paul is very ill.'

The third subcontext covers graded comparatives as in (66). For gradating comparatives both – French as well as German – use a different degree expression than for the positive form of adjectives. French uses *beaucoup* and German uses *viel*. This subcontext does not really fit with the other two subcontexts since in the other two cases the degree expression specifies the frequency of an event. In case of comparatives, the degree expression does not specify a frequency, but the difference that obtains between the two compared NPs.

(66) a. *Paul est beaucoup plus grand que Daniel.*
　　　 Paul is a lot   more tall than Daniel
　　　 'Paul is much taller than Daniel.'
　　b. *Paul ist viel   größer als Daniel.*
　　　 Paul is much taller than Daniel
　　　 'Paul is much taller than Daniel.'

The last two contexts distinguished by Doetjes are non-predicatively used mass (67) and count nouns (68). Neither French nor German has a distinction between mass and plural count quantity expressions similar to the English one between *much* and *many*. In French, adnominal quantity expressions require the partitive article *de*. The partitive article is not required if the graded noun is used predicatively (62a). In German, *viel* agrees with its head noun in case and number and therefore inflection differs depending on whether the head noun is a mass noun, which is morphologically singular, or a plural count noun.

(67) a. *beaucoup de   soupe*
　　　 a lot   of.the soup
　　　 'much soup'
　　b. *viel Suppe*
　　　 much soup
　　　 'much soup'
(68) a. *beaucoup de   livres*
　　　 a lot   of.the books
　　　 'many books'
　　b. *viele Bücher*
　　　 much books
　　　 'many books'

Table 2 summarizes the distribution of high degree expressions in French and German. French uses *très* only with gradable adjectives and *beaucoup* in all other contexts. German makes use of *sehr* with gradable adjectives and for verbal degree gradation, whereas *viel* is used in all other contexts. Doetjes claims that degree expressions are only used in adjacent contexts, hence the distribution of German *sehr* and *viel* contradicts this assumption.

As table 2 shows, *sehr* is not found in adjacent contexts, but is restricted to contexts (i) and (iii). A solution for this problem would be to rearrange

2.4 Cross-categorical distribution of degree expressions

Context of use	French	German
(i) gradable adjectives	très	sehr
(ii) gradable nominal predicates		viel
(iii) gradable verbs	beaucoup	sehr
(iv) eventive verbs, eventive adjectives, comparatives		viel
(v) mass nouns		
(vi) plural nouns		

Table 2: Degree expression continuum for French and German high degree expressions, based on Doetjes (2008).

the contexts but Doetjes argues that the order in contexts is a natural one based on the diachronic development of degree expressions. A further problem for Doetjes' degree expression continuum is provided by the distribution of the Persian degree expressions *kheyli* 'very' and *ziad* 'much.' *Kheyli* is used for degree gradation of adjectives (69a) as well as verbs (69b). Hence, *kheyli* is very much like German *sehr*, and *ziad*, which is used for extent gradation (70) and as an adnominal quantity expression (71), is much like German *viel*. The difference between the Persian and German degree expressions is that *kheyli* is also used with comparatives (72). Thus Doetjes' fourth context is split in Persian as *ziad* is used for extent gradation of verbs and adjectives but not for comparatives. This further indicates that this context consists of rather heterogeneous subtypes.

(69) Persian (Indo-Iranian <Indo-European)
    a. *Ou kheyli ghadboland ast.*
        3SG very tall   is
        'S/he is very tall.'
    b. *Oura kheyli dustdarad.*
        3SG.ACC very like.3SG
        'S/he likes him/her very much.'

(70) *Ou ziad knoonrizi dasht.*
        3SG much bleeding has
        'S/he bled a lot.' (= extent)

(71) a. *Dar daryache ab ziad ast.*
        in.the lake   water much is
        'There is a lot of water in the lake.'

2 Gradation and degree expressions

    b.   Ou ketabhaye ziadi darad.
         3SG books   much has
         'S/he has many books.'

(72)   In pesar kheyli bozorg-tar as dushash ast.
        DEM boy very tall-COMP as his friend is
        'The boy is much taller than his friend.'

The distribution of *ziad* and *kheyli* is summarized in table 3. Two contexts discussed for French and German are missing: gradable nominal predicates and eventive adjectives. Nevertheless, the distribution of degree expressions in Persian is problematic for Doetjes' continuum hypothesis.

Based on the German and Persian data, I reject Doetjes' continuum claim and go into a broader cross-linguistic comparison of the distribution of degree expressions in the next section. I will use different contexts to Doetjes and do not assume that they are naturally ordered in a degree expression continuum.

Context of use	Persian
(i) gradable adjectives	kheyli
(iii) gradable verbs	kheyli
(iv.a) eventive verbs	ziad
(iv.b) comparatives	kheyli
(v) mass nouns	ziad
(vi) count nouns	ziad

Table 3: Degree expression continuum for Persian.

2.4.2 Cross-linguistic distribution of degree expressions

As argued in section 2.1, there are two different subtypes of verb gradation, which are degree and extent gradation. Extent gradation can itself be subdivided into two subtypes: frequentative and durative extent gradation. Hence, we have to distinguish three different contexts for verb gradation, which yields five different strategies for marking these contexts. Table 4 summarizes these five different possibilities. The first option is that a language uses the same degree expression for all three contexts. As a general second option, a language could mark two contexts in the same way and

2.4 Cross-categorical distribution of degree expressions

employ a different degree expression for the third context. Either degree gradation could be marked differently from extent gradation or one of the subtypes of extent gradation could be marked in the same way as degree gradation, whereas the other one requires a different degree expression. The last option would be to mark all three contexts differently.

degree gradation	extent gradation$_{Frequency}$	extent gradation$_{Duration}$
A	A	A
A	B	B
A	A	B
A	B	A
A	B	C

Table 4: Possible distribution of adverbial degree expressions.

French uses the first option since *beaucoup* is uniformly used for degree as well as extent gradation. German on the other hand uses the second option: degree gradation is marked differently from extent gradation. Both subtypes of extent gradation are marked in the same way. Table 5 lists the distribution of adverbially used degree expressions in 27 languages, including French and German. The language sample is neither geographically nor genetically well balanced and only contains languages from Eurasia. Although the sample covers languages from different language families (Indo-European, Afro-Asiatic, Altaic, Kartvelian, Sino-Tibetan, Finno-Ugric, Bantu), most of the languages belong to the Indo-European family. Therefore no valid typological generalizations can be proposed; nevertheless the data discussed in this section provide, as far as I know, the first large cross-linguistic comparison of the distribution of degree expressions.[23]

The languages in table 5 display only two of the possible strategies distinguished above. The languages either show the same distribution as French – option 1 – or they employ the strategy used in German, which was the second one. There is no language in the sample that uses one of the other three strategies. It could simply be chance that no other patterns have been attested by the data, probably due to the limited set of languages in

---

[23] When I am speaking of the distribution of degree expressions, I am only concerned with the distribution of the neutrally high degree adverbials mentioned in the table. Different adverbials may have different distributions.

2 Gradation and degree expressions

the sample. Therefore, I do not claim that the other types cannot be found, they simply do not show up in my sample.

Language	Verb gradation		
	Degree gradation	Extent gradation (frequency)	Extent gradation (duration)
German	*sehr*	*viel*	*viel*
Dutch	*erg/veel*[24]	*veel*	*veel*
Russian	*cčen'*	*mnogo*	*mnogo*
Polish	*bardzo*	*duzo*	*duzo*
Persian	*kheyli*	*ziad*	*ziad*
Mandarin Chinese	*hěn*	*hěn dūo*	*hěn dūo*
Estonian	*väga*	*palju*	*palju*
Tatar	*bik*	*küp*	*küp*
Croation	*jako*	*mnogo*	*mnogo*
Georgian	*žalian*	*bevri*	*bevri*
Hebrew	*meʔod*	*harbe*	*harbe*
Japanese	*totemo*	*takusan*	*takusan*
Korean	*acwu*	*manhi*	*manhi*
French	*beaucoup*	*beaucoup*	*beaucoup*
Romanian	*mult*	*mult*	*mult*
Spanish	*mucho*	*mucho*	*mucho*
Italian	*molto*	*molto*	*molto*
Bulgarian	*mnogo*	*mnogo*	*mnogo*
English[25]	(*very*) *much, a lot*	(*very*) *much, a lot*	(*very*) *much, a lot*
Swedish	*mycket*	*mycket*	*mycket*
Turkish	*čok*	*čok*	*čok*
Finnish	*paljon*	*paljon*	*paljon*
Khalka Mongolian	*ix*	*ix*	*ix*
Nepali	*dherai*	*dherai*	*dherai*
Arabic	*k-θ-r*	*k-θ-r*	*k-θ-r*
Swahili	*sana*	*sana*	*sana*
Kikuyu	*monɔ*	*monɔ*	*monɔ*

Table 5: Cross-linguistic distribution of degree expressions used for verb gradation.

---

[24] Doetjes (1997, 2008) mentions that *erg* and *veel* are in complementary distribution, *erg* should only be used for degree gradation, whereas *veel* is restricted to extent gradation. But according to my information (both from the Nederlands and Belgium) *veel* can also be used as a degree modifier and sometimes is even preferred to *erg*.

[25] See (Quirk et al., 1985, 469ff.) for a discussion of English intensifiers and Gonzáles-Díaz (2008) on a discussion of recent developments of English intensifiers.

2.4 Cross-categorical distribution of degree expressions

I will use the terms 'French-type' and 'German-type' to refer to the two attested types distinguished above. 'German-type' languages use different degree expressions for degree and extent gradation, whereas 'French-type' languages make use of the same expression for both. To refer to the expressions used for verb gradation, I introduce the notions 'd-,' 'e-' and 'd/e-' adverbials. 'd(egree)-adverbials' are adverbial degree expressions that are only used for degree gradation. 'e(xtent)-adverbials' are restricted to extent gradation, whereas 'd(egree)/e(xtent)-adverbials,' like French *beaucoup*, can be used for degree as well as extent gradation. 'German-type' languages distinguish between 'd-' and 'e-adverbials,' whereas 'French-type' languages employ 'd/e-adverbials' for verb gradation. I take Swahili and Kikuyu as a special subtype of the 'French-type languages' as they differ in one important aspect from the other languages of this type. I call this special subtype 'Swahili-type languages.'

Starting with 'German-type' languages, table 6 shows the cross-categorical distribution of 'd-' and 'e-adverbials.' The table summarizes how these adverbials extend to the adjectival and nominal domain. For each domain, I only distinguish two subcontexts, which are (i) positive vs. comparative for adjectives and (ii) mass vs. count for nouns. Some of the contexts discussed by Doetjes, such as gradable nominals and eventive verbs, are not taken into consideration.

As indicated in the table, all the languages use the same expression for verbal degree gradation as well as intensifying the positive form of adjectives. The expression used for verbal extent gradation is always also used as an adnominal quantity expression. 'German-type' languages treat degree gradation, irrespective whether it is related to adjectives or verbs, in the same way. On the other hand, the expression of quantity, in the verbal as well as the nominal domain, is also treated in the same way. All of these languages, except Persian and Japanese, use the expression used for extent gradation also for grading comparatives. Comparatives seem to be the only context that shows variance in marking, whereas all the languages are uniform with regard to the other gradation contexts.

2 Gradation and degree expressions

Language	Adjectival domain		Nominal domain		Verbal domain
	Positive	Comparative	Mass	Count	
German	sehr	viel	viel	viel	$sehr_D$/$viel_E$
Russian	očen'	mnogo	mnogo	mnogo	$očen'_D$/$mnogo_E$
Dutch	erg	veel	veel	veel	erg_D/$veel_{(D)E}$
Polish	bardzo	duzo	duzo	duzo	$bardzo_D$/$duzo_E$
Mandarin Chinese	hěn	hěn duō	hěn duō	hěn duō	$hěn_D$/$hěn\ duō_E$
Tatar	bik	küp	küp	küp	bik_D/$küp_E$
Croatian	jako	mnogo	mnogo	mnogo	$jako_D$/$mnogo_E$
Georgian	žaljan	bevri	bevri	bevri	$žaljan_D$/$bevri_E$
Estonian	väga	palju	palju	palju	$väga_D$/$palju_E$
Korean	acwu[26]	manhi	manhi	manhi	$acwu_D$/$manhi_E$
Hebrew	meʔod	harbe	harbe	harbe	$meʔod_D$/$harbe_E$
Persian	kheyli	kheyli	ziad	ziad	$kheyli_D$/$ziad_E$
Japanese	totemo	totemo	takusan	takusan	$totemo_D$/$takusan_E$

Table 6: Cross-categorical distribution of 'd'- and 'e'-adverbials.

The cross-categorical distribution of 'd/e-adverbials' is summarized for 'French-type' languages in table 7. As shown in the table, 'French-type' languages differ with regard to the marking of the positive form of adjectives. Either the verbal degree expression extends to all contexts, including the positive form, like Bulgarian or Italian, or different degree expressions are required for the positive form of adjectives as in French and Spanish. Further variance exists with regard to the mass/count distinction. Most languages use the same quantity expression for mass and count

---

[26] Whether there is a distinct class of adjectives in Korean is highly disputed and I do not want to take a stance on that issue.

nouns; only English and Khalka Mongolian show a split in marking of both types of nouns. In both languages, the quantity expression used with mass nouns has a broader distribution than the one used with count nouns. But it should be noted that in English the split between mass and count only shows up with *much* and *many* but not with *a lot*, which can be used with mass and count nouns alike. Hence, the mass/count distinction does not extend throughout the whole system of nominal quantity expressions in English but only holds for particular lexical items.

Language	Adjectival domain		Nominal domain		Verbal domain
	Positive	Comparative	Mass	Count	
French	trés	beaucoup	beaucoup	beaucoup	beaucoup$_{D/E}$
Spanish	muy	mucho	mucho	mucho	mucho$_{D/E}$
Romanian	foarte	mult	mult	mult	mult$_{D/E}$
English	very	much, a lot	much, a lot	much, a lot	much, a lot$_{D/E}$
Finnish	hyvin	paljon	paljon	paljon	paljon$_{D/E}$
Bulgarian	mnogo	mnogo	mnogo	mnogo	mnogo$_{D/E}$
Italian	molto	molto	molto	molto	molto$_{D/E}$
Swedish	mycket	mycket	mycket	mycket	mycket$_{D/E}$
Turkish	čok	čok	čok	čok	čok$_{D/E}$
Khalka Mongolian	ix	ix	ix	olon	ix$_{D/E}$
Nepali	dherai	dherai	dherai	dherai	dherai$_{D/E}$
Arabic	dʒidd	k-θ-r	k-θ-r	k-θ-r	k-θ-r$_{D/E}$

Table 7: Cross-categorical distribution of 'd/e'-adverbials.

The following tentative generalizations can be derived from the data in the tables shown above:

(73)　(i.)　If a language uses different adverbials for extent and degree gradation ('d-' vs. 'e-adverbials'), the expression that is used for verbal degree gradation ('d-adverbial') is also used for in-

2 Gradation and degree expressions

tensifying the positive form of adjectives.[27]

(ii.) If a language uses different adverbials for extent and degree gradation ('d-' vs. 'e-adverbials'), the expression that is used for extent gradation ('e-adverbial') is also used in the nominal domain.

(iii.) If a language uses the same adverbial for extent and degree gradation ('d/e-adverbial'), the expression used as 'd/e-adverbial' extends – at least – to the nominal domain and to comparatives.

(73ii) and (iii) allow for the generalization in (74):

(74) (iv) Expressions used for extent gradation of verbs are also used in the nominal domain, irrespective whether the language distinguishes between 'd-' and 'e-adverbials' or not.

A short note on the nominal mass/count distinction is appropriate. Doetjes (2012, 2565) mentions that adnominal quantity expressions in English can be extended to adverbial uses, i.e., they function as an expression of extent gradation. Either these adnominal expressions are insensitive to the mass/count distinction as, for example, *a lot* or if they are sensitive to this distinction, as in the case of *much* and *many*, the expression used with mass nouns is used in the adverbial context too. This observation is also confirmed by the Khalka Mongolian data mentioned above.

Two classes of languages contradict – at least some – of the generalizations made above. The first class, just presenting an apparent contradiction, is Tagalog. The second class, presenting a real contradiction, is formed by the 'Swahili-type' languages. Tagalog uses different grading devices for different lexical categories. In (75) it is shown how the positive form of an adjective is graded and intensification of a comparative form is shown in (76). The positive form takes the prefix *napaka-*, which indicates a high degree. There is no corresponding way to intensify comparatives; rather an element meaning *truly* has to be used, which is ambiguous between indicating a high degree and an epistemic reading expressing certainty.

---

[27] This claim is supported by Muroi (2010) who shows, based on a corpus study, that in German the positive and the comparative form of adjectives mostly take different degree expression.

2.4 Cross-categorical distribution of degree expressions

(75) Tagalog (Central Philippine < Austronesian)
 Napaka-tangkad ng bata.
 INTS-tall NSUB child
 'The child is very tall.'

(76) *Talaga-ng mas ma-tangkad ang bata sa kaniya-ng kapatid.*
 true-LNK COMP ADJ-tall SUB child DAT 3GEN-LNK sibling
 'The boy is much taller than his brother.'

A high quantity with regard to nouns is expressed by an adjective meaning plenty (77). The affix *napaka-* cannot be used with nouns but is restricted to adjectives. As the example shows, there is no mass/count distinction that is reflected in the choice of the adnominal quantity expression.

(77) *Kumain siya ng ma-rami-ng saping/sopas.*
 eat<PST.AV> 3SG.SUB NSUB ADJ-plenty-LNK banana/soup
 'He ate many bananas/soup.'

There are two different ways of expressing verbal degree gradation. Either the same construction as used for comparatives can be used (78), or a degree expression which is uniquely linked to the predicate by the linker *(na)ng* can be employed (79). *Husto* also expresses a high degree but is restricted to adverbial contexts and therefore can neither used with adjectives nor nouns.

(78) *Talaga-ng ginulat ng leon ang bata.*
 true-LNK frighten<PST.UV> NSUB lion SUB child
 'The lion frightened the child a lot.'

(79) *Ginulat ng leon (na)ng husto ang bata.*
 frighten<PST.UV> NSUB lion LNK INTS SUB child
 'The lion frightened the child a lot.'

The examples in (80) and (81) illustrate that *(na)ng husto* is also used for extent gradation. In (80) this is illustrated for the durative subtype and in (81) for the frequentative one. *Talaga-ng* cannot be used for expressing extent gradation rather with the verbs for *sleep* and *go* only an epistemic interpretation is possible.

(80) *Na-tulog (na)-ng husto ang bata kagabi.*
 PST.UV-sleep LNK INTS SUB child last.night
 'The boy slept a lot last night.'

2 Gradation and degree expressions

(81)   *Pumunta   siya   sa   sine-han   (na)-ng husto.*
       go<PST.UV>   3SG.SUB   DAT   movie-LOC   LNK   INTS
       'He went to the cinema a lot.'

In Tagalog, degree expressions do not extend across lexical categories, taking constructions as shown in (76) and (77) aside, which make use of lexical items that are functionally not restricted to the expression of gradation. This seems only to hold for native degree expressions, since *sobra* 'too much,' which is a loan from Spanish, can be used with adjectives, verbs as well as nouns. The case of grading the positive form of adjectival concepts (75) is not a counterexample as gradation is morphologically and not syntactically expressed and therefore is not covered by the generalizations made above.

The 'Swahili-type' languages Swahili and Kikuyu show the distribution of degree expressions as summarized in table 8.[28] The relevant deviation concerns the nominal domain; unlike 'German-type' and 'French-type' languages, 'Swahili-type' languages do not use the expression used for extent gradation in nominal domain too. Instead, Swahili *sana* is restricted to the adjectival and verbal domain, whereas *-ingi* is used with mass and count nouns. Kikuyu is special in having a distinct form for grading comparatives which is not used in the other contexts.

Language	Adjectival domain		Nominal domain		Verbal domain
	Positive	Comparative	Mass	Count	
Swahili	sana	sana	-ingi	-ingi	$sana_{D/E}$
Kikuyu	monɔ	makeria	-inge	-inge	$monɔ_{D/E}$

Table 8: Cross-categorical distribution of degree expressions in 'Swahili-type' languages.

The 'Swahili-type' languages contradict the generalization expressed in (73), namely that languages with 'd/e-adverbials' use this expression also in the nominal domain and with comparatives. Hence, the generalizations

---

[28] See Krifka & Zerbian (2008) for a broader discussion of quantity expressions and quantifiers across Bantu languages.

made above are restricted to 'German-type' and 'French-type' languages and do not hold for 'Swahili-type' languages.

The generalizations for 'German-type' and 'French-type' languages give rise to a couple of questions: first, is there any particular reason why degree expressions used for extent gradation (German *viel*, French *beaucoup*) are also used as adnominal quantity expressions and those restricted to degree gradation (German *sehr* and French *très*) are not? Second, does German display a difference between extent and degree gradation that does not overtly exist in French as such? Or does French display the same distinction as German does but masked by using the same degree expression? In chapter 4, I will argue that 'German-' as well as 'French-type' languages show the same distinction between extent and degree gradation. I will argue that extent and degree gradation are realized in two different syntactic configurations, irrespective whether a language distinguishes between 'd-' and 'e-adverbials' as in German, or if it does not, as is the case with French. This syntactic difference will also provide a natural explanation to the first question. I will argue that quantity is expressed in the same kind of syntactic configuration irrespective whether it is in the nominal or verbal domain.

A further question is why, in all languages that obey the above generalizations (except Persian and Japanese), comparatives are graded with expressions that are not restricted to degree contexts. In 'French-type' languages comparatives pattern with all other contexts, whereas in 'German-type' languages they are graded by using extent/quantity expressions. An answer to this question is beyond the limits of the thesis.

At last, it is surely a question whether more languages obey the generalizations made above than contradict them like the 'Swahili-type' languages do. A broader cross-linguistic comparison could reveal more strategies for expressing gradation across categories, and this would require a principal explanation for why these differences arise.

2.5 Conclusion

In the first section, the notion of gradation was defined as a linguistic process of comparing degrees. Degrees represent measurement values of a scale; hence, gradation is best analyzed with regard to scales. A second essential element of gradation is degree expressions, which introduce the

2 Gradation and degree expressions

degree of comparison. In a broad sense, the notion of a 'degree expression' covers all devices used for gradation ranging from comparative degree morphology to degree expressions such as German *sehr*.

Verb gradation shows an additional complexity not shared with adjectival or nominal gradation. If verbs are eventive, gradation can either affect a gradable property related to the verb or a gradable property of the respective event. This results in a distinction between degree and extent gradation. Two basic types of languages have been identified with regard to the expression of verb gradation. 'German-type' languages use different degree expressions for extent and degree gradation, whereas 'French-type' languages use the same expression for both. It was shown that expressions used for extent gradation, in 'German-' as well as 'French-type' languages, are also always used in the nominal domain as adnominal quantity expressions. It was argued that neither extent gradation nor the specification of an adnominal quantity requires a quantificational analysis. A quantificational analysis was uniformly rejected for all degree expressions. Nevertheless, the specification of the exact mode of semantic composition, i.e., modification vs. argument saturation, is postponed until chapter 5.

3 Verb classification

An analysis of verb gradation requires a discussion of the properties of the verb, which is the graded expression. As will be shown in this chapter, the interpretation of verb gradation depends on the semantic class of the verb. This means that a different interpretation of verbal degree gradation applies for different semantic verb classes. Examples are provided in (1). In (a), *sehr* specifies the increase of width, whereas in (b) it is the intensity of his love.

(1) a. *Der Riss hat sich sehr verbreitert.*
        the crack has REFL very widened
        'The crack has widened a lot.'
    b. *Er liebt Angela sehr.*
        he loves Angela very
        'He loves Angela very much.'

This chapter aims at discussing different types of verb classification. In 3.1, I will start with a classification of verbs based on argument alternations, as it is explicated in the work of Levin (1993). Section 3.2 discusses aktionsart-based event structural representations of verb meaning. 'Manner/result complementarity,' which builds on an event structural classification of verbs and provides a lexicalization constraint on verbal roots, is discussed in 3.3. Manner/result complementarity is of relevance since it introduces the notion of 'scalar verbs.' Since scales are an essential component for gradation, this provides a natural link between verb gradation and verb semantics. Section 3.4 finally discusses the notion of the 'degree verb.' This term was introduced by Bolinger (1972) to denote gradable verbs, i.e., verbs that license degree gradation. This leads to the question what such 'degree verbs' have in common; in other words: what makes a verb gradable? Is gradability dependent on some other semantic property, like an aktionsart property, or is it independent from other semantic properties?

There are two proposals in the literature on that topic, which will be discussed in that section. The chapter closes with a general discussion on the notion of 'gradability.'

The current chapter provides the background for later chapters by introducing relevant aktionsart properties as well as other related properties which will be relevant in chapters 6 to 8. At the same time, the chapter presents different views on the relationship between scalarity/gradability and the lexical semantics of verbs. An essential question of this chapter is which verbs lexicalize scales, and are there any semantic constraints with respect to verbal degree gradability? The chapter will demonstrate that verbal scalarity is a much more common phenomenon than often assumed in literature, i.e., more verbs than usually thought have scales as components in their lexical semantics.

3.1 Semantic verb classes

In her 1993 monograph "English Verb Classes and Alternations," Beth Levin provides a classification of several thousand English verbs depending on the semantic class they belong to. The basis for her classification is diathesis alternations, i.e., alternations in the expressions of the arguments and adjuncts of a verb. The rationale of such a verb classification is characterized by Levin (1993, 11) as follows: "Studies of diathesis alternations show that verbs in English and other languages fall into classes on the basis of shared components of meaning. The class members have in common a range of properties, including the possible expression of certain morphologically related forms." The key idea is that the syntactic behavior of a verb depends on two properties: first, general principles of grammar and second, the meaning of the verb (Levin, 1993, 11). Whether a certain verb undergoes a diathesis alternation or not depends on the meaning of the verb, since each alternation requires the presence of a certain meaning component such as 'change of state' or 'change of location.' Therefore, verbs participating in the same alternations have to share some meaning component.

Levin uses argument alternations such as the causative/inchoative alternation in (2) or the middle alternation in (3) for her classification of verbs.

3.1 Semantic verb classes

(2)   a.   *The child broke the window.*
       b.   *The window broke.*
(3)   a.   *The boy cuts the bread.*
       b.   *The bread cuts easily.*

The range of argument alternations Levin uses for her classification of English verbs is rather extensive and I am not going to discuss them in detail. Levin mentions that not all languages show the same range of alternations but if they do, the alternations are licensed by the same meaning components (Levin, 1993, 10f.). Frense & Bennett (1996), for example, compare verbal alternations in German and English and show that they lead to a corresponding classification of verbs in both languages (see also Hale (2000) for a discussion of verbal alternations in O'odham (Uto-Aztecan), which also includes a broader cross-linguistic comparison). Schulte im Walde (2006) demonstrates for German that an automatic induction of semantic verb classes is possible. This automatic classification of verbs is in agreement with manually done classifications, such as the one by Levin.

Members of semantic verb classes share some properties, which include the realization of arguments, the interpretation of the arguments, the existence of morphologically related forms and – most importantly – some semantic components such as, for example, causing a change of state. But semantic verb classes such as those proposed by Levin are not unquestioned. Rosen (1996) – among others – argues that these classes face several problems; for example, semantically similar verbs participate in different alternations, or the syntactic behavior of verbs is not fully governed by their lexical semantics but also depends on context. She claims that semantic verb classes are "an epiphenomenon of descriptive work on lexical semantics, argument structure, and verbal alternations" (Rosen, 1996, 193). Even if event-based accounts, as claimed by Rosen, provide a better explanation of argument linking, the concept of semantic verb classes is relevant in the context of verb gradation. What makes these classes important in the context of verb gradation is that they share the same interpretation of verbal degree gradation (this claim goes back to Ropertz (2001) and is crucial for Löbner's (2012b) claim of 'subcompositionality,' which will be discussed in chapter 9). The German examples in (4) illustrate the relevance of semantic verb classes for verbal degree gradation. In (4a) we have a change of state verb for which *sehr* specifies the extent of the change. *Bluten* 'bleed' is a verb of substance emission and in this case *sehr* indicates a great quantity of the emitted substance. Finally, *ängstigen* 'frighten' is a psych verb and *sehr* is related to the intensity of the feeling.

(4)   a.   *Das Kind ist sehr gewachsen.*
             the child is very grown
             'The child has grown a lot.'
      b.   *Die Wunde blutet sehr.*
             the wound bleeds very
             'The wound is bleeding a lot.'
      c.   *Der Hund ängstigt das Kind sehr.*
             the dog frightens the child very
             'The dog frightens the child a lot.'

Degree gradation is related to different scales for all three verbs in (4). It is not only that the respective verbs in (4) differ with regard to the scale they are related to and therefore with respect to the interpretation of verbal degree gradation, but we can only observe a uniform pattern for verbs belonging to the same semantic class. This is due to the fact that degree expressions do not lexically encode a scale but require the graded predicate to contribute a suitable gradation scale. All gradable change of state verbs (e.g,. *widen, broaden, lengthen*) receive the same interpretation of degree gradation, the same holds for all gradable verbs of substance emission (e.g., *rain, fester, hail*) and gradable psych verbs (e.g., *fear, love, amuse*) respectively. Gradation scales can be seen as a further semantic component shared by members of certain semantic classes. But it is a semantic property that is not related to argument realization, since argument alternations do not affect verbal degree gradation. In (5) the experiencer, the one having the feeling, is realized as the subject of the verb and *sehr* specifies the intensity of the experiencer's feeling, whereas in (4c) it is the intensity of the feeling of the referent of the argument in object position that is indicated by *sehr*. *Lieben* 'love' as well as *ängstigen* 'frighten' are psych verbs; they differ in argument realization but nevertheless degree gradation shows the same effect on both verbs.

(5)   *Die Frau liebt den Mann sehr.*
        the woman loves the man very
        'The woman loves the man very much.'

3.1 Semantic verb classes

For psych verbs, it can be said that – irrespective of the heretogeneity of this verb class – they give access to INTENSITY scales.[1] But not all semantic verb classes license a certain type of scale. This holds in two different ways: first, some semantic verb classes, like verbs of change of possession (*give, take, sell, buy*), reject degree gradation completely.[2] These verbs, at least in German, take neither *sehr* nor other degree expressions. Second, verb classes can be heterogeneous regarding scales such that some verbs accept degree expressions, whereas others do not. In German, *rennen* 'run' and *laufen* 'walk, run' can be graded by *sehr* (6) but *gehen* 'go,' as one example, cannot. Grading *rennen* affects the velocity of the moving entity and probably verbs of motion that do not admit degree gradation either give not access to a velocity scale or inherently specify the value of that scale in a way that is incompatible with further degree gradation. I will not speculate further on this point and not go into further detail.

(6) Übrigens ich habe den Aufstieg in der vorgegebenen Zeit
 by the way I have the climb in the prescribed time
 geschafft, muss aber zugeben, dass ich sehr gerannt bin [...].[D]
 managed have to but admit that I very ran am
 'By the way, I managed the climb in the prescribed time but have to admit that I ran very fast [...]'

The question of gradability will be discussed in more detail in section 3.5. Lastly, it has to be noted that the notion of 'semantic verb class' is relevant for the description of verbal degree gradation but that the classes I discuss throughout this thesis do not directly correspond to semantic classes identified by Levin. Several classes distinguished by Levin will be taken together since they exhibit uniform behavior with regard to verbal degree gradation. For each of the case studies in the later part of the thesis, I will specify how the respective classes are related to those of Levin.[3]

---

[1] Psych verbs are heterogeneous with regard to argument realization as well as aktionsart, as will be shown in detail in chapter 8

[2] Beavers (2006) in fact argues for a scalar analysis of verbs of change of possession but discussing this in detail would go beyond the limits of the thesis.

[3] See Croft (2012, 369ff.) for a recent comparison of Levin's verb classification with the FrameNet approach and related work.

3.2 Event structure

The term 'event structure' is used to refer to a structured lexical semantic representation of verb meaning. Verbs "individuate and name events" (Levin & Rappaport Hovav, 2011, 424) and hence lexicalize properties of events. Event structures are, as mentioned by (Levin & Rappaport Hovav, 2005, 4), couched within a theory of event conceptualization which determines the properties of events that are encoded in verbs. Event structures are used for structured representations of grammatically relevant properties of event descriptions.[4] Such structured representations go by different names as 'semantic forms' Wunderlich (1997), 'logical structures' (Van Valin & LaPolla 1997; Van Valin 2005), 'event structures' (Rappaport Hovav & Levin 1998; Levin & Rappaport Hovav 2005) and others (cf. Levin & Rappaport Hovav 2011). All these approaches share a common aim, namely to explain the verb's grammatical behavior, such as argument realization or verbal alternations by their inherent event structural properties. But these approaches also differ from each other in details. In the remainder, I concentrate on semantic representations as used in Role & Reference Grammar and Levin & Rappaport Hovav's event structures. The notion of 'event' does not occur in Role & Reference Grammar, whereas it figures prominently in Levin & Rappaport Hovav's work. What the authors mean by 'event' are what Bach (1986) and others call 'eventualities.' 'Eventuality' is a cover term for all situation types: states, processes and events. I will use the term 'event' to refer to non-stative situation types and use 'eventuality' to cover states as well as events.

Approaches to event structure differ with regard to the question which properties of event descriptions determine the grammatical behavior of verbs. A large number of researchers, including Van Valin and Levin & Rappaport Hovav, take aktionsart to be the basic properties of event descriptions. Others, like Croft (1991), assume that causal relationships are the most important element in determining the grammatical behavior of verbs (cf. Levin & Rappaport Hovav (2005) for a discussion of different approaches to event structure). Since event structures represent structured representations of grammatically relevant elements of the lexical semantics of verbs, they are usually combined with predicate decomposition. Systems

---

[4] Verbs only lexicalize properties of event descriptions but not of events as such.

3.2 Event structure

of predicate decomposition use a small set of semantic primitives "to represent components of meaning that recur across significant sets of verbs" (Levin & Rappaport Hovav, 2005, 69). Those components used in predicate decomposition are chosen to represent the grammatically relevant elements in the verb's lexical semantics. I will start by discussing aktionsart in section 3.2.1 and move on to a discussion of predicate decomposition in 3.2.2.

3.2.1 Aktionsart

Vendler (1957, 1967) proposed a four-way distinction of verbs according to their inherent temporal characteristics and distinguished the following four aktionsart classes: states, activities, achievements and accomplishments. As often mentioned in the literature, aktionsart classification does not always apply to verbs as such but rather to verbal predications[5], that is verbs and arguments/adjuncts.

Three semantic features can be used to distinguish between the four Vendlerian classes: dynamicity, durativity and telicity. Dynamicity is the property that a verb refers to a situation which is conceived as a happening in the world. Stative predications are non-dynamic, while all other aktionsart classes are dynamic. States simply hold in the world, whereas events, which are dynamic, always entail some change. This notion of 'change' builds on Dowty (1979), who assumes that dynamic predications can only be evaluated over an interval of time, whereas states can be evaluated at a single moment. The second property, durativity, describes whether a verbal predication describes an eventuality that is conceived as to be extended in time. The last property is telicity, which captures the fact whether the verbal predication is taken to entail the reaching of a natural endpoint. Different theoretical explanations of the notion of 'telicity' exist – see for example the discussion in Borik (2006) – and I turn to a deeper theoretical discussion of telicity in chapter 6.

Table 9 lists the feature specifications for Vendlerian aktionsart classes. The list contains a fifth aktionsart class – semelfactive predicates – which

---

[5] I use the term 'verbal predication' for referring to the respective object of an aktionsart classification, which can be either a verb or the combination of a verb with its argument(s) or adjunct(s).

3 Verb classification

has been introduced by Smith (1997). All five classes are uniquely determined by the combination of the three features dynamicity, durativity and telicity.[6]

	dynamic	durative	telic
State predicate	no	yes	no
predicate	yes	yes	no
Achievement predicate	yes	no	yes
Accomplishment predicate	yes	yes	yes
Semelfactive predicate	yes	no	no

Table 9: Feature matrix of aktionsart properties.

The table lists stative predicates as the only stative, i.e., non-dynamic, type of predication. A state holds without a certain time limit, hence it is durative, and does not entail the reaching of an inherent endpoint. Activity predicates express a dynamic situation which also does not entail an endpoint. The two types of verbs that entail the reaching of a natural endpoint – accomplishment predicates and achievement predicates – differ with regard to durativity. The reaching of an endpoint, i.e., telicity, always implies a change in a certain property (but not *vice versa*). The telos, which is the entailed endpoint, can be understood as a state that holds at the end of the event but not at its beginning. Accomplishment predicates describe temporally extended changes[7], whereas achievement predicates denote punctual and thereby instantaneously occurring changes. In a more restricted sense, the term 'achievement' is used for "terms that denote the culmination of a process" (Löbner, 2013, 145), i.e., punctual changes that presuppose "a dynamic initial condition" (Löbner, 2013, 145). I will not delimit the term 'achievement' in this sense and use it for punctual change verbs irrespective of whether they presuppose a certain process such as *arrive* or not like *turn on (the light)*. Semelfactives, as the last class, are punctual activ-

---

[6] Croft (2012, 33f.) summarizes eleven aktionsart classes from literature, which cover at least four different types of states. Also Mori et al. (1992) argue for a finer distinction of aspectual classes and identify nine distinct classes for Japanese verbs.

[7] Note that this notion of 'change' differs from the notion of 'change' that is used to characterize dynamic predicates. An explication of the former notion of 'change' will be done in section 6.

ity predicates. English examples of semelfactive verbs are *cough* or *knock*. These verbs are ambiguous between a semelfactive – single event reading – and an activity reading. In their activity reading these verbs denote an iteration of single events.

Before turning to the discussion of aktionsart tests, a remark regarding the use of the terms 'accomplishment' and 'achievement' is required. Above I mentioned that accomplishment predicates describe durative changes, whereas achievement predicates are punctual ones. This is in accordance with Vendler's original classification and also the use of terminology in Van Valin (2005). There is also a use of these terms that goes back to Dowty (1979). Dowty uses 'accomplishment' for causative changes, whereas 'achievements' are their non-causative counterparts. Rappaport Hovav & Levin (1998) – among others – follow this use of terminology. I go with Vendler's original proposal and consider durativity to be the factor distinguishing between accomplishment predicates and achievement predicates rather than causativity. In fact, causativity is not taken to be a relevant aktionsart feature.

Turning now to the test criteria, different proposals in the literature exist how to test for dynamicity, durativity and telicity. The respective tests are language specific but test for the same semantic properties. For English, as one example, the progressive aspect is used to distinguish stative from non-stative predicates.[8] As Comrie (1976) mentions, the progressive aspect not only requires an ongoing but also a dynamic eventuality. Since stative predicates are not dynamic, they cannot be used in the progressive aspect. Languages without a grammaticalized progressive construction cannot make use of this test criterion. In the following, I discuss test criteria which will be used throughout the remainder of the thesis. I rely on German examples to illustrate the criteria. There is much debate with respect to (i) the validity of aktionsart tests and (ii) the question as to what they are testing (e.g. Nicolay (2007) for an extensive discussion of aktionsart tests in German). I will not get into this debate and only use more or

---

[8] To be more specific, the progressive aspect distinguishes between stage-level stative and individual-level stative predicates (Carlson 1977, Van Valin 2005, 35n3) on the one hand and between individual-level stative predicates and non-stative but durative predicates, as dynamic and punctual predicates, i.e., achievement predicates, require some type-shifting operation to be compatible with a progressive interpretation (cf. Rothstein 2004, chapter 2).

3 Verb classification

less well accepted test criteria.

The distinction between stative and non-stative, i.e., dynamic, predicates has gained a lot of attention in the linguistic literature (Dowty 1979, Katz 1995, Rapp 1997, Maienborn 2003, Rothmayr 2009 among others). In her discussion of aktionsart classification in German, Nicolay states that most of the tests mentioned in the literature are either unreliable or test for a different property than stativity. The test she considers to be the most reliable was introduced by Gabbay & Moravcsik (1980). This test is based on the fact that states, if they hold for a certain period of time, do so without gaps or interruptions. The authors write: "if someone knows something, then forgets, and then knows it again, we say that he rediscovered the relevant item; we count two states of knowing. Likewise, if someone is sick on a day, recovers, and becomes sick again, we say that the person was sick twice during the day" (Gabbay & Moravcsik, 1980, 63). After an interruption, a state cannot simply continue, but a new state of the same kind begins. Rapp (1997) argues for German that if an interruption is predicated of a state, the predicate can only combine with *wieder* 'again' but not with *weiter* 'further.' Activities on the other hand, which are dynamic, are compatible with *wieder* as well as *weiter*. The examples in (7) and (8) illustrate this test for the stative predicates *wohnen* 'to live, to reside' and *achten* 'to respect.'

(7) *Er wohnte drei Jahre lang in Köln,   nachdem er weggezogen*
    he lived   three years long in Cologne after   he moved.away
    war, wohnte er später wieder/ *weiter in Köln.
    was   lived   he later again   further in Cologne
    'He lived in Cologne for three years, after he moved away, he lived in Cologne again.'

(8) *Nachdem er sich entschuldigt hatte, achtete   ich ihn *weiter/*
    after   he REFL apologized   had   respected I   him further
    wieder.
    again
    'After he apologized, I respected him again.'
    (Nicolay, 2007, 77)

3.2 Event structure

The verbs *brüllen* 'yell' (9) and *regnen* 'rain' (10) denote dynamic eventualities and after a break the respective eventuality can either be continued or a new event of the same kind can start.⁹ As shown by the examples above (7)/(8), stative predications can only combine with *wieder*.

(9) *Er brüllte 10 Minuten, und nach einer Pause brüllte er weiter/*
he yelled 10 minutes and after a break yelled he further
wieder.
again
'He yelled for ten minutes and, after a short break, he continued yelling/yelled again.'
(Rapp, 1997, 37)

(10) *Es regnete, hörte eine Weile auf, und regnete dann weiter/*
it rained stopped a while PART and rained than further
wieder.
again
'It rained, stopped for a while, and then it continued raining/rained again.'

Maienborn (2003) mentions two further test criteria for stativity which she considers to be relatively reliable. The first criterion is that only dynamic predicates allow an anaphoric reference with *geschehen/passieren* 'happen occur,' whereas states reject it. The examples in (11) to (13) are taken from Maienborn (2003). In (11) and (12), taken from Maienborn (2003, 59f.), it is shown that eventualities denoted by dynamic predicates like (*Klavier*) *spielen* 'play (piano)' and *umherlaufen* 'walk around' can be anaphorically picked up by *geschehen/passieren*. Stative predications do not refer to eventualities which allow an anaphoric reference by *geschehen/passieren* as illustrated in (13) and (14), taken from Maienborn (2003, 59f.). A similar test for English by using *happen* for anaphoric reference is discussed in Jackendoff (1983) (also cf. Rappaport Hovav & Levin 2000, 284).

---

9   Nicolay (2007) mentions that one has to control carefully for agentivity. A construction such as *nach einer Pause* 'after a break/pause' expresses an agentive interruption of the respective eventuality. One has to be careful not to mix up dynamicity with agentivity.

3 Verb classification

(11) *Shirin spielte Klavier. Das geschah/passierte während...*
Shirin played piano   this happened/occurred while
'Shirin played piano. This happened/occurred while...'

(12) *Angela lief im Garten umher. Das geschah/passierte*
Angela walked in.the garden around this happened/occurred
während...
while
'Angela walked around in the garden. This happened/occurred while...'

(13) *Heidi stand am Fenster. *Das geschah/passierte während...*
Heidi stood at.the window this happened/occurred while
'Heidi was standing at the window. This happened/occurred while...'

(14) *Britta besaß ein Haus am See. *Das geschah/passierte*
Britta owned a house at.the lake this happened/occurred
während...
while
'Britta owned a house at the lake. This happened/occurred while...'

The second criterion Maienborn mentions is that manner adverbs like *fast* and *slowly* are restricted to dynamic predicates and therefore are not compatible with stative predications. If they are combined with states, the state is coerced towards a dynamic reading, i.e., coming into the respective state. Maienborn's (2003: 61) examples in (15) indicate the difference in acceptability of the manner adverb *schnell* 'fast' for dynamic (a, b) and stative predicates (c, d).[10]

(15) a. *Heidi lief schnell im Garten umher.*
Heidi walked fast in.the garden around
'Heidi walked around quickly in the garden.'
b. *Die Lampe blinkte schnell.*
the light blinked fast
'The light blinked quickly.'

---

[10] Mittwoch (2013, 28) mentions that iterative activity predicates, i.e., semelfactives, receive a different interpretation than non-iterative ones when combined with manner adverbials like *fast*.

c. #*Renate wartete schnell auf Eva.*
   Renate waited fast   on Eva
   'Renate waited quickly for Eva.'
d. #*Die Briefmarke klebte schnell auf dem Brief.*
   the stamp   stuck fast   on the letter
   'The stamp stuck quickly on the letter.'

Not all activity predicates receive the same interpretation if combined with the adverb *schnell*, as illustrated by the example in (16). The only admissible interpretation in (16) is that the wound starts bleeding easily. *Schnell* does not indicate the speed of the emitted blood, in contrast to (15a), in which case *schnell* specifies the speed of Heidi.

(16) *Die Wunde blutet schnell.*
      the wound bleeds fast
      'The wound bleeds easily.'

The three test criteria mentioned above can be used together to distinguish stative predicates from activity predicates. Activity predicates, which are atelic predications, can be distinguished from accomplishment predicates by a whole battery of tests. Accomplishment predicates and activity predicates can combine with time-span adverbials like *in X Zeit* 'in X time' but differ in the interpretations they allow. For activity predicates, as in (17), the time-span adverbial indicates the time until the respective event starts ('ingressive reading').

(17) *Der Junge schläft in einer Stunde.*
      The boy   sleeps in one hour
      'The boy sleeps in an hour.'
      → After an hour, the boy starts sleeping.
      ↛ After an hour, the boy finishes sleeping.

This reading is also possible for accomplishment predicates but in addition they allow a second interpretation in which the time-span adverbial indicates the time after which the event stops (18). Since accomplishment predicates are telic, the time-span adverbial can specify the time it takes to reach the telos ('egressive reading').

(18)   Der Mann repariert das Auto in einer Stunde.
       the man   repairs the car in one hour
       'The man repairs the car in an hour.'
       → After an hour, the man starts repairing the car.
       → After an hour, the man finishes repairing the car, i.e., after an hour the car is repaired.

Dowty (1979) mentions that expressions like *almost* (German *fast*) allow two different interpretations with accomplishment predicates (19a) – an ingressive as well as an egressive one – but only for an ingressive reading with activity predicates (19b).[11] As (19c) also shows, state predicates only license an ingressive reading of *fast*, since they lack a telos like activity predicates do. The most obvious interpretation of sentence (19c) would be: The man lived very close to Cologne (almost in the city, but a little outside). Nevertheless, in the example I focus on the aspectually relevant ingressive reading and ignore the local reading of the sentence.

(19)   a.   *Der Mann hat den Wagen fast   repariert.*
            the man   has the car   almost repaired
            'The man almost repaired the car.'
            → The man almost started repairing the car.
            → The man almost finished repairing the car, i.e., the car is almost repaired.
       b.   *Der Mann hat fast   geblutet.*
            the man   has almost bled
            'The man almost bled.'
            → The man almost started bleeding.
            ↛ The man almost finished bleeding.
       c.   *Der Mann hat fast   in Köln   gewohnt.*
            the man   has almost in Cologne lived
            'The man almost lived in Cologne.'
            → The man almost started to live in Cologne.
            ↛ The man almost finished living in Cologne.

---

[11] See, among others, von Stechow (1996) and Beck (2005) for an analysis of the different readings of *wieder* in German.

3.2 Event structure

A third criterion that is useful in distinguishing activity predicates from accomplishment predicates is what Dowty (1979) calls the 'imperfective paradox' (also cf. Bennett & Partee's 1972 'subinterval property'). Activity predicates license an entailment from the progressive (20a) to the perfect (b). As soon as someone is running, it can be said that he ran. Garey (1957, 156) states that such predicates describe situations which are realized as soon as they begin.

(20) a. *Der Mann war am Laufen, als er hinfiel.*
the man was at.the running when he tumbled
'The man was running, when he tumbled.'
b. *Der Mann ist gelaufen.*
the man is run
'The man ran.'

The entailment does not go through for accomplishment predicates; the progressive sentence in (21a) does not entail the perfect one in (b). The respective process has to reach the telos to yield a true predication, thus the predication is not true as soon as the denoted event starts. It is not true that as soon as the process of stabilization has started, the condition has stabilized. Situations denoted by telic predicates are not realized as soon as they begin.

(21) a. *Der Zustand des Patienten war sich am Stabilisieren,*
the condition of.the patient was REFL at.the stabilizing
als er verstarb.
when he died
'The condition of the patient was stabilizing when he died.'
b. *Der Zustand des Patienten hat sich stabilisiert.*
the condition of.the patient has REFL stabilized
'The condition of the patient has stabilized.'

At last, criteria to distinguish punctual predications, i.e., achievements and semelfactives, from durative ones need to be introduced. Punctual predicates get an iterative interpretation if they are combined with durative time adverbials such as *X Zeit lang* 'for X time.' The verb *klopfen* 'knock' can have a semelfactive reading, meaning that a single knock was produced (22a). By adding the time-adverbial *zehn Minuten lang* 'for ten minutes,' the

3 Verb classification

only interpretation is that the man knocked repeatedly for ten minutes. No one would make the interpretation that it took him ten minutes to make a single knock. For activity predicates, as in (22b), the durative adverbial measures the temporal extent of the event (cf. Mittwoch 2013). This is also the effect for (22a) but requires an iterative and therefore activity reading of the predicate.[12]

(22)   a.   *Der Mann klopfte zehn Minuten lang an die Tür.*
               the man knocked then minutes long at the door
               'The man knocked at the door for ten minutes.'
      b.   *Der Mann lief zehn Minuten lang.*
               the man ran ten minutes long
               'The man ran for ten minutes.'

Also some achievement predicates get an iterative interpretation if combined with durative time adverbials. Sentence (23a) has the reading that Angela scared her friend repeatedly for ten minutes. If an accomplishment predicate is combined with a durative adverbial, telicity is canceled and the verb is shifted towards an activity reading (cf. Engelberg (1994) for a discussion of the combination of accomplishment predicates and durative time adverbials in German). In (23b) it is only expressed that the man was engaged in the activity of reparing his car for an hour but it is not entailed that after an hour the car is repaired. In contrast to achievement predicates, the durative adverbial does not induce a repetitive interpretation of the process.

(23)   a.   *Angela erschreckte ihren Freund zehn Minuten lang.*
               Angela scared her friend ten minutes long
               'Angela scared her friend for ten minutes.'
      b.   *Der Mann reparierte das Auto eine Stunde lang.*
               the man repaired the car one hour long
               'The man repaired the car for an hour.'

---

[12] Further criteria for identifying semelfactive predicates are discussed in Rothstein (2004).

3.2.2 Predicate decomposition

Predicate decompositions are "representations of meaning formulated in terms of one or more primitive predicates chosen to represent components of meaning that recur across significant sets of verbs" (Levin & Rappaport Hovav, 2005, 69). The aim of using predicate decompositions is to provide a structured representation of grammatically relevant meaning components of verbs. These meaning components are not stipulated for each verb separately, but capture meaning elements which are shared by verbs showing similar grammatical behavior. Predicate decompositions are used for representing event structures. There are different ways of using these structures for representing events: events can either be left implicit represented as predicate decompositional structures are understood as event descriptions or events can be explicitly introduced into these representations — as an event variable — and thereby function as an argument of the decompositional predicates. Van Valin as well as Rappaport Hovav and Levin go the first way, for the second option see, for example, Rothstein (2004).

Each system of predicate decomposition makes use of a limited set of primitive predicates such as for example **do'** in RRG or ACT in Levin & Rappaport Hovav's account. These predicates (or operators as they are called in RRG) are used to represent the relevant aktionsart characteristics even if they do not directly represent the aktionsart properties discussed in the last section. So there is no predicate expressing stativity or telicity; nevertheless, the set of basic predicates is used to represent aktionsart classes. Beside these predicates, each decompositional system has a way of expressing the idiosyncratic content which distinguishes verbs belonging to the same aktionsart classes. For example, *know* and *believe* are both stative predicates and share the same structural representation, but they are differentiated by their idiosyncratic content. Van Valin (2005) uses the term 'predicate' to refer to the elements expressing the idiosyncratic content, whereas Levin & Rappaport Hovav (2011) and Rappaport Hovav & Levin (2010) call it 'root.'

As a starting point, I take Van Valin's predicate decomposition, which is based on Dowty (1979). One reason for choosing this approach is that I will make use of Role & Reference Grammar (RRG; Foley & Van Valin 1984; Van Valin & LaPolla 1997; Van Valin 2005) in later parts of the thesis (especially chapter 4). Van Valin assumes two basic types of predicates, which function as the building blocks for other predication types. These are states on the one hand and activities on the other hand.[13] This means that achievements, accomplishments and semelfactives are derived from state or activity predicates. States are represented as plain predicates, as in (24). The general scheme for states is shown in (a), whereas (b) and (c) shows its instantiation for two example verbs.

(24) STATE: **predicate'**(x) *or* **predicate'**(x, y)
    a. *know*: **know'**(x, y)
    b. *believe*: **believe'**(x, y)

Activity predicates are always marked by the two-place predicate **do'**. The first argument of **do'** is the actor, which is x in (25) and the second argument is itself a one- or two-place predicate that introduces the idiosyncratic content of the overall predication. In (25) the general scheme for activities is shown in (a), as well as two sample instantiations for that predicate type (b, c).

(25) ACTIVITY: **do'**(x, [**predicate'**(x)]) *or* **do'**(x, [**predicate'**(x, y)])
    a. *run*: **do'**(x, [**run'**(x)])
    b. *kiss*: **do'**(x, [**kiss'**(x, y)])

The predicates that show up as the second argument of **do'** are always preceded by it and never occur alone. **do'** itself functions merely as a marker for activities and evidence for such an operator is provided by Basque (26) taken from Van Valin & LaPolla (1997, 104). They mention that Basque makes use of a light verb construction consisting of the verb *egin* 'do' and a noun for predications which in English are expressed as intransitive activities.

(26) Ni-k   lan-∅   egin d-u-t.
      1SG-ERG work-ABS do 3SG.ABS-AUX-1SG.ERG
      'I worked.' (literally: 'I did work.')

---

[13] In the remainder, I use the terms 'state', 'activity', 'accomplishment', 'achievement' and 'semelfactive' as a short form for 'stative predicate', 'activity predicate', and so on. But one has to carefully keep in mind that *die*, for example, is not an achievement but an achievement predicate.

The other aktionsart classes are derived by adding further operators to the basic predicate types. Achievements are derived by adding the INGR (ingressive) operator, which is used to mark punctual changes of state (27a) or punctual onsets of activities. An example of the first type is shown in (27a), whereas a punctual onset of an activity is shown by the Russian example in (27b).

(27) ACHIEVEMENT: INGR **predicate'**(x) or (x,y)
　　　　　　　　　INGR **do'**(x, **predicate'**(x) or (x,y))
　　a. *pop*: INGR **popped'**(x) [intransitive]
　　b. *zaplakat'*: INGR **do'**(x, **cry'**(x))
　　　('burst out crying')
　　　(Van Valin, 2005, 42)

The operator BECOME, which is defined in Dowty (1979, 76), is used to derive accomplishment predicates. BECOME can be added to a state or activity predicate to mark a temporally extended change of state (28a) or a non-punctual onset of an activity. The latter is illustrated by the Russian example in (28b), which is taken from Van Valin (2005, 42).

(28) ACCOMPLISHMENT: BECOME **predicate'**(x) or (x, y)
　　　　　　　　　　　BECOME **do'**(x, **predicate'**(x) or (x,y))
　　a. *melt*: BECOME **melted'**(x)
　　b. *zagovarit'*: BECOME **do'**(x, **speak'**(x))
　　　('start talking')

If an accomplishment or achievement is derived from a state predicate, the state predicate stands for the attained result state. An activity predicate stands for the respective activity into which the actor goes over.[14] A last operator is SEML, which is used to mark punctuality of states or activities. In Van Valin's approach, stative as well as activity predicates can serve as the basis for semelfactives (29).

(29) SEMELFACTIVE: SEML **predicate'**(x) or (x, y)
　　　　　　　　　　SEML **do'**(x, **predicate'**(x) or (x,y))
　　a. *glimpse*: SEML **see'**(x, y)
　　b. *cough*: SEML **do'**(x, **cough'**(x))

---

[14] I leave out the discussion of 'active accomplishments' but see Van Valin (2005).

3 Verb classification

Russian has a morphological marking of semelfactives. By adding the morpheme *-nu* to a non-punctual activity, a semelfactive is derived (30). *Prygat'* 'jump' and *kričat'* 'shout' are imperfective verbs; the derived semelfactives, on the other hand, are perfective. Hence, the affix *-nu* not only changes the aktionsart of the predicates, but also affects the grammatical aspect.

(30)   a.   *prygat' prygnut'*
            'jump' 'jump once'
       b.   *kričat' kriknut'*
            'shout' 'shout once'

CAUSE is a further operator within the decompositional approach but it is not used to derive an aktionsart class from a basic state or activity predicate. Rather it is an additional operator which represents a grammatically relevant meaning component. The operator CAUSE is used to represent a causal relationship between two subevents. The operator takes two formulas – α and β – as its arguments (31). Examples of causative predicates are shown in (a) and (b), which are the causative uses of *melt* and *pop* respectively. The non-causative uses have been represented above in (27a) and (28b). In both cases, the causing subevent is unspecified, it is merely expressed that some activity causes the respective change of state. '∅' is used to represent an unspecified activity.

(31)   CAUSATIVE α CAUSE β
       a.   *melt*: [**do'**(x, ∅)] CAUSE [BECOME **melted'**(y)]
       b.   *pop*: [**do'**(x, ∅)] CAUSE [INGR **pop'**(y)]

Since causality is not an aktionsart property, test criteria for causality have not been discussed in the last section. At this stage, I would like to introduce two criteria that can be used for testing for causality. First, causative predicates allow for an explicit causative paraphrase (Van Valin, 2005, 38). In English, the verb cause explicitly shows up in such a paraphrase, as can be seen in (32a). Such a causative paraphrase is appropriate for *frighten*, but as (b) indicates it is not for *fear*. To be an appropriate paraphrase, the number and order of arguments have to be the same in the paraphrase and the paraphrased predication. Causativity is independent from agentivity as *the dog* in (32a) can either be agentively engaged in frightening the boy

3.2 Event structure

or merely the source of the boy's fear without doing something to cause the fear. It could probably be merely the presence of the dog that causes the boy to feel fear.

(32) a. *The dog frightened the boy.*
→ The dog caused the boy to feel fear.
b. *The boy feared the dog.*
↛ The dog caused the boy to feel fear.

A second criterion is based on VanValin & Wilkin's (1996) distinction between 'implements' and 'instruments.' Instruments are "manipulated inanimate effectors" (Van Valin, 2005, 59), which are embedded in a causal chain. In (33) the logical structure for the sentence *Leslie shattered the window with a rock.* is shown. The instrument *rock* is embedded in a causal chain, since it can be taken as an intermediate causer of the shattering of the window. Typically, instruments allow the instrument-subject alternation (cf. Levin 1993, 80) as in (34).

(33) [**do'**(Leslie, ∅)] CAUSE [[**do'**(rock, ∅)] CAUSE [INGR **shattered'**(window)]]
(Van Valin, 2005, 59)

(34) a. *Leslie shattered the window with a rock.*
b. *The rock shattered the window.*

Implements are not embedded in a causal chain and are added to an activity structure, which is further modified by the implement. This is illustrated with the example sentence *Chris ate the soup with a spoon.* in (35). The implement is added to the structure by the predicate **use'** and the connective '∧,' which in this case means 'and simultaneously.'

(35) **do'**(Chris, [**eat'**(Chris, soup) ∧ **use'**(Chris, spoon)])
(Van Valin, 2005, 59)

Evidence for a different treatment of instruments and implements is provided by the fact that implements do not participate in the subject-instrument alternation (36).

(36) a. *Chris ate the soup with a spoon.*
b. *#The spoon ate the soup.*

3 Verb classification

The decompositional system employed by Levin & Rappaport Hovav is similar to Van Valin's and also based on Dowty (1979). Levin & Rappaport Hovav distinguish between structural and idiosyncratic components of verb meaning and write: "The structural part of a verb's meaning is that part which is relevant to determining the semantic classes of verbs that are grammatically relevant, whereas the idiosyncratic part of a verb's meaning distinguishes that verb from other members of the same class" (Rappaport Hovav & Levin, 1998, 106). Idiosyncratic parts of verb meaning are also called 'roots' and function either as the modifier of a structural component or as its argument. In (37) a slightly revised version of Rappaport Hovav & Levin's (1998, 108) event schema is shown. Roots are written in angled brackets and come in two basic types. They either denote a state, which functions as the sole element of a stative predicate, or as the argument of BECOME. In the latter case, the root is called 'result root.'[15] The second type is called 'manner root' and functions as a modifier of an ACT predicate. The distinction between 'manner' and 'result' will be discussed in the next section, at the current stage only a description of Rappaport Hovav & Levin's event schemata is intended.

(37) a. State: $[x\langle\text{STATE}\rangle]$
      b. Activity: $[x \text{ ACT}_{\langle\text{STATE}\rangle}]$
      c. Achievement: $[\text{BECOME }[x \langle\text{RESULT}\rangle]]$
      d. Accomplishment: $[x \text{ CAUSE }[\text{BECOME }[y \langle\text{RESULT}\rangle]]]$

The differences between Van Valin's approach and the one of Rappaport Hovav & Levin consist basically in a different analysis of achievements and accomplishments on the one hand and on the other hand in the use of different operators for activity predicates.[16] Rappaport Hovav & Levin (1998) follow Dowty in assuming that causality is the differentiating factor between achievements and accomplishments and not durativity. With regard to the second point, Rappaport Hovav and Levin use a one-place

---

[15] The authors do not specify whether result roots are a subtype of plain state roots or whether they are distinct types. I assume result roots, which denote result states, to be a subytpe of states in general.

[16] Although Levin (1999) identifies semelfactives as a separate class, she assigns them the same event structural template then activities. Following Levin, the difference between semelfactives and activities is not in the structural but in the idiosyncratic meaning component.

predicate ACT instead of Van Valin's two-place predicate **do'**. This goes together with the notion of a root and how the root is integrated into the decompositional structure. Van Valin does not make use of the term 'root' but it corresponds to the predicates in his decompositional system. In the case of activities, the root is taken to be a modifier by Rappaport Hovav & Levin, whereas Van Valin takes it to be the second argument of **do'**. For the following discussion, I equate Van Valin's predicates with Rappaport Hovav & Levin's notion of a 'root.' Roots are the central target in the discussion of manner/result complementarity to which I turn in the next section.

3.3 Manner/result complementarity

'Manner/result complementarity' is a constraint on the lexical content of monomorphemic predicates.[17] It is not so much this lexicalization constraint that is relevant for the current thesis but Rappaport Hovav & Levin's explication of result verbs as 'scalar verbs.' They propose a natural link between the notion of 'result' and scalarity. The assumption behind the manner/result complementarity is that a constraint of the following type holds: each monomorphemic predicate only lexicalizes a single root Rappaport Hovav & Levin (1998, 2010). This classification only applies to dynamic verbs; it does not cover stative predications. The manner/result complementarity means that each monomorphemic verb either lexicalizes a manner or a result root and not both at the same time. Manner/result complementarity imposes a constraint on possible event structures. The event structures in (38a) to (c) are possible for monomorphemic verbs; in each case the structure contains just one root. In (c) the root indicates the result state, since result roots are arguments of BECOME, whereas manner roots are modifiers of ACT. Structures (d) and (e) are excluded for monomorphemic verbs, since in this case two roots would be lexicalized.

(38)   a. $[\text{x ACT}_{\langle \text{ROOT} \rangle}]$
         b. $[\text{BECOME } [\text{x } \langle \text{ROOT} \rangle]]$

---

[17] For a critical discussion of the manner/result complementarity cf. Beavers & Koontz-Garboden (2012), also see the discussion in Levin & Rappaport Hovav (2013) and the literature cited therein.

c. [x ACT] CAUSE [BECOME [x ⟨ROOT⟩]]
d. *[[x ACT⟨ROOT1⟩] CAUSE [BECOME [x ⟨ROOT2⟩]]]
e. *[[x ACT⟨ROOT1⟩] CAUSE [**BECOME** [**x ⟨ROOT1⟩**]]]
(based on Beavers & Koontz-Garboden 2012, 333)

The structure in (d), unlike the one in (e), is possible for complex, i.e., derived verbs. (38e) is excluded since a single root would simultaneously specify manner and result. A case in which manner and result are contributed by different elements in a complex verb is indicated by the Lakhota examples in (39). The result root is contributed by the stem *t'a* 'die, be dead' and the manner component is added by the instrumental prefix. The instrumental prefix *ya-* indicates an action with the mouth, *wa-* an action with a sawing motion/a knife, *wo-* an action from a distance and *yu-* an action with the hands.[18]

(39) Lakhota (Siouan; Foley & Van Valin 1984, 41ff.)
 a. *ya-t'a* 'bite to death'
 b. *wa-t'a* 'stab to death'
 c. *wo-t'a* 'shoot to death'
 d. *yu-t'a* 'strangle to death'

The German examples in (40) show the opposite pattern to the Lakotha one. It is the verb in (40) that specifies the manner, whereas the result is derived in the process of prefixation.

(40) *stechen er-stechen*
 'stab' 'stab to death'

For this thesis, it is relevant that manner/result complementarity provides a classification of dynamic verbs into 'manner verbs' and 'result verbs.' But even more interesting is Rappaport Hovav & Levin's explication of the notions of 'manner' and 'result' in terms of 'scalar changes.' As mentioned in 3.2, all dynamic predicates express changes. But manner and result verbs differ with respect to the nature of the change they express. Result verbs express scalar changes, which are directed changes in a single, specified dimension. This kind of change can be characterized as progression along

---

[18] The examples in (39) are not exhaustive as Lakhota has further instrumental prefixes see Van Valin (1977, 19ff.) and Foley & Van Valin (1984, 41ff.).

a scale. Explicating the notion of 'non-scalar change,' Rappaport Hovav & Levin (2010, 32) write: "A non-scalar change is any change that cannot be characterized in terms of an ordered set of values of a single attribute." Two different types of non-scalar changes can be distinguished: (i) undirected changes and (ii) changes in multiple dimensions. An example of an undirected change is provided by the verb *cross*. Rappaport Hovav & Levin (2010, 30) state that the direction of the crossing is unspecified and hence the change not directed. A crossing of the British Channel may either occur from England to France or from France to England. The verb itself is compatible with a movement in both directions. Scalar change verbs are directed, a change expressed by *grow* always entails an increase in size and is not compatible with a decreasing size of the changing entity. The second type of non-scalar change can be illustrated by the verb *jog*. Rappaport Hovav & Levin (2010, 33) write: "[E]ven though there is a sequence of changes specified by *jog*, collectively these changes do not represent a change in the values of a single attribute, nor is any one element in the sequence of changes privileged as being the necessary starting point of motion." *Jog* expresses changes in different dimensions, as – among other changes – changes in the positioning of the arms of the jogger, of the legs and of the entire location. Hence, the verb does not isolate a single dimension for which it expresses a change. Based on this interpretation of the notions of 'manner' and 'result,' the manner/result complementarity might be rephrased as I do in (41).

(41) Rephrasing of manner/result complementarity:
All dynamic (monomorphemic) verbs either express non-scalar or scalar changes. No such verb encodes both at the same time.

Rappaport Hovav (2008) lists three properties that are characteristic of scalar change verbs. These characteristics, which can be used to separate scalar and non-scalar change verbs from each other, are listed in (42), based on the formulation by Fleischhauer & Gamerschlag (2014, 35).

(42) a. Scalar verbs are restricted to result-XPs that are compatible with the lexicalized scale.
b. Scalar verbs can be telic without a measure phrase or explicit event delimitation.

3 Verb classification

c. Scalar verbs do not allow for the deletion of the theme argument.

The basic idea underlying the properties in (42) is that the presence of a scale measuring a change affects the grammatical behavior of verbs. I discuss the three properties separately, beginning with the one in (a). Rappaport Hovav states that scalar change verbs are more restricted regarding possible result-XPs than non-scalar change verbs. The rationale behind this idea is that result-XPs are taken to be scale-denoting expressions. A result-XP is either an adjectival phrase as in (43a) or a prepositional phrase like in (b). The adjective denotes an endpoint on a scale, in this case a two-point scale consisting of the two values 'alive' and 'dead.' In (b), the change occurs along a multivalue scale and ends up at a value of 80 degrees.

(43) a. *Der Mann schlägt seinen Nachbarn tot.*
the man hits his neighbor dead
'The man beats his neighbor to death.'
b. *Das Wasser erhitzt sich auf 80 Grad.*
the water heats REFL up 80 degrees
'The water heats up to 80 degrees.'

The notions of 'two-point' and 'multivalue scales' is used by different authors such as Beavers (2008, 2013), Rappaport Hovav (2008) or Rappaport Hovav & Levin (2010). Chief (2007, 11) uses instead the notions of 'complex scale,' which consists of at least three values, and 'simple scale,' consisting of merely two degrees. A two-point scale only has two values, which are contradictory to each other; in the case of (43a) the man is either dead or alive and there is no further possibility. In case of a multivalue scale, the values form a contrary set. Two-point scales are nominal scales and therefore do not qualify as scales in the sense of Kennedy & McNally (cf. the discussion in section 2.2).[19]

Beavers (2008, 2013, 690) explicitly states that two-point scales are not gradable and gradable terms are related to multivalue scales. Beavers, Rappaport Hovav and Rappaport Hovav & Levin use scale for an explication of the notion of 'change' and Beavers (2013, 684) writes: "[...] change is defined

---

[19] See Bolinger (1967, 7) for the view that scales have to consist of at least three values and hence two opposed values do not constitute a scale.

as some theme transitioning to and maintaining a new value along some property scale [...]". The reason for postulating two-point scales in addition to multivalue scales is to provide a uniform analysis of result verbs as scalar, irrespective of whether they are punctual or not. A punctual change is a change on a two-point scale, whereas a temporarily extended change progresses along a multivalue scale. I adopt this broad notion of scalarity as it allows characterizing all change of state verbs as scalar verbs, but degree gradation, as will be shown in chapter 5, is restricted to multivalue scales. Therefore, the notion of a 'two-point scale' will be not of crucial relevance for the analysis and nothing hinges on this notion.

Going back to resultative constructions as in (43), the common core of (43a) and (b) is that in both cases a change of state is predicated. In (a) the neighbor changes from being alive to being dead, whereas in (b) the temperature of the water changes up to 80 degrees. The difference between (a) and (b) is that only in the latter case a change of state, i.e., a scalar change, is already entailed by the verb *erhitzen* 'heat up.' Even without a result-XP, the verb *erhitzen* expresses a scalar change in a single dimension of the referent of the theme argument *Wasser* 'water.' This is different for (a), the verb *schlagen* 'hit' does not express a scalar change. No specific result is entailed by the verb and a change of state predication only arises by the addition of the result-XP. Washio (1997) and Kaufmann & Wunderlich (1998) call resultative constructions as in (43a) 'strong resultatives' whereas those of the type in (b) are called 'weak resultatives.' In the case of weak resultatives, the result-XP further specifies an already lexically encoded result.

Rappaport Hovav claims that verbs which do not lexically encode a scalar change are less restricted with regard to result-XPs than those which do. The reason is that if a verb expresses a scalar change, the result-XP has to be compatible with the change denoted by the verb. This means that the result-XP has to denote a value that belongs to the scale lexicalized by the verb. Since non-scalar change verbs do not express a change measured on a scale, they do not provide such a restriction on result-XPs and hence allow a broader range of resultative-XPs. In (44) the contrast between a scalar and two non-scalar verbs regarding resultative-XPs are shown. The scalar verb *gefrieren* 'freeze' in (a) is very restricted with respect to possible resultative-XPs. *Essen* 'eat' on the one hand and *schreien* 'cry' are compatible with a broader range of result-XPs. The relevant fact is that *zu Eis* 'to ice' denotes a natural endpoint of a change denoted by *gefrieren*. In (c), for example, the resultative-XPs belong to different types of scales; *hoarse* and *to sleep* do not denote values that belong to the same dimension. Thus the verb does not provide such a neat restriction on resultative-XPs than found by scalar verbs.[20]

(44) a. *Der Fluss gefror zu Eis/ #breit/ #tief.*
         the river froze to ice wide deep
         'The river froze solid/#wide/#deep.'
     b. *Peter aß sich #groß/ krank/ fett/ zu Tode/ glücklich.*
         Peter ate REFL tall ill fat to death happy
         'Peter ate himself #tall/sick/fat/to death/happy.'
     c. *Das Kind schrie sich heiser/ in den Schlaf.*
         the child cried REFL hoarse in the sleep
         'The child cried itself hoarse/to sleep.'
         (Fleischhauer & Gamerschlag, 2014, 35)

The second property of scalar verbs is that they allow a telic interpretation even without explicit event delimitation. This clearly holds for verbs like *repair* in (45), but as Rappaport Hovav & Levin (2010, 27) mention telicity fails to appropriately distinguish between scalar and non-scalar change verbs. Some clearly scalar verbs denote atelic changes of state, as for example German *wachsen* 'grow' (46).

(45) *The man repaired the car in one hour.*

(46) a. *#Das Kind ist in einem Jahr gewachsen.*
         the child is in one year grown
     b. *Das Kind ist in einem Jahr zehn Zentimeter gewachsen.*
         the child is in one year ten centimeters grown
         'The child has grown ten centimeters in one year.'

---

[20] The first criterion only holds for Talmy's (2000) 'satellite-framed languages' like German and English but it does not hold for 'verb-framed languages' such as French or Spanish. The latter only allow strong resultatives, i.e., resultative constructions with scalar verbs (see Gehrke 2008 among others).

Change of state verbs like *wachsen*, which are either atelic or show variable telicity, are called 'degree achievements' following Dowty (1979).[21] Many degree achievements as German *verbreitern* 'broaden,' *verlängern* 'lengthen' or *verkleinern* 'diminish' are derived from gradable adjectives and provide the prototypical instances of scalar verbs. I will discuss these verbs in more detail in chapter 6. The relevant aspect shown by these verbs is that Rappaport Hovav's second property of scalar verbs is merely a sufficient but not a necessary one, since all telic verbs are scalar but not all scalar verbs are telic.

The third property is concerned with argument realization patterns of scalar and non-scalar verbs. Scalar verbs do not license the omission of the undergoer argument, whereas non-scalar verbs often do. Taking (47) as an example, the transitive verb denotes a caused change in the undergoer, which is *die Straße* 'the street.' During the event denoted by the verb, the street increases in width. The change is measured on a width-scale and the entity that is measured on the scale is *die Straße*. As (b) shows, if the actor *die Arbeiter* 'the workers' is realized as the single argument of the verb, the sentence is odd. Example (c) shows that the undergoer can be the single argument of the verb without turning the sentence to ungrammaticality.

(47)   a.   *Die Arbeiter$_{Causer}$ verbreiterten die Straße$_{Theme}$.*
            the workers   widened   the street
            'The workers$_{Causer}$ widened the street$_{Theme}$.'
      b.   **Die Arbeiter$_{Causer}$ verbreiterten.*
            the workers   widened
      c.   *Die Straße$_{Theme}$ verbreiterte sich.*
            the street   widened   REFL
            'The street$_{Theme}$ widened.'
            (Fleischhauer & Gamerschlag, 2014, 36)

The reflexive pronoun *sich* in (47c) marks the causative/inchoative alternation with change of state verbs in German. This alternation and the marking by the reflexive will be discussed in more detail in chapter 6. But note that the use of the reflexive in (47c) differs from fake reflexives as in

---

[21] As mentioned above, Dowty's use of the term 'achievement' differs from how I use that term. But I stay with the notion of 'degree achievement' since it is well established, even if 'degree accomplishments' would be more correct.

the resultative constructions in (44b) and (c). In the latter cases, the change is predicated over the referent of the reflexive, whereas in (47) it does not function as an argument but merely as a marker of the anticausative.

Non-scalar change verbs freely allow the omission of the undergoer argument (called 'unspecified object alternation' in Levin (1993, 33) and 'antipassive' in Löbner (2013, 137) as exemplified in (48). In contrast to scalar change verbs, an ungrammatical sentence arises if only the undergoer argument is realized (48c). A further difference from scalar verbs is that the non-scalar verbs do not require a special marking – for example, in terms of the reflexive pronoun *sich* – for an intransitive use. Following Rappaport Hovav, the reason for the non-omissability of the undergoer argument of scalar verbs is that the entities measured on a scale need to have an overt realization.

(48)   a.   *Peter$_{Agent}$ aß das Brot$_{Theme}$.*
            Peter   ate the bread
            'Peter$_{Agent}$ ate the bread$_{Theme}$.'
     b.   *Peter aß.*
            Peter ate
            'Peter$_{Agent}$ ate.'
     c.   **Das Brot$_{Thema}$ aß (sich).*
            the bread   ate   REFL
       (Fleischhauer & Gamerschlag, 2014, 36)

There is some debate as to whether incremental theme verbs are lexically scalar (e.g. Beavers 2012; Kardos 2012 or whether the respective scale is introduced by the incremental theme argument via argument composition. Rappaport Hovav and Rappaport Hovav & Levin advocate the latter position, since incremental theme verbs do not show the characteristics of scalar change verbs, as the examples above have shown. Hence, these verbs are not lexically scalar, but express a change on a scale that is compositionally derived. Scalar change verbs, i.e., verbs that lexically express a scalar change, comprise the class of change of state verbs and also some directed motion verbs like *enter* or *exit*. Incremental theme verbs as well as some other directed motion verbs, for example *cross*, are not lexically scalar but, in some of their uses, express changes on compositionally derived scales. The presence and nature of the scale is dependent on the (incremental) theme argument (see Rappaport Hovav 2008; Rappaport Hovav & Levin 2010; Kennedy 2012).

Rappaport Hovav relates the three mentioned classes of verbs (change of state verbs, incremental theme verbs and verbs of directed motion) to different types of scales as summarized in table 10.

scale type	verb class	examples
property scale	change of state verbs	*widen, darken, grow*
path scale	verbs of directed motion	*enter, exit, cross*
volume/extent scale	incremental theme verbs	*eat N, drink N, read N*

Table 10: Scale type and verb class relationship, based on Rappaport Hovav (2008).

Change of state verbs are related to property scales that represent some property as 'size' or 'weight' of the referent of the theme argument. Such scales are always lexicalized by the respective verbs. Volume/extent scales are always compositionally derived and introduced by the incremental theme argument. These scales measure the volume/extent of the referent of the incremental theme argument and how much of it is affected by the event. Path scales, to which verbs of directed motion are related, are lexicalized by some verbs but not by others. If the verb denotes a movement to a definite endpoint, Rappaport Hovav as well as Rappaport Hovav & Levin assume that the verb lexicalizes a path scale. If no such definite spatial transition is expressed, the verb is taken to be non-scalar and scales are compositionally derived.

In chapter 6, I discuss change of state verbs in detail and raise the question of what it means that a verb lexicalizes a scale. For the current discussion, the focus is put on the claim that only change of state verbs (and a subset of verbs of directed motion) are scalar verbs and that the notion of 'scalarity' is relativized to the expression of directed changes in a single dimension.

3.4 Degree verbs

The notion 'degree verbs' goes back to Bolinger and is negatively defined: "[a] nondegree verb does not accept intensifiers" (Bolinger, 1972, 160). Hence, degree verbs are verbs that accept what Bolinger calls 'intensifiers,' as indicated by his examples in (49). The sentences marked with an asterisk contain nondegree verbs, whereas those without an asterisk contain degree verbs.

(49)   a.   Why do you hesitate so?
         b.   *Why do you wait so?
         c.   Don't struggle so.
         d.   *Don't perform so.
         e.   Why did you bury it 'get it so deep'?
         f.   *Why did you inter it so?
               (Bolinger, 1972, 160)

Bolinger is well aware of the distinction between extent and degree gradation, which in fact goes back to his work. He writes that extent gradation is almost universal among verbs and so he considers extent gradability not to be a relevant property for being a degree verb. Rather he writes: "Verbs like *talk, dance, swim, reach, leave, sleep,* etc. are nondegree and normally intensified, like plural and mass nondegree nouns, only for extensibility" (Bolinger, 1972, 161). In (50) *dance* is intensified for the extent of the event, or the amount of dancing as (Bolinger, 1972, 161), puts it. But, as he further states, it rejects degree gradation and therefore does not qualify as degree verb.

(50)   a.   Such dancing all the time.
         b.   I wish they wouldn't dance so all the time.
               (Bolinger, 1972, 161)

Similar to the adjectival domain, Bolinger conceives gradability as a property to classify verbs. Gradability can be used to distinguish between gradable and non-gradable adjectives, gradable adjectives admitting degree morphology as the comparative morpheme in languages such as English and German, whereas non-gradable adjectives either reject it or require some coercion (cf. chapter 2). Bolinger's distinction between degree and nondegree verbs is similar, verbs that accept expressions for degree gradation are degree verbs, and those that do not are nondegree verbs. This leads to the questions which property, beyond the acceptability of degree expressions, is shared by the class of degree verbs, if they share some relevant property at all. There are two actual proposals, by Tenny (2000) and Tsujimura (2001), on the semantic properties licensing degree expressions. Both proposals make use of event structure and are discussed sequentially in the following sections. In this chapter, I concentrate on 'degree gradability' and will not discuss the conditions licensing extent gradation; but see Doetjes (1997, 2007) for a discussion of extent gradability.

3.4.1 Tenny (2000) on 'measure adverbs'

Tenny (2000), based on the work of Travis (2000), argues basically that event structure is reflected in syntax, meaning generative grammar style syntax. Different parts of syntactic trees are associated with different event structural components. A basic distinction she is arguing for is the one between inner and outer events. Outer events are associated with causation, whereas inner (or core) events are the expression of stativity and inchoativity (Tenny, 2000, 292). This distinction can be illustrated by using example (51). The outer event is the sweeping of the floor that constitutes the first subevent. It is linked via a causal relation to the inner event which is a change into a state of being clean.

(51)   *He sweeps the floor clean.*
       (He sweeps the floor) CAUSE (BECOME (the floor is clean))
       (Dowty, 1979, 93)

Tenny associates inner/core events with the expression of changes and the achievement of a final state. Classes of verbs that contain inner events are those which also have a BECOME predicate in their event structural representation: change of state verbs, (transitive) incremental theme verbs , verbs of motion to a goal (*to run*) and verbs of putting (*to put*). The class of verbs which Tenny considers contain an inner event is not coextensive with Rappaport Hovav & Levin's class of result/scalar change verbs but Rappaport Hovav & Levin's result verbs form a subclass of those verbs that have a core event.

3 Verb classification

Different test criteria for the presence of core events are mentioned by Tenny. First, only verbs that have a core event allow for the causative/inchoative alternation (52). Incremental theme verbs, as already mentioned, do not participate in this alternation but they can be used in the middle construction (53) which is also considered to be a diagnostic of core events.

(52) a. The workers widened the gap.
 a' The gap widened.
 b She darkened the photograph.
 b' The photograph darkened.

(53) a. This book reads easily.
 b. The soup that eats like a meal.
 (Tenny, 2000, 298)

The further criterion mentioned by Tenny is telicity. If a predication is telic, then it contains a core event. The reason is that telicity always requires some change towards the telos. But, as mentioned above, not each expression of a property change results in a telic predication. This is, for example, the case with degree achievements. Verbs that contain a core event differ with regard to the criteria mentioned above and my aim is not to evaluate this part of Tenny's analysis. Rather I am focusing on her claim that verbs which have a core event in their event structure also have a measure or path as part of their lexical meaning. She writes: "If it [the verb] contains a measure or path, the final state for the core event is a gradable predicate, admitting degree modification" (Tenny, 2000, 296). A measure/path represents a gradable property with respect to which a change is expressed. Tenny assumes that change of state verbs, incremental theme verbs and verbs of motion towards a goal have a measure/path as part of their lexical meaning, whereas verbs of putting do not. The first three classes of verbs allow measuring the progression in the gradable property, which can be illustrated by combining them with measure adverbs (54). In cases such as (54a), measure adverbs "modify the endstate of the core event in the verb's lexical meaning" (Tenny, 2000, 303).

(54) a. Jessie ran partway to the drugstore.
 b. *Jessie put the book partway on the table.
 (Tenny, 2000, 300)

Tenny claims that measure adverbs only combine with verbs that contain a core event as well as a measure/path in their event structure. Hence, these verbs need to have a BECOME predicate in their event structural representation and therefore denote a change that leads to the achievement of a specific result. As verbs of putting reveal, core events alone are not sufficient for licensing measure adverbs, also a measure is required. Tenny restricts her discussion of measure adverbs to such English expressions as *completely, partly* and *halfway*. Ernst (2002) builds on Tenny's work and includes degree expressions as (*very*) *much* in the analysis. Neither Tenny nor Ernst make use of Bolinger's term 'degree verbs' but if they are right, the class of degree verbs – at least in English – should be limited to such verbs that contain a core event as well as a measure in their event structure. Hence, neither state predicates nor activities should be gradable, since they do not contain a core event. But this assumption is contrary to examples like those in (55). In (a) and (b) *very much* grades the stative verbs *like* and *believe*. Those verbs do not have a core event, as argued above, but they do lexicalize some scale, i.e., 'measure' in Tenny's terminology.

(55) a. *John likes Mary very much.*
 b. *John believes very much in Mary's innocence.*

As shown in (56), *like* does not pass one of the three core event tests. First, *like* does not participate in the causative/inchoative alternation; second, it does not allow the middle constructions, and third, a telic reading of *like* (without coercion) is not possible. This shows that adverbials such as *very much* are not restricted to verbs containing core events.

(56) a. **Mary likes.*
 b. *#John likes easily.*
 c. *#John likes Mary in ten minutes.*

Originally, Tenny only discussed such adverbs as *completely* or *partially*, hence her analysis could probably be rescued by restricting the discussion to these adverbs.[22] But as the examples in (57) reveal *completely* can combine with stative predicates such as *cover* and *consist*. I take the examples in

---

[22] Cf. Piñón (2005) for a discussion of the syntax and semantics of adverbs of completion with a short critical discussion of Tenny's account on these adverbs.

3 Verb classification

(57) as counterevidence against Tenny's analysis, knowing that the verbs in (57) could possibly be analyzed as denoting result states which presuppose a change of state. Such a change of state could be existentially bound in the verb's event structure (cf. Koontz-Garboden 2012) and therefore the predicates could be in agreement with the requirement of a core event in their event structure.

(57)   a.   *In contrast, an embedded tooth is an unerupted tooth that is covered, usually completely, with bone.*[23]
        b.   *The album consists completely of original Dan Band songs, with no covers.*[24]

The examples discussed above show that Tenny's account is too restrictive and so I turn to the less restrictive account of Tsujimura (2001) in the next section.

3.4.2 Tsujimura's (2001) analysis of Japanese degree verbs

Tsujimura (2001) provides a discussion of Japanese degree verbs, which she considers to be verbs that license the degree expression *totemo* 'very, very much.' Like German *sehr*, *totemo* is a degree expression that can be used to intensify adjectives (58a) as well as verbs (58b). Like *sehr*, *totemo* is restricted to degree gradation and does not function as a device for extent gradation.

(58)   Japanese (isolate; Tsujimura 2001, 32f.)
        a.   *totemo takai*
            very   expensibe
            'very expensive'
        b.   *Taroo-wa totemo kurusinda.*
            Taro-TOP very   suffered
            'Taro suffered very much.'

Tsujimura identifies the three conditions in (59) that have to be fulfilled by a verb to license *totemo*. Only the first condition is directly related to event structure and restricts the adverbial modification by *totemo* to such verbs

---

[23] http://en.wikipedia.org/wiki/Tooth_impaction (30.11.2012)
[24] http://en.wikipedia.org/wiki/The_Dan_Band (30.11.2012)

3.4 Degree verbs

that have a state component. The other conditions are concerned with scale structure. I discuss these conditions consecutively using Tsujimura's examples for illustration.

(59) a. A verb must have a STATE component in its event structure.
b. The STATE component must refer to a gradable property.
c. The gradable property defined over scalar structure must be with nontrivial standard.
(Tsujimura, 2001, 47)

The first condition states that all aktionsart classes except activities potentially admit gradation by *totemo*.[25] Tsujimura provides the examples in (60) to show that activities really reject *totemo*.

(60) a. *Taroo-wa totemo hasitta.*
Taro-TOP very   ran
'Taro ran very much.'
b. *Taroo-wa totemo waratta.*
Taro-TOP very   laughed
'Taro laughed very much.'
c. *Taroo-wa doa-o   totemo tataita.*
Taro-TOP door-ACC very   hit/knocked
'Taro hit/knocked on the door very much.'[26]
(Tsujimura, 2001, 38)

Not all verbs that contain a state component in their event structural representation license *totemo* (61). The second criterion states that the state component has to be related to a gradable property. Tsujimura does not further discuss the notion of 'gradable property' and hence does not provide any test criterion to distinguish between states that are related to gradable properties and those which are not. The verbs in (61) are achievements in the sense of Vendler and express changes on a two-point scale. Tsujimura

---

[25] Tsujimura (2001) builds on Rappaport Hovav & Levin's (1998) event structure account. They follow Dowty (1979) in assuming that causativity is the relevant factor distinguishing achievements and accomplishments rather than durativity.

[26] Tsujimura's data judgement is not shared by all native speakers of Japanese, as one of my informants judged at least (b) as totally acceptable. For illustrating her argumentation, I follow Tsujimura's data judgement but will show later that her analysis is not warranted.

3 Verb classification

does not raise the question whether the rejection of *totemo* depends on the fact that these verbs are related to two-point but not multivalue scales.

(61) a. **Omotya-ga totemo kowareta.*
toy-NOM very broke
'The toy broke very much.'
b. **Neko-ga totemo sinda.*
cat-NOM very died
'The cat died very much.'
(Tsujimura, 2001, 39)

The third condition in (61) is a scale structural one. Tsujimura claims that for some verbs the non-acceptability of *totemo* cannot be explained by assuming that the state component that is part of the verb's event structure refers to a non-gradable property. Rather it seems intuitive that the respective property can be graded, which does not hold for the state of being broken or dead. With regard to the latter examples Tsujimura (2001, 39) writes: "the dead of a cat and the broken state of a toy do not convey gradable properties." For the verbs in (62) she assumes that the respective scales block an application of *totemo* because the scales are related to the wrong kind of standard.

The gradable properties of verbs as those in (62) are related to a nontrivial standard (the notion of 'non-trivial standard' is taken from Kennedy & McNally (1999), which entails that the respective scale has to be closed. A non-trivial or absolute standard is per default one of the endpoints of the scale. That the examples in (62) are related to a non-trivial standard can be seen by the fact that they license the endpoint modifier *kanzenni* 'completely' (63).

(62) a. **Harigane-ga totemo magatta.*
wire-NOM very bent
'The wire bent very much.'
b. **Toosuto-ga totemo kogeta.*
toast-NOM very burned
'The toast burned very much.'
(Tsujimura, 2001, 40)

(63) a. *Harigane-ga kanzenni magatta.*
       wire-NOM completely bent
       'The wire bent completely.'
   b. *Toosuto-ga kanzenni kogeta.*
       toast-NOM very burned
       'The toast burned completely.'
       (Tsujimura, 2001, 40)

The third condition in (59) could be paraphrased as: *totemo* does not combine with closed-scale predicates and does combine with those that are related to open scales. This results in a complementary distribution of *totemo* and *kanzenni* as the data in (62)/(63) on the one hand and (64)/(65) on the other hand show.

(64) a. *Taroo-wa totemo kurusinda.*
       Taro-TOP very suffered
       'Taro suffered very much.'
   b. *Hosi-ga totemo hikatta/kagayaita/kirameita.*
       star-NOM very shone/glittered/sparkled
       'The star shone/glittered/sparkled very much.'
   c. *Suupu-ga totemo atatamatta.*
       soup-NOM very warmed
       'The soup got warmed very much.'
       (Tsujimura, 2001, 34)

(65) a. **Taroo-wa kanzenni kurusinda.*
       Taro-TOP completely suffered
       'Taro suffered completely.'
   b. **Hosi-ga kanzenni hikatta/kagayaita/kirameita.*
       star-NOM completely shone/glittered/sparkled
       'The star shone/glittered/sparkled completely.'
   c. **Suupu-ga kanzenni atatamatta.*
       soup-NOM completely warmed
       'The soup got warmed completely.'
       (Tsujimura, 2001, 43)

Tsujimura's class of degree verbs covers all verbs that contain a state component that is related to a gradable property. In difference to Tenny, also

3 Verb classification

stative predicates are taken to be degree verbs, since the mere presence of a state component is less restrictive than the presence of a core event. But similarly to Tenny, Tsujimura predicts that activities do not admit degree gradation.

Contrary to Tsujimura's claim, activities can be graded by *totemo*; examples are *totemo okotta* 'bluster a lot' or *totemo yorokonda* 'rejoice very much.'[27] As also mentioned above, some native speakers of Japanese disagree with Tsujimura's judgement of the data and conceive examples like the one in (66) as absolutely acceptable. This furthermore shows that activities are gradable by *totemo* and that Tsujimura's event structural analysis of the distribution of adverbial *totemo* is not tenable.

(66)   *Taroo-wa totemo waratta.*
         taro-TOP very   laughed
         'Taro laughed very much.'

Even if Tsujimura's analysis were warranted for Japanese, it is not possible to extend Tsujimura's analysis to German, French or Russian. In those languages, degree gradation is not restricted to verbs containing a state component, as many activities admit degree gradation without undergoing some process of coercion. In (67) a German example of a graded activity predicate is shown, in this case it is the manner of motion verb *rennen* 'run' which is modified by *sehr*. Russian and French examples of graded activities are shown in (68). In the case of Russian (68a), only a degree reading arises, whereas the French example in (b) is ambiguous between an extent and a degree reading.

(67)   *Er musste sehr zum Bus rennen, um nicht zu spät zu kommen.*
         he must very to.the bus run so as not to late to come
         'He had to run very fast to the bus in order not to be late.'

(68)   a. *Segondja očen' doždil.*
             today   very rained
             'It rained a lot today.'
        b. *Il a plu beaucoup.*
             it has rained a lot
             'It rained a lot.'

---

[27] I owe these data to Sebastian Löbner (p.c.), who also reports that the Japanese verbs are really activities since corresponding states would be expressed by adjectival forms.

The examples in (67) and (68) reveal that event structure does not provide a restriction on degree gradation since some activities can be graded like verbs belonging to all other aktionsart classes. Furthermore, gradable properties are not solely expressed by state components, which is evident in the case of activity predicates. I turn to a short general discussion of gradability in the conclusion of this chapter.

3.5 Conclusion

The aim of the current chapter was twofold: on the one hand the chapters provide relevant background for latter chapters by introducing the notions of, for example, 'aktionsart' and 'event structure.' The second aim was to present a discussion of the conditions licensing degree gradation of verbs. Two different event-structural proposals have been discussed and it has been shown, by discussing the work of Tenny and Tsujimura, that degree gradability of verbs does not depend on event structure. Degree gradation is not restricted to verbs of a certain aktionsart class; rather verbs of all aktionsart classes are gradable (69). In (a) it is shown that states can be graded, and (b) shows the same for accomplishments. The example in (c) shows degree gradation of an achievement, whereas an activity and a semelfactive are graded in (d) and (e). The presence of *einmal* 'once' in (e) focuses on a semelfactive reading of *bellen* 'bark' that otherwise also allows an iterative reading in which it is used as activity verb.

(69)   a.   *Maria liebt Peter sehr.*
            Maria loves Peter very
            'Maria loves Peter very much.'
       b.   *Der Zustand hat sich sehr stabilisiert.*
            the condition has REFL very stabilized
            'The condition stabilized a lot.'
       c.   *Maria hat Peter sehr erschreckt.*
            Maria has Peter very scared
            'Maria scared Peter very much.'
       d.   *Maria ist sehr gerannt.*
            Maria is very ran
            'Maria ran very fast.'

e. *Der Hund hat (einmal) sehr gebellt.*
   the dog has once very barked
   'The dog once barked very much.'

It is not only the case that aktionsart classes do not constrain degree gradability of verbs but also Rappaport Hovav & Levin's disctinction between scalar and non-scalar verbs is also independent from degree gradability. In (69) examples of gradable scalar and non-scalar change verbs are shown. *Stabilisieren* 'stabilize' in (69b) is a result verb, i.e., scalar change verb, and admits degree gradation. The verbs *rennen* 'run' in (d) and *bellen* 'bark' in (e) are manner verbs, i.e., non-scalar verbs, and also admit degree gradation. In Rappaport Hovav & Levin's work, the notion of 'scalarity' is restricted to directed changes in a single dimension. They do not claim any relationship between scalarity and gradation and in fact the discussion in this chapter reveals that degree gradation is not restricted to scalar changes. This demonstrates that, for verbs, access to a scale is not dependent on the expression of directed changes in a single dimension. Instead scales are lexical componnets of a much broader set of verbs which cannot be covered by Rappaport Hovav & Levin's class of 'scalar change verbs.' Nevertheless, Rappaport Hovav & Levin's class of scalar (change) verbs is relevant for the latter discussion, as these verbs form a special subtype of verbal degree gradation that interacts with grammatical aspect as well as with telicity. This will be discussed in more details in chapters 6 and 9.

The discussion in this chapter revealed that the only relevant factor for licensing degree gradation is the presence of a suitable gradation scale. Whether a verb is related to a scale that is admissible for gradation or not does not depend on such factors as telicity, durativity, dynamicity or whether the verb encodes 'manner' or 'result.' Even if the presence of a scale is not predictable, as it is not dependent on some other semantic property, verbs belonging to the same semantic class show remarkable uniformity regarding degree gradation (as indicated in 3.1). Hence, the notion of 'semantic verb classes,' in the sense of Levin (1993), plays an essential role in the analysis of verbal degree gradation and the case studies presented in chapter 6 to 8 are organized around such a semantic classification of verbs.

4 Syntax of verb gradation

The discussion in chapter 2 revealed that verb gradation is not uniformly expressed across languages. 'German-type' languages use 'd-adverbials' for degree gradation and a distinct set of 'e-adverbials' for extent gradation. 'French-type' languages – on the other hand – use 'd/e-adverbials' both for extent as well as degree gradation. Based on this distinction, the question emerges whether there is a principal difference between the realization of verb gradation in 'German-type' and 'French-type' languages. A second question that arises is: why are the adverbials used for extent gradation – in 'German-' as well as 'French-type' languages – also used as adnominal quantity expressions?

I will propose a syntactically based answer to both questions in this chapter. With regard to the first question I will argue that degree and extent gradation are uniformly expressed in both types of languages. The distinction between extent and degree gradation is syntactically reflected in German- as well as French-type languages. For the latter type this results in a syntactic ambiguity of 'd/e-adverbials.' For the second question, I will propose that 'quantity' is uniformly expressed in a certain syntactic configuration. This is independent of whether quantity in the nominal or verbal domain is concerned: which is not surprising given that the same expressions can be used for the expression of nominal as well as verbal quantity.

In 4.1, I will start with a discussion of French *beaucoup* and argue for the view that it is syntactically ambiguous between an extent and degree use. Two other proposals on the syntax of adverbial *beaucoup* will be reviewed, before presenting the crucial data that show the syntactic ambiguity of *beaucoup*. Section 4.2 introduces the syntactic framework – Role & Reference Grammar – that is used for the analysis. In 4.3, I am concerned with scope relationships, which can be used to explore the syntactic differences between extent and degree gradation. This section also provides a discussion of grammatical aspect, since verb gradation and grammatical aspect show interesting scope relationships. A concrete syntactic analysis of degree expressions within the framework of Role & Reference Grammar will be presented in section 4.4.4. The analysis will concern adverbially used degree expressions as well as adnominally used ones.

4.1 Syntactic analysis of adverbial *beaucoup*

Before presenting my own analysis of the syntax of degree expressions, I want to discuss some previous analyses of adverbial *beaucoup*. A considerable amount of work has been done on French adverbial and adnominal *beaucoup*. At this point, I want to briefly mention the discussion of the so-called 'quantification at a distance'-construction (QAD-construction) in French. In a QAD-construction the adnominal quantity expression *beaucoup* is placed at a distance from to the noun it modifies, which means that it is realized outside of the NP to which it belongs.[1] This can best be seen by comparing (1a) and (b). In (a) *beaucoup* directly precedes the NP *de livres*, which it modifies. In (b) *beaucoup* is in adverbial position, as argued for example by Obenauer (1984). Nevertheless, *beaucoup* still modifies the NP, which can be seen by the presence of the partitive article *de*, which would be replaced by a non-partitive definite or indefinite article if the quantity expression does not modify the noun.

(1)   a.   *Jean a lu beaucoup de livres.*
                 Jean has read a lot of books
                 'Jean has read many books.'
        b.   *Jean a   beaucoup lu   de livres.*
                 Jean has a lot   read of books
                 'Jean has read many books.'
                 (Doetjes, 1997, 252)

Obenauer (1984) argues for a relationship between the possibility of having a QAD-construction and the type of verb gradation – extent vs. degree gradation – that a verb allows. He states that "the verbs that do not allow

---

[1] Quantification at a distance is not restricted to *beaucoup* but is also possible with other degree expressions as for example *trop* 'too much' or *peu* 'little' (see Obenauer 1984). See Doetjes (1997) for a discussion of the relationship of QAD-constructions with 'floating quantifiers.'

QAD are those whose meanings impose the 'intensely'-type interpretation for *beaucoup, peu*, etc., excluding at the same time the 'often'-type interpretation" (Obenauer, 1984, 162). I will not discuss this type of construction further (for a critical discussion of Obenauer's analysis cf. Doetjes (1997) since it is only indirectly related to the analysis of verb gradation.[2] Instead, I will focus on two other analyses that aim to explain the two different readings of adverbially used *beaucoup*: I first discuss Doetjes' (1997) explanation of the verbal extent/degree in terms of theta selection (section 4.1.1) and then continue with Vecchiato's (1999) syntactic analysis of adverbial b*eaucoup* (section 4.1.2). The critical examination of these approaches will be the basis for my own analysis in the following sections.

4.1.1 Doetjes (1997)

In her work on degree expressions, Doetjes (1997) aims at explaining the cross-categorical distribution of these expressions on the one hand and how the differences in their interpretations arise on the other. In the following, I will concentrate on her explanation of the differences between the three examples in (2). Example (2a) shows that *très* rather than *beaucoup* is used for grading adjectives in the positive. How can the distribution of both expressions be explained? The second question, which will be the more important one, is: how do the different interpretations of verb gradation in (b) and (c) arise? What is responsible for getting an extent (frequency) reading in (b) but a degree reading in (c)?

(2)   a.   *Paul est très/* beaucoup malade.*
           Paul is   very/a lot   ill
           'Paul is very ill.'
     b.   *Paul va   beaucoup au   supermarché.*
           Paul goes a lot   to.the supermarket
           'Paul goes to the supermarket a lot.'
     c.   *Paul aime beaucoup cette pièce de theàâtre.*
           Paul loves a lot   this   play of theater
           'Paul loves this play a lot.'

---

[2]   Further discussions of this construction can be found in, for example, Vinet (1996) or Bouchard & Burnett (2007).

Doetjes claims that *beaucoup* is not ambiguous between being a frequency and an intensity adverb. Rather, the difference in interpretation results from different scales to which *beaucoup* applies. If it applies to an intensity scale, a degree reading results. And if the scale is a quantity scale, it leads to an extent reading.[3] Both types of scales are syntactically related to different theta positions. For intensity scales, Doetjes assumes a grade position (g-position), which is inherently scalar and represents a lexicalized gradable property. Gradable adjectives and verbs do have such a g-position and its saturation results in adjectival, or verbal degree gradation.

The grammatical reflex of a quantity scale is the quantity position (q-position) which can be found in verbs and nouns. Q-positions are not inherently scalar but depend on the referential properties of the nouns, or verbs at hand. In the case of singular count nouns, the q-position is non-scalar, whereas mass and plural count nouns have a scalar q-position. 'Once-only' predicates like *write the letter* only have a singular interpretation and therefore have a non-scalar q-position. Such predicates do not allow for a plural reading since a single letter (token) can only be written once. Verbal predications that allow for a plural interpretation like *go to the supermarket* and the verbal equivalent of mass predicates Bach (1986), which are atelic verbs such as *sleep* and *rain*, have a scalar q-position. Extent gradation is possible in the event that a verb has a scalar q-position. For atelic verbs a mass-to-count shift is required; otherwise they do not induce a criterion for counting events (cf. Abeillé et al. 2004, 187). For a more detailed discussion of such shifts, see Bach (1986), among others.

Doetjes argues that *beaucoup* is not categorically restricted as it modifies nouns as well as verbs. But, she states, it is restricted to scalar theta positions, which are either inherently scalar g-positions or scalar q-positions. The fact that *beaucoup* is not used with adjectives in the positive form is explained by the 'elsewhere condition.' It states that an expression is blocked for a certain context if a more specific expression of that context exists. This is the case with *très* in French as it is restricted to the positive form and therefore blocks the application of *beaucoup*. For German, one can argue that the degree expressions *sehr* and *viel* show stronger restrictions than *beaucoup* does. *Sehr* is restricted to g-positions and *viel* to scalar

---

[3] Doetjes (2007) speaks of 'quantitative' and 'qualitative scales' instead of 'quantity' and 'intensity scales' which basically covers the same distinction.

q-positions. This would explain the complementary distribution of these expressions with respect to verbal degree and extent gradation.

Since the difference between verbal extent and degree gradation is related to the saturation of two different theta positions and therefore two different types of scales, Doetjes does not need to propose a semantic ambiguity of *beaucoup*. She also does not assume a syntactic ambiguity of *beaucoup*, but analyzes *beaucoup* uniformly as a VP-adjunct that can show variable ordering with respect to the VP.[4] Relying on the examples in (3), she writes: "In French the DQ [degree quantifier] is ordered quite freely with respect to the elements of the VP. The only restriction seems to be that it cannot occur to the left of the inflected verb" (Doetjes, 1997, 118). This seems to hold only for lexical verbs but not for auxiliaries as (3c) shows.

(3) a. *Jean beaucoup voit Marie.
         Jean a lot   sees Marie
     b. Jean voit beaucoup Marie.
         Jean sees a lot   Marie
     c. Jean beaucoup a   vu   sa petite sœur.
         Jean a lot   has seen his little sister
     d. Jean a   beaucoup vu   sa petite sœur.
         Jean has a lot   seen his little sister
     e. ?Jean a   vu   beaucoup sa petite sœur.
         Jean has seen a lot   his little sister
     f. Jean a   vu   sa petite sœur.
         Jean has seen his little sister

Doetjes mentions that *beaucoup* is flexible in its positioning but does not relate the syntactic positioning to the difference between extent and degree gradation. I will show in section 4.1.3 that the interpretation of *beaucoup* is constrained by its syntactic position, which speaks in favor of a syntactic ambiguity of the degree expression. This will also be the major point that separates Doetjes' and my analysis. Essentially, I follow her assumption that *beaucoup* is semantically non-ambiguous and that extent and degree gradation are each related to different scales. But I reject the view that ex-

---

[4] Abeillé & Godard (2003) also argue for an adjunct analysis of degree adverbials in French but assume that they are complements and occur to the right of the predicate they modify.

4 Syntax of verb gradation

tent gradation is related to a quantity scale, whereas degree gradation is dependent on an intensity scale. This assumption is too simplistic, since degree gradation can also be related to a quantity scale as the German example in (4) shows. In this example, *sehr* specifies the quantity of rain that has fallen but not the extent of the event. Therefore, the distinction between quantity and intensity does not coincide with the distinction between extent and degree gradation. The crucial difference seems to be that for extent gradation the quantity scales measure the quantity of an event, i.e., its temporal duration or frequency, whereas in (4) it is the quantity of an implicit argument of the verb, namely 'rain,' which is measured on the quantity scale.

(4)   *Gestern   hat es sehr geregnet.*
      yesterday has it very rained
      'Yesterday it rained a lot.'

In the next subsection, I turn to Vecchiato's syntactic analysis of *beaucoup*, which indicates that there is indeed a syntactic difference between verbal degree and extent gradation in French.

4.1.2 Vecchiato (1997)

Vecchiato (1999) is working in the cartographic enterprise (cf. Cinque & Rizzi (2008) for an overview) that was used by Cinque (1999) for a cross-linguistic investigation of the order of adverbs. Her aim is to cover French degree expressions – such as *beaucoup* and *peu* 'little' – within Cinque's hierarchy. Cinque derives a universal hierarchy of adverbs by investigating the relative order of adverbs. This is illustrated in (5) for the Italian habitual adverb *solitamente* 'usually' and the negative adverb *mica*. As the examples show, only the order that *solitamente* precedes *mica* is acceptable. Based on such pairs of sentences, Cinque (1999, 106) derives the hierarchy in (6).

(5)   Italian (Romance <Indo-European; Cinque 1999, 4)
   a.   *Alle due, Giannai non ha solitamente mica mangiato, ancora.*
        'At two, Giannai has usually not eaten yet.'
   b.   **Alle due, Gianni non has mica solitamente mangiato, ancore.*
        'At two, Gianni has not usually eaten yet.'

108

4.1 Syntactic analysis of adverbial beaucoup

(6) [frankly MOOD$_{speech-act}$
[fortunately MOOD$_{evaluative}$
[allegedly MOOD$_{evidential}$
[probably MOOD$_{epistemic}$
[once T(PAST)
[then T(FUTURE)
[perhaps MOOD$_{irrealis}$
[necessarily MOOD$_{necessity}$
[possibly MOOD$_{possibility}$
[usually ASP$_{habitual}$
[again ASP$_{repetitive(I)}$
[often ASP$_{frequentive(I)}$
[intentionally MOD$_{volitional}$
[quickly ASP$_{celerative(I)}$
[already T(ANTERIOR)
[no longer ASP$_{terminative}$
[still ASP$_{continuative}$
[always ASP$_{perfect(?)}$
[just ASP$_{retrospective}$
[soon ASP$_{proximative}$
[briefly ASP$_{durativ}$
[characteristically (?) ASP$_{generic/progressive}$
[almost ASP$_{prospective}$
[completely ASP$_{SgCompletive(I)}$
[tutto ASP$_{PlCompletive}$
[well VOICE
[fast/early ASP$_{celerative(II)}$
[again ASP$_{repetitive(II)}$
[often ASP$_{frequentative(II)}$
[completely ASP$_{SgCompletive(II)}$]]]]]]]]]]]]]]]]]]]]]]]]]]]]]

Each semantic class of adverbs, such as 'evaluative mood' or 'durative aspect,' is related to its own functional projection in the clause. Adverbs are analyzed as specifiers of functional heads and have their base position in the specifier position of the respective functional projection. All the different semantic classes of adverbs are strictly ordered with respect to the other classes.

4 Syntax of verb gradation

Vecchiato aims at extending Cinque's universal hierarchy of adverbs by investigating the exact base positions of degree expressions. I restrict myself to her discussion of *beaucoup* in which she says that it allows for two different interpretations: 'intensity' vs. 'frequentative.' With regard to these two interpretations she states that they "are apparently associated with two different positions in the hierarchy" (Vecchiato, 1999, 262n4). She presents two arguments in favor of the apparent association of *beaucoup* with two different positions. The first argument is that *beaucoup* can be realized twice in a sentence. Since each functional projection only has one specifier position, a multiple realization of *beaucoup* requires that it is related to different functional projections. Vecchiato uses the example in (7) to demonstrate the multiple realization of *beaucoup*. However, my native speaker consultants rejected the example in (7) as ungrammatical. I will present grammatical examples of multiple realization of *beaucoup* in the next section.

(7) La pièce a beaucoup été beaucoup changée.
the play has a lot been a lot changed
'The play has been changed a lot many times.
(Vecchiato, 1999, 263)

The second argument she raises is that *beaucoup* in its frequentative reading can occupy more positions in the sentence than if it is used in its degree reading. Vecchiato presents the examples in (8) and (9) to illustrate the differences in the positioning of frequentative *beaucoup* (8) and intensity *beaucoup* (9). Following her analysis, *beaucoup* used as an extent degree expression can directly follow the participle (8b), which is not possible for intensity *beaucoup* (9b). I will discuss the difference in the syntactic positions extent and degree *beaucoup* can occupy in more detail in the next section.

(8) a. On a beaucoup discuté ce projet ces dernier
3SG.IPS has a lot discussed this project these latest
jours.
days
'We have discussed this project a lot of times the latest days.'
b. On a discuté beaucoup ce projet ces dernier jours.

4.1 Syntactic analysis of adverbial beaucoup

    c. *On a discuté ce projet beaucoup ces dernier jours.*
       (Vecchiato, 1999, 263)

(9) a. On a beaucoup discuté ce projet á la réunion.
          3SG.IPS has a lot   discussed this project at the meeting
          'We have discussed this project a lot at the meeting.'
    b. *On a discuté beaucoup ce projet á la réunion.*
    c. *On a discuté ce projet beaucoup á la réunion.*
       (Vecchiato, 1999, 264)

Vecchiato uses the methodology employed by Cinque and compares the relative order of adverbs to determine their position in Cinque's universal adverb hierarchy.[5] For adverbial *beaucoup* she claims that it is located between *tout* 'everything' and *bien* 'well.'[6] The examples in (10a) and (11a) are intended to show that *beaucoup* follows *tout* but precedes *bien*, whereas the examples in (10b) and (11b) show that the reverse order results in ungrammaticality.

(10) a. *Pierre a tout   beaucoup aimé.*
           Pierre has everything a lot   liked
           'Pierre liked everything a lot.'
     b. **Pierre a **beaucoup** tout aimé.*
        (Vecchiato, 1999, 271)

(11) a. ?*Il a beaucoup bien analysé la pièce de théâtre.*
           he has a lot   well analyzed the play of theater
           'He analyzed the play a lot and well.'
     b. **Il a bien beaucoup analysé la pièce de théâtre.*
        (Vecchiato 1999, 271; slightly adapted)

The examples in (10) and (11) are problematic since in (10) *beaucoup* is used for degree gradation, whereas in (11) it functions as an extent degree expression. Since Vecchiato claims that frequentative and intensity *beaucoup*

---

[5] Cinque is not the first person to make use of the relative order of adverbs to explore their syntax. This idea goes back to Jackendoff (1972) and is also used in Van Valin & LaPolla (1997).

[6] Vinet (1996, 215f.) argues that in Quebec French *beaucoup* has to precede *bien* as well as *tout* and therefore would occupy a different position in Cinque's universal hierarchy of adverbs which would contradict the claim that there really is a universal and strictly ordered hierarchy of functional heads.

111

4 Syntax of verb gradation

differ and are apparently associated with two different positions in the hierarchy, the examples in (10) and (11) do not support her analysis. Finally, she claims that there is only one functional projection for adverbial *beaucoup*, thereby ignoring the arguments she raised for the assumptions that both are related to two different positions in the hierarchy.

Vecchiato presents arguments for syntactic differences of extent and degree *beaucoup*, but the data she presents are either ungrammatical or inconclusive. In the next section I will present further data that demonstrate the syntactic ambiguity of *beaucoup*.

4.1.3 Preliminary observations of the syntactic ambiguity of *beaucoup*

In the last section, I reviewed Vecchiato's arguments in favor of the view that extent and degree *beaucoup* occupy different positions in the sentence. I will build on her arguments and finally conclude, unlike her, that adverbial *beaucoup* is in fact syntactically ambiguous. The first argument she put forth is that *beaucoup* can be realized twice in a single sentence. In the last section, I pointed out that my native speaker informants rejected the example Vecchiato gave but there are other examples of a double realization of *beaucoup*. An example illustrating this point is (12). In this sentence, the frequency of bleeding events as well as the quantity of emitted blood is specified.

(12) Il a   beaucoup saigné beaucoup du   nez.
      he has a lot   bled   a lot   from.the nose
      'He often bled a lot out of his nose.'

There is an explanation why *saigner* 'bleed' allows for a multiple realization of *beaucoup* but *changer* 'change' – the verb used in Vecchiato's example in (7) – does not. Change of state verbs only allow the degree reading of *beaucoup* but do not license the extent interpretation of *beaucoup* (cf. Fleischhauer 2013). In (13) *beaucoup* indicates the degree to which the condition improved but neither its temporal duration nor its frequency.

4.1 Syntactic analysis of adverbial beaucoup

(13) Si mon etat   s'est beaucoup amélioré depuis quelques
      if my condition CL=is a lot   improved since several
      moins [...]
      months
      'If my condition has greatly improved since several months [...]'
      (Fleischhauer, 2013, 147)

Saigner licenses both the extent and the degree reading of *beaucoup*. Sentence (14) is ambiguous between the interpretations that the subject referent often bled (frequentative reading), that he bled for a long time (durative reading) or that he emitted a lot of blood (degree reading). A multiple realization of *beaucoup* is possible if both a degree and an extent reading are available for *beaucoup*. If a verb licenses only one of these interpretations, a multiple realization of *beaucoup* is impossible.

(14) Il a beaucoup saigné.
      he has a lot   bled
      'He bled a lot.'

It can be determined even more precisely which of the two *beaucoup*'s in (12) licences the extent and which the degree interpretation. It is the second, the post participle *beaucoup*, that specifies the quantity of emitted substance. The first one – placed between the auxiliary and the participle – specifies the frequency of the event. This is shown by the examples in (15). If *beaucoup* is located between the auxiliary and the participle it can either be interpreted as indicating the extent or the degree (15a). Placed directly after the participle, *beaucoup* only allows for a degree interpretation (b). And if *beaucoup* follows the direct object, as in (c), it only gets the extent reading. There is one ambiguous position for *beaucoup*, which seems to be the preferred one, and two unambiguous positions.

(15) a. Il a   beaucoup admiré cette chanteuse à l'opera.
          he has a lot   admired this chanteuse at the=opera
          'He has (often) admired this chanteuse (very much) at the opera.'
      b. Il a admiré beaucoup cette chanteuse à l'opera.
          'He has admired this chanteuse very much at the opera.'
      c. Il a admiré cette chanteuse beaucoup à l'opera.
          'He has often admired this chanteuse at the opera.'

4 Syntax of verb gradation

The examples in (15) contradict Vecchiato's claim that *beaucoup* in its degree interpretation is blocked in the position directly following the participle. In fact, example (15b), in which *beaucoup* directly follows the participle, only allows for the degree reading. In addition, with intransitive verbs the position directly after the participle is restricted to the degree reading of *beaucoup* (16b), whereas located between the auxiliary and the participle *beaucoup* is ambiguous (16a).

(16) a. *Il a beaucoup saigné du nez.*
he has a lot bled from.the nose
'He bled a lot out of his nose.'
b. *Il a saigné beaucoup du nez.*
he has bled a lot from.the nose
'He bled a lot out of his nose.'

The frequency adverb *souvent* is restricted to the position between the auxiliary and the participle and cannot be placed directly after the participle (17). This is not surprising given the synonymy of frequentative *beaucoup* and *souvent*.

(17) a. *Il a souvent saigné du nez.*
he has often bled from.the nose
'He often bled out of his nose.'
b. **Il a saigné souvent du nez.*

Further proof that the position between the auxiliary and the participle is ambiguous, whereas the one directly after the participle is not, is presented in the examples in (18). If one adds the subordinated sentence *mais seulement un peu* 'but only a little bit' to the sentence in (18a), a contradiction arises. In the main sentence it is expressed that the referent of the subject argument emitted a large quantity of blood, whereas in the subordinated sentence it is expressed that the emitted quantity of blood was merely small. The quantity of blood the subject referent emitted would be specified twice by different degrees. Sentence (18b) is not contradictory since *beaucoup* is in a syntactically ambiguous position. Ergo, the sentence allows for the non-contradictory interpretation that the referent of the subject argument often bled but emitted only a small quantity of blood.

(18) a. #Il a saigné beaucoup du nez, mais seulement un peu.
 he has a lot bled from nose but only a little bit
 'He bled a lot out of his nose, but only a little bit.'
 b. Il a beaucoup saigné du nez, mais seulement un peu.
 he has bled a lot from nose but only a little bit
 'He often bled out of his nose, but only a little bit.'

The data in this section have shown that the interpretation of *beaucoup* is syntactically constrained. Its position in the sentence determines its interpretation. In section 4.4, I will provide a theoretical explanation of the syntactic differences observed in this section, which will also extend to other languages such as German. The next section introduces the theoretical framework for the analysis.

4.2 Role & Reference Grammar

Role & Reference Grammar (RRG; Foley & Van Valin 1984; Van Valin & LaPolla 1997; Van Valin 2005) is a grammatical framework that attempts to describe and analyze the interplay between form (syntax), meaning (semantics) and communication (pragmatics). RRG – in contrast to e.g. the Minimalist Program (e.g., Chomsky 1995) or Relational Grammar (e.g., Perlmutter 1980) – provides a monostratal account of syntax and therefore only one level of syntactic representation is assumed. A central element of Role & Reference Grammar is a semantically motivated layered structure of the clause, which is built on the distinction between predicates and arguments on the one hand and between arguments and non-arguments, i.e., adjuncts, on the other hand. The predicate, which can be a verb but also another predicating expression, is contained in the smallest syntactic layer called 'nucleus.' The core, which is the next layer up, contains the nucleus and its arguments. The highest layer is the clause and it contains the core and some optional elements that are not of further relevance for the following analysis. For each layer, there is an optional periphery that contains adjuncts and adverbials.[7] A further relevant distinction is the one

---

[7] Throughout this chapter, I use the terms 'adverbs' and 'adverbials' interchangeably for adverbially used expressions irrespective of whether they belong to a lexical class of adverbs or not.

4 Syntax of verb gradation

between constituents and operators. Nucleus, core and periphery are the primary constituents that make up the clause (Van Valin, 2005, 4). Operators are expressions for grammatical categories such as aspect and tense. They are treated as modifiers of different layers of the clause. Two different structural representations for constituents and operators are assumed which are labeled 'constituent projection' and 'operator projection.'[8] Constituent and operator projection are a mirror image of each other and connected through the nucleus. A schematic representation of these structural representations is shown in figure 3.

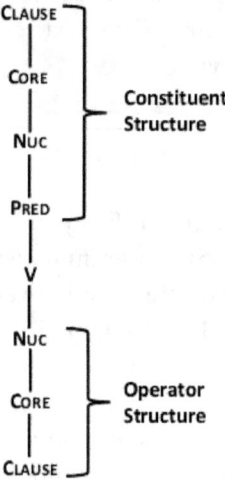

Figure 3: Schematic representation of constituent and operator structure in RRG (following Van Valin 2005, 12).

Two essential differences between RRG and generative approaches to syntax – such as the Minimalist Program or Government and Binding – need to be mentioned. First, there is no notion 'verb phrase' (VP) in RRG. In those languages that seem to have VPs, this is due to a grammaticalization of focus structure (cf. Van Valin 2005, 80f.). Instead of distinguishing between VP-internal and VP-external arguments, RRG locates all the pred-

---

[8] A third projection – the focus structure – is also assumed in RRG but is not of further relevance for the current discussion.

icate's arguments equally in the core. Second, RRG does not make use of the traditional notion of 'subject,' since it is not a cross-linguistically valid grammatical function (see Schachter 1976; Van Valin 1980). Instead, RRG employs the notion of a 'privileged syntactic argument' which is not a general grammatical relation but can be specific for certain constructions. For Germanic, Slavic and Romance languages, the privileged syntactic argument corresponds to the traditional notion of subject. For convenience, I continue using the term 'subject.'

Within RRG, adverbs are located in the periphery of the constituent structure and can attach to all three layers of the clause. Although adverbs are uniquely assigned to a certain syntactic layer, it is not assumed that they have a fixed base position (contrary to Cinque 1999, for example). Rather the positioning of adverbs is constrained by the layered structure of the clause. If multiple adverbs are realized in a single sentence, then nuclear adverbs have to be located closer to the nucleus than core adverbs and core adverbs have to be closer to the nucleus than clausal adverbs (Van Valin, 2005, 21). This ordering constraint only holds if the adverbs are located on the same side of the verb, otherwise they cannot be brought into a relative order to each other. In (19) this constraint is illustrated for the English nuclear adverb *completely*, the core adverb *slowly* and the clausal adverb *evidently*. If all three adverbs are located on the same side of the verb, as in (a), then the order has to be *evidently* > *slowly* > *completely* > 'verb.'[9] A different order, as in the other examples except (b), is ungrammatical. Sentences (a) and (b) show that *completely* and *slowly* can be placed in the same position, directly in front of the participle. But if *slowly* is in that position, *completely* has to be located to the right side of the verb. This indicates that there is no fixed position for these adverbs but that the order of adverbs is only constrained relatively to each other.

(19) a. *Evidently, Leslie has slowly been completely immersing herself in the new language.*
      b. *Leslie has evidently been slowly immersing herself completely in the new language.*

---

[9] Note that also the reverse order 'verb' > *completely* > *slowly* > *evidently* is possible, but the relative order of the adverbs remains the same (cf. Van Valin 2005, 20f. for examples).

> c. *Evidently, Leslie has completely been slowly immersing herself in the new language.
> d. *Slowly, Leslie has evidently been completely immersing herself in the new language.
> e. *Slowly, Leslie has completely been evidently immersing herself in the new language.
> f. *Completely, Leslie has evidently been slowly immersing herself in the new language.
> g. *Completely, Leslie has slowly been evidently immersing herself in the new language.
> (Van Valin, 2005, 20)

Even if there is no base position for adverbs in a sentence, this does not mean that syntax provides no constraints for adverbs. One constraint, the relative order of multiple adverbs, has been mentioned above. A further constraint is that the position of an adverb within a sentence may affect its interpretation. This has been demonstrated in the last section for *beaucoup* and is illustrated for a different example from English in (20). In (20a) *cleverly* is in the immediate pre-verbal position and the sentence is ambiguous between the following two interpretations: (i) the manner in which Ruth hit the cash was clever or (ii) the fact that Ruth hit the cash was clever. Examples (b) and (c) are unambiguous; (b) only has the first interpretation and (c) only has the second one.[10] The examples in (20) indicate that operators like the tense operator in English and adverbs interact in such a way that their placement relative to each other constrains the interpretation.

> (20) a. Ruth cleverly hit the cash.
> b. Ruth hit the cash cleverly.
> c. Cleverly, Ruth hit the cash.
> (Van Valin, 2005, 20)

In many cases, adverbs and operators function as expressions for the same grammatical category. This, for example, is obvious if one compares the morphological and adverbial marking of tense within and across languages. English uses morphological as well as adverbial devices (e.g., *yesterday*) for expressing temporal relationships, whereas languages such as Cantonese

---

[10] This observation goes back to McConnell-Ginet (1982).

express tense solely through adverbial expressions, as indicated in (21). Tense can also be marked on an auxiliary verb, as the English example in (22) reveals. In this example, the main verb is infinite and tense is merely expressed on the auxiliary. In an RRG analysis, the auxiliary would not be part of the constituent structure but is treated as an operator, indicating – among other things – tense.

(21) Cantonese (Sinitic <Sino-Tibetan; Matthews & Yip 1994, 190)
 Gwok yīsàng yíhchìhn jyuh Sāan Déng.
 Kwok doctor before   live Peak
 'Dr. Kwok used to live on the Peak.'

(22) *Peter had left yesterday.*

Tense operators are analyzed as clausal operators, whereas Van Valin & LaPolla (1997, 162) consider temporal adverbials to be core adverbs.[11] This shows that there does not have to be a close match between the layers at which adverbials and their corresponding operators are realized. Furthermore, operators are closed-class items, whereas adverbials form an open-class (Van Valin, 2005, 26n7). But the order of operators is constrained in the same way as the order of adverbs. Nuclear operators are closer to the stem than core operators, which are closer to the stem than clausal operators. A summary of different operators is shown in (23).

(23) **Nucleus operators**: aspect, negation, directionals (that modify orientation of an action without reference to participants)
 Core operators: directionals (that modify the orientation or motion of an participant), event quantification, modality, internal negation
 Clause operators: status, tense, evidentiality, illocutionary force
 (Van Valin, 2005, 9)

Scope relationships of operators are reflected in the logical representation of predications. (24) shows a partial semantic representation of the sentence *Has Kim been crying?*, which contains three operators. INT(*errogativ)*

---

[11] It is questionable whether such adverbs as Cantonese *yíhchìhn* 'before' differ from English *tomorrow* in being clausal operators since they express a relation between speech time and event/reference time which makes them different from English *tomorrow* and more similar to tense operators.

expressing illocutionary force, PRES(ent) for tense and PERF(ect) PROG(essiv) as aspectual operators. The scope of operators is reflected in their linear order in the logical structure.

(24) ⟨_IF_ *INT* ⟨_TNS_ *PRES* ⟨_ASP_ *PERF PROG* ⟨do'(Kim, [cry'(Kim)])⟩⟩⟩⟩
(Van Valin, 2005, 50)

A relevant factor in the ordering of affixed morphemes is the distinction between inflectional and derivational morphemes. Derivational morphemes are closer to the stem than inflectional ones (cf. Watters 2009, 264 on the impact of the derivational vs. flectional distinction on the order of affixed operators).

With regard to gradation, RRG does not mention an operator that corresponds to degree gradation. But there is one operator that seems to be semantically very close to extent gradation, this operator is called 'event quantification' in RRG. An example for 'event quantification' is provided in (25) from Amele. Amele has the distributive morpheme -*ad* which expresses a multiplicity of actions in (25a). The corresponding sentence in (b) without the distributive morpheme only expresses a single action.

(25) Amele (Papua-New Guines; Roberts 1987, cited after Van Valin 2005, 11)
 a. *Age bel-ad-ein.*
    3PL go-DISTR-3PL-REMPST
    'They went in all direction.'
 b. *Age bel-ein.*
    3PL go-3PL-REMPST
    'They went.'

What the Amele example shows is that the distributive morpheme – the event quantificational operator – is closer to the stem than the tense operator, which is a clausal operator. What is called 'event quantification' by Van Valin is often discussed under the notion of 'pluractionality.'[12] Yu (2003) demonstrates that pluractionality marking in Chechen (Nakh-Dagestanian) may have a frequentative (26a) but also a durative (26b) in-

---

[12] See Armoskaite (2012) and literature cited therein for a discussion of the relationship between verbal plurality and distributivity.

terpretation, which is quite similar to the different readings of extent gradation that we find.

(26) Chechen (Nakh-Dagestanian; Yu 2003, 293, 299)
    a. *molu myylu*
       'drink' 'drink repeatedly'
    b. *xowzhu xiizha*
       'ache' 'ache for a while'

The short discussion of the Amele and Chechen data reveals that event quantification/pluractionality can be seen as corresponding to verbal extent gradation. Hence, I consider distributive markers like those in Amele as operators expressing extent gradation.[13]

The Slave example in (27) shows that aspectual operators (in this case inceptive and perfective markers) are closer to the stem than the distributive morpheme *yá-*. Rice (2000), discussing the order of verbal affixes in Athapaskan languages, mentions that the same ordering of distributive and aspectual markers also holds for other Athapaskan languages such as Koyukon, Athna and Deni'ina.

(27) Slave (Athapaskan; Rice 1989, 678, Rice 2000, 52)
    yá-d-į-ta
    DISTR-INCEP-PF-kick
    'I kicked it many times.'

The data in (25) and (27) reveal that event quantificational operators are affixed closer to the stem than clausal operators, but that nuclear operators like aspect are closer to the stem than event quantificational ones. The described order of operators is in accordance with Van Valin's (2005, 11) claim that event quantification is an operation at the core layer. A second argument for this claim is that the core is the minimal expression and therefore syntactic realization of an event (Van Valin 2005, 11; Bohnemeyer & Van Valin 2013). Whereas the event predicate is already present at the nucleus layer, the event participants are realized at the core layer. This fits well with Chung & Ladusaw's (2004, 11) claim that at the event level all

---

[13] I do not want to claim that distributive markers solely function as pluractionality markers or expressions of extent gradation as they clearly have other functions too. In Chechen, the pluractionality markers also have a distributive reading Yu (2003).

4 Syntax of verb gradation

arguments except the event argument have to be saturated, which requires a realization of the event participants. Therefore, the lowest layer for event quantification has to be the core.

I argued above that event quantification can be semantically equated with extent gradation. At this stage, I claim that expressions used for extent gradation are realized at the same syntactic layer as event quantificational operators which is at the core layer. Based on this claim, we can formulate the prediction in (28).

(28)   Adverbial extent degree expressions are core adverbials.

There are also good candidates for degree operators as the examples from Jalonke in section 2.3 or the Maricopa example in (29) show. Unfortunately, neither the Jalonke nor the Maricopa data allow determining the syntactic layer of the degree operator due to a lack of relevant data.

(29)   Maricopa (Yuman <Hokan; Gordon 1986, 141)
       mhay-ny-sh ny-aham-hot-m
       boy-DEM-SJ 3/1-hit-very-real
       'The boy hit me hard.'

Within RRG there is no discussion of degree expressions. Van Valin & LaPolla and Van Valin briefly discuss the adverb *completely* by introducing the syntactic analysis of adverbs in RRG. But the authors consider *completely* being an aspectual adverb rather than a degree adverbial. The reason for doing this is that *completely* conveys the meaning specification of 'completeness' similar to perfective aspect. Since *completely* is taken to be an adverbial correspondent to aspectual operators, it is analyzed as a nuclear adverb. Such an argumentation cannot easily be transferred to degree adverbials such as German *sehr* or French *beaucoup*, which are not that close in meaning to aspectual operators.

Since there is no RRG analysis of degree expressions, we need criteria to decide to which layer expressions used for degree gradation belong. As mentioned above, Van Valin uses the relative order of multiple adverbs as an indication of their syntax. I will not make use of this test criterion since many factors may influence the relative order of adverbs. One relevant factor is information structure. Thus the sentences in (30) show that *sehr* and the directional PP *aus der Nase* 'out of the nose' are not uniquely constrained in their relative order.[14] There is no semantic difference between the sentences in (a) and (b): native speakers of German accept both sentences but prefer the one in (a) due to pragmatic reasons.

(30)   a.   *Er hat sehr aus der Nase geblutet.*
              he has very out the nose bled
              'He bled a lot out of his nose.'
      b.   *Er hat aus der Nase sehr geblutet.*
              he has out the nose very bled
              'He bled a lot out of his nose.'

Maienborn (1996, 2003) also mentions that in German the order of locative adverbials is affected by information structure. For an investigation of the relative order of adverbs one needs to take information structure into account but this would go beyond the limits of this thesis. Therefore, my syntactic analysis is based on scope relationships between adverbs and operators rather than on the relative order of adverbs.

4.3 Scope relationships

The aim of this section is to demonstrate that expressions used for degree and extent gradation differ in their scope relationships with respect to grammatical aspect. More precisely, extent degree expressions have scope over grammatical aspect, whereas grammatical aspect has scope over expressions of degree gradation. de Swart (1998, 29) defines scope informally as "a relational notion, where the interpretation of one expression depends on another one in a certain way." To say that grammatical aspect has scope over expressions of degree gradation means that the interpretation of degree gradation is dependent on grammatical aspect. This is the case if two sentences that only differ in aspect result in two different readings of degree gradation. The same holds for extent gradation having scope over grammatical aspect. If the interpretation of the aspectual operator differs depending on the presence of an extent degree expression, it can be said that extent gradation has scope over aspect. Before I demonstrate that these

---

[14]   Van Valin (p.c.) mentions that *aus der Nase* is probably an argument-adjunct rather than an adverbial. I leave this question open for future work.

4 Syntax of verb gradation

scope relationships hold, I will shortly discuss the formal expression of aspect in Russian, French and German.

4.3.1 Grammatical aspect in German, French, and Russian

Grammatical aspect, also called viewpoint aspect by Smith (1997), is basically concerned with the way how a particular situation is described. A basic aspectual distinction can be drawn between perfective and imperfective aspect. The imperfective aspect can itself be subdivided into habitual, continuous and progressive aspect.[15] This aspectual typology is shown in figure 4.

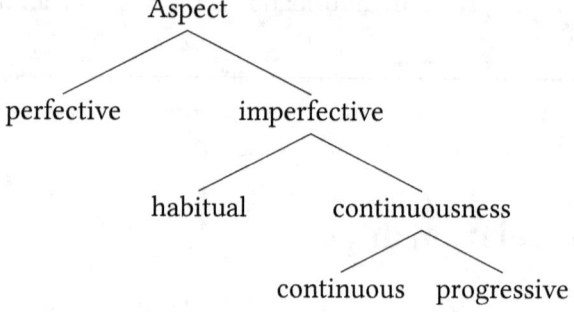

Figure 4: Aspect typology based on Comrie (1976, 25).

By using the perfective aspect, a situation is described as complete but not necessarily as completed. Perfective aspect does not entail resultativity (cf.Comrie 1976), rather it describes a situation as a whole. This means that there is an abstraction from the internal constituency of a situation and neither the end nor the beginning or some other part of the situation is focused on. Imperfective aspect, on the other hand, is used to describe non-complete situations which can be conceived in different ways. With habitual aspect a situation is described as pertaining over an extended period of time" (Comrie, 1976, 27f.). A second major use of the imperfective aspect is to describe situations as ongoing. This can either be done by using a progressive or by using a continuous form. Comrie notes that the

---

[15] Filip & Carlson (1997), for example, argue against the view that 'habitual' is a subtype of imperfective aspect.

4.3 Scope relationships

progressive requires a dynamic predicate and is incompatible with stative predicates. Continuous aspect is conceived by Comrie as semantically close to the progressive but without a restriction to dynamic situations.

German does not have a grammaticalized aspectual system but it has a perfect form like English. As Comrie (1976, 52) mentions, the perfect is different from the imperfective/perfective aspectual distinction as it is not concerned with the internal temporal constitution of a situation. Rather the perfect expresses a relation between a situation and a proceeding eventuality. An illustrative example is the resultative use of the perfect as exemplified in (31). In contrast to a plain past tense *John arrived* the perfect form allows the inference that John is still there. "A present state is referred to as being the result of some past situation," as Comrie (1976, 56) states it.

(31)   *John has arrived.*

A resultative reading of the perfect is one use of the perfect form, for a detailed discussion of the perfect see Comrie (1976, chap. 3) and especially Löbner (2002) for a discussion of the perfect in German. I will come back to the German perfect by discussing the expression of aspect in German.

The aspectual system of Russian and Slavic languages in general forces a lot of discussion that I will not review in this thesis (but see Filip 1999). In Russian, all verbs are either perfective or imperfective with some verbs, so-called biaspectual verbs, which allow either a perfective or an imperfective reading. An example of such a biaspectual verb is *stabilizirovat'* 'stabilize' which is a loan like many other biaspectual verbs. In Russian, there is no distinct marker for perfective or imperfective aspect. We find simplex verbs that are imperfective (32) but also ones that are perfective (33). For the perfective verbs in (33) imperfective simplex verbs exist.

(32)   a.   *znat'*$_{\text{IMPF}}$
            'know'
       b.   *pisat'*$_{\text{IMPF}}$
            'write'
       c.   *govorit'*$_{\text{IMPF}}$
            'say'

4 Syntax of verb gradation

(33) a. *izičat'*_{IMPF} – *izičit'*_{PF}
'learn, study'
b. *govorit'*_{IMPF} – *skazat'*_{PF}
'say'

For the examples in (33), it can be said that suppletive stems for imperfective and corresponding perfective verbs exist (33b). But most perfective verbs are derived by prefixation, examples are shown in (34).

(34) a. *delat'*_{IMPF} – *s-delat'*_{PF}
'do, make'
b. *rezat'*_{IMPF} – *raz-rezat'*_{PF}
'cut'
c. *krast'*_{IMPF} – *u-krast'*_{PF}
'steal'

Verbal prefixes in Russian cannot be considered as inflectional markers of perfective aspect as they quite often change the meaning of the derived verb. An example is shown in (35). Using *pro-* adds a temporal specification to the base verb but also derives a perfective verb from an imperfective one.

(35) a. *čitat'*_{IMPF}
'read'
b. *pro-čitat'*_{PF}
'read for a while'

Filip (1999, 2000) presents many more arguments for considering verbal prefixes in Russian but also in Slavic languages in general as derivational rather than inflectional affixes. Nevertheless, there is also an inflectional marker of aspect which is the so called secondary imperfective illustrated in (36). The secondary imperfective *-(i)va* only affects the aspectual interpretation and always yields on imperfective reading of derived and underived perfective base verbs.

(36) a. *pisat'*_{IMPF}
'write'
b. *vy-pisat'*_{PF}
'write out'
c. *vy-pis-yva-t'*_{IMPF}
'write out/be writing out'

4.3 Scope relationships

French has a less grammaticalized aspectual system since a systematic perfective vs. imperfective distinction only exists in the past tense. The imperfective past – *imparfait* – is expressed by an affix that combines information on aspect 'imperfective,' tense 'past' and subject agreement (number and person). Such an imperfective form is shown in (37a). The perfective past is expressed by the so-called *pass'e compose* which is formed by a present form of the auxiliary *avoir* 'have' or *être* 'be' and a participial form of the main verb (37b).

(37) a. *nous aim-ions*
    we love-1PL.PST.IMPF
    'we loved'
   b. *nous avons   aimé*
    we have.1PL love.PARC
    'we have loved'

Neither the auxiliary nor the participle can be considered to be the exponent of perfective aspect but both together express temporal, aspectual as well as agreement information. Imperfect is a general imperfective form that can be used for expressing the continuous as well as habitual reading. But there is also a dedicated periphrastic progressive construction formed by the inflected auxiliary *être* and the form *en train de* 'in the process of' followed by an infinitival form of the main verb (38).

(38) *Nous sommes en train de rénover   norte maison.*
    we   AUX   PROG   renovate.INF our   house
    'We are renovating our house.'

German has a periphrastic progressive construction that is somewhat similar to the progressive construction found in French. This form is called *rheinische Verlaufsform*[16] which is formed by the inflected auxiliary *sein* 'be,' a prepositional phrase consisting of a contracted form of the preposition *an* 'at, on, by' and the dative form of the definite article and followed by a nominalized infinitive.[17] The form is illustrated in (39).

---

[16] See Andersson (1989) for a discussion of the *rheinische Velaufsform* and a comparison with other devices for expressing progressive aspect in German.

[17] If one takes the presence of the contracted form of the preposition and the definite article seriously, the infinitive should be seen as a nominalized form. This is not accepted by everyone (see the discussion in Andersson 1989) but if one does, it should be reflected in the orthography as in German nouns are written with a capital letter.

4 Syntax of verb gradation

(39)   a.   *Ich bin am Essen.*
           I   AUX at.the.DAT eating
           'I am eating.'
     b.   *Ich bin (das) Brot am Essen.*
           I   AUX the bread at.the.DAT eating
           'I am eating (the) bread.'

Ebert (2000) shows that the use of the progressive form is unevenly distributed in Germany and the form has developed farthest in the Rhineland. In this area (39b) is acceptable, whereas speakers of other areas do not accept transitive verbs in this construction and they accept the combination with a definite direct object even less.

For those speakers who accept the *rheinische Verlaufsform*, German has a grammaticalized progressive aspect but it still lacks a grammaticalization of perfective aspect. As mentioned above, German has a perfect form which is formed in the same way as the French *passé composé* by a combination of an inflected auxiliary (either *haben* 'have' or *sein* 'be') and a participial form of the main verb. In fact, in many cases – mostly in southern Germany – the perfect simply expresses past tense and it is used instead of the inflectional past tense form. The perfect is not simply reduced to an expression of past tense but still shows up in regular perfect uses. I will not focus on the specific functions of the perfect (in contrast to perfective and imperfective aspect) but take it as a way to force a perfective interpretation. In its non-past but perfect use the perfect form expresses a relation between a situation and a preceeding state. Thereby the situation denoted by the base verb is taken as completed and therefore licenses a perfective reading of the described situation. To be clear, I do not assume that the perfect form in German is a way to express perfective aspect, I merely assume that it can be used to emphasize that a certain situation is described as completed. Nevertheless, the aspectual interpretation is context-dependent as can be illustrated by examples like those in (40) and (41) which are taken from Löbner (2002, 374).

(40)   *Als ich die CD gebrannt habe, stürzte der Computer ab.*
          when I   the CD burned have crashed the computer PART
          'While I was burning the CD, the computer crashed.'

(41) Als   der Computer abgestürzt ist, habe ich gerade eine CD
      when the computer crashed   is have I just   a   CD
      gebrannt.
      burned
      'When the computer crashed, I was just burning a CD.'

In (40) the perfect shows up in the subordinated sentence and describes the background (what I was doing when something else happened). Both events (the burning of the CD and the crash of the computer) happened simultaneously and so although the verb is used in the perfect form, the described situation is understood as ongoing. In (41) the subordinate clause as well as the main clause contain a verb used in the perfect form. The main clause describes the background of what I did and therefore receives an imperfective interpretation. The verb used in the subordinate clause gets a perfective interpretation; it does not describe an ongoing event but takes the crashing of the computer as a single whole which is located relative to the burning of the CD.

4.3.2 Grammatical aspect and verb gradation

The starting point of this section is Ropertz' (2001) observation that the interpretation of degree gradation interacts with grammatical aspect. The interaction between degree gradation and grammatical aspect is illustrated by the example in (42). In (a) the verb is intended to be used in a perfective context and it shows up in an explicit progressive construction in (b). It is in (a) that *sehr* specifies the total quantity of rain which has fallen during the event. The interpretation of the (b) example is different, in this case it is not the total quantity of rain that is specified, but the quantity of rain that is falling at a single stage of the event.[18]

(42) a. *Gestern   hat es sehr geregnet.*
          yesterday has it very rained
          'Yesterday it rained a lot.'
      b. *Es ist sehr am   Regnen.*
          it is very at the raining
          'It is raining hard.'

---

[18] See Landman (1992, 23) on the notion of 'event stages'.

4 Syntax of verb gradation

Both sentences in (42) require different paraphrases. An appropriate paraphrase for (42a) is (43a). The quantity of rain is explicitly specified by the adnominal quantity expression *viel* 'much'. (43b) is an appropriate paraphrase for (42b); the meaning of the sentence is at best paraphrased by the manner adverbial *stark* 'strongly, hard.'

(43)   a.   *Gestern ist viel Regen gefallen.*
               yesterday is much rain fallen
               'Yesterday, much rain has fallen.'
      b.   *Es ist stark am Regnen.*
               it is strongly at.the rain
               'It is raining hard.'

In the perfective as well as progressive case, *sehr* specifies the quantity of rain. But since the progressive describes an event as ongoing and not completed, *sehr* cannot specify the total amount of rain. Both readings in (42a) and (b) do not entail each other. That the total amount of rain is large does not mean that at each stage of the event a lot of rain was falling. Rather it is possible that at each stage it rained moderately but the total amount of rain in the overall event amounts to a large quantity. The same holds in the opposite direction: that it rains hard at a certain stage of the event does not entail that the overall amount of rain is large. Rather it could rain hard at a certain short interval but the total amount does not sum up to a large quantity. This would simply be the case if it is raining hard at one stage of the event but only very softly at all other stages. Even if both readings do not entail each other, they are very closely related.

In French, grammatical aspect has the same scope effect on degree gradation as in German. An example similar to the German one discussed above is shown in (44). In the case of a perfective verb (a) *beaucoup* specifies the total quantity of blood that is emitted during the event. If the verb is used in the progressive aspect (b) *beaucoup* indicates the quantity of blood emitted at a certain stage of the event.

(44)   a.   *Il a beaucoup saigné.*
               he has a lot bled
               'He bled a lot.'
      b.   *Il est en train de saigner beaucoup.*
               he is PROG to bleed a lot
               'He is bleeding a lot.'

Only the perfective example in (44a) allows for an extent interpretation of *beaucoup*. The sentence in (a) is ambiguous between the extent reading that he bleeds often and the degree reading specifying the quantity of emitted blood. The progressive sentence in (b) only licenses the degree reading but not the extent reading of *beaucoup*. Given the fact that the extent reading requires a multiplicity of events and the progressive describes a single, ongoing event, it is expected that the extent reading of *beaucoup* is excluded in (44b). This is independent of the position *beaucoup* occupies in the sentence. As mentioned above, if *beaucoup* is placed between the auxiliary and the participle, it is ambiguous between a degree and an extent reading. In (44b) *beaucoup* follows the infinitive, but in (45) it is positioned between the auxiliary and the infinitive.[19] Also in this case, the only possible interpretation is the degree reading of *beaucoup*, which demonstrates that aspect constrains the interpretation of verb gradation as an otherwise possible interpretation of *beaucoup* is excluded in the progressive aspect.

(45) Il est en train de beaucoup saigner.
      he is PROG   a lot   bleed
      'He is bleeding a lot.'

It is not the case that the progressive construction is in general incompatible with verbal extent gradation. This is shown, for example, by the German sentences in (46). In (46a), the degree expression *viel* 'much' is combined with a verb in a perfective context and with an explicit progressive construction in (46b). In both sentences, *viel* indicates a high frequency of raining events. This requires a shift from the single event reading of the progressive to an iterative interpretation for (b).

(46) a. *Letzte Woche hat es viel geregnet.*
          last   week has it much rained
          'Last week, it rained a lot.'
      b. *Letzte Woche war es viel am Regnen.*
          last   week was it much at.the raining
          'Last week, it was raining a lot.'

---

[19] *Être en train de* is one constituent and it is not possible for *beaucoup* to be placed within the construction.

4 Syntax of verb gradation

Comrie (1976, 37) discusses a similar case from English which is shown in (47a). He states that in the sentence the reading of the progressive aspect changes towards a habitual reading which happens due to the presence of *a lot*. Like *viel*, *a lot* requires, in its adverbial extent use, a multiplicity of events and therefore is incompatible with a single event interpretation of the progressive. As (b) shows, the interpretation of extent gradation is the same, irrespective of whether the verb is used in the perfect or the progressive form.

(47)   a.   *We're going to the opera a lot these days.*
             (Comrie, 1976, 37)
       b.   *We have gone to the opera a lot.*

In the examples in (46) and (47) it is the grammatical aspect that is affected in its interpretation by extent gradation. It was the other way round for the interaction between grammatical aspect and degree gradation. As the German and English data show, the progressive construction is, in general, compatible with extent gradation but for some reason the shift towards a habitual reading of the progressive aspect is blocked for the periphrastic progressive construction in French.

Russian, as a language with a fully grammaticalized aspectual system, shows the same interaction between extent gradation and grammatical aspect as has been observed for German, French and English. Since Russian has a general imperfective aspect, the sentence in (48a) allows for a progressive as well as a habitual interpretation. A further reading, which will be ignored in the following, is that the subject referent has the ability to play guitar. By adding *mnogo* 'much' to sentence (b) only the habitual but not the progressive interpretation of imperfective aspect is possible.

(48)   a.   *On igraet na gitar-e.*
             he plays PREP guitar-LOC
             'He is playing guitar.' or 'He usually plays guitar.'
       b.   *On mnogo igraet na gitar-e.*
             he much plays PREP guitar-LOC
             'He is playing guitar a lot.'

The data discussed in this section showed that the scope relationships summarized in (49) obtain. Extent degree expressions, or 'd/e-adverbials' used for extent gradation, have scope over grammatical aspect, whereas grammatical aspect has scope over degree intensifiers, resp. 'd/e-adverbials' used for degree gradation.

(49) 'extent' degree expression > grammatical aspect > 'degree' degree expression[20]

In 4.4, I present a syntactic analysis of verb gradation based on the asymmetrical scope relationships identified in this section.

4.4 Syntactic analysis of degree expressions

This section is split into two subsections: I will start with a syntactic analysis of verbal degree and extent gradation and in the second subsection extend this analysis to adnominal quantity expressions.

4.4.1 Syntactic analysis of verb gradation

In section 4.2, I predicted that extent degree expressions are core adverbials, since (i) event quantificational operators are analyzed as core operators and (ii) RRG assumes that the core is the minimal syntactic expression of an event. The previous section showed that expressions used for degree gradation and those used for extent gradation differ in scope with respect to grammatical aspect. Extent degree expressions have scope over grammatical aspect, whereas grammatical aspect has scope over expressions used for degree gradation. Aspect, as shown in section 4.2, is a nuclear operator.

Adverbs and adverbials are represented as modifiers in the semantic representation and take different components of these representations as their arguments (cf. Van Valin 2005, 49). In (50) the semantic representation for the verb *bluten* 'bleed' is shown.

(50) *bluten*: **do**'(x, **bleed**'(x))

In (51) the aspectual operator *PERF*, for perfective aspect, as well as degree expressions are added to the representation. Scope relations are indicated by the angled brackets in the semantic representations. Since aspect has scope over degree gradation, *sehr* in (b) has to be located closer to the pred-

---

[20] '>' is used to indicate scope relationships.

icate than the aspectual operator, whereas the aspectual operator is closer to the predicate than the extent degree expression in (a).

(51) a. *hat viel geblutet*: **viel'**($\langle_{\text{ASP}}$ PERF (**do'**(x, **bleed'**(x))))⟩
 b. *hat sehr geblutet*: ($\langle_{\text{ASP}}$ PERF (**sehr'** (**do'**(x, **bleed'**(x))))⟩

An operator can have scope over another expression if that expression is on the lower syntactic layer or a syntactic layer further below. As aspect is a nuclear operator and the nucleus forms the lowest syntactic layer, expressions used for degree gradation must be located on that layer too. That expressions used for extent gradation have scope over aspect does not entail that these expressions are located on a specific layer. This scope relationship is compatible with extent degree expressions located at the core or the nucleus layer. But arguments for the view that extent degree expressions are core adverbials have been presented above.

The syntactic representations I assume for extent and degree gradation are depicted in figures 5 and 6. The tree in figure 5 shows the syntactic structure of the sentence *Er hat sehr geblutet* 'He bled a lot.' The syntactic structure for *Er hat viel geblutet* 'He bled a lot' is shown in figure 6. Both trees only differ with respect to the syntactic layer on which the degree expression is located. Scope relationships are not directly visible in the trees but only in the logical representations in (51) above. A note on the representation of grammatical aspect is required. I assume that each sentence has an aspectual interpretation and therefore I assume an aspectual operator present in the syntactic structure of each sentence. But perfective aspect in German is not grammaticalized, so that the operator cannot be linked to a certain element in the constitutent structure. The reason to represent the operator is simply that it shows scope relationships with degree expressions.[21]

Figures 7 and 8 show the syntactic structures for the corresponding French example sentences. *Beaucoup* in its degree use is shown in figure 7, whereas the syntactic structure for an extent reading of *beaucoup* is shown in figure 8. There is one major difference to the representation of the German sentences, namely aspect is grammaticalized in the French past tense

---

[21] Van Valin (2008) introduces the notion of a 'referential phrase' (RP) instead of the more traditional term 'nominal phrase' (NP). Nothing in this thesis hinges on this distinction, so I will stick to the more familiar term NP.

4.4 Syntactic analysis of degree expressions

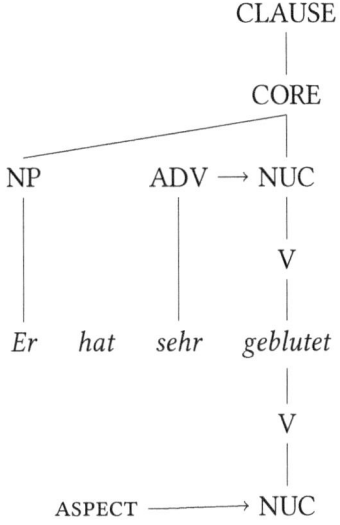

Figure 5: Syntactic representation of degree gradation in German.

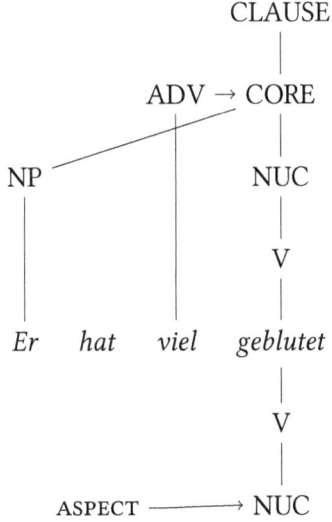

Figure 6: Syntactic representation of extent gradation in German.

and therefore the aspectual operator is linked to an element in the constituent structure. In this case, aspect is contributed by the combination of the auxiliary and the participle. In German, on the other hand, there is no

4 Syntax of verb gradation

overt exponent of the perfective aspect since the perfect construction does not always lead a perfective interpretation but only in certain contexts. Hence, there is no link between the aspectual operator and the auxiliary and main verb in the syntax tree.

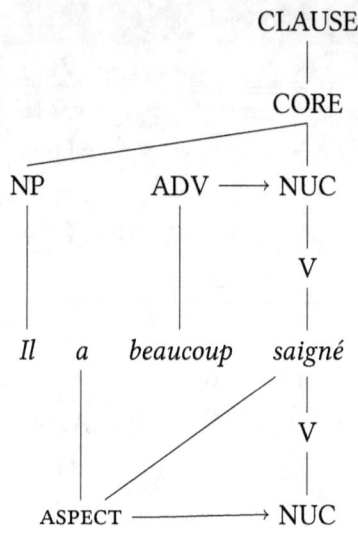

Figure 7: Syntactic representation of degree gradation in French.

Syntactically, degree and extent gradation are related to two different syntactic layers, as indicated by the differences in scope with respect to aspect. This syntactic difference is independent of the fact whether a language uses different adverbial expressions of extent and degree gradation, as German does, or if it uses the same as French. Semantically, this syntactic ambiguity between extent and degree gradation can be explained by relying on different sources that contribute the respective scales for gradation. In case of degree gradation, it is the verb that contributes the scale, whereas for extent gradation the scale is contributed by the event description.

The syntactic analysis presented above does not directly explain the relationship between the positioning of *beaucoup* and its interpretation as expression of degree/extent gradation. To present a full syntactic explanation of these data, a deeper syntactic analysis of French sentence structure has to be undertaken, which clearly goes beyond the limits of this thesis.

4.4 Syntactic analysis of degree expressions

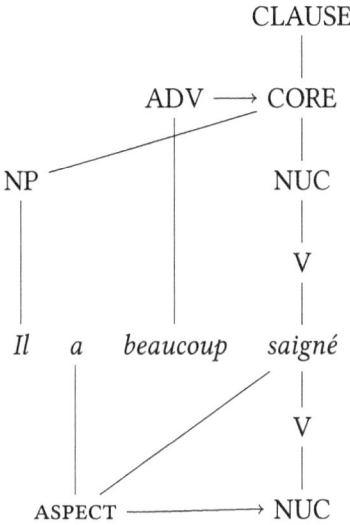

Figure 8: Syntactic representation of extent gradation in French.

4.4.2 Syntax of adnominal degree expressions

A central finding of the cross-categorical comparison of degree expressions was that those expressions used for extent gradation also function as adnominal quantity expressions. This holds irrespective of whether a language distinguishes between extent and degree adverbials or not. In addition, it turned out that expressions restricted to degree gradation cannot be used for indicating an adnominal quantity. This section aims in presenting a syntactic explanation for these findings.

I take the RRG approach to noun phrase structures as a starting point of the analysis. In analogy to the layered structure of the clause, Role & Reference Grammar assumes a layered structure for noun phrases. This structure consists of the layers: nominal nucleus, nominal core and NP. The nominal nucleus is the head noun, whereas the nominal core contains the nucleus and possible arguments of a complex derived noun. The NP-level corresponds to the clause level of the sentence. As in the case of clauses, RRG assumes a periphery for each layer of the noun phrase. There is also a distinction between operator and constituent structure for NPs. Van Valin (2005, 24) mentions the nominal operators listed in (52).

4 Syntax of verb gradation

(52) **Nucleus operators**: nominal aspect
Core operators: number, quantification, negation
NP operators: definiteness, deixis

As for adverbs, adjectives are not conceived of as operators and therefore are not located in the operator structure. Rather adjectives are located in the nominal periphery. Restrictive adjectives, like restrictive adjunct modifiers in general, are located in the nuclear$_N$ periphery, whereas non-restrictive ones are placed in the NP-level periphery. The core-level periphery contains "adjunct setting PPs and adverbials of complex event expressions" (Van Valin, 2005, 26). A further similarity between adjectives and adverbs is that adjectives underlie the same kind of ordering constraint as adverbs do: "they [adjectives] must occur closer to the nominal nucleus than core$_N$- and NP-level operators and modifiers" (Van Valin, 2005, 26).

The question as to whether adnominal quantity expressions are quantifiers or adjectives has a direct consequence for the syntactic analysis. If adnominal quantity expressions were quantifiers, they would be core operators. But if they are quantity adjectives rather than quantifiers, they would be located in the nominal periphery and not in the operator structure. In the following, I will show that adnominal quantity expressions are adjectives rather than quantifiers.

Starting point for the discussion is the linear order of elements within the German NP. As (53) reveals, a quantifier like *einige* 'some' is in NP initial position, followed by the definite article, which precedes an adnominal quantity expression as *viel* 'much'. Other adjectives, like *groß* 'tall,' follow the adnominal quantity expression and directly precede the head noun.

(53) *einige der vielen großen Kinder*
some of.the many tall children
'some of the many tall children'

As Löbner (1990, 42) states, adnominal quantity expressions and adjectives occupy different positions within the NP. The examples in (54) demonstrate that the adjective has to follow the quantity expression; the reverse order is not possible. Löbner (1990, 69, also Löbner to appear) states that adjectives have to be in the scope of quantity expressions if they add further sortal specifications to the noun they modify.

(54) a. *viele große Kinder*
         many tall   children
         'many tall children'
    b. **großе viele Kinder*
         tall many children

There is not only a fixed order for quantity expressions and adjectives but also for quantifiers as *einige* 'some' and vague quantity expressions like *viel* 'much.' This is shown by the data in (55a) and (b). The quantifier is in NP-initial position, but if no quantifier is present, other elements, such as quantity expressions, can occupy that position (55c).

(55) a. *einige der großen Kinder*
         many the tall   children
         'some of the tall children'
    b. **der einige großen Kinder*
         the some tall   children
    c. *viele der großen Kinder*
         many the tall   children
         'many of the tall children'

In NPs that contain a quantifier as well as a vague quantity expression, the quantifier has to precede the quantity expression. In (56), a definite article in genitive case, expressing partitivity, is placed between the two elements. Only definite articles in partitive function can follow quantifiers and quantity expressions. Non-partitively used definite articles can only precede vague quantity expressions in their cardinal interpretation (57) but not quantifiers (55b) or partitively interpreted quantity expressions.

(56) *einige der vielen Kinder*
     some of.the many children
     'some of the many children'

(57) *die vielen Kinder im Zimmer*
     the many children in.the room
     'the many children in the room'

4 Syntax of verb gradation

The order of elements is quite strict and can be summarized as in (58).[22] This indicates a difference between quantity expressions and quality adjectives on the one hand but also between quantity expressions and quantifiers on the other hand.

(58)   Definite Article/Quantifier >Quantity Expression >Quality Adjective >Noun

A further difference between quantity expressions and quantifiers and at the same time a similarity between quantity expressions and quality adjectives can be observed with regard to inflexion. German has different adjective declensions, a weak and a strong one (there is also a mixed declension which I will not mention further). Table 11 shows the two declensions for the plural.

plural	strong declension	weak declension
Nominative	groß-e Männer viel-e Männer	die groß-en Männer die viel-en Männer
Accusative	groß-e Männer viel-e Männer	die groß-en Männer die viel-en Männer
Dative	groß-en Männer-n viel-en Männer-n	den groß-en Männer-n den viel-en Männer-n
Genitive	groß-er Männer viel-er Männer	der groß-en Männer der viel-en Männer

Table 11: Adjective declension in German, plural forms for the weak and strong declension type.

The weak declension is used if the adjective is preceded by, for example, the definite article. If, on the other hand, the adjective is the first element in the NP or if it is preceded by the indefinite article, the strong declension is used (see Esau 1973 for a discussion of the different adjectival declen-

---

[22] '>' is used to indicate linear order, the element on the left precedes the element on the right. The term 'quality adjective' is used instead of plain 'adjective' to indicate that the respective adjectives do not specify the quantity of the head noun. (58) is not exhaustive and does not indicate the relative order of all functional elements within the NP (cf. Löbner to appear for a more detailed discussion of the NP).

sion paradigms in German). As shown in the table, *viel* shows the same pattern for weak and strong declension as the quality adjective *groß* 'tall.' Quantifiers such as *einige* 'some' only show the strong declension type; the reason is simply that quantifiers are always the first element within an NP. Hence, the difference between weak and strong declension is only used for elements that can be placed in the initial position of the NP and can also be preceded by quantifiers or the definite article.

Based on morphosyntactic concerns, it is reasonable to state that quantity expressions show more similarities to adjectives than to quantifiers (this view is also held by Löbner (1985, 1990), Eschenbach (1995) and Solt (2009) among others). Hence, I take them to be adjectives rather than operators. I assume that quantity expressions are realized at the core layer rather than the nuclear layer like quality adjectives. The reason is that quantity expressions are sensitive to nominal number. As the examples in (59) show, *viel* cannot apply to singular count nouns (a) but only to plural count nouns (b) and mass nouns (c). The mass noun *Bier* 'beer' is morphologically singular and triggers singular agreement, whereas the plural count noun triggers plural agreement. This is reflected by different declensions of *viel* in (b) and (c). The mass/count distinction is only relevant with regard to agreement marking, whereas nominal numbers provide a restriction on the applicability of quantity expressions. They require a plural or transnumeral noun, as in (b) and (c).

(59) a. #*viel Mann*
       much man
    b. *viele Männer*
       many men
       'many men'
    c. *viel Bier*
       much beer
       'much beer'

In RRG, number is considered to be a nominal core operator and since *viel* is sensitive to number marking, the core operator has to be within the scope of the quantity expression. This is further substantiated by the fact that singular nouns are coerced if they are modified by quantity expressions. Well known examples are those in (60), which are discussed under the label

141

4 Syntax of verb gradation

of 'universal grinder' (e.g., Bach 1986). In cases like (60), the count meaning of the nouns shifts towards a mass reading which denotes the 'stuff' of car in (a) or missionary in (b). The same holds for cases as (59a), which require coercion due to the singular form of the count noun.

(60)   a.   *Viel   Auto für wenig Geld.*
           much car for little money
           'Much car for little money.'
       b.   *Much missionary was eaten at the festival.*
            (Bach, 1986, 10)

In figure 9, the syntactic representation of the NP *die vielen großen Männer* 'the many tall men' is shown.

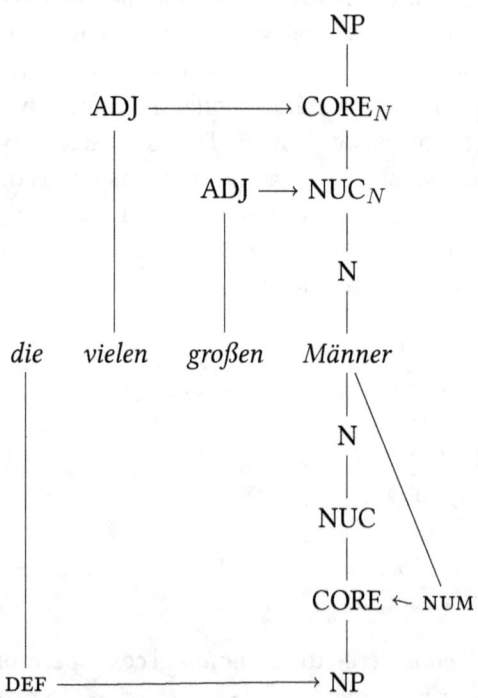

Figure 9: Syntactic representation of the complex NP *die vielen großen Männer* 'the many tall men'.

In this section, it has been shown that adnominal quantity is expressed at the nominal core layer. This provides an answer to the question why expressions which are used for verbal extent gradation are also used as adnominal quantity expressions. Extent degree gradation as well as nominal quantity is expressed at the core layer. German *viel* is not restricted with regard to lexical categories but only with respect to the syntactic configuration it can be used in. It has to be realized at the core layer, which leads to an indication of a nominal quantity in adnominal contexts, whereas it leads to extent gradation in adverbial contexts. Hence, the expression of quantity/extent is done in the same syntactic configuration.

4.5 Conclusion

In this section, I argued that the difference between extent and degree gradation is basically a syntactic one. In the case of degree gradation, the degree expression directly modifies the predicate in the nucleus and the scale to which it applies is contributed by the verb. Extent gradation is located at the core layer and the scale is contributed by the event description. The different sources of the scales match with the different syntactic configurations which are used for degree and extent gradation.

As shown in the last section, the syntactic analysis also extends to the nominal domain and can be used to explain the cross-categorical distribution of degree expressions. But it still remains open whether and how the analysis can be extended to the adjectival domain. Is there also a layered structure of the adjective? Van Valin (2008, 172) argues that modifier phrases, heading adjectives and adverbs, could have a layered structure too. One of the arguments he presents is that these modifiers can themselves be modified. Besides suggesting such an analysis, Van Valin does not further develop the proposal, which also would surely go beyond the limits of this thesis. More work within RRG on the syntactic structure of adjectival phrases would be required to decide whether the analysis presented above also allows explaining why in languages like German adjectives in the positive take *sehr* but comparatives take *viel* as intensifier.

In the next chapter, I turn to the semantics of verb gradation. The results presented in this chapter will be relevant for discussing the (syntax-driven) compositional semantics of verb gradation.

5 Gradable predicates and intensifiers

The aim of the current chapter is twofold: on the one hand it contains a discussion of the semantics of gradable predicates and on the other hand, it presents an analysis of degree expressions. In the process, it provides the background for the following chapters. The starting point for the discussion of gradable predicates is gradable adjectives. In section 5.1, I will start with a discussion of the semantics of gradable adjectives, focusing on the analyses of Kennedy (1999b, 2007) and Kennedy & McNally (2005a) on the one hand, and Löbner (1990) on the other.

In 5.2, I will turn to the analysis of degree expressions, starting with a discussion of their semantic type and a subclassification of different types of degree expressions. The focus of 5.3 is the semantics of intensifiers like English *very* and German *sehr*. Finally, I turn in 5.4 to verbs and discuss how verbs fit into the analysis of gradable predicates. On the one hand, similarities and differences with regard to gradable adjectives are discussed, on the other hand specific questions with respect to the encoding of scales in verbs are formulated.

5.1 Gradable adjectives

Different analyses of gradable adjectives have been proposed in the literature (e.g. Cresswell 1976; Klein 1980, 1982; Bierwisch 1989; Löbner 1990; Kennedy 1999b,a; Kennedy & McNally 2005a).[1] In 5.1.1, I will start with a discussion of Kennedy's and Kennedy & McNally's approach of the semantics of gradable adjectives. Then I will turn in 5.1.2 to Löbner's (1990) approach, which makes use of a different theoretical framework.

---

[1] See Kennedy (1999b) as well as Morzycki (2013, chap. 3) for a summary of previous accounts on the semantics of gradable adjectives and see Carstensen (2013) for a comparison of Bierwisch's and Kennedy's approach.

5 Gradable predicates and intensifiers

5.1.1 Kennedy & McNally (2005a)

In their subsequent work, Kennedy (1999b,a, 2007) and Kennedy & McNally (2005a,b) present a degree-based analysis of gradable adjectives.[2] Degrees figure prominently in this analysis as an ontological type 'd' for degrees is assumed. Degrees, as abstract representations of measurement, are conceived of the logical type 'd.' The nature and status of degrees has been discussed by authors like Cresswell (1976) and von Stechow (2008), who analyze degrees as equivalence classes of objects which are indistinguishable with regard to a certain property.[3] The definition of equivalence classes is based on the transitive and antisymmetric 'more than' relation ('>'). '$>_{beau}$', for example, stands for the empirical relation 'more beautiful/prettier than.' Basically, an equivalence relation ('$=_{beau}$') expresses that two individuals x and y are of equal beauty. This holds in the case that for any y, if x is more beautiful than z, y is also more beautiful than z. And also the reverse holds: if z is more beautiful than x, z is also more beautiful than y. This means that x and y are indistinguishable with respect to beauty. A formal definition is presented in (1); $F(>=_{beau})$ is the field of the relation 'more beautiful/prettier than.'

(1) $x =_{beau} y$ "x is exactly as beautiful as y"
 $(\forall x, y \in F(>_{beau}))$ $[x =_{beau} y]$ iff $(\forall z \in F(>_{beau}))$ $[x >_{beau} z$ iff $y >_{beau} z]$ & $[z >_{beau} x$ iff $z >_{beau} y]$
 (von Stechow, 2008, 3)

Degrees of beauty can be defined as all the equivalence classes generated by $=_{beau}$, as shown in (2). Applied to a concrete example such as *Angela is beautiful* we get the equivalence class $[Angela]_{beau}$ as the degree of her beauty, which, following von Stechow (2008, 3), is tantamount to 'Angela is beautiful to the degree she is.' One the one hand, this is a trivial statement,

---

[2] Bochnak (2015) and Beltrama & Bochnak (2015) discuss languages which either do not have degree constructions, such as Washo, or make use of modifiers which apparently look like intensifiers but are also used in non-degree contexts. The authors propose an analysis, for these constructions/languages, which does not rely on degrees. Such languages are not in the scope of this thesis.

[3] See Morzycki (2013, 115) for some problems with this account of 'degrees' and also for other analyses of this notion. See, for example, Anderson & Morzycki (2015) for an explication of degrees as kinds (of states).

one the other hand it is exactly this triviality which shows, as von Stechow (2008, 3) says, that introducing degrees is innocuous.

(2) Degrees of beauty:
$(\forall x \in F(>_{beau})) [x]_{beau} = \{y | y =_{beau} x\}$
$Deg_{beau} = \{[x]_{beau} | x \in F(>_{beau})\}$
(von Stechow, 2008, 3)

By taking degrees to be equivalence classes, hence as sets of objects, they do not necessarily represent a new ontological type. Since they denote sets of objects, we can assign them the type of set denoting expressions $\langle e, t \rangle$. Therefore, type 'd' could be conceived as an abbreviation for equivalence classes. Kennedy (2001, 34n1) follows the analysis of degrees as equivalence classes but also seems to assume that 'd' is an irreducible ontological type. I follow von Stechow's explication of the notion of 'degrees' but remain uncommitted as to whether degrees should be conceived of as an irreducible ontological type or not.

In Kennedy's and Kennedy & McNally's approach, gradable adjectives are analyzed as measure functions. Measure functions map individuals onto scales and return the degree of the individuals on the scale. Such measure functions are of type $\langle e, d \rangle$. The adjective *warm* can be analyzed as the measure function WARM(x), which is a function from the domain of individuals that have temperature to degrees of temperature. Measure functions do not express properties of individuals but need to be converted into such expressions by degree morphology. "Degree morphemes serve two functions: they introduce an individual argument for the measure function denoted by the adjective and they impose some requirement on the degree derived by applying the adjective to its argument, typically by relating it to another degree" (Kennedy, 2007, 5). One of the degree morphemes assumed by Kennedy and Kennedy & McNally is the positive morpheme *pos* which turns a measure function into the positive form of an adjective. There is a type-theoretic and thereby theory-internal reason to postulate the morphological null *pos* morpheme, as it is required to convert measure functions into properties of individuals. By applying *pos* to a measure function of type $\langle e, d \rangle$ we get an expression of the type $\langle \langle e, d \rangle, t \rangle$. Before we turn to the semantics of pos, I would like to discuss the linguistic evidence for the assumption of *pos*.

5 Gradable predicates and intensifiers

Several authors, for example Cresswell (1976); von Stechow (1984); Kennedy (1999b,a) as well as Kennedy & McNally (2005a,b), assume a morphological null *pos* morpheme. Sinitic languages provide evidence for such a morpheme as they require an explicit marking of the positive form of adjectives. In these languages a degree expression is required for a positive reading of adjectives as bare uses of (some) adjectives results in a comparative reading. This is illustrated for Mandarin Chinese, Cantonese and Fuyang Wu in (3) to (5). The Mandarin Chinese example in (3a) only yields a comparative reading; if no comparandum is realized, it is contextually supplied. The addition of the degree expression *hěn* 'very' yields a positive reading (cf. the discussion in chapter 2). Matthews & Yip (1994) mention that in Cantonese a predicatively used adjective also requires the addition of a degree expression to yield a positive interpretation (4). The same is shown by the data from Fuyang Wu (5), in which case the degree expression *man* 'very' is required for a positive reading. Unlike Mandarin Chinese, Fuyang Wu requires the addition of a different degree expression for a comparative reading if no comparandum is realized (5b).

(3) Mandarin Chinese (Sinitic < Sino-Tibetian; Sybesma 1999, 27)
    a. *Zhāngsān gāo.*
       Zhangsan tall
       'Zhangsan is taller (than someone else known from context).'
    b. *Zhāngsān hěn gāo.*
       Zhangsan very tall
       'Zhangsan is tall.'

(4) Cantonese (Sinitic < Sino-Tibetian; Matthews & Yip 1994, 158)
    Léih go jái hóu gōu.
    you CLA son very tall
    'Your son is tall.'

(5) Fuyang Wu (Sinitic < Sino-Tibetian; Xuping Li, p.c.)
    a. *kɤ ɕiɔpi xɔkɛn ɕin*
       CLA girl good-looking a bit
       'The girl is better looking.'
    b. *kɤ ɕiɔpi man xɔkɛn*
       CLA girl very good-looking
       'The girl is good-looking.'

5.1 Gradable adjectives

The assumption of a positive morpheme is not crucial for Kennedy's proposal and he mainly proposes that the positive morpheme keep the compositional analysis of the positive form parallel to other forms that make use of overt degree morphology (like the comparative or superlative constructions). Kennedy (2007, 7) states that one can either assume a zero positive morpheme or one can take the absence of overt positive morphology seriously and simply assume a type-shifting rule that turns a measure function into a property of individuals (see Neeleman et al. 2004 for such a solution). I will discuss the question whether we need to assume a verbal *pos* morpheme in section 5.4 and turn now to the semantics of *pos*.

The semantics of *pos* looks like in (6). *g* is a variable for gradable adjectives and *s* is "a context-sensitive function from measure functions to degrees that returns a standard of comparison based both on properties of the adjective *g* (such as its domain) and on features of the context of utterance" (Kennedy, 2007, 16).[4] Kennedy further states that *s* chooses a standard of comparison which ensures that the positive form is true in the context of utterance.[5] The standard is the cutoff point which determines of which degrees the positive form is true and of which it is not. This cutoff point is determined by the degree returned by *s*, and therefore *s* specifies the minimal degree for an individual such that the predication is true.

(6) $\llbracket pos \rrbracket = \lambda g \lambda x.(g(x) \geq s(g))$
(Kennedy, 2007, 17)

Applying *pos* to the gradable adjective tall yields the denotation in (7). An individual *x* is tall if its degree on the scale associated with *tall* exceeds the contextual standard for *tall*.

(7) $\llbracket [pos[tall]] \rrbracket = \lambda x.tall(x) \geq s(tall)$

For gradable absolute adjectives such as *full*, for example, the standard is not context-dependent. Instead, these adjectives lexically indicate an

---

[4] One has to keep in mind that different types of standards or norms, as Leisi (1971) calls it, need to be distinguished. As I argued in chapter 2.2, all the types of norms identified by Leisi are context-dependent and can probably be captured by Kennedy's analysis.
[5] See Kennedy (2007, 16ff.) for a discussion of domain restrictions with respect to standards of comparison.

5 Gradable predicates and intensifiers

appropriate comparison degree. For absolute adjectives that are closed at the lower end like *straight*, d is '> min(S_A)', which means that the degree has to exceed the minimal degree on the adjective's scale. For absolute adjectives that are closed at the upper end, d is equated with the maximal degree on the associated scale. The truth conditions for adjectival phrases headed by absolute adjectives are shown in (8). The representations are based on Kennedy & McNally (2005a, 358) but adapted to the representational format of Kennedy (2007). S_g stands for the scale associated with the adjective and **min** and **max** for functions that return the minimal and maximal degree of the scale.

(8)   a. $[\![AP_{min}]\!] = \lambda x.g(x) > \min(S_g)$
        b. $[\![AP_{max}]\!] = \lambda x.g(x) = \max(S_g)$

Kennedy (2007) assumes that gradable adjectives directly denote measure functions. The degree argument, meaning the standard of comparison, and the relational component (whether the degree of x has to exceed the standard or not) are introduced by degree morphology. Kennedy & McNally (2005a) take a different stance and follow Cresswell (1976); von Stechow (1984) and Bierwisch (1989) among others in assuming that gradable adjectives express relations between individuals and degrees. They propose the denotation in (9) for an adjective like *expensive*. The degree returned by the measure function EXPENSIVE is compared to a comparison degree d. In this case, the function of degree expressions is to saturate the degree argument and thereby to specify the standard of comparison.

(9) $[\![\text{expensive}]\!] = \lambda d \lambda x.\textbf{expensive}(x) = d$
       (Kennedy & McNally, 2005a, 349)

A simplified version of their (Kennedy & McNally, 2005a, 350) representation of *pos* is shown in (10). *pos* binds the degree argument and thereby specifies the comparison degree. The **standard** relation holds "of a degree d just in case it meets a standard of comparison for an adjective G with respect to a comparison class determined by C, a variable over properties of individuals whose value is determined contextually" (Kennedy & McNally, 2005a, 35). As Bochnak (2013a, 51) writes: "the norm-related interpretation of the bare form [i.e., positive form] is not lexicalized in the gradable adjectives themselves, but rather is contributed by *pos*."

(10) $[\![\text{pos}]\!] = \lambda G \lambda x.\exists d[d > \textbf{standard}_C(G) \wedge G(d)(x)]$

5.1 Gradable adjectives

Kennedy & McNally (2005a) propose a general template for degree expressions and assume that all degree expressions convert measure functions into properties of individuals by introducing a standard of comparison. Degree expressions, as they state, impose restrictions on the comparison degree. The general degree expressions template can be formulated (based on the proposal in Kennedy & McNally 2005a, 367) like in (11). The idea is that a degree expression takes a gradable adjective G as its argument and provides a restriction R on the comparison degree.

(11) $[\![DEG(P)]\!] = \lambda G \lambda x. \exists d [R(d) \wedge G(d)(x)]$
(Kennedy & McNally, 2005a, 367)

Pos is an instantiation of the general template in (11) and imposes a restriction on d in terms of the **standard** relation. The semantic representations of two other degree expressions are shown in (12). (12a) shows the representation of the measure phrase *two meters* and (b) shows it for the degree expression *completely*. The measure phrase *two meters* restricts the degree to a value which is equal or higher than two meters, whereas *completely* equates it with the maximal degree on the scale.

(12) a. $[\![\text{two meters}]\!] = \lambda G \lambda x. \exists d [d \geq \textbf{two meters} \wedge G(d)(x)]$
b. $[\![\text{completely}]\!] = \lambda G \lambda x. \exists d [d = \textbf{max}(S_G) \wedge G(d)(x)]$
(Kennedy & McNally, 2005a, 368f.)

In accordance with the view that *pos* is an instatiation of the general degree template in (11) and therefore behaves like other degree expressions, one can say that the morphologicaly null *pos* morpheme completes "a paradigm whose other members do have overt counterparts" (Bochnak, 2013a, 59) and therefore can be seen as "an appropriate technical solution for a unified analysis of the paradigm" (Bochnak, 2013a, 60). But I will show later that not all degree expressions are of the same type and therefore the general template is not adequate for capturing the compositional semantics of the various degree expressions.

5.1.2 Löbner (1990)

In his 1990 monograph, Löbner describes the conceptual format of 'phase quantification.' In his view, phase quantification is a general mechanism

5 Gradable predicates and intensifiers

which can be applied to a semantic analysis of genuine quantifiers, gradable adjectives, aspectual particles like German *schon* 'already' and *noch* 'still'[6] but also grammatical operators such as aspect or modality (cf. the overview in Löbner 1990, 2011b). As Löbner (2011b) states, the notion of 'phase quantification' is somewhat misleading and in fact it is essentially a unifying scalar approach to the aforementioned phenomena.

Löbner (2011b, 504) describes phase quantification as follows: "Phase quantification is about some first-order predication p; the truth value of p depends on the location of its argument on some scale; for example p may be true of t only if t is located beyond some critical point on the scale." Basically, phase quantification is about the location of an argument on a scale and concerns the question how the argument is located with regard to the critical point on that scale. This critical point separates a scale into a phase for which the predication is true and one for which it is false. Four types of phase quantifiers can be distinguished with regard to the order of the phases and the location of the argument.

Figure 10 is a graphical illustration of the four types of phase quantifiers. *P* marks the respective phase on the scale for which the predication holds true. *t* is the argument assigned to one of the phases. In (a) the predication is true for higher cases on the scale, but false for lower ones. The argument *t* is assigned to the phase for which *P* is true. (b) presents the reversed order of phases; the predication is true for lower cases on the scale, and *t* is assigned to the phase for which the predication is true. Both types in (c) and (d) equal (a) and (b) respectively in the order of the two phases, but *t* is assigned to different phase respectively. Natural language examples taken from the domain of gradable adjectives that illustrate the four types in figure 10 are *tall* for (a), its antonym *short* for (b), *not tall* for (c) and finally *not short* for (d). For *tall* the predication is true for degrees higher on the scale than the critical point. Phase quantification leads to a contrast between those higher degrees, which are marked for size, and lower degrees that count as 'not-tall.' *Small* on the other hand provides a contrast between those degrees that count as 'small' in a certain context of use and higher degrees on the scale which do not count as 'small' anymore. The four types

---

[6] These particles are also often called 'Gradpartikel' (degree particles) in German, which seems to be rather misleading terminology since they are not used as gradation devices.

5.1 Gradable adjectives

of phase quantification, illustrated in figure 10, are not all lexicalized. With respect to adjectives only the types illustrated in (a) and (b) are lexicalized (*tall* vs. *short*), whereas those in (c) and (d) are expressed by negation (cf. Löbner 1985, 1990 for a discussion of the differences in lexicalization of the four types of phase quantifiers).

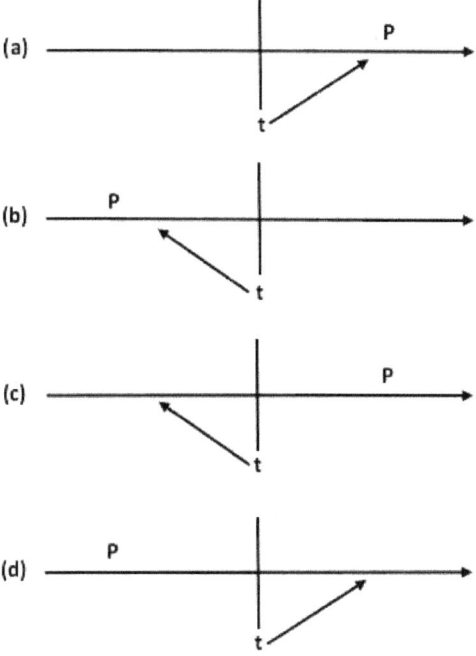

Figure 10: Graphical representations of the four different types of phase quantifiers.

Löbner (1990, 2011b) bases his explication of phase quantification on a definition of 'admissible α-intervals' (13). An admissible α-interval is a section of a scale which is divided into at most one positive and one negative phase. A positive phase is one for which the predication is true, a negative one for which it is false. α represents the truth value of p for the first section on the phase.

5 Gradable predicates and intensifiers

(13) Let p be a predicate expression with domain D, < a partial ordering in D, t ∈ D and $\alpha = 0$ or 1. The set of admissible α-intervals in terms of <, p and t – AI(α, <, p, t) – is the set of all subsets of D which
(i) are linearly ordered by <
(ii) contain t and some t' < t
(iii) start with a phase of [p] = α
(iv) contain at most one transition from not-p to p below t.
(Löbner, 2011b, 503)

The partial ordering in D is, in the case of gradable adjectives, lexically specified by the predicate. Each gradable adjective specifies a scale on which the elements in D can be ordered. Based on this definition, a general definition of phase quantification is given in (14).

(14) Phase quantification:
Given the conditions of definition (13), PQ(α, <, p, t) $\equiv_{df}$ ∃∀I(I ∈ AI(α, <, p, t) : p(t)).
(Löbner, 2011b, 503)

The definition in (14) makes use of the homogenous quantifier ∃∀, which is defined in (15). It is a quantifier that takes two arguments and essentially expresses that "the b's are p" as Löbner (2011b, 491)) states.

(15) ∃∀x(b : p) $=_{df}$ ∃x(b ∧ p) iff [∃x(b ∧ p) = ∀x(b → p)], otherwise undefined.
(Löbner, 2011b, 491, Löbner, 1990, 28)

For the definition of phase quantification this warrants that each phase leads to a homogeneous predication regarding the crucial property p. Gradable adjectives like *small* and *tall* provide an ordering of their (shared) domain with respect to the size of the elements in the domain. In the case of *tall*, α is 0. Hence, it starts with a phase for which the predication p does not hold and then there is a transition to a phase for which it holds. The argument of the predication is assigned to the second phase. For *small* it is reversed, its partitioning of the scale starts with a phase for which the predication holds and then there is a transition to a phase for which the predication is false. This leads to a contrast between lower degrees, for which *small* is true, and higher degrees for which it is not. The argument of the predication is assigned to the first phase. (16) shows the semantic representation for gradable adjectives as phase quantifiers. t is bound by a lambda operator and represents the syntactic argument of the adjective. The respective predication is expressed by $\lambda t'(gt' = x)$, which specifies that the degree of t' is either 1 or 0, meaning that it is either marked with regard to the expressed property or not.

(16) $\lambda t\ PQ1(<, t, \lambda t'(gt' = x))$
    (based on Löbner, 1990, 161)

Degree expressions can be conceived as phase quantifiers similarly to gradable adjectives. Löbner (1990, 162, 166) presents a formal analysis of, for example, the comparative construction but also of degree expressions like German *viel* 'much, many' and *wenig* 'little'. These degree expressions are analyzed as gradable adjectives, and with respect to *viel* Löbner assumes that it makes a predication about the quantity of its argument. But neither Löbner nor Ropertz (2001) provide an analysis of *sehr* in terms of phase quantification but suggest that such an analysis should be straightforwardly possible (see Fleischhauer (2013) for a first attempt of analyzing *sehr* as a phase quantifier). The main advantage of the phase quantificational approach is that it provides a general format for the semantic analysis of apparently unrelated linguistic expressions such as genuine quantifiers, gradable adjectives and aspect. So far the structural properties of scales – the presence vs. absence of minimal/maximal scale values – have not been integrated into the phase quantificational approach.[7]

As Löbner's approach is less widely used than the one from Kennedy and Kennedy & McNally, I opt for the latter account as it is currently one of the most widely used approaches to degree semantics.

5.2 Semantic type of degree expressions

In this section, the semantic type of degree gradation is discussed. In 5.2.1, I will discuss the question whether gradation has to be conceived of as quantification or rather as modification. A classification of different types of degree expressions is presented in 5.2.2.

---

[7]   See Naumann (2014) for an integration of phase quantification within the frame approach of Löbner (2012a, 2014).

5 *Gradable predicates and intensifiers*

5.2.1 Quantification vs. modification

In chapter 2, the question emerged whether there is a deeper connection between gradation and quantification. The question has been raised by examples like those in (17). As demonstrated, German *viel* can be used for adverbial extent gradation as well as to indicate a nominal quantity. Examples such as (17b) are conceived by many authors as falling under the notion of 'quantification.'

(17)   a.   *Er schläft viel.*
                he sleeps much
                'He sleeps a lot.'
       b.   *viele Bücher*
                much books
                'many books'

Bosque & Masullo (1998) extend the notion of 'quantification' to all instances of normally adnominally used quantity expressions like *mucho* 'a lot' or *un poco* 'a bit' in Spanish. In their view, examples like (18), taken from Spanish, are considered to be instances of 'inherent quantification.'

(18)   *Me   gusta un poco.*
           CL.to.me like   a bit
           'I like it a little bit.'
           (Gallego & Irurtzun, 2010, 5)

In chapter 4, I concentrated on the syntactic status of adnominal quantity expressions and argued for treating them as adjectives rather than quantifiers. The aim of the current section is to discuss the semantic type of degree expressions, focusing on their adverbial uses. Two different questions arise regarding the semantic type of (adverbial) degree expressions: (i) of which type can (adverbial) degree expressions be? and (ii) are all (adverbial) degree expressions of the same semantic type?

de Swart (1993) distinguishes between two basic types of adverbs; they are either quantifiers or modifiers. She is working in the format of Generalized Quantifier Theory (GQT, Barwise & Cooper 1981) which analyses determiners like *much* or *many* as two-place expressions. Each such determiner takes two set denoting expressions (which are of type

⟨e, t⟩) as its arguments and makes a predication about the intersection of both sets. Hence, determiners are of the semantic type ⟨⟨e, t⟩⟨⟨e, t⟩, t⟩⟩ and are generalized quantifiers.

Following de Swart (1993, 5), the function of quantificational adverbsis to indicate a quantity of events. This is opposed to the semantic function of adverbial modifiers, which do not indicate a quantity of events but add a "further specification to the identity of the event itself" (de Swart, 1993, 5). Modifiers take an unsaturated expression and form another unsaturated expression of the same type (McNally, to appear, 2).[8] Hence, they are of the semantic type ⟨X, X⟩, whereby X can be any simple or complex type.[9] De Swart states that (adverbial) modifiers map sets onto subsets. This is illustrated by example (19) where an entailment relationship between the sentences *John runs fast* and *John runs* holds. If John is running fast, he necessarily is running. The situations in which he is running fast form a subset of those situations in which he is running.

(19)   *John runs fast.* ⇒ *John runs.*

Following de Swart, quantificational adverbs differ from manner adverbs like *fast*. She discusses the sentences in (20) and says that if the sentence in (a) is true, the one in (b) is true too but "the relation [between the sentences] is not an implicational one [...]. We cannot claim that Anne's going to the movies [often] is a subset of Anne's going to the movies." (de Swart, 1993, 5).

(20)   a.   *Anne est souvent alleé au cinema.*
              Anne is often gone to.the cinema
              'Anne has often been to the movies.'
        b.   *Anne est alleé au cinema.*
              Anne is gone to.the cinema
              'Anne has been to the movies.'
              (de Swart, 1993, 5)

---

[8] Also see the discussion of the notion of 'modifier' in Morzycki (2013), who advocates the view that modification is not a unitary concept (p. 262).
[9] As Wunderlich (1997) and McNally (to appear), among others, show, not all modifiers are of the semantic type ⟨X, X⟩.

5 Gradable predicates and intensifiers

In (21a) and (b), *souvent* 'often' and *beaucoup* indicate the frequency of Jean's going to the movies. Both sentences are truth conditionally equivalent and therefore *beaucoup* in its use as extent intensifier could be conceived of as an adverb of quantification. Following de Swart's argumentation, the situation where Jean goes to the movies a lot should also not form a subset of those situations where Jean goes to the movies. *Beaucoup* used as an expression for degree gradation differs from its extent use. In (22), we have the same entailment relationship between the sentences as observed for the manner adverb in (19).

(21) a. Jean va   souvent au   cinema.
          Jean goes often   to.the movies
          'Jean often goes to the movies.'
      b. Jean va   beaucoup au   cinema.
          Jean goes a lot   to.the cinema
          'Jean goes to the movies a lot.'

(22) Il aime beaucoup cette langue. ⇒ Il aime cette langue.
      he loves a lot   this language   he loves this language
      'He loves this language very much. ⇒ He loves this language.'

It is doubtful whether de Swart's characterization of the relationship between the sentences in (21), and therefore those in (22) too, is correct. It is the case that the situations where (21a) is true form a subset of those situations where (21b) is true. Hence, (21a) entails (21b); if one has gone to the movies often, it must be the case that one has gone to the movies. What de Swart wants to say is that *beaucoup* in its extent use is not a modifier of the event, whereas *beaucoup* in its degree use really functions as a modifier analogous to manner adverbs. De Swart also claims that extent *beaucoup*, like the frequency adverb *souvent*, is an adverbial quantifier. If this is true, *beaucoup* would be ambiguous between functioning as adverbial quantifier and degree modifier. Abeillé et al. (2004), based on the work of de Swart (1993) and Doetjes (1997), argue against such an ambiguity. Adverbs of quantification show scope ambiguities and license two different readings: a 'relational' and a 'non-relational' one de Swart (1993). De Swart argues that only the relational reading requires a quantificational analysis similar to the distinction between 'cardinal' and 'proportional' readings of adnominal quantity expressions. In (23), (i) is the relational reading of *souvent*, whereas (ii) indicates the non-relational reading. In the relational reading of the example, the *quand* clause provides the restriction for the adverbial quantifier, whereas the subordinated sentence functions as the domain of quantification in the non-relational use.

(23) Quand elle est à Paris, Pauline va souvent au Louvre.
      when she is in Paris Pauline goes often to.the Louvre
      (i) 'Many of the times she is in Paris, Pauline goes to the Louvre.'
      (ii) 'Whenever she is in Paris, Pauline often goes to the Louvre.'
      (Abeillé et al., 2004, 191)

The cardinal reading of (24) is that a high number of third-year students signed up, whereas the proportional reading is that a high number of all the third-year students signed up. The proportional reading allows for a partitive paraphrase like *many of the third-year students signed up for class*, whereas the cardinality reading does not (cf. Löbner 1987b, 192).

(24) *Many third-year students signed up for class.*

Partee (1988), too, argues that adnominal quantity expressions like *many* are ambiguous between a quantificational use, which leads to the proportional reading, and an adjectival use that licenses the cardinal reading.[10] In the latter use, quantity expressions are similar to cardinal numbers, with the only difference being that the first-mentioned are vague and context-dependent, the latter are not. Partee argues for a type ambiguity of adnominal quantity expressions, only the proportional use giving rise to a quantificational analysis. Hoeksema (1983); Löbner (1987a,b, 1990) and Solt (2009, 2011) argue against an ambiguity analysis and assume that quantity expressions never require a quantificational analysis.[11] What is relevant at this stage is that de Swart's argumentation regarding adverbs of quantification resembles Partee's argumentation regarding the type ambiguity of adnominal quantity expressions: only proportional/relational readings require a quantificational analysis, whereas cardinal/non-relational ones do not.

---

[10] Partee does not explicitly state whether it is a lexical or contextual ambiguity but only writes that "the ambiguity has both syntactic and semantic repercussions" (Partee, 1988, 384f.).

[11] See the mentioned literature for the details of the argumentation and an explanation of how the difference between the proportional and the cardinal reading results.

5 Gradable predicates and intensifiers

Abeillé et al. (2004) show that extent *beaucoup* only allows for a non-relational interpretation (25).[12] The authors take this contrast between *souvent* and *beaucoup* as an argument against a quantificational analysis of the latter.

(25)   *Quand il est à Paris, Paul va beaucoup au Louvre.*
        when he is in Paris Paul goes a lot to.the Louvre
        'Whenever he is in Paris, Paul goes to the Louvre a lot.'
        (Abeillé et al., 2004, 191)

I follow Abeillé et al. (2004) in rejecting a GQT analysis of extent degree expressions but this does not necessarily mean that such degree expressions are modifiers. As a further option, such expressions could function as argument saturating expressions. Such an analysis is proposed by Kennedy & McNally (2005a). In their analysis, degree expressions are of the type $\langle\langle d, \langle e, t\rangle\rangle, \langle e, t\rangle\rangle$ and saturate the degree argument of a gradable expression. In a different work, Kennedy & McNally (2005b) argue that not all degree expressions are of the same semantic type, some are argument saturating, whereas others are plain modifiers. The classification of degree expressions regarding their semantic type is discussed in some detail in the next section.

5.2.2 Classification of degree expressions

The starting point for Kennedy & McNally's (2005b) subclassification of degree expressions are examples like those in (26). In these sentences, multiple degree expressions are used. (26a), for example, uses the measure phrase *10 feet* for a further modification of the comparative construction and it specifies the degree to which the new tower exceeds the height of the Empire State Building.

(26)   a.   *a new tower 10 feet taller than the Empire State Building*
       b.   *an old department store a lot less taller than the city hall building*
       c.   *an engineer very much more afraid of heights than the architect*
           (Kennedy & McNally, 2005b, 178)

---

[12]   Fortuin (2008, 239) shows that the same contrast observed between *souvent* and *beaucoup* obtains between Russian *často* 'often' and *mnogo* 'much'.

The examples in (27) further show that degree expressions, in this case we have a combination of *quite* and *very* in (a) and of *rather* and *very* in (b), can be stacked.

(27) a. *He specializes in swimwear and is quite very popular for it.*
      b. *Lola rennt, or Run Lola Run in English, is the first German film I've ever seen. It's rather very inventive.*
          (Kennedy & McNally, 2005b, 180)

If degree expressions are of the semantic type $\langle\langle d, \langle e, t\rangle\rangle, \langle e, t\rangle\rangle$, as Kennedy & McNally (2005a) state, then the stacking of degree expressions cannot be easily explained. Going back to (26a), the comparative morpheme takes a gradable adjective (type $\langle d, \langle e, t\rangle\rangle$,) as its argument and returns an expression of type $\langle e, t\rangle$. But this would be of the wrong input type for the measure phrase *10 feet*, which also requires an argument of type $\langle d, \langle e, t\rangle\rangle$. The same is true for the other examples in (26) and (27).

At the same time, restrictions regarding the order of stacked degree expressions can be found. As the examples in (28) show, the order (*very*) *much* > *more* is possible, whereas *more* > (*very*) *much* is not.

(28) a. *This new building will give the university (very) much more effective support.*
      b. **This new building will give the university more (very) much effective support.*
          (Kennedy & McNally, 2005b, 181)

Kennedy & McNally claim that these data can best be explained by assuming that different classes of degree expressions exist, which are of different semantic types. The different classes of degree expressions are summarized in figure 11.

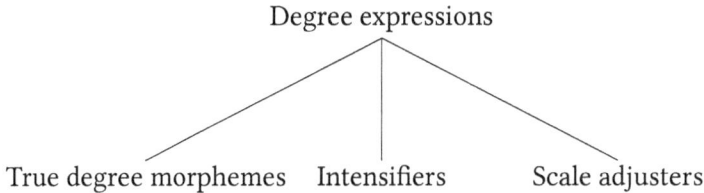

Figure 11: Types of degree expressions Kennedy & McNally (2005b).

5 Gradable predicates and intensifiers

The class of 'true degree morphemes' includes measure phrases as well as the positive morpheme. These expressions are of the type $\langle\langle d, \langle e, t\rangle\rangle, \langle e, t\rangle\rangle$ and fit Kennedy & McNally's (2005a) analysis of degree expressions. They saturate the degree argument and thereby change the semantic type of its argument. The second class are 'intensifiers' like *very*. Kennedy & McNally take intensifiers to be predicate modifiers, which apply to expressions that have an already saturated degree argument. The semantic function of intensifiers is to manipulate the standard introduced by the positive morpheme (Kennedy & McNally, 2005b, 183). As mentioned in the last section, the comparison class for *very* consists of those individuals for which the positive form of the respective predicate is true. Hence, *very* combines with the adjective after its degree argument is saturated by the positive morpheme. Since the composition of the positive morpheme and an adjective result in an expression of type $\langle e, t\rangle$, intensifiers are of type $\langle\langle e, t\rangle, \langle e, t\rangle\rangle$. The comparative is a 'scale adjuster,' which manipulates the measure function of an adjective. In the case of the comparative, a minimal scale value is introduced. Kennedy & McNally (2005a) assume that in the case of a comparative a new scale is derived by introducing a derived minimal scale value, which is the degree of the comparandum. Hence, comparatives can be considered as functions from measure functions to measure functions and since measure functions are of the type $\langle d, \langle e, t\rangle\rangle$, scale adjusters are of type $\langle\langle d, \langle e, t\rangle\rangle, \langle d, \langle e, t\rangle\rangle\rangle$.

Only intensifiers and scale adjusters are true modifiers since modifiers take an unsaturated expression as its argument and return an unsaturated expression of the same type (cf. McNally to appear). This means that modifiers do not change the type of its argument, which is not the case for true degree morphemes, as they are argument saturating expressions. That intensifiers and scale adjusters are modifiers is supported by the fact that "a number of combinations of multiple intensifiers [and scale adjusters] are possible," (Kennedy & McNally, 2005b, 186) meaning that they allow stacking.[13] This is shown for (29) where multiple comparatives are combined.

(29) a. *Dole isn't as much more conservative than Clinton as Buchanan is.*

---

[13] For further examples of comparative stacking, see Bhatt & Pancheva (2004, 4n6).

5.2 Semantic type of degree expressions

b. *Maverick's is more too dangerous to surf than it was yesterday.*[14]
    (Kennedy & McNally, 2005b, 186)

The examples in (30) show stacking of degree expressions in German. *So* 'so' introduces an equative construction and allows for a deicitic as well as non-deicitic use (b). In the latter case, a subordinated sentence indicates the compared degree. *Zu* 'too' in (c) introduces an excessive construction, expressing that the respective degree is too high for some purpose. In both cases, the equative/excessive element precedes *sehr*.[15]

(30) a. *Er blutet so sehr.*
          he bleeds so very
          'He is bleeding so much.'
      b. *Er ist so groß, dass er nicht durch die Tür passt.*
          he is so tall that he not through the door fits
          'He is so tall that he does not fit through the door.'
      c. *Er schluchzt zu sehr, um sprechen zu können.*
          he sobs too very for speak to can
          'He is sobbing too much to speak.'

The constructions in (30) differ from ordinary degree constructions with *sehr* in being not factitive anymore (Ropertz, 2001, 5). Although being *sehr groß* 'very tall' entails being *groß* 'tall,' such an entailment does not apply to (30a) and (b), as Ropertz points out. That someone sobs too much does not mean that he also sobs much. Hence, *zu sehr schluchzen* 'sob too much' does not entail *sehr schluchzen* 'sob much.'

In (31) we have stacking of two intensifiers which further specify the difference degree expressed by the comparative. First, *viel* indicates that the difference in size between the brothers is large and then *sehr* further indicates that it is not only large but very large. The addition of *sehr* does not affect the factitivity of the construction, being *sehr viel größer* 'very much taller' entails being *viel größer* 'much taller.'

---

[14] Several native speakers I consulted did not accept the sentences in (29). For the sake of the argument, I follow Kennedy & McNally's judgements of the sentences' acceptability.
[15] See Löbner (1990) for a deeper discussion of these degree constructions.

(31) Der Junge ist sehr viel größer als sein Bruder.
    the boy is very much taller as his brother
    'The boy is really a lot taller than his brother.'

There is much more to say regarding the combination of multiple degree expressions as they show more restrictions than those discussed in this section. But a deeper discussion of this topic would go beyond the scope of the current thesis. The relevant point of the discussion is to indicate the heterogeneity of degree expressions with respect to their semantic type. This entails that the different types of degree expressions enter the compositional process at different stages. Scale adjusters are the first degree expressions that combine with gradable adjectives, as they are functions from measure functions to measure functions. True degree morphemes take measure functions as their arguments and saturate the degree argument. Intensifiers enter the compositional process after the degree argument has been saturated. In the remaining discussion, I am focusing on intensifiers as defined above. The term 'degree expression' will be used as a general term for gradation devices.

5.3 Semantics of intensifiers

This section aims at discussing the semantics of the intensifiers *sehr* and *very*. In this section, I am concentrating on adjectival degree modification and turn to the discussion of verbs in section 5.4. A crucial property distinguishing between intensifiers is factivity (Bierwisch 1989; Löbner 1990), also called 'extensionality' by Piñón (2005) or evaluativity (Neeleman et al. 2004; Rett 2007). Factivity is exemplified by the examples in (32) taken from Piñón (2005, 153).

(32) a. *Rebecca completely solved the problem.* ⇒ *Rebecca solved the problem.*
      b. *Rebecca partly (half) solved the problem.* ⇏ *Rebecca solved the problem.*

Piñón states that dropping *completely* preserves the truth of the predication, whereas dropping *partly/half* does not. Or to put it another way, *completely* requires the truth of the embedded predication (*to solve the problem*), whereas *partly/half* require that the embedded predication is not true. *Sehr* – but the same holds for its correspondents in other languages – is also factitive, meaning that it requires the embedded predication to be true. If, as in example (33), a boy is *sehr groß* 'very tall,' it entails that he has to be *groß* 'tall.' You cannot be 'very tall' without being 'tall.' This is shown in (34), where the negation of being tall leads to a contradiction.

(33)   *Der Junge ist sehr groß.* ⇒ *Der Junge ist groß.*
       the boy is very tall   the boy is tall
       'The boy is very tall. ⇒ The boy is tall.'

(34)   #*Der Junge ist sehr groß, aber er ist nicht groß.*
       the boy is very tall but he is not tall
       'The boy is very tall but he is not tall.'

Factivity is an important property of *sehr* since on the one hand it requires the truth of the embedded predicate; on the other hand, it determines at which part of the scale the intensifier induces a partitioning. Following Löbner (1990, 2012b, 233) and Ropertz (2001, 21) the partitioning of the scale induced by *sehr* can be illustrated as in figure 12.

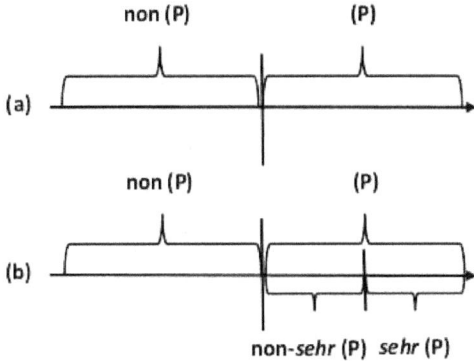

Figure 12: Scale partitioning by an ungraded gradable relative predicate (a) and by one graded by *sehr* (b).

In (a), the partitioning of a scale induced by a gradable relative predicate P like *groß* 'tall' is shown. The adjective applies to a height scale and separates those degrees for which *groß* is true, in the respective context, and those for which it yields a false predication, i.e. for which *non* (P) is true. As shown in (b), *sehr* applies to the part of the scale for which the predicate is true and separates between those individuals which are *sehr groß* 'very tall' and those which are *groß* but not *sehr groß*, i.e. for which *non-sehr groß* is true.

Factivity does not only hold for adadjectival *sehr* but similarly for its adverbial use, as stated by Löbner (2012b, 234) and illustrated in (35). If someone *wächst sehr* 'grows a lot,' he has to *wachsen* 'grow' at all, hence *sehr wachsen* entails the truth of *wachsen*.

(35) Das Kind ist sehr gewachsen. ⇒ Das Kind ist gewachsen.
 the child is very grown the child is grown
 'The child has grown a lot. ⇒ The child has grown.'

The fact that *sehr* is factive and leads to a partition between 'non-high' and 'high' degrees imposes restrictions on graded predicates. An ungraded predication has to be true for at least two degrees otherwise a partitioning of degrees is impossible. Kennedy & McNally (2005a) do not explicitly discuss factivity for *very* but base their analysis of the intensifier on that property as the following quote shows: "whereas the regular contextual standard [for the ungraded adjective] is a degree that exceeds a norm or average of the relevant property calculated on the basis of an arbitrary, contextually determined comparison class, the *very* standard is a norm or average calculated in the same way but just on the basis of those objects to which the unmodified predicate truthfully applies" (Kennedy & McNally, 2005a, 369f.). It follows that an ungraded but gradable adjective and one graded by *very* apply to two different domains. An adjective like *big* applies to all entities that have some size, whereas *very big* applies only to those for which – in a certain context – *big* is true. This is what is illustrated in figure 12 and it also was the reason to claim in section 5.2 that intensifiers enter the compositional process only after the gradable predicate's degree argument has been saturated. Saturation of the degree argument is required to decide whether the ungraded predicate is true of an individual or not and this is what is presupposed by *very*, *sehr* and similar degree expressions.

Based on the proposal in Kennedy & McNally (2005a, 370), the denotation of *very* can be represented as in (36). *Very* takes two arguments, a gradable property g and an individual x and expresses that the degree of x in g exceeds the standard of comparison. The standard for *very* depends on the standard of the positive form of g. (36) states that *very A* is true of x, if the degree of x in the property g exceeds the standard for the ungraded positive form of A. This ensures factivity of the construction *very A*.

(36) $[\![very]\!] = \lambda g \lambda x.(g(x) > s(\lambda y.[\![pos(g(y))]\!]))$

In (37), it is shown how *very* combines with the gradable adjective *tall*. First, the adjective combines with *pos* to convert the measure function into a property of individuals and then *very* applies to the positive form.

(37) $[\![tall]\!] = [\lambda x.tall(x)] ([\![pos]\!])$
$[\![pos[tall]]\!] = [\lambda x.tall(x)] \geq s(tall)] ([\![very]\!])$
$[\![very[pos[tall]]]\!] = [\lambda x.tall(x) > s(\lambda y.tall(y) \geq s(tall))]$

Regarding the truth conditions of *very*, Kennedy & McNally write: "Thus *very* is true of an object if the degree to which it is A exceeds a norm or average of the A-scale for a comparison class based on those objects that have the property of *pos A* in the context of utterance" (Kennedy & McNally, 2005a, 370). The effect of *very* is to raise the standard to a 'high' degree on the respective scale. What counts as a 'high' degree is context-dependent. In (38a), it is expressed that the size of the tree has increased a lot, whereas in (b) it is stated that the height of the boy increased by a large degree. Whatever counts as a large degree in these situations is dependent on the respective comparison class. An increase in size by one centimeter in a month could be a lot for a child of a certain age but not for a tree (or vice versa). As the comparison class and therefore also the respective standard is dependent on the argument of the gradable property, this type of context-dependency is part of the calculation of the standard of comparison.

(38)   a.   Der Baum ist sehr gewachsen.
            the tree   is very grown
            'The tree has grown a lot.'
       b.   Der Junge ist sehr gewachsen.
            the boy   is very grown
            'The boy has grown a lot.'

5 Gradable predicates and intensifiers

Kennedy & McNally argue at length that *very* only modifies relative adjectives but not absolute ones. The reason is that absolute adjectives restrict the standard to an endpoint of the scale and it would have no semantic effect adding *very* as it could not further raise the standard (cf. Kennedy & McNally 2005a, 372). In their analysis, Kennedy & McNally also mention apparent counterexamples like *This region of the country is very dry* (Kennedy & McNally, 2005a, 371), in which case the absolute adjective *dry* is interpreted as being a relative one. In their view, *dry* only allows for a relative reading if it denotes a permanent and stable property but has an absolute reading if it denotes a transient property. The authors remain uncommitted as to whether this is a case of polysemy, vagueness regarding the adjectival standard or coercion. What is essential is merely the fact that both readings, the relative and the absolute one, can be disambiguated. There are similar examples in German, as discussed by Ropertz (2001, 28f.). One case is the adjective *leer* 'empty,' which, as shown in (39a), is compatible with an endpoint modifier but also with *sehr* (b). In the first case, the sentence means that nobody or nothing is in the theater. This is not the interpretation of (b), which rather means that the theater is not only empty, compared to some standard of comparison, but rather empty to a high degree. This relative reading of *leer* does not entail that nobody or nothing is in the theater but that the number of persons or things is less compared to, for example, some expectation.

(39)   a.   Das Theater ist vollständig leer.
                 the theater is completely empty
                 'The theater is completely empty.'
       b.   Das Theater ist sehr leer.
                 the theater is very empty
                 'The theater is very empty.'

The discussion on the distribution of degree expressions always presupposes that *sehr/very* and endpoint modifiers such as *vollständig/completely* are in complementary distribution. This is true in many cases, such as those in (40) and (41). *Groß* 'tall' rejects the endpoint modifier but takes *sehr*, whereas the adjectival participle *geschlossen* 'closed' takes the endpoint modifier but rejects *sehr*.

5.3 Semantics of intensifiers

(40) a. *Das Kind ist sehr groß.*
the child is very tall
'The child is very tall.'
b. #*Das Kind ist vollständig groß.*
the child is completely tall
'The child is completely tall.'

(41) a. *Die Tür ist vollständig geschlossen.*
the door is completely open
'The door is completely open.'
b. #*Die Tür ist sehr geschlossen.*
the door is very open
'The door is very open.'

If one assumes that *very/sehr* and *completely/vollständig* are in complementary distribution, examples like (39) are in need of an explanation. But one could also argue that it is only an apparent complementary distribution. I assume that there are at least two types of maximal absolute adjectives: adjectives that are only true at the maximal value of the scale and adjectives that truthfully denote the region adjacent to the maximal scale value (including the maximal scale value). *Geschlossen* 'closed' would only be true at the maximal degree on the respective scale, whereas *voll* 'full' would yield a true predication if the degree falls within a range before the maximal scale value. This distinction can be substantiated by two linguistic differences between the two types of adjectival predicates. In (42) it is shown that *voll* 'full' allows for a comparative construction, whereas *geschlossen* 'closed' does not. The examples in (43) show that the positive use of *voll* is compatible with the statement that a still higher degree could be achieved, which is not possible for *geschlossen*.

(42) a. *Dieses Glas ist voller als das andere.*
this glass is fuller than the other
'This glass is fuller than the other one.'
b. #*Diese Tür ist geschlossener als die andere.*
this door is more.closed than die other
'This door is more closed than the other one.'

(43) a. *Das Glas ist voll, aber es könnte noch voller sein.*
the glass is full, but it could still fuller be
'The glass is full but it could be even fuller.'
b. #*Die Tür ist geschlossen, aber sie könnte noch geschlossener*
the door is closed but she could still more.closed
sein.
be
'The door is closed but it could be even more closed.'

The distinction between 'endpoint' and 'end range' absolute adjectives is crucial for the analysis of degree gradation of change of state verbs in the next chapter. This distinction allows predicting which telic change of state verbs admit degree gradation and which reject it. Hence, I take a different stance on the restrictions of intensifiers like *very*, *sehr* with respect to scale structure. As long as the adjective denotes more than a single degree on the scale, a standard raising effect of intensifiers such as *very* or *sehr* should be possible irrespective of whether the scale is closed or not.

5.4 Degrees, scales, and verbs

So far, the discussion of degree gradation has centered around adjectives and intensifiers of adjectives. The question of the current section is whether the analysis of gradable adjectives can easily be extended to gradable verbs. In their analysis of gradable adjectives, Kennedy & McNally (2005a) assume measure functions to be the semantic core of gradable relative and absolute adjectives. A central assumption of this approach is that degree morphology is required to turn measure functions into predications of individuals. Degree morphology, like the *pos* morpheme, introduces a standard of comparison by saturating the degree argument of the adjective.

Gradable adjectives can be conceived of as scalar predicates par exellence as they directly express a scalar predication. The adjective *wide*, for example, is a function that returns the width degree of its argument and compares it to a standard of comparison. Closely related to gradable adjectives are deadjectival change of state verbs like *widen*. Such verbs express a scalar change of state and will be discussed in more detail in chapter 6.

5.4 Degrees, scales, and verbs

But there is also another class of verbs that is similar to gradable adjectives; namely scalar stative dimensional verbs Gamerschlag (2014). Stative dimensional verbs lexically encode a single dimension; in (44), examples of scalar (a) and non-scalar stative dimensional verbs (b) are shown.

(44) a. *The book costs ten dollars.*
      b. *She is called Ava.*
          (Gamerschlag, 2014, 275f.)

The verb *cost* encodes the dimension PRICE, the measure phrase *ten dollars* is required as an argument of the verb. *Cost* equates the price of the book with the price denoted by the measure phrase. PRICE is a scalar dimension, as its values are linearly ordered. *Be called* encodes the non-scalar dimension NAME (for the distinction between scalar and non-scalar dimensions see chapter 2.2). *Ava* functions as an argument of the verb and specifies the value of the dimension encoded in the verb.

An external value specification by an argument-like NP is not required in each case as some verbs allow absolute uses (45). In (a) the value of the weight of the suitcase is specified externally by the measure phrase *zehn Kilo* 'ten kilos.' (45b) illustrates the absolute use; in which case it expresses that the suitcase has a contextually 'high' degree of weight (see Gamerschlag 2014 for a more extensive discussion of absolute uses of stative dimensional verbs).

(45) a. *Der Koffer   wiegt   zehn Kilo.*
          the suitcase weighs ten   kilo
          'The suitcase weighs ten kilos.'
      b. *Der Koffer   wiegt.*
          the suitcase weighs
          'The suitcase weighs a lot/is heavy.'
          (Gamerschlag, 2014, 283)

In the absolute use, *weigh* makes a scalar predication, as it expresses that the degree on the scale exceeds some context-dependent standard. This shows that the scalar predication is not only invoked by a degree expression but it is really anchored in the lexical semantics of the verb. Therefore, a semantic representation for *wiegen* 'weigh' can be proposed, as in (46).

(46)   ⟦wiegen⟧ = λdλxλv.WEIGHT(x, v) ≥ d[16]

There are two reasons to assume a degree argument for *wiegen* and other scalar stative dimensional verbs. First, in its absolute use the verb requires an external value specification in terms of a measure phrase. Hence, there is an argument slot for this type of expression. Second, in their absolute use, scalar stative dimensional verbs express a comparison of the degree of its argument and a context-dependent standard. A scalar predication also arises if no explicit degree construction is used. For the absolute use, one can assume existential binding of the degree argument. Following the analysis of Kennedy & McNally (2005a), one could also propose a verbal positive morpheme that saturates the degree argument in the absolute use. But as far as I know, there is no evidence for an overt expression of such a verbal morpheme in any language (in contrast to the overt expression of adjectival *pos* in Sinitic languages). Due to the absence of linguistic evidence for verbal *pos*, I will not assume such a null morpheme for scalar verbs in contrast to Kennedy & Levin (2008).

The discussion reveals that there are some verbs which express a scalar predication in all of their uses. But verbal degree gradation is not restricted to these verbs and (to be more precise) not all scalar stative dimensional verbs accept intensifiers. Some of them take *viel* 'much' as an intensifier but reject *sehr* (47), others license neither (48). For *dauern* 'to last,' the adjective *lang* 'long' is used for indicating a 'high' degree and therefore blocks the use of more general degree expressions like *sehr* or *viel*.

(47) a. *Der Koffer wiegt viel/*sehr.*
          the suitcase weighs much/very
          'The suitcase weighs a lot.'
      b. *Das Buch kostet viel/*sehr.*
          the book costs much/very
          'The book costs a lot.'

(48) *Der Film dauert *viel/*sehr/lang.*
       the film lasts much/very/long
       'The film lasts a long time.'

---

[16]   I use 'v' as a variable for eventualities, covering both states and events. 'e' is used for events if the respective verb is clearly eventive.

5.4 Degrees, scales, and verbs

Many gradable verbs belong neither to the class of change of state verbs nor to the class of scalar stative dimensional verbs. Two examples are the verbs *stinken* 'stink' and *regnen* 'rain.' Degree gradation of *stinken* (49a) results in a specification of the degree of the intensity of the emitted smell. With regard to *regnen*, it is the quantity of the emitted rain that is specified by the intensifier (49b).

(49) a. *Der Hund stinkt sehr.*
          the dog stinks very
          'The dog really stinks.'
      b. *Gestern hat es sehr geregnet.*
          yesterday has it very rained
          'Yesterday, it rained a lot.'

The ungraded verb *regnen* in (50) only expresses the emission of rain but does not make a predication about the quantity of rain. Hence, the quantity scale, to which *sehr* applies, is not an active meaning component of *regnen* in each context of use. It is clearly the case that if it is raining, some quantity of rain must be emitted but this does not entail that the ungraded verb makes a predication about the quantity of emitted rain. Rather, the quantity of emitted rain is only relevant in a gradational context.

(50) *Gestern hat es geregnet.*
      yesterday has it rained
      'Yesterday, it rained.'

The same argumentation holds for *stinken*. Clearly, it is the case that if a dog stinks, the emitted smell needs to have some intensity as it is not possible to have smell without any intensity. But with *regnen*, the ungraded verb does not make a predication about the degree of the intensity of the emitted substance. If the verb did this, a sentence like (51) would always contain an (implicit) comparison between the intensity of the smell of the dog and some standard for the intensity of stinking.

(51) *Der Hund stinkt.*
      the dog smells
      'The dog smells.'

5 Gradable predicates and intensifiers

We do not interpret a sentence like (51) with respect to an (implicit) comparison class like 'the dog smells for a dog,' 'the dog smells more than a standard dog smells' or 'the dog smells more than he normally smells.' Given these facts, there is no reason to conclude that the measure functions QUANTITY or INTENSITY are active meaning components of these verbs in sentences like (50) and (51). I propose the definition in (52) for the notion of a 'lexically scalar verb':

(52)   Lexically scalar verb: A verb is lexically scalar iff it expresses a scalar predication in every context of use.

As argued above, *wiegen* 'weigh' is a lexically scalar verb, as it provides a comparison between the weight of its argument and some other degree of weight. Another class of lexically scalar verbs are change of state verbs, as discussed in 3.3. But note that the definition proposed in (52) does not rely on Rappaport Hovav's characteristics of scalar verbs, as they would not be appropriate for stative verbs like *wiegen*. *Stinken*, as the discussion above revealed, is a lexically non-scalar verb that does not encode a scale in its lexical semantics. Rather *stinken* and lexically non-scalar verbs in general require an explicit degree context for expressing a scalar predication.

Even if verbs like *stinken* are lexically non-scalar, it is not arbitrary that *sehr* indicates the intensity of the emitted smell in (49a) but the quantity of the emitted rain in (49b). The verb determines the respective scale which is 'activated' if required by the (linguistic) context. Activation of attributes is not a process of coercion as the meaning of the verb is not shifted to fit the context. Rather, the meaning is enriched by a gradable attribute.

A neo-Davidsonian representation of the lexical semantics of *stinken* is shown in (53). The representation consists of five conjuncts, the first one is a predicate of the eventuality argument. The next two other conjuncts link the explicit and implicit event participants to the eventuality. EMITTER links the emitter argument, which is the only syntactic argument of the verb, to the eventuality. EMITTEE represents an implicit semantic argument of the verb, namely the stimulus emited in the eventuality.[17] The emitee is specified as being smell and being unpleasant by the predicates in the last two conjuncts.

---

[17]   The notion of an 'implicit argument' is discussed in more detail in chapter 7.

5.4 Degrees, scales, and verbs

(53) $[\![\text{stinken}]\!] = \lambda x \lambda v \exists y.\text{emit}(v) \wedge \text{EMITTER}(v) = x \wedge \text{EMITTEE}(v) = y \wedge \text{smell}(y) \wedge \text{unpleasant}(y)$

EMITTER and EMITTEE are attributes in the sense of frame theory (Petersen 2007; Löbner 2014). This notion of 'frame' is based on Barsalou's (1992a; 1992b) frame account and differs from the one employed by Fillmore (1968), for example. The frame theory proposed by Löbner uses recursive attribute-value structures for representing lexical and conceptual meaning. What is essential is the notion of 'attribute,' which comprises partial functions that assign a unique value to its argument (Löbner, 2014, 26f.). As he states: "Value specifications may be more or less specific, but at the most specific level of description, the value is uniquely determined" (Löbner, 2014, 26.). In the following, all attributes are written in small capitals. The attribute EMITTER takes the eventuality and returns the individual that bears the emitter role in that eventuality. Similarly, for the attribute EMITTEE which returns the individual that functions as emittee in the respective eventuality. Such role attributes are functional; for each eventuality there is only one emitter, emittee, agent or theme respectively.[18] I integrate attributes in a neo-Davidsonian account of verb semantics and do not use a frame-based representation since up to now no well-established frame approach to verb meaning exists. Nevertheless, there have been some attempts to represent verbal concepts in frames (e.g. Kallmeyer & Osswald 2013; Gamerschlag et al. 2014; Fleischhauer et al. 2014; Fleischhauer 2015; Kawaletz & Plag 2015).

Gradable properties are also attributes in the sense discussed above. But INTENSITY is not an attribute in the lexical entry of the verb *stinken*. Rather, the attribute is retrieved from the conceptual knowledge associated with the (implicit) emittee argument *stink*. Part of our conceptual knowledge associated with the nominal concept *stink* is 'is emitted by something/someone,' 'has a certain aroma,' 'has a certain intensity.' The central idea is that lexical representations can be enriched by additional attributes if this is required by the linguistic context. With respect to verbal degree gradation, this idea can be spelled out as follows: an intensifier requires a gradation scale, and if there is no scale in the lexical representation of the

---

[18] See Löbner (2014, 42ff.) for an analysis of semantic roles as attributes in the sense of frame theory.

5 Gradable predicates and intensifiers

verb, a suitable scale has to be retrieved from the conceptual knowledge associated with the verb. The verb is not arbitrarily linked to conceptual knowledge, but only components that are part of the verb's lexical semantics give access to conceptual knowledge. With regard to the representation in (52), only the attribute specified in the lexical entry gives access to conceptual knowledge. As only the implicit EMITTEE argument is specified, it is only *stink* that allows the activation of concrete conceptual knowledge and hence it is only possible to retrieve a gradable property from the knowledge about *stink*. Since the intensifier combines with the verb before the syntactic arguments are saturated (cf. chapter 4), the EMITTER attribute does not license access to conceptual knowledge as it is unspecified. Hence, the lexicalized meaning components constrain the possible attributes that can be activated, and therefore the lexical meaning of the verb constrains activation of suitable gradation scales. Based on this discussion, it is possible to give a more precise characterization of the notion of 'degree gradable verb': a verb admits degree gradation if it either lexicalizes a suitable gradation scale or if the activation of a suitable gradation scale is licensed by the conceptual knowledge associated with a meaning component lexically specified in the verb.

But it is not always the case that degree gradation specifies the degree of a gradable property of an implicit argument of the verb. An example where this is not the case is (54). The gradable property is DIFFERENCE of the subject referent's size at two different points in time and therefore the argument of the measure function is a syntactic argument of the verb.

(54)   Das Kind ist sehr gewachsen.
       the child is very grown
       'The child has grown a lot.'

The cases discussed above illustrate two different sources of verbal scales. The first option is that the scale is lexicalized by the verb as in (54) or (46). A second option is that the scale is retrieved from our conceptual knowledge associated with one of the attributes of the verb, for example, an implicit argument. There is also a third option: the scale can be introduced by a morphosyntactic device like a resultative predicate. For verbs that do not lexically encode a change of state, the resultative construction introduces a change of state predication. The construction in (55) denotes a change which leads to the result that the child is hoarse at the end of the event. Following the analysis in chapter 3, the construction introduces a scale measuring the change of the subject referent.

(55)   Das Kind schrie sich heiser.
         the child cried REFL hoarse
         'The child cried itself hoarse.'

Only verbs that lexicalize a scale express a scalar predication (in every context); the other two types of scales require a special (morphosyntactic) context. The diversity regarding verbal gradation scales makes it impossible to postulate one general rule of semantic composition for verbal degree gradation. Löbner (2012b) claims that verbal degree gradation is a subcompositional construction. A syntactic construction is subcompositional if there is no uniform rule of semantic composition for this construction (Löbner, 2012b, 224). Löbner's general claim is that there is not a single rule of semantic composition for the construction 'sehr + verb' but different rules depending on the semantic class of the graded verb.

In the last section, a single compositional rule for the construction 'very/sehr + adjective' has been presented. Hence, adjectival degree gradation is not subcompositional and therefore subcompositionality is the crucial factor distinguishing verbal degree gradation from adjectival degree gradation. The case studies on degree gradation of three different classes of gradable verbs, in the chapters 6 to 8, will illustrate the different compositional patterns in more detail. After presenting the case studies, I will come back to the notion of 'subcompositionality' in chapter 9.

Due to subcompositionality, I will not provide a compositional analysis of verbal degree gradation in the following chapter but only indicate the outcome of the subcompositional process. Therefore, I will also not discuss the standard of comparison in verbal degree gradation but restrict myself to the interpretation of verbal degree gradation and the question how the gradation scales are related to the lexical meaning of the graded verbs.

Subcompositionality of verbal degree gradation is deeply connected with the fact that many gradable verbs are lexically non-scalar. The scale is activated from the conceptual knowledge associated with the verb and there is a different functional relation between the scale and the eventuality denoted by the verb from different classes of verbs. Furthermore, the fact that

5 Gradable predicates and intensifiers

many gradable verbs do not lexically encode a scale makes a big difference between verbal degree gradation and gradation of adjectives. As discussed in 5.1, gradable adjectives are lexically scalar and based on Kennedy (1999b) and Kennedy & McNally (2005a) it is reasonable to assume that they have a degree argument. Due to this big difference regarding lexical scalarity, the analysis of adjectival degree gradation cannot be adopted for the case of verbal degree gradation.

5.5 Conclusion

Starting from a discussion of adjectival degree gradation, the current chapter revealed two essential differences between adjectical and verbal gradation. First, verb gradation is subcompositional, whereas adjectival gradation is not. Second, the scale is the semantic core of gradable adjectives but it is not a meaning component of most gradable verbs. Rather, the scale has to be retrieved from the conceptual knowledge associated with the verb. Most gradable verbs do not express a scalar predication and so there is no need to postulate a degree argument for these verbs. But it is a different question for lexically scalar verbs such as change of state verbs and scalar stative dimensional verbs. I will turn to a discussion of change of state verbs as a prototypical example of scalar verbs in the next chapter.

6 Change of state verbs

Change of state verbs are one of the prototypical examples of scalar verbs. There are two reasons for this: first, some of the verbs are derived from gradable adjectives, and second, the verbs are result verbs in the sense of Rappaport Hovav & Levin (2010) and therefore express a change along a scale.

This chapter is organized as follows: in 6.1, I will present a general overview of the class of change of state verbs and distinguish between different subtypes of change of state verbs. Section 6.2 is more closely concerned with argument realization and argument alternations. Scales are the topic of section 6.3, which elaborates on the notion of scalar change and discusses in detail the question whether all change of state verbs lexicalize a scale. A scalar analysis of telicity will be the topic of section 6.4, and I will turn to the discussion of degree gradation of change of state verbs in section 6.5. Finally, a discussion of telicity with regard to verbal degree gradation is provided in 6.6, before I turn to a conclusion in 6.7.

6.1 Change of state verbs – a general perspective

Change of state verbs express a change in an attribute of one of the verb's arguments. To be more precise, it is always the referent of the theme argument that undergoes a change in a certain property. In (1) *the gap* is the theme argument of the verb, which is realized as the subject of the intransitive verb (a) but as the direct object of the transitive verb (b).

(1)   a.   *The gap widened.*
       b.   *The earthquake widened the gap.*

The dimension of change is specified by the verb.[1] *Widen* specifies the property of change as the theme argument's WIDTH, whereas a verb such

---

[1] The dimension of change is not always specified by the verb. I turn to such cases in chapter 6.3.

as *stabilize* expresses a change in the theme argument's STABILITY. As discussed in chapter 3, Rappaport Hovav & Levin (2010) classify change of state verbs as result verbs rather than manner verbs. Result verbs express the attainment of a result but do not specify how that result comes about. Taking *widen* as an example, the verb expresses that the referent of its theme argument increases in width but the manner in which this happens is not specified. The way Rappaport Hovav & Levin analyze the difference between result and manner verbs is in terms of scalarity. Result verbs express scalar changes, whereas manner verbs express non-scalar changes (cf. the discussion in chapter 3). A scalar change can be explicated as a change progressing along a certain scale. I will discuss the scalarity of change of state verbs in more detail in 6.3; for the moment it suffices to assume that change of state verbs lexically encode a scale at which they measure the change of the referent of the theme argument.

The changes expressed by these verbs can be classified in several respects: (i) they can be lexically classified with respect to the kind of change expressed by the verb, (ii) they can be distinguished with respect to the opposition between extensional and intensional changes and finally, (iii) they can be aspectually classified in terms of durativity and telicity. The verbs can also be classified with respect to the lexical specification of the scale. I will discuss this point in detail in section 6.3. Levin (1993) proposes a lexical classification of changes as she puts forward a distinction of lexical subclasses of change of state verbs. Among others, she distinguishes the following classes: 'break verbs,' 'bend verbs,' 'cooking verbs' and 'verbs of entity-specific changes of state.' Break verbs, for example, describe a change in the material integrity of the theme argument (Levin, 1993, 242), whereas bend verbs denote a change in the shape of the referent of the theme argument.[2] Verbs of entity-specific changes are not so much classified by expressing a certain kind of change but rather by imposing strong selectional restrictions on their theme arguments. One example is the verb *blossom*, which is restricted to plants.

The classification discussed above applies to verbs as such, but the opposition extensional vs. intensional changes applies to uses of verbs.

---

[2] This is merely a partial classification of dimensions of change. A more extensive typology of dimensions encoded in (stative dimensional) verbs can be found in Gamerschlag (2014).

6.1 Change of state verbs – a general perspective

Verbs such as *steigen* 'rise' have two different uses, which are called 'extensional' and 'intensional' Montague (1973); Löbner (1979, 1981). Example (2a) is an extensional use of *steigen*, whereas in (2b) the verb is used intensionally. In the extensional use a change in a single dimension of the referent of the theme argument is expressed. In (2a) this is the HEIGHT of the balloon. *Steigen* – in its extensional use – expresses an upward motion along a vertical path.

(2) a. *Der Ballon steigt.*
 the balloon rises
 'The balloon is rising.'
 b. *Die Temperatur steigt.*
 the temperature rises
 'The temperature is rising.'

In the intensional use, the respective dimension of change is specified by a functional noun like *Temperatur* 'temperature' in (2b). Although in (2a) only a partial change of the referent of the theme argument is predicated – the only relevant change of the balloon is the height of his position – a total change of the referent of the theme argument is expressed in the intensional use of *steigen*. In the case of intensional verbs the subject argument cannot be replaced *salva veritate* by an expression with the same reference. *Die Temperatur* in (2b) cannot be replaced by an expression that refers to the referent of the subject to a specific time point, which is a specific degree on the temperature scale, as shown in (3). On the other hand, it is possible to replace the subject referent of the extensionally used verb with an expression that has the same reference as in (4).

(3) #*26 Grad Celsius steigen.*
 26 degrees Celsius rise
 '26 degrees Celsius are rising.'

(4) *Das Gefährt der Brüder Montgolfier steigt.*
 the vehicle the brothers Montgolfier rises
 'The vehicle of the Montgolfier brothers is rising.'
 (Fleischhauer & Gamerschlag, 2014, 33)

Verbs such as German *steigen* can be considered as change of state verbs only in their intensional uses. If they are used extensionally, they have to be conceived as verbs of directed motion that express a directed change of position. In their motion sense, i.e., the extensional use, these verbs fully specify the dimension of the positional change. But it is the intensional use which requires an external specification of the dimension, as in (2b), in which the noun *Temperatur* indicates that the change progresses along the temperature scale.

The contrast between extensional and intensional uses of change of state verbs is discussed less often in the literature than aktionsart-related distinctions between change of state verbs. All change of state verbs are dynamic and express a directed change, but they differ with respect to whether this change is temporally extended (durative) or whether it is punctual. Beavers (2008); Rappaport Hovav (2008) and Rappaport Hovav & Levin (2010) argue that the contrast between durative and punctual change of state verbs is reflected in their scales. Durative change of state verbs are related to multivalue scales, whereas punctual ones express changes on two-point scales. Two-point scales merely consist of two degrees which form a contradictory pair such as 'alive' and 'dead' in the case of the German achievement predicate *sterben* 'die.' The values of multivalue scales form a set of contrary degrees which consists of at least three values.

It is a defining feature of achievements and accomplishments that they express telic predications. Degree achievements, the term goes back to Dowty (1979), form a distinct subclass of change of state verbs which display variable telicity like English *cool*. The English verb *cool* is compatible with time-frame and time-span adverbials, as the example in (5a) shows. In its telic reading in (5a) *cool* entails that the soup became cool, whereas in the atelic reading it only entails that the soup got cooler.[3] Some degree achievements are even basically atelic like *grow* in (5b) which does not license the in-adverbial (cf. Dowty 1979 and Hay et al. 1999 among others for a discussion of aspectual properties of degree achievements.).

(5)   a.   *The soup cooled for/in an hour.* (Hay et al., 1999, 127)
       b.   #*The child has grown in one year.*

---

[3] Languages differ with regard to aspectual properties of degree achievements like English *cool*. Kardos (2012, 111) states, for example, that in Hungarian the corresponding verb only has an atelic reading; the telic reading requires an explicit delimitation of the event.

Degree achievements display variable telicity, like incremental theme verbs.[4] But they differ from incremental theme verbs as it is not the referential properties of the theme argument that determine telicity (cf. Dowty 1979; Levin & Rappaport Hovav 2005; Kennedy & Levin 2008; Kennedy 2012). If an incremental theme argument has cumulative reference, the incremental theme predication is atelic, and if it shows quantized reference, the whole predication is telic (cf. Verkuyl 1972; Mourelatos 1978; Bach 1986; Krifka 1986, 1998; Filip 1999, 2000). The incremental theme argument in (6a) is a singular count noun, which has a quantized reference, therefore the predication is telic. We get an atelic predication in (6b) where the incremental theme argument is a mass noun that has cumulative reference (cf. Krifka 1991 for a discussion of different properties of count and mass nouns). A/telicity of degree achievements like *cool* is not affected by the referential properties of the theme argument as (5a) illustrates. The theme argument is explicitly quantized by the use of the definite article, but irrespective of this fact the verb only licenses an atelic reading.

(6) a. *Paul ate an/the apple in ten minutes.*
    b. #*Paul ate soup in ten minutes.*

With respect to degree achievements, telicity is dependent on whether the extent of the change is specified or not (Hay et al. 1999; Levin & Rappaport Hovav 2005; Kennedy & Levin 2008; Fleischhauer 2013). In (7a), it is an unspecified change which leads to an atelic interpretation, whereas the measure phrase *five degrees* specifies the extent of the change in (b) and this results in a telic interpretation.

(7) a. *Sandy warmed the solution for three minutes.*
    b. *Sandy warmed the solution five degrees in three minutes.*
       (Rappaport Hovav & Levin, 2005, 280)

In English, there is no difference between the telic and the atelic use of the verb. In (7b) it is merely the measure phrase that 'marks' telicity. In other languages, such as Mparntwe Arrernte, the contrast between a telic and an atelic predication is explicitly marked at verb level. In the atelic reading in

---

[4] Deo et al. (2013) argue that change over time should be seen as an instance of obtaining a value difference, which also allows for capturing extent readings of degree achievements like in *The trail narrowed at the summit* (Deo et al., 2013, 98).

(8a), -*irre* marks the process of getting colder, whereas -*arle* in (b) indicates the termination of the process, i.e., reaching the endpoint.

(8)   Mparntwe Arrernte (Australian; Wilkins 1989 cited after Van Valin 2005, 43)
    a.   *Ayenge   irrernt-irre-ke.*
         1SG.NOM cold-PROC-PST
         'I got colder/cooler/*cold.'
    b.   *Ayenge   irrernte-arle-irre-ke.*
         1SG.NOM cold-RES-PROC-PST
         'I got cold.'

Telic and atelic change of state verbs – or uses of change of state verbs as in (5a) – differ with regard to their truth conditions. The telic ones entail the reaching of an endpoint (telos) and in languages such as English and German the result state is often denoted by the positive form of an adjective (9a). Atelic change of state verbs equal comparatives in their truth conditions and the result state is often denoted by the comparative form of an adjective (9b).

(9)   a.   *The soup cooled in an hour.* → *The soup got cool.*
       b.   *The soup cooled for an hour.* → *The soup got cooler.*

German shows a morphological reflex of this distinction, since many deadjectival degree achievements, but not all, are derived from the comparative form of the adjective. Table 12 lists some deadjectival degree achievements, the first three verbs in the table are derived from the comparative form of their adjectival base, whereas the later three are derived from the positive form.[5] Irrespective of the adjectival base, all degree achievements in table 12 show comparative truth conditions, i.e., merely indicating that a change occurred without entailing the reaching of a specific endpoint. Also Bobaljik (2012, 181) states that "variable telicity is not a function of the presence or absence of comparative morphology."

---

[5]   Bobalijk (2012) shows that if a language has suppletive comparative forms, deadjectival change of state verbs are derived from the suppletive comparative stem and not from the positive stem. An English example is *bad – worse – worsen* and not **badden*. Also cf. Kriz (2011, 51f.) for a discussion of different derivational patterns for deadjectival change of state verbs in German and English.

6.1 Change of state verbs – a general perspective

Deadjectival degree achievement	Positive form of base adjective	Comparative form of base adjective
vergrößern 'enlarge'	*groß* 'tall'	*größer* 'taller'
verkleinern 'diminish'	*klein* 'small'	*kleiner* 'smaller'
verbreitern 'broaden'	*breit* 'broad'	*breiter* 'broader'
verteuern 'increase in price'	*teuer* 'expensive'	*teurer* 'more expensive'
vertiefen 'deepen'	*tief* 'deep'	*tiefer* 'deeper'
verengen 'narrow'	*eng* 'narrow'	*enger* 'narrower'

Table 12: Deadjectival degree achievements and their corresponding adjectival bases.

I will use the term 'accomplishment' for all telic uses of change of state verbs, irrespective whether the verb also has an atelic use or not. The term 'degree achievement' will be used for atelic uses of change of state verbs (this differs from the use of the notion of 'degree achievement' in the literature as the term is commonly used to refer to change of state verbs that are either atelic or show variable telicity.). Paraphrases for accomplishments and degree achievements are given in (10). An accomplishment like *open* can be paraphrased as *become open*, whereas a degree achievement like *grown* is paraphrased is *become taller*. The comparandum, in the case of degree achievements, is the initial size of the argument of the verb and not the size of some other entity. Note that the paraphrases are only intended to capture the inchoative reading of change of state verbs, causality will be discussed in the next section.

(10) a. Accomplishment: BECOME ADJ$_{POS}$
      b. Degree Achievement: BECOME ADJ$_{COMP}$

The distinction between degree achievements and accomplishments will turn out to be relevant for the discussion of degree gradation of change of state verbs. Therefore, I will discuss telicity in more detail in section 6.4. In the next section, I first will turn to a discussion of the argument realization of change of state verbs.

6.2 Argument realization

In German, change of state verbs basically show the argument realization patterns in (11). There are intransitive change of state verbs like *wachsen* 'grow' (11a), which do not have a transitive variant with the same root (b). There are also change of state verbs which are basically transitive, as *verbreitern* 'widen' in (c).

(11)   a.   Das Kind wächst.
               the child grows
               'The child is growing.'
       b.   *Die Eltern wachsen das Kind.
               the parents grow the child
       c.   Das Erdbeben verbreitert den Riss.
               the earthquake widens the crack
               'The earthquake is widening the crack.'

The single argument of intransitive change of state verbs is a theme argument. The theme denotes the participant that is affected by the change. Transitive change of state verbs realize the theme argument as direct object, whereas the subject argument is semantically a causer or the cause. The causer is responsible for bringing about the change in the theme argument. Verbs such as *wachsen* do not have a causative variant; Levin & Rappaport Hovav (1995) argue that *wachsen* and other verbs like it express an internally caused event. *Verbreitern* and other transitive change of state verbs denote externally caused events. In such a case, an event participant who is distinct from the referent of the theme argument is responsible for initiating the event. In the case of internally caused events, it is a property of the referent of the theme argument, for example, a biological predisposition, which causes the event. For a critical examination of this analysis see, for example, McKoon & MacFarland (2000). The event structural representation of both types of change of state verbs is shown in (12).

(12)   a.   externally caused change of state verb $[\mathbf{do'}(x, \emptyset)]$ CAUSE [BECOME **pred'**(y)]
       b.   internally caused change of state verb BECOME **pred'**(y)

6.2 Argument realization

The distinction between internally and externally caused change of state verbs is, among other things, intended to explain which verbs participate in the causative/inchoative alternation and which do not. Internally caused change of state verbs are always intransitive, whereas externally caused change of state verbs show up in a transitive argument realization pattern. Many causative change of state verbs also have a derived inchoative use, in which the causer is not expressed anymore and the theme argument is realized as the subject of the verb. In German, two different derivational patterns can be found for derived inchoative change of state verbs. We have zero derivation in (13a) and (b); neither the inchoative nor the causative use of *schmelzen* is explicitly marked. This kind of derivation is the usual one in English, whereas in German a marking of the derived inchoative verb by the reflexive *sich* is more common.[6] The examples in (11c) vs. (13c) illustrate the derivation of the inchoative verb from the causative by means of reflexive marking.

(13) a. *Der Käse schmilzt.*
the cheese melts
'The cheese is melting.'
b. *Die Sonne schmilzt den Käse.*
the sun melts the cheese
'The sun is melting the cheese.'
c. *Der Riss verbreitert sich.*
the crack widens REFL
'The crack is widening.'

Russian, as well as French, also derives inchoative change of state verbs from causative ones. French uses a reflexive pronoun like German to mark the inchoative verb (14). Russian does not use a reflexive pronoun, but instead the reflexive affix *-sja* is attached to the verb to mark the derived inchoative verb (15).[7]

(14) a. *Le tremblement de terre est en train d' élargir la fissure.*
the earthquake PROG widen the crack
'The earthquake is widening the crack.'

---
[6] Cf. Haspelmath (1993) for an overview of different strategies for the realization of causative/inchoative verb pairs.
[7] Beside the bounded form, Russian also has a free reflexive pronoun. The free form is not used for marking the causative-inchoative alternation, however.

b. *La fissure est en train de s'élargir.*
    the crack PROG   REFL=widen
    'The crack is widening.'

(15) a. *Mal'čik plavit syr.*
        boy   melts cheese
        'The boy is melting cheese.'
     b. *Syr   plavit-sja.*
        cheese melt-REFL
        'The cheese is melting.'

Different analyses for the causative/inchoative alternation have been proposed in the literature. The decausativation analysis assumes that the inchoative verb is derived from the causative one by means of a decausativizing process. In this case, the causal subevent is deleted from the event structure of the verb and at the same time the verb is detransitivized. Such an analysis is, for example, assumed by Löbner (2013, 138). A different view is that the inchoative verb is derived from the causative one by existential binding of the causer. In this case, the causative subevent is not deleted from the event structure of the verb. This results in the derivation of an intransitive verb, which otherwise does not differ semantically from the causative one. Such an approach is advocated by, for example, Levin & Rappaport Hovav (1995).[8] A third account is the reflexivization analysis of Koontz-Garboden (2009). According to this account, it is assumed that the reflexive pronoun really has a reflexive interpretation such that the causer and theme argument are taken to be coreferential.[9] Beavers & Zubair (2013, 32f.) state that a non-agentive causer cannot act on itself and in such a case we get the reading that something internal to the theme argument causes its change. Hence, we have a derived internally caused change of state interpretation. If the causer is agentive, then a plain causative use of the change of state verb remains, as in (16). The verb allows a reflexive marking, but it does not derive an inchoative reading. Rather the causer is interpreted as acting on itself. For a critical discussion of this approach

---

[8] Rappaport Hovav & Levin (2012) argue against their 1995 analysis and reject the view that inchoative change of state verbs are derived from causative ones by a lexical rule that existentially binds the causer.

[9] Cf. Koontz-Garboden (2009, 83ff.) for a formal representation of the reflexivization approach based on Chierchia's (2004) reflexive operator.

see Horvath & Siloni (2011) and the replies in Beavers & Zubair (2013) and Beavers & Koontz-Garboden (2013).

(16) *Der Mann hat sich getötet.*
the man has REFL killed
'The man killed himself.'

Koontz-Garboden's approach does not apply to languages such as English, which do not make use of a reflexive marking in deriving inchoative change of state verbs. An account of the causative/inchoative alternation needs to explain why some verbs, such as English *sterilize*, do not alternate (17).

(17) a. *The nurse sterilized the instruments.*
b. **The instruments sterilized.*
(Levin & Rappaport Hovav, 1995, 95)

Heidinger (2012) claims – based on Haspelmath (1993) – that only verbs referring to spontaneously occurring events can participate in the causative/inchoative alternation. Changes that cannot be considered to occur spontaneously – i.e. they can also occur without an external causation – can only be expressed by causative verbs. Rappaport Hovav & Levin (2012) claim that if a verb requires an agentive causer, it cannot participate in the causative/inchoative alternation. The exact analysis of the nature of the causative/inchoative alternation does not matter for a discussion of degree gradation of change of state verbs and therefore I will stay uncommitted about it. Relevant for causative/inchoative verbs is that both variants require the realization of the theme argument. Rappaport Hovav (2008) uses this as one of the defining criteria for scalar change verbs (see chapter 3.3 and next section). As was previously discussed, the explanation she provides is that the entity undergoing a scalar change has always to be realized overtly in a sentence. Crucially, the theme argument cannot be deleted by an argument alternating process. Intensionally used verbs deviate from the argument realization pattern observed above. As (18a) shows, the theme argument *Buch* 'book' is realized as the possessor of the scale-denoting noun *Preis* 'price.' Fleischhauer & Gamerschlag (2014, 41) write that "[t]aken literally, the change denoted by *steigen* is predicated of the referent of the subject *Preis* which therefore can also be characterized as a theme. However, the theme relevant to Rappaport Hovav's deletabil-

6 Change of state verbs

ity criterion is contributed by the possessor DP which refers to the participant whose property is measured on the scale." *Preis* does not refer to that participant. Rather, it introduces the scale on which the change is predicated. Hence, it can be considered as a scale-denoting noun and the contrast between (18b) and (c) shows, it is the theme argument but not the scale-denoting noun that can be deleted.

(18)   a.   *Der Preis des Buchs$_{Theme}$ ist gestiegen.*
              the price of.the book.GEN is risen
              'The price of the book has risen.'
     b.   *Der Preis ist gestiegen.*
              the price is risen
              'The price has risen.'
     c.   #*Das Buch ist gestiegen.*
              the book is risen
              (Fleischhauer & Gamerschlag, 2014, 38)

Following Löbner (1979, 1985, 2011a), scale-denoting nouns such as *Preis* 'price' or *Temperatur* 'temperature' are functional nouns. Functional nouns are relational, which means that they take one or more arguments and, due to functionality, provide a unique mapping between the referent of the noun and its argument(s). In the case of *Preis*, it takes the argument *Buch* 'book' in (18a) and assigns it a unique value on the price scale. This value is the referent of the noun *Preis*. Not all functional nouns are scalar: *mother*, for example, is a functional noun, too. In (19) it expresses a unique relation between *John* and a further individual, who is the mother of John. The 'mother of'-relation between John and his mother is unique but the value assigned is not a degree on a scale.

(19)   *the mother of John*

In the case of *Preis*, the noun assigns a price value to the object it takes as possessor argument. Fleischhauer & Gamerschlag analyze such scale-denoting nouns as measure functions; they are functions from individuals to degrees. A semantic representation for such scalar functional nouns is shown in (20). *Preis* is represented as the measure function PRICE that maps individuals onto price degrees. The index indicates the parameters (dimension, set of degrees and linear order) of the scale onto which the concept maps the individual. The *x* argument is saturated by the possessor argument of the functional noun.

(20) *Preis* 'price' $\lambda x \lambda t.\text{PRICE}_{\langle Price, PriceDeg.,<\rangle}(x, t)$
(Fleischhauer & Gamerschlag, 2014, 43)

The argument of a functional noun can be omitted if it is recoverable from context (18b). This explains why the theme argument of intensionally used verbs can be deleted. Intensionally used verbs also undergo the possessor-subject alternation (cf. Levin 1993, 77f., also Löbner 1979) as shown in (21) taken from Fleischhauer & Gamerschlag (2014, 41). In (21b) the possessor argument is realized as the subject of the sentence and the functional noun is realized within a PP.

(21) a. *Der Preis des Buchs ist gestiegen.*
the price of.the book.GEN is risen
'The price of the book has risen.'
b. *Das Buch ist im Preis gestiegen.*
the book is in.the price risen
'The book has risen in price.'

Change of state verbs like *wachsen* 'grow' differ in argument realization from intensionally used verbs (22). The theme argument cannot be realized as the possessor argument of a scale-denoting noun (a) and the possessor-subject alternation is not possible with such verbs (b). As (23) shows, this holds similarly for the extensional uses of verbs like *steigen*.

(22) a. **Die Größe des Kindes wächst.*
the size of.the child.GEN grows
b. **Das Kind wächst in der Größe.*
the child grows in the size
(Fleischhauer & Gamerschlag, 2014, 42)

(23) a. *Der Balloon steigt.*
the balloon rises
'The balloon is rising.'
b. **Die Höhe des Balloons steigt.*
the height of.the balloon.GEN rises

c. *Der Balloon steigt in der Höhe.
       the balloon rises in the height

A reason why *wachsen* rejects the realization of a scale-denoting noun is that the verb itself specifies a scale, which is not the case with intensionally used *steigen*. In the next section, I will discuss the lexicalization of scales in more detail and argue that verbs like intensional *steigen* are scalar even if the scale is determined by its subject argument.

6.3 Scalar changes and the lexicalization of scales

As mentioned above and discussed in detail in chapter 3, Rappaport Hovav & Levin (2010) classify change of state verbs as result verbs. Result verbs express scalar changes, which distinguishes them from manner verbs which express non-scalar changes. A central assumption made by Rappaport Hovav & Levin is that result verbs lexicalize a scale along which the respective change is measured. This claim can be formulated as in (24), which Fleischhauer & Gamerschlag (2014) call the 'strong version of the lexicalization of scales hypothesis.' The reason why it is called a 'strong version' is that it requires that the verb lexically specifies all scale parameters. The weaker version of this hypothesis will be presented below.

(24) Lexicalization of scales (strong version): If a change of state verb lexicalizes a scale, all scale parameters are specified in the lexical meaning of the verb.
      (Fleischhauer & Gamerschlag, 2014, 33)

There are clear cases for which the strong version of the lexicalization of scales hypothesis seems to be true. These are, for example, the German change of state verbs *verteuern* 'increase in price' and *wachsen* 'grow.' The scale parameters lexicalized by these verbs are shown in (25).

(25) a. *verteuern* 'increase in price' Δ: PRICE, D: price degrees, R: $<$[10]
      b. *wachsen* 'grow' Δ: SIZE, D: size degrees, R: $<$

---

[10] To repeat the abbreviations which are taken from Kennedy & McNally's (2005a) analysis of scales: 'Δ' is the measurement dimension, 'D' is the set of degrees and 'R' is the linear order of these degrees (cf. section 2.2).

6.3 Scalar changes and the lexicalization of scales

Taking *verteuern* as an example: the verb specifies the dimension (Δ) of change as PRICE. The dimension restricts the values to price values and there is a linear ordering relation for the values of that scale ($<$). The scale is inherited from the base adjective *teuer* 'expensive' from which the verb is derived. Since *wachsen* 'grow' is not derived from an adjective, it cannot be said that the lexicalization of all scale parameters is only due to the fact that these parameters are already specified by the base adjective.

Other verbs are more problematic for the strong lexicalization hypothesis. First, intensionally used verbs like *steigen* 'rise' provide a problem for the hypothesis since such verbs require a scale-denoting noun to specify the respective scale of change. As the examples in (26) show, the respective scale of change is dependent on the nominal argument and varies in all three sentences ('pressure' in (a), 'price' in (b) and 'temperature' in (c)). The verb is underspecified regarding the scale parameters and depends on the noun that specifies the scale of change.

(26)   a.   *Der Druck steigt.*
               the pressure rises
               'The pressure is rising.'
      b.   *Der Preis steigt.*
               the price rises
               'The price is rising.'
      c.   *Die Temperatur steigt.*
               the temperature rises
               'The temperature is rising.'

Second, there are verbs such as German *verfärben* 'change color' or *verformen* 'form into' which specify a dimension of change as well as possible values but do not impose a linear order on them. *Verfärben* expresses a change in the dimension COLOR and specifies that the respective values are color values. Although the color space is structured Gärdenfors (2000), colors are not linearly ordered and hence do not form a scale. Rather, *verfärben* expresses an undirected change through color space, which is compatible with a change from, for example, red to blue or blue to red. Rappaport Hovav & Levin report a similar case in the domain of motion verbs. They write with regard to the verbs cross and traverse: "Although they [*cross* and *traverse*] lexically specify motion along a path defined by a particular axis on the ground, the direction of motion along this path is not lexically specified and, hence, they do not impose an ordering on the points on the path. [...] the verb *cross* is equally applicable whether a traversal of the England Channel is from England to France or from France to England" (Rappaport Hovav & Levin, 2010, 30). The verbs *cross* and *traverse* are similar to *verfärben* in expressing an arbitrary and undirected change in a specified dimension. Rappaport Hovav & Levin conclude that *cross* and *traverse* are non-scalar change verbs. This raises the question as to whether *verfärben*, as well as intensionally used change of state verbs, qualify as scalar change verbs or not.

In chapter 3.3, different properties that are characteristic of scalar change verbs but not of manner verbs have been discussed. Based on Rappaport Hovav (2008) it has been shown that scalar change verbs are restricted to result-XPs that are compatible with the lexicalized scale. Also scalar change verbs do not allow omission of the theme argument. Piñón (2005) further mentions that only scalar change verbs can combine with *gradually* without requiring coercion. Non-scalar change verbs need to be coerced towards a scalar change reading to combine with *gradually*.[11] A case in point, discussed by Piñón, is *He gradually loves her*, which means that the referent of the subject argument gradually fell in love with someone. Also plural arguments, as in *He gradually rescued the children*, license the addition of *gradually*. In this case, a gradual affection of the plural referents is expressed (cf. Piñón 2005 for a deeper discussion of these examples). In (27), it is shown that the German adverb *graduell* 'gradually' can combine with a scalar change verb (*verteuern*) but not with non-scalar change verbs like *essen* 'eat' and *schreien* 'cry.'[12]

(27)   a.   *Das Apartment hat sich graduell verteuert.*
               the apartment has REFL gradually increase.in.price
               'The apartment has gradually increased in price.'
       b.   **Das Kind hat graduell gegessen.*
               the child has gradually eaten
       c.   **Das Kind hat graduell geschrien.*
               the child has gradually cried

---

[11]   Cf. Gawron (2009, 7) for a discussion of the combination of *gradually* with stative verbs.
[12]   German also has the adverb *allmählich*, meaning *gradually*, but this also has a temporal interpretation and is therefore not used in this test construction.

6.3 Scalar changes and the lexicalization of scales

As the following examples show, both *verfärben* and *steigen* show the same properties as scalar change verbs do. The examples in (28) show that *verfärben* and *steigen* are restricted with respect to admissible result-XPs. *Verfärben* only allows for color adjectives as result predicates, whereas in the case of *steigen* the result-XP has to be compatible with the scale denoted by the functional noun.

(28) a. Das Laub verfärbt sich rot/ #nass/ #alt/ #welk.
the leave change.color REFL red wet old limp
'The leaves change color to red/#wet/#old/#limp.'
b. Der Preis des Buchs steigt auf 10 Euro/ #neu/ #rot.
the price of.the book rises to 10 euro new red
'The price of the book is rising to 10 euros/#new/#red.'
(Fleischhauer & Gamerschlag, 2014, 37)

Deletion of the theme argument is not possible in the case of *verfärben*, as shown in (29). Intensionally used verbs differ with regard to argument realization and allow the deletion of the theme argument (cf. section 6.2).

(29) a. Der Regen$_{Causer}$ verfärbt die Hausfassade$_{Theme}$.
the rain changes.color the house.front
'The rain changes the color of the front of the house.'
b. *Der Regen$_{Causer}$ verfärbt (sich).
the rain changes.color REFL
c. Die Hausfassade$_{Theme}$ verfärbt sich.
the house.front changes.color REFL
'The color of the front of the house changes.'
(Fleischhauer & Gamerschlag, 2014, 38)

Fleischhauer & Gamerschlag (2014, 38) cite the examples in (30) to show that both *verfärben* and *steigen* can combine with *graduell*. Neither *verfärben* nor *steigen* requires coercion to combine with the adverb.

(30) a. [...] *eine Beschichtung [...], die sich bei Einwirkung eines Desinfektionsmittels auch graduell verfärbt [...].*[13]
'[...] a surface coating which gradually changes color if impacted by germicide [...].'

---

[13] http://www.patent-de.com/20010913/DE10065941A1.html (15.7.2012)

b. *Juncker sagte dazu am Rande des Treffens, der Euro-Kurs habe sich nicht "brutal" nach oben bewegt, er sei graduell gestiegen.*[14] 'On this point, Juncker said in the margins of the meeting that the Euro exchange rate has not moved "dramatically" upwards, it has risen only gradually.'

The data discussed above reveal that *verfärben* and *steigen* exhibit the properties of scalar change verbs. Hence, these verbs qualify as scalar and therefore lexicalize a scale. But this assumption is in conflict with the strong version of the lexicalization of scales hypothesis proposed in (24). Instead, the data warrant a weaker version of the lexicalization assumption, such as the one proposed in (31).

(31)   Lexicalization of scales (weak version): A change of state verb lexicalizes a scale, even if one or more of the scale parameters remain unspecified in the meaning of the verb.
(Fleischhauer & Gamerschlag, 2014, 34)

The weak version allows for an underspecification of scale parameters in the lexical semantics of the verb. Table 13 provides a typology of scalar underspecification of change of state verbs.

Verb(s)	Unspecified in the verb meaning	Specified in the verb meaning
verteuern 'increase in price', *wachsen* 'grow'	- - -	all scale parameters
verfärben 'change color', *verformen* 'form into'	order of values	dimension, values
steigen 'rise', *fallen* 'fall', *verändern* 'change'	all scale parameters	- - -

Table 13: Typology of scalar (under)specification (Fleischhauer & Gamerschlag, 2014, 39).

---

[14] http://m.faz.net/aktuell/wirtschaft/wirtschaftspolitik/wirtschaftspolitik-euro-laender-verpflichten-sich-zum-sparen-1435278.html (15.7.2012)

6.3 Scalar changes and the lexicalization of scales

Verbs such as *verteuern* and *wachsen* lexically specify all scale parameters, whereas *verfärben* and *verformen* only specify the dimension and values. The third type of verbs, which include verbs such as *steigen*, *fallen* 'fall' and *verändern* 'change,' leave all scale parameters underspecified.

There is a further property distinguishing *steigen* from *fallen* on the one hand and *verändern* on the other. The first two verbs lexically specify the direction of change, whereas *verändern* does not. As shown in (32) and (33), *steigen* is only compatible with an increase of values. In the case of (32), the temperature degree has to increase and cannot decrease. It is the opposite for *fallen* in (33), which is only compatible with a decrease in temperature.

(32) *Die Temperatur steigt.*
 the temperature rises
 'The temperature is rising.'
 → The temperature is increasing.
 ↛ The temperature is decreasing.

(33) *Die Temperatur fällt.*
 the temperature falls
 'The temperature is falling.'
 → The temperature is decreasing.
 ↛ The temperature is increasing.

Verändern on the other hand is compatible with an increase as well as a decrease of the temperature degree (34). The verb only indicates that there is some difference in temperature but leaves open whether it gets warmer or cooler.

(34) *Die Temperatur verändert sich.*
 the temperature changes REFL
 'The temperature is changing.'
 → The temperature is increasing.
 → The temperature is decreasing.

Considering direction of change as independent from the three scale parameters, which can be justified by the fact that (32) and (33) differ only with respect to the direction of change but not with respect to the scale, we get a fourth parameter which can be lexically specified by change of state verbs. This produces the revisited table in 14, which adds the direction of change as a further parameter lexically (under)specified in change of state verbs. Most change of state verbs seem to be fully specified with regard to all scale parameters and the set of verbs totally underspecified with regard to all scale parameters and the direction of change seems to be rather restricted. An open question is whether the typology in table 14 covers all types of scalar underspecification; so far, some possible types do not seem to be attested, such as verbs specifying all scale parameters but leaving the direction of change underspecified. Also, there do not seem to be any verbs which specify the dimension of change but not the set of values. This could be due to logical reasons as the set of values does not seem to be independent from the dimension of change. But the first type does not seem to be logically excluded, so it is an empirical question whether some language lexicalizes such verbs.

Verb(s)	Unspecified in the verb meaning	Specified in the verb meaning
verteuern 'increase in price', *wachsen* 'grow'	- - -	all scale parameters, direction of change
verfärben 'change color', *verformen* 'form into'	order of values	dimension, values, direction of change
steigen 'rise', *fallen* 'fall'	all scale parameters	direction of change
verändern 'change'	all scale parameters, direction of change	- - -

Table 14: Typology of scalar (under)specification (based on Fleischhauer & Gamerschlag 2014).

Fleischhauer & Gamerschlag discuss two strategies for the resolution of scalar underspecification. First, missing scale parameters can be introduced by a scale-denoting noun as is the case with intensionally used change of state verbs. Second, missing scale parameters can be supplied by context. In the following, I will merely concentrate on the first strategy,

6.3 Scalar changes and the lexicalization of scales

but for contextual issues in the resolution of scalar underspecification see Fleischhauer & Gamerschlag (2014). Starting with *verteuern*, the semantic representation of a totally specified change of state verb can be assumed to look like in (35). The representation makes use of the measure function PRICE, which returns a degree on a price scale for some argument x to a certain time. The time is given by the function BEGIN(e), which returns the first time point of the event denoted by the verb, respectively END(e) returns the last time point of the event. Basically, the verb expresses an inequality between the degree of x on the price scale at the initial moment of e and the degree of x on the price scale at the final moment of e. The bracketed index at the measure function represents the three lexically specified scale parameters.

(35) *verteuern* 'increase in price'
$\lambda x \lambda e.\text{PRICE}_{\langle Price, PriceDeg., < \rangle}(x, \text{BEGIN}(e)) < \text{PRICE}_{\langle Price, PriceDeg., < \rangle}(x, \text{END}(e))$

For intensionally used *steigen*, Fleischhauer & Gamerschlag (2014, 43) assume the semantic representation in (36). Like *verteuern*, the verb has two arguments but it differs in the nature of its arguments from the former one. Unlike *verteuern*, it does not take an individual but rather a measure function f as its argument. Semantically, *steigen* expresses that the degree delivered by the measure function is higher at the end of the event than it was at its beginning.

(36) *steigen* 'rise'
$\lambda f_{\langle \Delta, D, R \rangle} \lambda e.f(\text{BEGIN}(e)) < f(\text{END}(e))$

Since *steigen* selects for a measure function, it can only combine with scale-denoting nouns, such as *Preis* 'price.' Based on the discussion in the last section, the semantic representation for functional nouns looks like that in (37). Since the functional noun is relational, it introduces its possessor as an argument.

(37) *Preis* 'price' $\lambda x \lambda t.\text{PRICE}_{\langle Price, PriceDeg., < \rangle}(x, t)$
(Fleischhauer & Gamerschlag, 2014, 43)

By combining (36) and (37) via functional application we get the representation in (38) for *der Preis des Buchs steigt* 'the price of the book is rising.'[15] *Preis* saturates the f-argument of the measure function and thereby introduces its own possessor argument. The x argument is the possessor of *Preis* and is specified by the ι operator due to the definite article.

(38) *der Preis des Buchs steigt* 'the price of the book is rising'
$\lambda e.\text{PRICE}_{\langle Price, PriceDeg.,<\rangle}(\iota x[\text{book}(x)], \text{BEGIN}(e)) < \text{PRICE}_{\langle Price, PriceDeg.,<\rangle}(\iota x[\text{book}(x)], \text{END}(e))$

The representation of *fallen* and *verändern* would differ from *steigen* in (36) mainly in the type of inequality lexically specified, which would be '>' for *fallen* and '≠' for *verändern*. Additionally, it is not the case that verbs such as *verändern* always take a scalar noun as their argument but rather that non-scalar functional nouns are possible, too (for a more detailed discussion of this point cf. Fleischhauer & Gamerschlag 2014).

The semantic representations used above are merely intended to capture the compositional process of scale composition but do not include a principled account of telicity (see Gamerschlag et al. 2014 for a frame-based representation of scale composition). In the next section, I turn to scalar approaches that aim at analyzing (i) variable telicity, (ii) telicity of accomplishments as well as (iii) providing an explanation of the relationship between scalar properties of adjectives and telicity of deadjectival change of state verbs.

6.4 Scalar analysis of telicity

Change of state verbs do not behave uniformly with respect to telicity. First, there are strictly telic change of state verbs like *open*, *close* and *stabilize*. Second, there are atelic change of state verbs such as *grow* and lastly verbs displaying the behavior of both. Such verbs show variable telicity, as demonstrated in (39).

(39) a. *The soup cooled for an hour.*
      b. *The soup cooled in an hour.*
          (Hay et al., 1999, 127)

---

[15] For the sake of simplicity, the event argument will be left unsaturated although the verb is used in a finite form.

6.4 Scalar analysis of telicity

Since Dowty (1979), the semantics of change of state verbs, more specifically the change denoted by these verbs, has been represented by a BECOME operator. In several approaches, refinements of this analysis have been proposed that decompose this operator and more explicitly represented changes as a progression along a scale. One reason for doing so is that verbs such as *cool* are variable in telicity and do not simply mean BECOME(cool'), in the sense of 'something changes till it reaches the state of being cool.' Rather, in the atelic reading it simply means 'become cooler than before.'

Borik (2006) distinguishes between the 'end-point approach' and the 'homogeneity approach' of telicity. The end-point approach relates telicity to the reaching of a temporal or other end-point, whereas the homogeneity approach focuses on the referential properties of (a)telic predicates. One special type of 'end-point approaches' are scalar analyses of telicity, such as those by Hay et al. (1999); Caudal & Nicolas (2005); Beavers (2006, 2008); Kearns (2007); Kennedy & Levin (2008); Piñón (2008), and others. In such degree-based analyses, the telos is equated with an endpoint on a scale. I will not provide a review of these approaches; rather, I restrict myself to a discussion of the influential work by Hay et al. (1999) and the proposal by Caudal & Nicolas (2005).[16] The aim is to introduce a degree-based analysis of telicity and to make the interaction between telicity and verbal degree gradation explicit. A revised degree-based analysis of telicity will be presented in section 6.6.

Telicity of change of state verbs is not dependent on the referential properties of the theme argument. Hay et al. state that telicity of degree achievements (strictly atelic ones as well as those showing variable telicity) depends on the fact whether the change on the scale is bounded or not. Since most degree achievements in English are deadjectival, as Hay et al. (1999, 130) state, the semantic core of these verbs is a gradable adjective. Kennedy's (1999a; 1999b) analysis of gradable adjectives is the basis for Hay et al.'s account of deadjectival verbs. They assume that the verb-forming morphology (either a zero form or *-en* in English) takes a gradable adjective as argument and returns a description of a change of state event. It is essen-

---

[16] For a review and comparison of different degree-based approaches see Piñón (2008) and Kriz (2011). See Fleischhauer (2013) for a comparison of 'end-point' and 'homogeneous approaches' with respect to degree gradation of change of state verbs.

6 Change of state verbs

tially the function INCREASE that is contributed by the verb-forming morphology. The truth conditions for this function are shown in (40), where φ is a gradable adjective meaning and SPO(e) and EPO(e) are functions that return the beginning, respectively end point of the event.

(40) $[\![\text{INCREASE}(\varphi)(x)(d)(e)]\!] = 1$ iff $\varphi(x)(\text{SPO}(e)) + d = \varphi(x)(\text{EPO}(e))$
(Hay et al., 1999, 132)

(40) states that INCREASE(φ)(x)(d)(e) is true, if the degree d of x in the property expressed by φ at the end of the event equals the degree of x at the beginning of the event plus some degree d.[17] Hence, d represents a difference value that specifies the increase of x with regard to φ.

The sentences in (41) are now given the representations in ScaleTelicity4. Causality is ignored in the representation as it does not influence telicity. The degree argument is existentially bound in ScaleTelicity4 and Hay et al. do not propose a verbal positive morpheme in difference to later work by, for example, Kennedy & Levin (2008).

(41) a. *Kim lengthened the rope.*
      b. *Kim lengthened the rope 5 inches.*
      (Hay et al., 1999, 130)

(42) a. $\exists e, d[\text{INCREASE}(\text{long}(\text{rope}))(d)(e)]$
      b. $\exists e[\text{INCREASE}(\text{long})(\text{rope})(5 \text{ inches})(e)]$
      (Hay et al., 1999, 132)

What (a) states is that the length of the rope increases by some amount, whereas in (b) the increase is explicitly bound by the measure phrase *5 inches*. If the difference value, the variable d, is bounded, a telic predication arises. If it is unbounded, the resulting predication is atelic. This is validated by the examples in (43). The entailment from the progressive to the perfect only holds in (a) but not in (b).

(43) a. *Kim is lengthening the rope.* → *Kim has lengthened the rope.*
      (Hay et al., 1999, 127)
      b. *Kim is lengthening the rope 5 inches.* ↛ *Kim lengthened the*

---

[17] For degree addition see von Stechow (1984); Rullmann (1995), Hay et al. (1999, 131) among others.

6.4 Scalar analysis of telicity

rope 5 inches. (Hay et al., 1999, 130)

The difference value can be bounded in different ways. One way, which is exemplified above, is by using a measure phrase. Another way is by using degree modifiers such as *slightly* or *significantly*. Example (44), taken from Hay et al. (1999, 134), shows the combination of a degree achievement with the intensifier *significantly*. As (b) indicates, the graded predication is telic.

(44)   a.   The independent counsel broadened the investigation significantly.
            b.   The IC is broadening the investigation significantly. ↛ The IC has broadened the investigation significantly.

A degree expression like *significantly* introduces a standard (minimum) value up to which the change has to progress. Based on such data, Hay et al. refine their explication of the notion of a 'bounded change': "a telic reading of a DA [degree achievement] requires that the difference value specify a lower bound on the degree to which an object must increase in the relevant property over the course of the event. Once this minimal point is reached, the truth conditions for the event description are met" (Hay et al., 1999, 134).

But how does a telic interpretation arise, if there is no measure phrase or degree expression that provides a bound on the difference value? Scale structure is crucial in determining telicity. Degree achievements derived from closed-scale adjectives are by default telic since the scalar endpoint provides a bound on the difference value and the change can progress until the endpoint is reached. If a degree achievement is derived from an open-scale adjective, it typically behaves atelically (Hay et al., 1999, 136). The reason is that if there is no endpoint, there is no lexical basis for inducing a bound on the difference value.

Hay et al. and also subsequent work by Kennedy & Levin (2008) restrict their analysis to degree achievements, basically deadjectival ones. Caudal & Nicolas (2005) propose a general degree-based analysis of telicity that is not restricted to degree achievements. Their definition of telicity is given in (45). The 'axiom BECOME,' which is mentioned in (c), defines a homomorphic mapping between a scale and an event such that each part of the event is mapped to a unique degree and vice versa. The temporal order of the event is matched by the order of the degrees (for details cf. Caudal & Nicolas 2005, 286, 293). The function of BECOME is to measure the progression of an event on a scale and to provide a strict mapping between the set of degrees and the event (the mapping between scales and events will be discussed in more detail in chapter 9).

(45) Telicity: A predication is telic if and only if,
(a) it has an associated set of degrees,
(b) a specified maximal degree, and
(c) its verbal predicate satisfies the axiom BECOME.
(Caudal & Nicolas, 2005, 294)

Following Caudal & Nicolas, a predication is telic if it expresses a change along a scale that has a maximal degree, i.e., forms a closed scale. Since there is a strict mapping between degrees and parts of an event, the event has to terminate if the maximal scale value is reached. They write: "the set terminal point of an event described by a telic predication is reached when the specified maximal degree is reached too; then the event cannot develop any further" (Caudal & Nicolas, 2005, 295). Caudal (2005) further states that atelic predications are related to open scales since there is no set terminal point which has to be reached.[18] Since Caudal & Nicholas equate the telos with a maximal scale value, they cannot provide an explanation for cases like (44). In this example, the telos cannot be equated with a maximal scale value and therefore a sentence like *The independent counsel broadened the investigation significantly* should result in an atelic predication.

The discussion of scalar approaches to telicity showed that intensifiers have an effect on the telicity of degree achievements. Change of state verbs that have an atelic interpretation have a telic reading if combined with intensifiers such as *significantly*. Hay et al. mention that such an effect only shows up with monotone-increasing intensifiers, whereas monotone-decreasing ones such as *slightly* do not make an atelic change of state predication telic (46).

(46) a. *The independent counsel broadened the investigation slightly.*
(Hay et al., 1999, 134)
b. *The independent counsel is broadening the investigation slightly.* → *The independent counsel has broadened the investigation slightly.*
(Hay et al., 1999, 135)

---

[18] For a critical examination of Caudal & Nicholas' approach see Piñón (2008).

6 Change of state verbs

Since monotone-increasing intensifiers affect telicity by bounding the difference value and introducing a lower bound that has to be reached, it is expected that *sehr* also has an effect on the telicity of degree achievements. I turn to this topic in the next section. In the degree-based analyses of telicity, discussed above, the telos of accomplishment predicates is equated with the maximum scale value. Therefore, such analyses give rise to the prediction that accomplishments should not be gradable by *sehr*. To explicate this prediction, the properties of accomplishments have to be taken into account:

(47)   Properties of accomplishments
(i) A telic change of state predication is true, if the telos is reached.
(ii) The telos is the maximal value on a scale.

Now we must take the properties of sehr into account (ii), which were discussed in chapter 5.3.

(48)   Properties of *sehr*
(iii) *Sehr* is factive, it entails the truth of the embedded predication.
(iv) *Sehr* can only apply to predicates which truthfully denote at least two non-zero degrees.

Since the telos is taken to be the maximal scale value, it should be the case that accomplishments do not license *sehr*. The reason is that on the one hand *sehr* presupposes the truth of the predicate it applies to (in the case of accomplishments the reaching of the maximal scale value) and on the other hand *sehr* requires that the predicate it applies to truthfully denotes at least two degrees and not just a single one. As the telos is equated with the maximum degree, this should lead to ungradability of accomplishments by *sehr*. In the next section, I will turn to a detailed discussion of degree gradation of change of state verbs which will show that the view on telicity sketched above is too restrictive and needs revision.

6.5 Degree gradation of change of state verbs

In this section, I will focus on degree gradation of change of state verbs. Degree achievements and accomplishments will be discussed separately since a degree-based account of telicity, which equates the telos with the maximal scale value, predicts that accomplishments should reject gradation by *sehr*. The following section is based on my discussion of degree gradation of change of state verbs in Fleischhauer (2013).

6.5.1 Degree gradation of degree achievements

Degree achievements, i.e. atelic uses of change of state verbs, are perfectly gradable by *sehr*.[19] The sentences in (49) to (51) are naturally occurring examples. Please note, that the English translations make either use of different verbs – *expand* in (49) instead of *widen* – and/or use different intensifiers. It is *a lot* in (50) and (51) but *greatly* in (49).

(49) *Das Angebot der   Pflege hat sich in den letzten Jahrzehnten in*
 the offer   of.the care has REFL in the last   decades   in
 Folge der   immer weiter zerfallenden Kleinfamilien   sehr
 course of.the ever   further decaying   nuclear families very
 verbreitert.
 widened
 'The range of care has expanded greatly over the last few decades as a consequence of the decay of the nuclear family.'[G]

(50) *Erst als   ich die Vorlage   sehr vergrößert hatte, konnte er den*
 first when I   the template very enlarged   had   could he the
 Text lesen.
 text read
 'It was not until I had enlarged the template a lot that he was able to read the text.'[G]

---

[19] Kriz (2011, 36f.) mentions that degree achievements allow for the same degree modifiers as adjectival comparatives and are only marginally acceptable with intensifiers of the positive form. But as shown in the examples, degree achievements do combine with *sehr* which does not apply to adjectival comparatives (see the discussion in chapter 2).

6 Change of state verbs

(51) Zu den Chancen einer kirchlichen Wiedervereinigung sagte
      to the chances a   churchly   reunification   said
      Lehman: "Sie sind natürlich sehr gewachsen, wie noch nie in
      Lehmann they are naturally very grown   like still never in
      der Geschichte vorher."
      the history   before
      'Speaking of the likelihood of a reunification of the churches, Lehmann said: "Of course, it has increased a lot, like never before".'[G]

In all three examples, the verbs are used in the perfect having a perfective interpretation and therefore expressing a completed situation.[20] The effect of *sehr* is to specify the amount of change. Taking (50) as an example, the sentence without *sehr* (52) has the interpretation that the speaker merely had to make the template larger. Clearly, not any increase in size would be sufficient for a true predication. The template needs to be enlarged enough to become readable for the speaker, which indicates the context-dependency of the difference value for degree achievements. But even if the difference degree is context-dependent, it is not specified and therefore the predication is atelic. By adding *sehr*, it is specified that the speaker increased the size of the template by a contextually large amount.

(52) Erst als   ich die Vorlage   vergrößert hatte, konnte er den Text
      first when I   the template enlarged   had   could he the text
      lesen.
      read
      'It was not until I had enlarged the template that he was able to read the text.'

As the contrast between (49), (51) and (50) shows, causativity does not affect degree gradation. In (50) we have a causative verb, whereas the verb in (51) does not have a causative variant and the one in (49) is a derived inchoative verb. In each case, it is the amount of change that is specified by

---

[20] Note that *wachsen* 'grow' takes *sein* 'be' as a perfect auxiliary, whereas *sich verbreitern* 'widen' takes *haben* 'have', which is due to the presence of the reflexive in the latter case. Syntactically, reflexive verbs behave like transitive verbs and therefore build the perfect with *haben* as transitive verbs do.

6.5 Degree gradation of change of state verbs

sehr. In (53a) the paraphrase of an ungraded but causative degree achievement is given. The paraphrase of a graded causative degree achievement is added in (b). As shown in (53b), the paraphrase indicates that gradation of degree achievements is very close to gradation of adjectival comparatives. This is also indicated by the choice of the intensifier in the paraphrase, which is *viel* in German and *much* in English. In (54), the paraphrases are applied to a concrete example, namely the causative use of *vergrößern* discussed in (50) and (52).

(53) a. ungraded (causative) DA: 'ADJ-COMP *machen*'
'make ADJ-COMP'
b. graded (causative) DA: '*viel* ADJ-COMP *machen*'
'make much ADJ-COMP'

(54) a. *vergrößern*: 'größer machen'
'enlarge' 'make larger'
b. *sehr vergrößern*: 'viel größer machen'
'enlarge a lot' 'make much larger'

The semantic representation of a degree achievement has already been introduced in section 6.3 and is repeated in (55) for the verb *vergrößern* 'enlarge.'

(55) 〚vergrößern〛 = $\lambda x \lambda e.\text{SIZE}_{\langle \Delta, D, R_< \rangle}(x, \text{BEGIN}(e)) < \text{SIZE}_{\langle \Delta, D, R_< \rangle}(x, \text{END}(e))$

Sehr, as discussed above, specifies the difference between the initial and the final degree but there is no explicit representation of this difference in (55). Therefore, I propose the equivalent representation in (56) which uses the DIFF function. DIFF returns the difference between the final degree on the price scale and the initial degree on that scale. The predication is true if the degree returned by the function is taller than zero.

(56) 〚vergrößern〛 = $\lambda x \lambda e.\text{DIFF}(\text{SIZE}_{\langle \Delta, D, R_< \rangle}(x, \text{END}(e)), \text{SIZE}_{\langle \Delta, D, R_< \rangle}(x, \text{BEGIN}(e))) > 0$

The effect of *sehr* is now to further specify the difference between those degrees as represented in (57). As for the positive form of adjectives, *sehr* introduces a standard of comparison 's' which is calculated based on the

6 Change of state verbs

positive – or in this case ungraded – predicate. *Sehr vergrößern* is true if the differential degree exceeds the standard based on the predicate *vergrößern*.

(57) $[\![\text{vergrößern}]\!] = \lambda x \lambda e.\text{DIFF}(\text{SIZE}_{\langle \Delta,D,R<\rangle}(x, \text{END}(e)),$
$\text{SIZE}_{\langle \Delta,D,R<\rangle}(x, \text{BEGIN}(e))) \geq s(\text{DIFF}(\text{SIZE}_{\langle \Delta,D,R<\rangle}(x, \text{END}(e)),$
$\text{SIZE}_{\langle \Delta,D,R<\rangle}(x, \text{BEGIN}(e)))$

Similar examples to those discussed above can be found in Russian and French. Examples of graded degree achievements from Russian are shown in (58). *Očen'* indicates the degree of change in these examples as *sehr* does in German. The verbs in (58) are perfective, and I will turn later to a comparison with imperfective change of state verbs.

(58)   a.   *Očen' vy-rosli zolotye zapas-y.*
           very VY-grew gold reserve-PL.NOM
           'The gold reserves grew a lot.'^{R}
    b.   *Pribor očen' na-grel-sja.*
           device.NOM very NA-heated-REFL
           'The device heated up a lot.'^{R}

French examples of graded degree achievements are shown in (59) to (61). *Beaucoup* indicates the degree of change in these examples; an extent reading of *beaucoup* is not possible in these cases.

(59)   *J'ai beaucoup grandi.*
       I=have a lot grown
       'I have grown a lot.'

(60)   *Si mon état s'est beaucoup amélioré depuis quelques*
       if my condition REFL=is a lot improved since several
       mois [...].
       months [...]
       'If my condition has greatly improved over the last few months [...].' (Fleischhauer, 2013, 147)

(61) […] *cette perfide   instabilité diminua   beaucoup la*
      […] this perfidious instability diminished a lot   the
      confiance et   l'amitié   que m'inspirait   la nature.
      confidence and the=friendship that REFL=inspired the nature
      '[…] this perfidious instability has greatly diminished the confidence and friendship that nature inspired in me.'
      (Fleischhauer, 2013, 147f.)

The verbs in the examples discussed above lexically specify the scale but the verbs in (62) and (63) are underspecified with regard to the scale of change. In these cases, *sehr* specifies the amount of change, too. The sentence in (62) expresses that the price of oil has not only risen by some amount but to a contextually large amount. The change is measured on a price scale which is specified by the functional noun *Preis* 'price.' (63) also has the reading that there is a contextually 'large' difference between the initial and the final degree but *Aussehen* 'appearance' is not a scale-denoting noun and therefore does not induce a scale. Rather, *sehr* applies merely to an unspecified difference scale, which measures the difference between two states.

(62)   *Der Preis des Öls ist sehr gestiegen.*
       the price of.the oil.GEN is very risen
       'The price of oil has risen a lot.'

(63)   *Sein Aussehen hat sich sehr verändert.*
       his appearance has REFL very changed
       'His appearance changed a lot.'

Verbs like *steigen* and *fallen* have extensional as well as intensional uses. In their intensional use, they denote a change of state and the respective scale is contributed by a functional noun. In their extensional use, these verbs denote a change of location. *Steigen* expresses an upward movement, whereas *fallen* denotes a downward movement. Following Fleischhauer & Gamerschlag (2014), I assume that extensional *steigen* expresses an increase with respect to the vertical location of an object, which means that the scale is lexically specified by the verb and measures the height of an object. The scale does not measure a property of the object as such but a path along which the object moves. Both, the intensional (62) as well as the

6 Change of state verbs

extensional use (64) can be graded by *sehr*. (64) has the interpretation that the height at which the object is located increased by a large amount.

(64)   Der Ballon   ist sehr gestiegen.
       the balloon is very risen
       'The balloon rose a lot.'

In constructions such as *die Treppen steigen* 'climb the stairs,' extensional *steigen* rejects gradation by *sehr* (65). *Die Treppen steigen* expresses an upstairs movement, combining direction and manner (see Gamerschlag et al. 2014 for a more detailed discussion of the differences between the extensional, the intensional as well as the manner use of *steigen* and a frame-based analysis of these uses). Gradation may be rejected since stairs have a natural end, whereas *steigen* in sentences as (64) expresses an upward movement without a linguistically specified endpoint.

(65)   *Ich bin die Treppen sehr gestiegen.
       I   am the stairs   very risen

In its extensional use *fallen* expresses a downward movement of the referent of the theme argument. The ground provides a natural endpoint for extensional *fallen* and *sehr* cannot be used to specify the change of the position of the theme argument. Nevertheless, as (66) shows, *fallen* can be graded by *sehr*; the sentence has the interpretation that the boy fell hard and not that the height at which the boy is located decreased by a large amount. *Sehr* specifies the effect of *fallen* on the boy, indicating that he hurt himself badly. Such a gradation construction is only possible with animate subjects and not with inanimate ones such as *Der Ball ist sehr gefallen* 'The ball fell very hard.'

(66)   Der Junge ist sehr gefallen.
       the boy is very fallen
       'The boy fell hard.'

For downward movement, there is a different verb *sinken* 'sink, fall' which can be used for an extensional description of a decrease of height (67). The example shows that the verb can be graded in its extensional use, indicating that a large decrease in height occurred. The difference between *sinken* and extensional *fallen* is that only the latter expresses a motion to the ground and therefore only *fallen* comes with a natural endpoint. In (64) and (67), the respective scale is a path rather than a property scale.

(67) Der Ballon ist sehr gesunken.
 the ballon is very sunk
 'The balloon fell a lot.'

Before I turn to accomplishments, the question whether grammatical aspect affects degree gradation needs to be discussed. In (68), the verb *wachsen* is used in a perfect (a) and a progressive construction (b). In (a), it is expressed that the size of the child increased by a contextually large amount. What is specified is the total amount of change accomplished in the event. This is different for (b) as the event is described as ongoing with respect to the reference time. The progressive aspect picks out one of the subevents of the whole event denoted by *wachsen* and specifies the degree of change at this subevent. We get the interpretation that at a certain part of the event, the size of the child increased a lot. This does not entail that in the total event the size increased a lot. The reverse does not hold either: if the size increased a lot over the entire course of the event, it does not entail that there was a large increase during any specific one of its subevents.

(68) a. Das Kind ist sehr gewachsen.
  the child is very grown
  'The child has grown a lot.'
 b. Das Kind ist sehr am Wachsen.
  the child is very at.the growing
  'The child is growing a lot.'

The effect of *sehr* is the same in the progressive as well as the perfectively interpreted perfect construction, namely specifying the degree of change. It is grammatical aspect that leads to the differences in the interpretation between (68a) and (b). Following Filip (1999, 172), we can assume a semantic representation for the progressive operator as shown in (69). The progressive restricts the predicate to a subevent. Since a subevent also has a beginning and an ending, we can specify the degree of change between these two moments. And this is what we find in a case like (68b).

6 Change of state verbs

(69) PROGRESSIVE $= \lambda P \lambda e' \exists e [P(e) \wedge e' \leq e]$ (Filip, 1999, 172)

This analysis fits the view that grammatical aspect has scope over degree gradation. First, *sehr* applies to the degree achievement and specifies the degree of change, then grammatical aspect is applied to the verb and either restricts the predication to a subevent – in the case of the progressive aspect – or to the total event if the verb is interpreted perfectively.

For Russian, we see the same difference as observed in German. In (70a), we have the perfective verb *vyrasti* 'grow' and in (b) the corresponding secondary imperfective *vyrastat'*. Like in (68), we see a difference between the indication of the total amount of change in (70a) and the specification of the degree of change at an instance of the event (b).

(70) a. *Rebënok očen' vyros.*
child.NOM very grew
'The child has grown a lot.'
b. *Rebënok očen' vyrastal.*
child.NOM very grew
'The child was growing a lot.'

6.5.2 Degree gradation of accomplishments

In section 6.4, it was stated that accomplishments should not be gradable since the requirement of reaching the telos leads to an incompatibility with intensifiers like *sehr*. But contrary to this expectation, telic change of state verbs can be graded by *sehr* (71). As was the case for degree achievements, English does not make use of one and the same intensifier with all these verbs. Rather it uses *a lot* in (a) but *very much* in the other two examples (b/c). The examples in (71) are collected from Sebastian Löbner's database. However, speakers do not usually reject gradation of accomplishments in general but only single examples.

(71) a. *In der Sonne trocknen Nacktschnecken sehr aus.*
in the sun dry slugs very out
'Slugs dry out a lot in the sun.'^{G}
b. *Die Verhältnisse haben sich wieder sehr normalisiert.*
the circumstances have REFL again very normalized
'The circumstances have very much normalized again.'^{G}

214

6.5 Degree gradation of change of state verbs

    c.   *Man könnte die beiden Gruppen noch sehr vereinheitlichen.*
           one could the both groups still very standardize
           'One could still standardize both groups very much.'^{G}

Before we consider the interpretation of degree gradation in cases like those in (71) in detail, it has to be shown that the ungraded verbs are telic. Taking the verb *normalisieren* 'normalize' as an example, (72) shows an ambiguity with the adverb *fast* 'almost.' The adverb either indicates that the event has almost started or that it has almost finished, as it is typical for telic predications.

(72)   *Die Verhältnisse   haben sich fast   normalisiert.*
        the circumstances have   REFL almost normalized
        'The circumstances have almost normalized.'

The sentence in (72) merely indicates that the ungraded verb is telic but does not allow inferring whether the graded verbs are telic too. It could be the case that the presence of the intensifier requires a coercion of a telic to an atelic predication. The time-span adverbial *in kurzer Zeit* 'within a short time' in (73) specifies the time it took to reach the telos in this case the state of being very stable. This shows that the graded sentence in (73) is telic like the ungraded verb in (74), too.

    If one assumes that telic predicates are related to closed scales, then two different strategies to explain the data are possible. First, one could assume that the application of *sehr* requires a shift from a closed scale to an open scale predication, which would also entail a shift from a telic to an atelic predication. By application of *sehr*, the shifted atelic predicate would again be shifted to a telic predicate since the graded predicate is telic. This argumentation is in accordance with the assumption that *sehr* can only apply to open scale predicates but it requires two steps of coercion. A second option would be to simply assume that *sehr* can also apply to closed scale predicates. This would not require coercion and therefore is the more parsimonious assumption. But this second option is not compatible with the view that the telos is a maximal scale value. In section 6.6, I will argue for the second option and present an analysis of telicity that does not require a telos to be (always) a maximal scale value.

6 Change of state verbs

(73) *Ich kam sehr instabil auf die Station* [...] *Dennoch wurde ich in*
I came very instable on the ward however become I in
kurzer Zeit sehr stabilisiert.
short time very stabilized
'In was in a very unstable condition when I arrived on the ward [...] but my condition stabilized a lot within a short time.'[21]

(74) *Der Zustand des Patienten hat sich in kurzer Zeit stabilisiert.*
the condition of.the patient has REFL in short time stabilized
'The condition of the patient stabilized within a short time.'

Degree gradation of accomplishment predicates leads to a specification of the result state. In sentences like those in (71) and (73) the intensifier indicates the degree of the result state, so if something *stabilisiert sich sehr* 'stabilizes a lot,' as in (73), it becomes 'very stable,' meaning stable to a high degree. Whereas the ungraded sentence (74) merely expresses that the referent of the theme argument becomes stable but not necessarily to a high degree since any degree of stability is sufficient.

A paraphrase for ungraded and non-causative accomplishments is given in (75a). Contrary to degree achievements it is not a comparative but an absolute result state that is achieved which, in German and English, at least in some cases, is denoted by an adjective. The paraphrase for graded accomplishments is given in (75b).

(75) a. ungraded accomplishment: 'ADJ$_{POS}$ werden'
'Become ADJ$_{POS}$'
b. graded accomplishment: 'sehr ADJ$_{POS}$ werden'
'Become very ADJ$_{POS}$'

As can be seen, degree gradation of accomplishments differs from degree gradation of degree achievements. In the case of degree achievements, *sehr* indicates the amount of change, i.e., the difference between the initial and the final degree. In the case of accomplishments, *sehr* does not bind a difference value, but provides a further specification of the resulting state. Since accomplishments are telic, there is already some degree up to which the change has (at least) to progress – the telos. Gradation by *sehr* indicates

---

[21] http://www.klinikbewertungen.de/klinik-forum/erfahrung-mit-krankenhaus-erlangen?bew_order=1&fac_id=psysom

6.5 Degree gradation of change of state verbs

that the change did not stop at the telos but progresses further till a 'high' degree of the resulting state has been achieved.

Based on the semantic representation of degree achievements, I propose the representation in (76) for accomplishments. For these predicates, a conjunct is added that represents the result state. The degree for the result state is equated with the telos, represented by 'd_{telos}'. The telos is lexically indicated and therefore specified by the verb, but as I will show later, the telos is not always the maximal scale value. In the case of degree gradation, the intensifier further specifies the degree of the result state, as shown in (77) for *sich sehr stabilisieren* 'stabilize a lot.'

(76) $\lambda\varphi\lambda x\lambda e.\varphi(x, \text{BEGIN}(e)) < \varphi(x, \text{END}(e)) \wedge \varphi(x, \text{END}(e)) \geq d_{Telos}$

(77)   ⟦sehr stabilisieren⟧ = $\lambda x\lambda e.\text{STABILITY}(x, \text{BEGIN}(e)) < \text{STABILITY}(x, \text{END}(e)) \wedge \text{STABILITY}(x, \text{END}(e)) = \text{high}$

Why does *sehr* take the second but not the first conjunct of the formula as its argument? The answer is that in the case of accomplishment predicates the degree of change is always specific as it is the difference between the initial degree and the telos. A double specification of the difference degree is not possible and therefore *sehr* cannot specify the amount of change directly. Rather, it modifies the result state and thereby indirectly indicates the amount of change. This coincides with the fact that degree gradation by *sehr* is not possible if the difference degree is explicitly bound by a measure phrase as in (78).

(78)   a.   Das Kind ist zehn Zentimeter gewachsen.
             the child is ten centimeters grown
             'The child has grown ten centimeters.'
         b.   *Das Kind ist zehn Zentimeter sehr gewachsen.
             the child is ten centimeters very grown

We also find graded accomplishments in Russian and also French: in (79) to (81) Russian examples are shown; French examples are listed in (82) and (83). The interpretation of these examples is the same as for the German cases, the intensifiers specify the degree of the resulting state.

(79) Esli očen' standartizirovat' i poctavit' na potok
when very standardize and put PREP stream.ACC
vozmočno, eta cifra snizitcja do 150-200
possible DEM.NOM number.NOM reduces PREP 150-200
tycjač.
thousand.GEN
'If you standardize it very much and put it on the assembly line,
the number could possibly decrease to 150-200 thousand.'[R]

(80) Sejčas my provodim konsul'tacii s tem, čto
now 3PL.NOM conduct consultations.ACC with DEM.INST what
vce-taki očen' unificirovat' tarify konsul'skix sborov
ultimately very unify rate.ACC consular.GEN tax.GEN.PL
'At the moment we are negotiating with the aim of standardizing
the consultant fares very much'[R]

(81) 1-oe, čto nužno sdelat' očen' stabilizirovat' sostojanie
first what need make very stabilize condition.ACC
bol'nogo [...].
ill.GEN
'The first thing that needs to be done is to stabilize the condition
of the injured a lot [...].'[R]

(82) [...] et le lexique c'est beaucoup standardisé en
[...] and the lexicon DEM=is a lot standardized by
s'alignant sur le haut-allemand de l'école et des
REFL=adapting to the high-German PREP the=school and PREP
medias.
media
'[...] and the lexicon has been mostly standardized by being adapted
to High German in school and in media.'
(Fleischhauer, 2013, 148)

(83) Le parti socialiste a   beaucoup homogénéisé sa   doctrine
      the party socialist has a lot   homogenized POSS doctrine
      lors de   l'adoption   de la déclaration de principe cet
      while PREP the=adoption of the declaration of principle this
      été.
      summer
      'The socialist party has greatly unified by adopting the principle declaration this summer.'[22]

The Russian verbs in (79) to (81) are biaspectual, they allow either for a perfective or an imperfective reading. In German, accomplishments can be used in the progressive (84a) but this construction sounds somewhat odd if combined with an intensifier. Most German native speakers I consulted rejected sentences like (84b). Degree gradation of telic predicates is dispreferred if the predicate is used in an explicit progressive construction. The reason is that the result state is canceled by the progressive aspect and therefore the target of *sehr* is not accessible.

(84) a. *Sein Zustand ist sich am   Stabilisieren.*
         his condition is REFL at.the stabilizing
         'His condition is stabilizing.'
      b. ??*Sein Zustand ist sich sehr am   Stabilisieren.*
         his condition is REFL very at.the stabilizing

6.6 Degree gradation and telicity

In the last section, I discussed degree gradation of degree achievements as well as accomplishments. I showed that both types of change of state verbs can be graded, which, for accomplishments at least, is unexpected. In this section, I will turn to a discussion of the interaction of telicity and degree gradation in change of state verbs. Two different questions arise: first, does degree gradation of degree achievements interact with telicity? And second, how can it be that (some) accomplishments admit degree gradation?

Starting with degree achievements, Hay et al. (1999) argue that monotone-increasing intensifiers affect their telicity. This effect is found

---

[22] http://www.france24.com/fr/20081125-je-pense-pas-quune-scission-ps-soit-possible-parti-socialiste?quicktabs_1=0; 21.08.2013

with *sehr*, too (85). *Wachsen* 'grow' is strictly atelic, but gets a telic reading if graded by *sehr*. *A lot* has the same effect on *grow*, as the English translation of the example shows.

(85)   a.   #*Das Kind ist in   einem Jahr gewachsen.*
              the child is grown in   one year
              'The child has grown in one year.'
       b.   *Das Kind ist in einem Jahr sehr gewachsen.*
              the child is in one   year very grown
              'The child has grown a lot in one year.'

The same holds for Russian, as the examples in (86) show. The verb *vyrastat'* 'grow' is atelic and as (b) shows, the intensifier licenses a telic interpretation of the predication.

(86)   a.   #*Rebënok   vyrastal za odin god.*
              child.NOM grew   in one year
              'The child has grown in one year.'
       b.   *Rebënok   očen' vyrastal za odin god.*
              child.NOM very grew   in one year
              'The child has grown a lot in one year.'

Caudal & Nicolas (2005) discuss similar examples and argue that verbs like *run* have an implicit quantity argument that can be bound by *a lot*. Sentence (87a) is atelic, whereas (b) is telic and *a lot* specifies the distance of the running.[23] The only difference is the intensifier *a lot* in (b). The authors write: "*A lot* apparently requires an open scale as its input, and yields a closed one as its output (cf. the telic predication *Yannig ran a lot in (*for) two hours*)" (Caudal & Nicolas, 2005, 284).

(87)   a.   *Yannig ran (for a long time).*
       b.   *Yannig ran a lot.*
            (Caudal & Nicolas, 2005, 284)

A crucial assumption of Caudal & Nicolas seems to be that if a graded predication is telic, the intensifier closes the scale. They write, with regard to a

---

[23] There is also a frequency interpretation of the sentence, which is irrelevant for the current discussion.

6.6 Degree gradation and telicity

similar example to the one in (87b), "the addition of *a lot* renders the scale closed" (Caudal & Nicolas, 2005, 288). This is based on the assumption that telic predications are always related to closed scales. However, all we can see is that the predication is telic but not that the scale is closed. The usual tests that are used to determine whether a scale is open or closed cannot be applied to (87b) but it is possible to say *Yannig already ran a lot and he is still running* which indicates that it is possible to further increase the distance Yannig ran.[24] Departing from Caudal & Nicolas and in accordance with Hay et al. (1999), I assume that a predication can be telic, even if the scale is not closed. *Sehr* but also *a lot* do not specify a fixed degree on a scale; rather they introduce a lower bound which has to be attained. Hence, the presence of a closed scale is a sufficient but not a necessary criterion for telicity.

I will now turn to the second question, namely why (at least some) accomplishments allow degree gradation. Caudal & Nicolas' definition of telicity, discussed in section 6.4, and similar accounts, predict that accomplishments are not gradable. This is contrary to the data discussed in 6.5.2, which show that accomplishments admit degree gradation. To account for these data, a more fine-grained distinction of types of telos is necessary. Following Kearns (2007), two types of telos can be distinguished – a maximum and a standard telos. A maximum telos can be equated with a maximal scale value and therefore coincides with the endpoint of a scale. A standard telos is a nonmaximal scale value that marks the onset of a result state. Maximum and standard telos are distinct if an accomplishment entails a result state that is not a single value on a scale, but covers a set of values. If the result state is a single scale value, standard and maximum telos coincide. Caudal & Nicolas' definition of telicity only covers the notion of a maximal telos.

To distinguish between both types of telos, Kearns introduces two test criteria. The first one tests whether the transition to a maximal degree can be negated without contradiction. If this is the case, the achievement of a maximal degree is merely an implicature but not entailed. As (88a) shows, the attainment of the result state cannot be negated without contradiction. But it is not contradictory to negate the transition to a maximal degree, i.e., to say that something stabilized but did not become completely stable

---

[24] I am thankful to Robert D. Van Valin, Jr. for bringing up this example.

6 Change of state verbs

(88b). *Stabilisieren* describes a transition to a telos which is not necessarily a maximal scale value.

(88) a. #*Der Zustand hat sich stabilisiert, er ist aber nicht stabil.*
the condition has REFL stabilized he is but not stable
'The condition has stabilized, but it is not stable.'
b. *Der Zustand hat sich stabilisiert, er ist aber nicht*
the condition has REFL stabilized he is but not
vollkommen stabil.
completely stable
'The condition has stabilized, but it is not completely stable.'
(Fleischhauer, 2013, 141)

The second test criterion asks whether it is possible that the result state is achieved but still higher degrees could be attained. Therefore, I use the test frame *X had V-ed, but could still be more ADJ*, whereby *ADJ* denotes the result state of the verb. If a verb can be used in such a test frame, it is related to a standard telos. Otherwise, the attainment of higher degrees should not be possible. *Stabilisieren* can be used in the test frame without a contradiction (89); something can be stabilized but still become more stable.

(89) *Der Zustand des Patienten hat sich stabilisiert, er könnte*
the condition of.the patient has REFL stabilized he could
aber noch stabiler sein.
but still more stable be
'The physical condition of the patient has stabilized, but it could still be more stable.' (Fleischhauer, 2013, 141)

As (90) shows, the verb *schließen* 'close' leads to a contradiction if used in the test frame. The verb is related to a maximum telos which excludes the possible attainment of a higher degree.

(90) #*Peter hat die Tür geschlossen, sie könnte aber noch geschlossener*
Peter has the door closed she could but still more closed
sein.
be
'Peter has closed the door, but it could still be more closed.'
(Fleischhauer, 2013, 141)

6.6 Degree gradation and telicity

Only accomplishment change of state verbs related to a non-maximal standard telos license degree gradation. *Stabilisieren* is gradable by *sehr*, as demonstrated in the last section, and as the two tests discussed above reveal, it has a distinct standard telos. *Schließen*, which, as demonstrated above, does not have a distinct standard telos, is also not gradable by *sehr* (91).

(91) #*Peter hat die Tür sehr geschlossen.*
Peter has the door very closed

The distinction between standard and maximum telos allows a prediction which accomplishments admit degree gradation and which reject it. Only those related to a standard telos admit it; those without a distinct standard telos reject it (see Fleischhauer 2013 for cross-linguistic testing of this prediction). The explanation for this is straightforward, since *sehr* requires that the predicate it modifies truthfully denotes a set of degrees and not only a single one. A standard telos marks the onset of an extended result state and it is the minimal degree that has to be achieved to yield a true predication. If an accomplishment does not have a distinct standard telos, its result state only covers a single point on the scale, which does not fit with the requirement of *sehr*. As a consequence, a telos is not necessarily the endpoint of a scale but any lower bound that has at least to be reached to yield a true predication. Therefore, Caudal & Nicolas' definition of telicity must be reformulated. It is given in (92).

(92) Telicity: A predication is telic if and only if,
    a. it has an associated range of degrees with,
    b. a specified standard value, and
    c. its verbal predication satisfies axiom BECOME [...]
    (Fleischhauer 2013, 142, slightly changed)

The crucial part of the reformulated definition is that a predication is telic if there is some specified standard value which has to be reached. This means that some lower bound up to which the change has to progress has to be specified. This is also the explanation Hay et al. present for the fact that monotone-increasing intensifiers lead to a telic reading of a degree achievement, whereas monotone-decreasing ones do not. They state: "a telic reading of a DA [degree achievement] requires that the difference

6 Change of state verbs

value specify a *lower* bound on the degree to which an object must increase in the relevant property over the course of the event" (Hay et al., 1999, 134). *Slightly*, which is monotone-decreasing, does not introduce a lower bound and therefore does not lead to a telic predication.

Different types of predications are related to different types of telos. A degree achievement does not have any telos, it is atelic. Graded degree achievements, i.e., achievements that are modified by a degree expression like *sehr*, are telic, as shown above. The telos is determined by the intensifier. Ungradable accomplishments are only related to a maximum telos, whereas gradable ones entail a standard telos and implicate a maximum telos.[25] Graded accomplishments, i.e., accomplishments that are modified by a degree expression like *sehr*, are telic, and it cannot be demonstrated that they differ with regard to telicity from gradable accomplishments. Table 15 summarizes the different types of predicates and the types of telos associated with these verbs.

Type of predication	Type of telos
degree achievement	no telos (= atelic)
graded degree achievement	derived standard telos (= standard induced by *sehr*)
ungradable accomplishment	maximum telos
gradable accomplishment	standard telos (entailed) and maximum telos (implicated)
graded accomplishment	like 'gradable accomplishment'

Table 15: Types of predicates and their associated types of telos (Fleischhauer, 2013, 142).

It is an open question whether gradable accomplishments always implicate a maximum telos. It seems that at least some verbs, such as *stabilisieren*, *normalisieren* 'normalize' and *austrocknen* 'dry out,' do. The reason for this assumption is that these verbs license endpoint intensifiers (93), which presuppose, following Kennedy & McNally (2005a), an endpoint of a scale.

---

[25] Ungradable means 'not gradable by *sehr*.' Correspondingly, I restrict the notion of 'gradable accomplishments' to those that admit degree gradation by *sehr*.

(93) a. *Der Zustand hat sich vollständig stabilisiert.*
the condition has REFL completely stabilized
'The condition has completely stabilized.'
b. *Die Situation hat sich vollständig normalisiert.*
the situation has REFL completely normalized
'The situation has completely normalized.'
c. *In der Sonne trocknen Nacktschnecken vollständig aus.*
in the sun dry slugs completely out
'Slugs dry out completely in the sun.'
(Fleischhauer, 2013, 143)

Adopting the semantic representation of accomplishments proposed in the last section, I assume two different semantic representations for gradable (94a) and ungradable accomplishments (b). The only difference is in the degree of the attained result state. For an ungradable accomplishment, which is related to a maximal telos, the reaching of the result state entails that the maximal degree on the scale is attained. For gradable accomplishments, it is merely entailed that the result state holds to a degree which is equal or larger than the standard telos.

(94) a. $\lambda\varphi\lambda x\lambda e.\varphi(x, \text{BEGIN}(e)) < \varphi(x, \text{END}(e)) \land \varphi(x, \text{END}(e)) = d_{MaxTelos}$
b. $\lambda\varphi\lambda x\lambda e.\varphi(x, \text{BEGIN}(e)) < \varphi(x, \text{END}(e)) \land \varphi(x, \text{END}(e)) \geq d_{StandardTelos}$

The data presented above reveal that gradable accomplishments are closed scale predicates and therefore the assumption that *sehr* is only compatible with open scale predicates is too strong. *Sehr* can intensify closed scale predicates as long as they denote a set of values on a scale and not merely a single scale value.

6.7 Conclusion

This chapter provided a discussion of degree gradation of change of state verbs. The discussion revealed that there are differences between degree achievements and accomplishments regarding degree gradation. In the case of degree achievements, *sehr* specifies the amount of change but it is

6 Change of state verbs

the result state that is modified in the case of graded accomplishments. For degree achievements, the facts that they admit degree gradation and also that monotonic-increasing intensifiers lead to a telic reading of otherwise atelic predications are uncontroversial.

For many degree-based accounts of telicity, degree gradation of accomplishments should be impossible. The treatment of a telos as a maximum scale value excludes the possibility for attaining a higher degree than the telos. Several examples from German, Russian and French showed that some accomplishments are gradable which led to a distinction between two types of telos.

Telicity turned out to be a relevant property affecting degree gradation. A different property of change of state verbs, namely whether the scale is fully specified in the verb's lexical semantics or not, does not affect degree gradation. There is a straightforward explanation for this fact. All change of state verbs are scalar but some do not fully specify the scale. Nevertheless, the expression of a scalar change builds the semantic core of these verbs and therefore is able to specify the obtaining difference on an unspecific scale.

The whole chapter centered on durative change of state verbs and I have not discussed degree gradation of punctual change of state verbs (achievements in the sense of Vendler). It seems that speakers reject degree gradation of punctual change of state verbs, at least if the theme argument denotes a single entity rather than a plurality or collection of things. As these verbs seem to reject degree gradation, I excluded them from the discussion. In the next chapter I will show that punctuality is not incompatible with degree gradation.

7 Verbs of emission

Verbs of emission are the second class of verbs that are discussed in detail with respect to verbal degree gradation. These verbs provide some interesting problems which will be highlighted during the following chapter. In 7.1, I will start with a general discussion of verbs of emission. The focus is on argument realization and a subclassification of verbs of emission. Degree gradation of each of the subclasses is separately discussed in the sections 7.2 to 7.5.

7.1 Emission verbs – a general perspective

Verbs of emission form a semantic class of verbs in Levin's (1993) classification. The verbs of this class describe the emission of a substance or stimulus by an entity (Levin, 1993, 233). Depending on the type of substance/stimulus emitted, four different subclasses of emission verbs can be distinguished. The four relevant subtypes are sound emission, light emission, smell emission and substance emission (cf. (1) for examples of each subclass and see Levin (1993, 233ff.) for more English examples).

(1) a. Verbs of sound emission: *beep, rattle, knock, jingle, ring*
 b. Verbs of light emission: *blink, sparkle, gleam, glitter, glow*
 c. Verbs of smell emission: *smell, stink*
 d. Verbs of substance emission: *bleed, sweat, fester*

A distinct class in Levin's (1993) lexical classification is the verbs of sounds made by animals, such as *bark, grunt* or *yowl*. As she mentions, some of these verbs also belong to the class of verbs of sound emission. I will not distinguish between them but subsume verbs of sounds made by animals under the label of verbs of sound emission. A further related, but somewhat different class of verbs is weather verbs such as *hail, rain, thunder* and *snow*. These verbs are used to describe weather phenomena which are related to the emission of a substance, a sound or light. Hence, at least some of these verbs are emission verbs. I take verbs such as *snow*, *hail* and *rain* as verbs of substance emission and a verb like *thunder* as a verb of sound emission.

Perlmutter (1978, 163) describes verbs of emission as unergatives that express a "non-voluntary emission of stimuli that impinge on the senses" (also Rappaport Hovav & Levin 2000; Potashnik 2012). Basically, emission verbs are intransitive and the single argument is the emitter. The emitter argument denotes the entity that emits the respective stimulus or substance. This is illustrated in (2) for a verb of substance emission (a) and a verb of smell emission (b). Even if the emitter is animated, as in the sentences in (2), emission of blood or smell is a non-voluntary process.

(2)   a.   *Peter blutet.*
           Peter bleeds
           'Peter is bleeding.'
     b.   *Der Hund stinkt.*
           the dog   stinks
           'The dog stinks.'

As Rappaport Hovav & Levin (2000, 280) further point out, the emitter argument is usually non-agentive and does not show control of the situation. The argument of verbs like *bark*, *grunt* and *yowl* is not a usual emitter as it has control of the situation and acts voluntarily. This indicates that non-volitionality and lack of control are not defining properties for the semantic role 'emitter' as some emitters behave like agents.

Weather verbs differ from verbs of emission in having, at least in German and English, one syntactic argument but no semantic one (Van Valin & LaPolla, 1997, 147). German requires an expletive pronoun in subject position (3) and no realization of an explicit emitter argument.

(3)   *Es regnet.*
      it rains
      'It is raining.'

Emission verbs are mainly used intransitively but there are some emission verbs that also license a transitive and thereby causative use. An example form German is the verb *läuten* 'ring' in (4). The subject is the causer of the emission, whereas the emitter is realized as direct object.

7.1 Emission verbs – a general perspective

(4)   a.   *Die Glocke läutet.*
            the bell   rings
            'The bell is ringing.'
      b.   *Der Küster läutet die Glocke.*
            the sexton rings the bell
            'The sexton is ringing the bell.'

Transitive uses of verbs of emission are very restricted and there is some debate regarding the exact restrictions and how they are determined (see Levin & Rappaport Hovav 1995 as well as Potashnik 2012 and the literature cited therein for this discussion). Many of the examples cited by Potashnik for English are not acceptable in German. For example, he mentions the sentence pairs *The tea-cups clattered* and *I clattered the tea-cups* (Potashnik, 2012, 263). As (5a) shows, the German verb *klappern* 'clatter' has the same intransitive use as its English equivalent but there is no direct transitive correspondent (b). Rather the emitter has to be realized in an instrumental-PP (c).

(5)   a.   *Die Teetassen klapperten.*
            the tea.cups   clattered
            'The tea cups clattered.'
      b.   **Ich klapperte die Teetassen.*
            I   clattered the tea.cups
      c.   *Ich klapperte mit den Teetassen.*
            I   clattered with the tea.cups
            'I clattered the tea cups.'

This kind of argument alternation is restricted to verbs of sound emission (5) and verbs of light emission (6), in which case the emitter functions as a manipulatable device that can be used for sound or light production.

(6)   a.   *Die Lampe leuchtet.*
            the lamp   shines
            'The lamp shines.'
      b.   *Peter leuchtet mit einer Taschenlampe.*
            Peter shines   with a   torch.light
            'Peter shines a torch light.'
      c.   **Peter leuchtet eine Taschenlampe.*
            Peter lights   a   torch.light

7 Verbs of emission

If the emitter cannot be manipulated, it is not possible to introduce an effector (7).[1] One cannot cause the sun to emit light hence it cannot be realized as an instrumental-PP in (7b).

(7) a. *Die Sonne scheint.*
the sun shines
'The sun shines.'
b. #*Peter scheint mit der Sonne.*
Peter shines with the sun

Verbs of substance as well as smell emission reject this kind of argument alternation, in which the emitter is demoted to direct object or oblique status and an effector argument is added in subject position. This is shown in (8) for the verb *bluten* 'bleed.' In (a) it is used with a non-agentive emitter argument, but as (b) and (c) show it is not possible to add an effector argument and to demote the emitter to be a direct object or oblique argument.

(8) a. *Die Wunde blutet.*
the wound bleeds
'The wound is bleeding.'
b. **Peter blutet die Wunde.*
Peter bleeds the wound
c. **Peter blutet mit der Wunde.*
Peter bleeds with the wound

There is also a set of verbs of sound emission which rejects that kind of alternation, namely those which take an agentive emitter as single argument. Examples include the verbs of sound produced by animals as well as such verbs as German *brüllen* 'roar, howl' or *schreien* 'yell.' The examples in (9) illustrate this point for the German verb *bellen* 'bark,' which takes an agentive emitter. That the requirement of an agentive emitter blocks the alternation shows that it is restricted to verbs for which the emitter does not have control over the situation.[2]

---

[1] Foley & Van Valin (1984) introduce the notion 'effector' as a cover term for dynamic event participants and subsumes the thematic roles 'agent,' 'force' and 'instrument' under this label (see also Van Valin & Wilkins 1996 on this point).

[2] Sentence (9c) is not ungrammatical but only allows for a comitative interpretation of *mit dem Hund* expressing that Peter barked togehther with the dog.

(9) a. *Der Hund bellt.*
 the dog barks
 'The dog is barking.'
 b. **Peter bellt den Hund.*
 Peter barks the dog
 c. #*Peter bellt mit dem Hund.*
 Peter barks with the dog

A further possible, but also restricted, alternation type is the realization of a cognate object. The cognate object construction allows making the emitted stimulus explicit but it requires a context in which the explication of something, which is already encoded in the verb, is relevant. This can be achieved by a further specification of the emitee as shown in (10).

(10) a. *Das Insekt blutet grünes Blut.*
 the insect bleeds green blood
 'The insect is bleeding green blood.'
 b. *Das Mädchen lacht ein heiseres Lachen.*
 the girl laughs a hoarse laugh
 'The girl is laughing a hoarse laugh.'

Verbs of emission vary according to the aktionsart classes they belong to. Rappaport Hovav & Levin (2000, 283) observed that "verbs of emission fall along a continuum of stativity, with verbs of smell emission being the most stative, verbs of light emission slightly less stative, followed by verbs of sound emission and substance emission, which are the most process-like." The *wieder/weiter* test discussed in chapter 3 reveals that verbs of smell emission and verbs of light emission are stative, whereas verbs of sound emission and verbs of substance emission express activities. Examples (11) to (14) illustrate this test for each subclass separately.

7 *Verbs of emission*

(11) Der Hund stank letzten Sommer, stank das restliche Jahr nicht
the dog stunk last summer stunk the remaining year not
und stinkt diesen Sommer wieder/ *weiter.
and stinks this summer again further
'The dog stunk last summer, didn't stink for the rest of the year but this summer he stinks again.'

(12) *Die Lampe leuchtete gestern Abend, war dann aus und*
the lamp shined yesterday evening was then out and
leuchtet jetzt wieder/ weiter.
shines now again further.
'The lamp was shining yesterday evening, it was turned out overnight but now it's shining again.'

(13) *Der Hund bellte vor dem Essen, war dann leise und bellt*
the dog barked before the meal was than silent but barks
jetzt wieder/ weiter.
now again further
'The dog barked before the meal, then it was silent and now it's barking again/it continues to bark.'

(14) *Die Wunde blutete gestern, hörte zwischenzeitlich auf zu*
the wound bleed yesterday stopped meanwhile PART to
bluten und blutet jetzt wieder/ weiter.
bleed and bleeds now again further
'The wound bled yesterday, meanwhile it stopped bleeding but now it's bleeding again/it continues to bleed.'

The activity status of verbs of sound emission is independent of the animacy of the emitter. This is illustrated by the examples in (13) and (15). The emitter is agentive in (13) but nonagentive in (15).

(15) *Der Motor dröhnte, war eine Weile leise und dröhnte dann*
the engine droned was a while silent and droned then
wieder/ weiter.
again further
'The engine droned for a while, was silent and then it droned again/continued droning.'

232

7.1 Emission verbs – a general perspective

At least in German, emission verbs do not fall in a continuum of stativity; rather, there is a clear distinction between stative verbs of emission, verbs of smell and light emission, and those that are activity predicates. Beside stative and activity predicates, there are also semelfactive verbs of emission of light and sound emission, such as *donnern* 'thunder' and *blitzen* 'light, flash.' The contrast between semelfactive and non-semelfactive emission verbs is shown in (16). The time adverbial *stundenlang* 'for hours' indicates that there was a single raining event that lasted for hours (16a) but in (b) it is required that it lightninged repeatedly. A single event interpretation – meaning a single lightening – is not possible for the sentence.

(16) a. Es hat stundenlang geregnet.
    it has hours.long rained
    'It rained for hours.'
  b. Es hat stundenlang geblitzt.
    it has hours.long lightninged
    'It lightninged for hours.'

Despite the difference in aktionsart, verbs of emission can uniformly be paraphrased with 'emitter emits stimulus/substance.' The paraphrases for all four subclasses of verbs of emission are listed in (17). The respective stimulus/substance emitted varies from verb to verb.

(17) a. Verbs of smell emission: Emitter emits smell
  b. Verbs of light emission: Emitter emits light
  c. Verbs of sound emission: Emitter emits sound
  d. Verbs of substance emissions: Emitter emits substance

Verbs of smell/sound/light emission differ with regard to the quality of the emitted stimulus. As an example, take the three German verbs of smell emission shown in (18). English paraphrases are shown for each verb, there is one verb describing the emission of an unpleasant smell (*stinken*), one that denotes the emission of a pleasant smell (*duften*) and one verb (*riechen*) which is neutral with regard to this feature. These verbs differ in the quality of the emitted smell but they have in common that they denote the emission of smell.

7 Verbs of emission

(18) a. *stinken* 'stink'
'emit unpleasant smell'
b. *riechen* 'smell'
'emit smell'
c. *duften* 'smell pleasantly'
'emit pleasant smell'

Verbs of substance emission differ with regard to the kind of substance emitted. *Bluten* 'bleed' denotes the emission of blood, *schwitzen* 'sweating' describes the emission of sweat and *ejakulieren* 'ejaculate' the emission of ejaculate. English and German are both quite productive in deriving new verbs of substance emission from nouns denoting substances. Ropertz (2001, 76) lists the following verbs, which illustrate the derivation of such verbs from nouns: *milchen* 'emit milk' derived from the noun *Milch* 'milk,' *mehlen* 'emit flour' from *Mehl* 'flour,' *sanden* 'emit sand' from *Sand* 'sand.' For other classes of emission verbs, such a derivational process is less productive. Only verbs of sound emission allow a productive derivation from onomatopoetic sound words. But even if many verbs of substance emission are denominal, not all of them are. Goldberg (2005, 22) mentions, for example, the English verbs *sneeze* and *blow* which do not have nominal counterparts. These examples are of particular importance for her discussion of 'implicit theme arguments.' Goldberg (2005, 20f.) lists the examples in (19) and states that "the theme argument is unexpressed despite the appearance of an overt directional." There is only one overt argument in the sentences but it is not the referent of this argument that moves into some direction, rather it is the referent of the unexpressed theme argument (19f). The unexpressed theme of (19f) is whatever Pat is vomiting.

(19) a. *Pat sneezed onto the computer screen.*
b. *Chris blew into the paper bag.*
c. *Don't spit into the wind.*
d. *The hopeful man ejaculated into the petri dish.*
e. *Sam pissed into the gym bag.*
f. *Pat vomited into the sink.*

Goldberg claims that in many of the examples in (19) the theme is semantically incorporated into the verb, "in the sense that the theme's existence and motion is entailed by the verb" (Goldberg, 2005, 21). But she uses the verbs *sneeze* and *blow*, which are not derived from nouns, as arguments against a syntactic incorporation (in the sense of Hale & Keyser 1993) of the theme argument.[3] Hale & Keyser assume that a nominal head is syntactically incorporated into a light verb construction to derive denominal verbs such as *bleed*. However, Goldberg argues that if no corresponding noun exists, such a derivational process is unlikely. I follow her argumentation and assume that all verbs of emission, not only verbs of substance emission, have an implicit argument which is semantically incorporated. The implicit argument is the emittee, i.e., the stimulus or substance emitted in the eventuality and therefore I speak of an implicit emittee argument rather than an implicit theme argument. The paraphrases in (17) make the incorporated semantic argument explicit. In the following, I will take the emitted stimulus/substance as a semantically incorporated and therefore implicit emittee argument. In the remainder, I will not go into a detailed discussion of the lexical differences of the verbs of emission within the different subclasses but see Atkins et al. (1988); Atkins & Levin (1991); Levin (1991); Levin et al. (1997) for (English) verbs of sound emission and Gerling & Orthen (1979) for a discussion of (German) verbs of light emission.

7.2 Degree gradation of verbs of smell emission

Verbs of smell emission form a rather limited set of verbs, the three most frequent German exponents of this subtype are *riechen* 'smell,' *duften* 'smell pleasantly' and *stinken* 'stink.' Gamerschlag (2014) lists further but very infrequent examples, which I will not include in the current discussion. A semantic representation for these three verbs is shown in (20). *Riechen* is characterized by four conjuncts; the first specifies the eventuality as being an emission. The emitter is represented as a syntactic argument as it is bound by the lambda operator. The emittee, which is the implicit semantic argument, is decribed by the last two conjuncts. In the first conjunct, the emittee is introduced and the predicate in the second one specifies it as

---

[3] Note that the notion of an 'implicit argument' is mostly used in a syntactic sense; cf. the discussion of this notion in Bhatt & Pancheva (2006).

7 Verbs of emission

being smell. Verbs of smell/sound/light emission differ with respect to the quality they attribute to the theme argument. This can be captured by a further predicate like 'pleasant(y)' and 'unpleasant(y)' in (20b) and (c).

(20) a. ⟦riechen⟧ = λxλv∃y(emit(v) ∧ EMITTER(v)=x ∧ EMITTEE(v)=y ∧ smell(y)
b. ⟦duften⟧ = λxλv∃y(emit(v) ∧ EMITTER(v)=x ∧ EMITTEE(v)=y ∧ smell(y) ∧ pleasant(y)
c. ⟦stinken⟧ = λxλv∃y(emit(v) ∧ EMITTER(v)=x ∧ EMITTEE(v)=y ∧ smell(y) ∧ unpleasant(y)

All three verbs of smell emission can be graded by *sehr*, as the examples in (21) to (23) reveal.

(21) *Also dass zwei Farbmäuse [...] sehr stinken, kann ich mir [...] nicht*
so that two mice very stink can I me not
vorstellen.
imagine
'I cannot imagine that two mice stink very much.'[G]

(22) *Er hat weißrose Blüten, die sehr duften.*
he has white.pink blossoms that very smell.pleasantly
'He has white and pink blossoms which smell very pleasant.'[G]

(23) *Die Wandfarbe stinkt sehr.*
the wall.paint stinks very
'The wall paint really stinks.'[G]

Sehr modifies the intensity of the emitted smell, which can be paraphrased as 'emitting a strong smell.' The paraphrases of ungraded (a) and graded verbs of smell emission are shown in (24). 'Intensity' is a property of the implicit emittee argument and provides a further specification of the theme.

(24) a. Verbs of smell emission: Emitter emits smell
b. *sehr* + Verbs of smell emission: Emitter emits intense/strong smell

Intensity of a smell is not the same as the quality of a smell. If something *stinkt sehr* 'stinks very much' the strength of the smell is 'high' but it does

7.2 Degree gradation of verbs of smell emission

not mean that the smell is of a worse quality than something else. So *sehr stinken* does not mean 'smell very unpleasant' rather it means 'smell unpleasant and very intense.' Therefore, I keep the quality specification of the smell and the indication of its intensity apart. A semantic representation of graded verbs of smell emission is shown in (25). The attribute INTENSITY takes the implicit emittee as its argument and returns the degree of its intensity. *Sehr* further specifies the intensity degree as 'high.' The INTENSITY attribute is retrieved from the conceptual knowledge associated with 'smell.' We know that smell is characterized by different attributes, one of them is INTENSITY. The degree context requires the activation of this attribute and as no appropriate scale is part of the lexical meaning of the verb, it is retrieved from the conceptual knowledge. The implicit emittee argument gives access to the conceptual knowledge as it is semantically incorporated and therefore part of the verb's lexical meaning.

(25) a. $[\![\text{sehr riechen}]\!] = \lambda x \lambda v \exists y(\text{emit}(v) \wedge \text{EMITTER}(v)=x \wedge \text{EMITTEE}(v)=y \wedge \text{smell}(y) \wedge \text{high}(\text{INTENSITY}(y)))$
b. $[\![\text{sehr duften}]\!] = \lambda x \lambda v \exists y(\text{emit}(v) \wedge \text{EMITTER}(v)=x \wedge \text{EMITTEE}(v)=y \wedge \text{smell}(y) \wedge \text{pleasant}(y) \wedge \text{high}(\text{INTENSITY}(y)))$
c. $[\![\text{sehr stinken}]\!] = \lambda x \lambda v \exists y(\text{emit}(v) \wedge \text{EMITTER}(v)=x \wedge \text{EMITTEE}(v)=y \wedge \text{smell}(y) \wedge \text{unpleasant}(y) \wedge \text{high}(\text{INTENSITY}(y)))$

The INTENSITY attribute is linked to the eventuality via an attribute chain which can be represented as in (26). INTENSITY is an attribute of the implicit emittee argument, which again is an attribute of the eventuality. I use representations like in (26) to illustrate the relevant attributes that link the attribute representing the gradable property to the eventuality.

(26) $\lambda v(\text{high}(\text{INTENSITY}(\text{EMITTEE}(v))))$

Like German, French and Russian also admit degree gradation of verbs of smell emission. This is shown in (27) for French and in (28) for Russian. As in German, the intensifier specifies the intensity of the emitted smell.

(27) Le chien pu beaucoup.
the dog stinks a lot
'The dog stinks very much.'

(28)   [...] *na stol-e stojala malen'kaja žestjanaja lampočka s*
          PREP table-LOC stood small   tin   lamp.NOM with
          kerosin-om kotoryj očen' vonjal.
          kerosine-INST which very stank
          'On the table stood a small tin lamp with kerosene, which stank very much.'[R]

Grammatical aspect does not have any effect on the gradation of verbs of smell emission. Since verbs of smell emission are stative, they require a shift to a non-stative interpretation if they are used in the perfective aspect. This is illustrated for Polish in (29). The verb *śmierdzieć* 'stink' is imperfective and denotes the state of stinking. Adding the prefix *za-* derives a perfective verb that means 'begin to stink.' The state denoted by the case verb is the result state of the change introduced by the prefix *za-*. *Bardzo* indicates in (a) the intensity of the smell, whereas in (b) it specifies the degree of change. The sentence in (b) expresses a change in the intensity of smelling, from some unspecified intensity to a high degree. This is similar to the effect of verb gradation in the case of degree achievements.

(29)   a.   *Jan bardzo śmierdział.*
              Jan very   stank
              'Jan stank very much.'
        b.   *Jan bardzo za-śmierdział.*
              Jan very   ZA-stank
              'Jan began to stink very much.'

The German verb *riechen* 'smell' can also be used in a perception verb sense. In this case, it is used transitively and an experiencer argument is added in subject position (30). Neither *duften* nor *stinken* can be used in such a construction. Constructions like the one in (30) are called 'subject-oriented' Whitt (2009). They are transitive and the experiencer is realized as the subject, whereas the stimulus is in object position.

(30)   *Ich habe Gas gerochen.*
        I   have gas smelled
        'I smell gas.'

7.2 Degree gradation of verbs of smell emission

Degree gradation is also possible in such a construction (31).

(31) Ich habe das Gas sehr gerochen.
      I   have the gas very smelled
      'I could really smell gas.'

Riechen not only licenses a subject-oriented perception verb use but also an object-oriented one (Viberg 1984, 2001 calls it 'phenomenon based'). Whitt (2009) describes such object-oriented perception verb uses as intransitive constructions in which the experiencer argument is optional, if it is possible at all. The meaning of such constructions is as follows: "the object-oriented perception verbs tend to indicate an assessment or value judgment made by the speaker that is based on perception" (Whitt, 2009, 1085). A German example is shown in (32).

(32) Die Jacke riecht nach Pferd.
      the jacket smells of   horse
      'The jacket smells of horse.'

Gamerschlag & Petersen (2012, 6) list the valency patterns in (33) as the major construction types of object-oriented perception verbs. The adjective in (a) specifies the type of smell of the subject referent. *Süß* 'sweet' can be taken as a direct specification of the type of smell. Petersen & Gamerschlag (2014), following Gisborne (2010), call this an attributive use of perceptions verbs. This use contrasts with more indirect constructions such as *The apples smell ripe*. *Ripe* does not indicate a kind of smell rather *ripe* is a state of the apples which can be inferred by the smell of the apples (for a discussion of such inferential uses of perception verbs cf. Gamerschlag & Petersen 2012). In (b) to (d) the type of smell is indicated by some reference object, which is introduced by a PP in (b) and (c) and by a complement clause in (d).

(33) a. Die Äpfel riechen süß.
          the apples smell   sweet
          'The apples smell sweet.'
      b. Die Äpfel riechen wie Bananen.
          the apples smell   like bananas
          'The apples smell like bananas.'

7 Verbs of emission

    c.   *Die Äpfel riechen nach Bananen.*
           the apples smell of bananas
           'The apples smell of bananas.'
    d.   *Die Äpfel riechen als ob sie Bananen wären.*
           the apples smell as if they bananas would.be
           'The apples smell as if they were bananas.'

All these constructions license the degree intensifier *sehr*, only (d) needs some refinement by adding the particle *so* 'so, as, like.' (34a) is not an instance of verbal degree gradation; rather the intensifier modifies the adjective *süß* 'sweet.' If there is an adjective present, it is not possible to relate *sehr* to an intensification of the verb. In all the other examples in (34) *sehr* intensifies the verb. But the interpretation of degree gradation in these examples differs from the one of plain verbs of smell emission. In (34b) to (d) it is not the intensity of the emitted smell that is specified, but the similarity relation induced by the object of comparison.

(34)   a.   *Die Äpfel riechen sehr süß.*
           the apples smell very sweet
           'The apples smell very sweet.'
      b.   *Die Äpfel riechen sehr wie Bananen.*
           the apples smell very like bananas
           'The apples smell very much like bananas.'
      c.   *Die Äpfel riechen sehr nach Bananen.*
           the apples smell very of bananas
           'The apples smell very much of bananas.'
      d.   *Die Äpfel riechen sehr so als ob sie Bananen wären.*
           the apples smell very so as if they bananas would.be
           'The apples smell very much as if they were bananas.'

What a sentence like (34c), for example, means is that the apples smell similar to bananas, or put differently, the smell of the apples is similar to the smell of bananas. *Sehr* indicates that the smell is not only similar but similar to a high degree. The construction introduces a new gradable property, namely 'similarity' between two objects and the intensifier applies to it.

This effect is not limited to the object-oriented perception verb uses of verbs of smell emission but also shows up with strong resultative constructions, which is exemplified by the verb of sound emission *schreien* 'shout' in (35). In (a), the verb is intensified by *sehr*, which specifies the loudness of the shouting.[4] A resultative construction is shown in (b) and in (c) the intensifier *sehr* and the resultative construction are combined. *Sehr* can only modify the resultant state – the boy shouts himself very hoarse – but not the loudness of the emitted sound. In English, it is obvious that in (35c) the resultative predicate rather than the verb is intensified. This is indicated by the use of *very*, which is restricted to adjectives and not possible with verbs.

(35) a. *Der Junge schreit sehr.*
 the boy shouts very
 'The boy shouts a lot.'
 b. *Der Junge schreit sich heiser.*
 the boy shouts REFL hoarse
 'The boy shouts himself hoarse.'
 c. *Der Junge schreit sich sehr heiser.*
 the boy shouts REFL very hoarse
 'The boy shouts himself very hoarse.'

If the resultative predicate is not gradable, *sehr* cannot be added to the sentence (36). This indicates that in resultative constructions only the resulting state can be graded, but the scale contributed by the verb is no longer admissible for degree modification.

(36) a. *Der Junge schreit sich in den Schlaf.*
 the boy shouts REFL in the sleep
 'The boy shouts himself to sleep.'
 b. **Der Junge schreit sich sehr in den Schlaf.*
 the boy shouts REFL very in the sleep

The fact that degree gradation applies to the similarity scale in the case of object-oriented perception verb uses of *riechen* and to the scale introduced by the resultative predicate depends on the fact that in these cases the scale is introduced by the morphosyntactic construction. Since the scale is overtly encoded, it is not required to retrieve a scale from the conceptual knowledge. If the scale is not suitable for *sehr*, as in (36b), degree gradation is not possible. This shows that overtly encoded scales block the retrieve-

---

[4] Degree gradation of verbs of sound emission is discussed in more detail in section 7.4.

ment of scales from conceptual knowledge and the activation of scales from conceptual knowledge seems to be a last resort strategy if neither the lexical semantics of the verb nor the morphosyntactic construction encodes a scale.

7.3 Degree gradation of verbs of light emission

Verbs of light emission are, like verbs of smell emission, stative predicates, but they are more numerous than verbs of smell emission. Gerling & Orthen (1979) provide a classification of German verbs of light emission that is based on features like 'continuous' vs. 'non-continuous light emission' or 'direct' vs. 'indirect emission.' Indirect light emission would cover light reflection phenomena, whereas direct light emission covers the production of light. A continuous light emission is denoted by such verbs as *leuchten, scheinen* 'shine,' whereas *flackern, flimmern* 'flicker' denotes a non-continuous one. I am not going into the details of Gerling & Orthen's work since it is not my aim to provide a lexicographic analysis of these verbs. But the feature 'continuous' vs. 'non-continuous' light emission indicates that this type of emission is less stative than smell emission. Hence, some verbs of light emission are more dynamic than others.

Verbs of light emission license degree gradation similarly to verbs of smell emission. Examples of graded verbs of light emission are shown in (37) and in each case, *sehr* modifies the intensity of the emitted light. INTENSITY, in the case of light emission, means the degree of brightness. (37c), for example, means that the eyes do not only sparkle but sparkle intensively and therefore brightly.

(37) a. *Von Geburt an habe ich sehr helle Augen, die sehr*
of birth on have I very bright eyes which very
leuchten in der Sonne.
shine in the sun
'Since birth I have had very bright eyes, which shine very much in the sun.'[G]
b. *Diamanten glänzen in der Sonne sehr.*
diamonds gleam in the sun very
'Diamonds gleam very much in the sun.'[G]

c. *Da die Steinchen sehr funkeln, ist diese Kette ein echter*
   since the stones very sparkle is this necklace a real
   Eye Catcher.
   eye-catcher
   'The necklace is a real eye-catcher because the stones sparkle very much.'^{G}

The verbs in (37) all express an indirect emission of light but we get the same effect with more direct cases of light emission, as those in (38). The emitted light is characterized as intensively and therefore brightly.

(38) a. *Die Lampe leuchtet sehr.*
       the lamp lights very
       'The lamp is very bright.'
    b. *Die Sonne scheint sehr.*
       the sun shines very
       'The sun is shining a lot [intensively].'

We find the same interpretation in Russian as shown with the perfective verb *iskrit'sja* 'sparkle' in (39). *Očen'* specifies the intensity of the emitted light.

(39) *Kogda letel sneg on očen' iskril-sja na svet-u.*
     when flew snow.NOM he very sparkled-REFL PREP light-LOC
     'When the snow was falling, it sparkled very much in the light.'^{R}

The meaning of the examples discussed so far can be partially paraphrased as indicated in (40). The paraphrase is the same as the one for verbs of smell emission; the only difference is that intensity is differently interpreted in the context of light and smell.

(40) a. Verbs of light emission: Emitter emits light
     b. *sehr* + Verbs of light emission: Emitter emits intense light

As the paraphrases for degree gradation of verbs of light emission, and verbs of smell emission do not differ, the semantic representation of these cases is also the same. I assume that verbs of light emission allow retrieving an intensity scale from the conceptual knowledge associated with the implicit emittee argument. (41) shows the semantic representation of the

7 Verbs of emission

graded verb *funkeln* 'sparkle.' The relevant attributes for verbal degree gradation and how they are linked to the eventuality is shown in (42).

(41) ⟦sehr funkeln⟧ = λxλv∃y(emit(v) ∧ EMITTER(v)=x ∧ EMITTEE(v)=y ∧ light(y) ∧ sparkling(y) ∧ high(INTENSITY(y)))

(42) λv(high(INTENSITY(EMITTEE(v))))

With regard to verbal degree gradation, the distinction between continuous and non-continuous light emission is relevant. Verbs like *flackern* 'flicker,' *blinken* 'twinkle' and *blitzen* 'light, flash' are semelfactive predicates which are ambiguous between a single event and an iterative reading. The sentences in (43) seem to license two different interpretations of verbal degree gradation: either the emitted light was very intense or the emission of light happened frequently. This looks as if *sehr* is ambiguous between degree and extent gradation with such verbs.

(43) a. *Ihr Paillettenkleid blinkt im Discolicht sehr.*
her pailette.dress twinkles in.the disco.light very
'Her sequined dress twinkles very much in the disco light.'[G]

b. *[...] man hat mir heute morgen gesagt, dass es sehr*
one had me today morning said that it very
geblitzt und gedonnert hat.
lightninged and thundered had
'[...] someone told me this morning that there was a lot of thunder and lightning.'[G]

We observe the same ambiguity in Russian, as shown by the example in (44). According to my informants, the default interpretation is that the LCD monitor flickered very intensely, meaning brightly. But there is also an interpretation that it flickered very often.

(44) *Popal-sja kak-to brakovannyj LCD monitor, očen' migal*
got-REFL once defective LCD-monitor.NOM very blinked
podsvetk-oi na nekotor-yx urovn-jax jarkost-i.
backlight-INST PREP some-LOC level-LOC brightness-GEN
'Got a defective LCD monitor once, its backlight flickered a lot on some brightness levels.'[R]

I will discuss degree gradation of semelfactive verbs of emission in more details in the next section, after presenting the relevant data on semelfactive verbs of sound emission.

7.4 Degree gradation of verbs of sound emission

Verbs of sound emission are activity predicates. The respective sound can be either produced by an agentive (*bark*) or a non-agentive emitter (*drone*). Agentivity of the emitter does not affect degree gradation of these verbs, as shown in (45) . *Dröhnen* 'drone' is a verb that takes non-agentive emitter, *lärmen* 'make noise' does not necessarily require an agentive emitter but the sentence in (b) can be understood in the sense that the guests voluntarily did something (e.g. talking) and thereby produced noise. In (c), the emitter – *Kreide* 'chalk' – is not agentive but there is an effector present in the sentence which is responsible for the chalk emitting some squeaking sound. *Das Kind* 'the child' is an active emitter in (d), who is responsible for emitting the scream. Degree gradation has the same effect in all four cases, namely to specify the intensity of the emitted sound. In (b), for example, the guests not only produce noise but the noise they produce is very intense. In the context of sound emission, intensity means 'loudness' or 'volume.' I will use the term 'loudness' to refer to 'sound intensity' in the remainder of the thesis.

(45) a. *Der Bass hat immer sehr gedröhnt und klang   unpräzise*
the bass has always very droned   and sounded imprecise
und weich.
and soft
'The bass always droned a lot and sounded imprecise and soft.'[G]

b. *In der letzten Nacht haben Gäste bis morgens um 2:00*
in the last   night have guests till morning at 2:00
Uhr   sehr gelärmt   [...].
o'clock very made noise
'Last night, guests made a lot of noise till 2 o'clock in the morning [...].'[G]

7 Verbs of emission

    c.   *Beim Schreiben an der Tafel hat er sehr mit der*
          at.the writing on the blackboard has he very with the
          Kreide gequietscht.
          chalk squeaked
          'While writing on the blackboard, he squeaked a lot with the chalk.'^{G}

    d.   *Das Kind hat sehr geschrien.*
          the child has very screamed
          'The child screamed a lot.'^{G}

As was the case for the other two subclasses of verbs of emission, degree gradation applies to an intensity scale which measures a gradable property of the implicit emittee argument. Degree gradation of verbs of sound emission can be paraphrased as in (46). Since we have the same pattern as for the other subclasses of emission verbs, the semantic representation of graded verbs is also the same (47). As agentivity does not affect degree gradation, it is ignored in the semantic representations. The attributes relevant for degree gradation is this case as shown in (48).

(46)   a.   Verbs of sound emission: Emitter emits sound
         b.   *sehr* + Verbs of sound emission: Emitter emits intense sound

(47)   ⟦sehr schreien⟧ = $\lambda x \lambda v \exists y (\text{emit}(v) \wedge \text{EMITTER}(v)=x \wedge \text{EMITTEE}(v)=y \wedge \text{shout}(y) \wedge \text{high}(\text{INTENSITY}(y)))$

(48) $\lambda v(\text{high}(\text{INTENSITY}(\text{EMITTEE}(v))))$

In the last section, it was mentioned that semelfactive verbs of light emission license a frequentative interpretation of verbal degree gradation. The same effect shows up with semelfactive verbs of sound emission, such as *schreien* 'scream' in (45d) or *bellen* 'bark' in (49a). *Sehr* either modifies the intensity of the emitted sound or the frequency of the emission of barking sounds. The intensity reading can be forced by a strictly semelfactive context like in (49b) in which a single emission is expressed. *Einmal* 'once' restricts the verb to a single event reading and in such a context *sehr* can only modify the intensity of the sound but not the frequency of its emission.

7.4 Degree gradation of verbs of sound emission

(49) a. *Ihr Hund bellt aber sehr!*
your dog barks but very
'Your dog barks a lot!'
b. *Ihr Hund hat einmal sehr gebellt.*
your dog has once very barked
'Your dog barked once very loudly.'[5]

As already mentioned with regard to semelfactive verbs of light emission, the same ambiguity in interpretation of degree gradation shows up in Russian. In (50), either the subject referent coughed loudly or often. The verb *kašljat'* 'cough' is imperfective and has an iterative interpretation; a semelfactive verb can be derived by adding the suffix *-nu* which yields the perfective verb *kašljanut'* 'cough once.' Grading the explicitly marked semelfactive verb does not give rise for a frequentative interpretation.

(50) *U menja byl bronxit, ja pozvonila doktoru Simony i*
by me was bronchitis I called doctor Simon and
skazala, čto ja očen' kašlaju.
said that I very cough
'I had bronchitis; I called Dr. Simon and told him that I cough a lot.'[R]

The question is whether examples such as those in (49) and (50) reveal that there is no strict separation between degree and extent gradation and that intensifiers such as *sehr* and *očen'* can be used for degree as well as extent gradation. I like to argue that this is not the case. A frequentative interpretation is an implicature but not the primary semantic effect of verbal degree gradation. This is shown by the German examples in (51) and the Russian ones in (52). The German examples show that *sehr bellen* 'bark very much' really means bark loudly and not barking for a long time. It is the degree and not the extent that is modified by *sehr* since it is possible to say that a dog barked very much but only shortly. At the same time, it cannot be negated that the dog barked loudly. Since the indication of a high frequency or long duration can be canceled, it is merely an implicature. The same is true for Russian since *očen' kašljat'* 'cough very much' does

---
[5] The sentence is ambiguous and either means 'The dog emitted a single bark' or 'At a single occasion, the dog barked'. I focus on the first reading.

7 Verbs of emission

not entail *mnogo kašljat'* 'cough a lot' which can be negated without contradiction. But a contradiction arises if one states that the subject referent coughed very much but not loudly (52b).

(51) a. ??*Gestern hat der Hund wieder sehr gebellt, aber nur*
yesterday has the dog again very barked but only
leise/ nicht laut.
silently not loud
'The dog barked a lot again yesterday, but not loudly.'
b. *Gestern hat der Hund wieder sehr gebellt, aber nicht*
yesterday has the dog again very barked but not
lange/ nur kurz.
long only short
'The dog barked a lot again yesterday, but not for long.'

(52) a. *On očen', no ne mnogo, kašljal.*
he very but not much coughed
'He coughed loudly [= very], but not for long [= much].'
b. #*On očen', no ne gromko, kašljal.*
he very but not loudly coughed
'He coughed a lot, but not very loudly.'

Why does the apparent ambiguity of the degree intensifier show up with verbs such as *bellen* 'bark' and *kašljat'* 'cough' but not with verbs such as *dröhnen* 'drone' or *wachsen* 'grow'? *Bellen* and *kašljat'* are compatible with the expression of an iteration of single sound emissions. Hence, they lexically license a frequentative reading since a scale measuring the frequency of the eventuality is grounded in the verb's meaning. A semantic representation for *sehr bellen* is given in (53), where we have an attribute FREQUENCY, which is a gradable property of the eventuality and measures the number of event occurences. This property has a minimal standard entailing that the frequency is greater than or equal to one. Russian has a grammaticalized device for restricting the the frequency to one – which is a single event –, by using the semelfactive affix *-nu*.

(53) $[\![\text{sehr bellen}]\!] = \lambda x \lambda v \exists y (\text{emit}(v) \wedge \text{EMITTER}(v){=}x \wedge \text{EMITTEE}(v){=}y$
$\wedge \text{bark}(y) \wedge \text{high}(\text{INTENSITY}(y)) \wedge \text{FREQUENCY}(v){\geq}1)$

7.4 Degree gradation of verbs of sound emission

For semelfactive verbs, I assume that FREQUENCY is a lexically encoded gradable property and therefore accessible for degree intensifiers, which operate on the level of the predicate. Verbs such as *dröhnen* or *wachsen* do not lexically encode a frequency scale and hence do not give rise to a frequency reading of *sehr*, resp. *očen'*. The picture looks different if we combine verbs of non-continuous sound emission with adverbial expressions of extent gradation like German *viel* (54). In this case, it is only the frequency or temporal duration which is modified but not the intensity of the emitted sound.

(54) *Der Hund hat viel gebellt.*
the dog has much barked
'The dog barked a lot.'

To conclude this discussion: degree gradation leads to an extent implicature with semelfactive verbs of light and sound emission. This is based on the fact that the verbs lexically encode a scale measuring the frequency of the eventuality.

Atkins et al. (1988); Atkins & Levin (1991); Levin (1991) and Levin et al. (1997) discuss further uses of verbs of sound emission which are illustrated for German in (55). In these cases, the emitter is not only producing a sound but does so with a communicative intention. In (a) and (b) the respective sound is emitted to warn someone. The difference then is that the intended receiver is explicitly realized in (b) but not in (a). In (c), what is emitted, i.e., the content of the communication, by the communicator is specified by the subordinate clause.

(55) a. *Er pfeift eine Warnung.*
he whistles a warning
'He whistles a warning.'
b. *Er schreit ihm eine Warnung zu.*
he shoutes him a warning PART
'He is shouting a warning to him.'
c. *Er grunzte, dass er gehen will.*
he grunted that he go wants
'He grunted that he wanted to go.'

These constructions do not license degree gradation by *sehr* as shown in (56). The verbs are not used as simple verbs of sound emission but rather

7 Verbs of emission

as communication verbs and the INTENSITY attribute cannot be activated in this kind of construction. Probably INTENSITY is not an attribute of a communicated message. To consolidate this claim a deeper investigation of degree gradation of communication verbs would be necessary, but this goes beyond the limits of this thesis.

(56)   a.   #*Er pfeift sehr eine Warnung.*
               he whistles very a warning
       b.   #*Er schreit ihm eine Warnung sehr zu.*
               he shouts him a warning very PART
       c.   #*Er grunzte sehr, dass er gehen würde.*
               he grunted very that he go would

Verbs of sound emission are not stative, and hence they show an aspectual opposition. This is demonstrated for German in (57). We have a contrast between a perfect (57a) and a progressive construction (b) but there is no contrast with regard to degree gradation. In both cases, *sehr* specifies the intensity of the emitted sound.

(57)   a.   *Der Motor hat sehr gedröhnt.*
               the engine has very droned
               'The engine droned very much.'
       b.   *Der Motor ist sehr am Dröhnen.*
               the engine is very at.the droning
               'The engine is droning very much.'

Again the same is true for Russian, as the examples in (58) show. In (a) we have the imperfective verb *lajat'* 'bark' and gradation affects the intensity of the emitted sound (leaving aside the extent implicature discussed above). The verb can be combined with various prefixes, not all of them licensing degree gradation. Adding the prefix *na-* derives a perfective verb with the meaning bark at someone; the prefix transitivizes the verb. In (a) and (b) it is both expressed that the dog barked at a girl. The interpretation of the perfective sentence, with regard to degree gradation, does not differ from the imperfective one. Hence, grammatical aspect does not affect degree gradation of verbs of sound emission.

(58)   a.   *Sobaka očen' lajala na devočk-u.*
            dog.NOM very barked PREP girl-ACC
            'The dog is barking very loudly at the girl.'
       b.   *Sokaba očen' na-lajala na devočk-u.*
            dog.NOM very NA-barked PREP girl-ACC
            'The dog barked very loudly at the girl.'

7.5 Degree gradation of verbs of substance emission

Verbs of substance emission are activity predicates. Their single argument, as for the other subtypes of emission verbs, is an emitter. But some variance with regard to the emitter argument can be observed. Taking *bluten* 'bleed' as an example, the emitter can either be a wound (59a), a person (b) or a body part (c). In (b) it is understood that the person is bleeding somewhere on his body, whereas in (a) and (c) it is understood that the wound or the body part belongs to a person or animal.

(59)   a.   *Die Wunde blutet.*
            the wound bleeds
            'The wound is bleeding.'
       b.   *Der Mann blutet.*
            the man bleeds
            'The man is bleeding.'
       c.   *Die Hand blutet.*
            the hand bleeds
            'The hand is bleeding.'

Other verbs of substance emission show less variation regarding the emitter argument. As (60) shows, the verb *eitern* 'fester' restricts the emitter to being either a wound or a body part but does not license a person as emitter. This is an interesting lexicographic contrast within the class of verbs of substance emission but will be ignored in the remainder of the analysis.

(60)   a.   *Die Wunde eitert.*
            the wound festers
            'The wound is festering.'

7 Verbs of emission

      b.   *#Der Mann eitert.*
           the man festers
      c.   *Die Hand eitert.*
           the hand festers
           'The hand is festering.'

Verbs that express an emission from a body also allow the so-called 'Body-Part Possessor Ascension Alternation' (Levin, 1993, 71) shown in (61). A body part and its possessor can either be realized in a single complex NP, as in (a), or the possessed body part can be expressed in a prepositional phrase (b). As (62) shows, this alternation is not restricted to body parts; nouns like *wound* can also be licensed as possessum.

(61)   a.   *Seine Hand blutet.*
            his hand bleeds
            'His hand is bleeding.'
       b.   *Er blutet an der Hand.*
            he bleeds on the hand
            'His hand is bleeding.' (lit. 'He is bleeding at his hand.')

(62)   a.   *Seine/Die Wunde blutet.*
            his/the wound bleeds
            'His/the wound is bleeding.'
       b.   *Er blutet aus der Wunde.*
            he bleeds out the wound
            'His wound is bleeding.' (lit. 'He is bleeding from his hand.')

As already mentioned for verbs like *donnern* 'thunder' and *blitzen* 'lightning, flash,' weather verbs do not have an emitter argument (63). Syntactically, they are atransitive Van Valin & LaPolla (1997). The atransitivity of these verbs is more obvious in languages such as Latin (64) where no expletive subject is required. Rather the verb can be used without any explicit argument. This is not simply a case of pro-drop since it can be observed with other intransitive verbs, as it is not possible to have an explicit argument. The same holds for Russian, as will be demonstrated later.

(63)   *Es regnet.*
         it rains
         'It is raining.'

7.5 Degree gradation of verbs of substance emission

(64) Latin (Romance < Indo-European; Eriksen et al. 2010, 566)
    Pluit.
    rain.3SG
    'It is raining.'

Eriksen et al. (2010, 567) state that "[m]eteorological events do not include distinct and salient participants" like agents or patient. This is why we observe the difference in the argument realization of *bleed* and *rain* in (59) and (63). It is cross-inguistically attested that meteorological events are denoted by complex predicates, as illustrated by the Basque example in (65). The complex predicate consists of a light verb and a nominal head which denotes the emitted substance.

(65) *Euri-a   bota   zuen.*
    rain-DET.ABS throw have.PST.ABS(3SG).ERG(3SG)
    'It rained.'
    (Alba-Salas 2004, 76; cited after Eriksen et al. 2010, 566)

Russian also makes use of such complex construction for the expression of meteorological events. Examples are *idti sneg* 'snow' (literally 'go snow') or *idti grad* 'hail' (lit. 'go hail'). Russian also uses such complex predicates for the expression of substance emission. An example is *idti krov'* 'bleed' (lit. 'go blood'). This is one similarity between weather verbs and verbs of substance emission; a further similarity is that they behave the same with regard to degree gradation. This is the reason why they are put together in this section.

Intransitive verbs of substance emission share some similarities to verbs of sound emission. First, the emitters of some verbs, for example *spucken* 'spit,' may get an agentive interpretation. But in contrast to verbs like *bellen* 'bark' the emitter of *spucken* is not necessarily agentive. The verb can denote an involuntary and therefore uncontrolled process of emission. Second, there is also a distinction between continuous and non-continuous substance emission. *Bluten* describes a continuous emission of substance, which can be interrupted, but is potentially temporally unbounded. *Spucken* refers to the emission of spit, which is not a continuous process. The addition of a durative adverbial indicates a repetition of single emission events (66).

7 Verbs of emission

(66) Der Mann spuckte zehn Minuten lang auf den Boden.
the man spat ten minutes long on the floor
'The man spat on the floor for ten minutes.'

Verbs of substance emission, which denote a continuous process of emission, can be graded by *sehr*. Examples are shown in (67). In each of the cases, *sehr* specifies the quantity of the emitted substance, which was already described by Ropertz (2001).

(67) a. *Da die Wunde sehr geblutet hat, sind meine Eltern mit*
as the wound very bled has are my parents with
mir ins Krankenhaus gefahren.
me in.the hospital driven
'As the was wound bleeding a lot, my parents took me to the hospital.'[G]
b. *Heute Nacht hat es sehr geregnet, [...].*
today night has it very rained
'Last night, it rained a lot [...].'[G]
c. *Ihre Haare fetten schon nach zwei Tagen sehr.*
her hairs grease already after two days very
'After two days her hair was already very greasy.'[G]

The sentences in (67) can be paraphrased as indicated in (68). As the paraphrase shows degree gradation affects the quantity of the emitted substance. The degree expression is paraphrased by the adnominal quantity expression *viel* 'much.'

(68) a. Verbs of substance emission: Emitter emits substance
b. *sehr* + Verbs of substance emission: Emitter emits much substance

The semantic representation of graded *bluten* is shown in (69).

(69) $[\![\text{sehr bluten}]\!] = \lambda x \lambda v \exists y (\text{emit}(v) \land \text{EMITTER}(v)=x \land \text{EMITTEE}(v)=y \land \text{blood}(y) \land \text{high}(\text{QUANTITY}(y)))$

The attribute chain that relates the gradation scale to the eventuality is shown in (70). QUANTITY is an attribute of the implicit emittee argument and retrieved from the conceptual knowledge associated with the referent

7.5 Degree gradation of verbs of substance emission

of the implicit emittee argument. In (70), we see a difference to the relevant attribute chains in verbs of smell/sound/light emission as we have the attribute QUANTITY instead of INTENSITY. Substances are not characterized by an INTENSITY attribute therefore INTENSITY is not a part of our conceptual knowledge of substances. The only admissible gradable property that can be retrieved from the conceptual knowledge associated with verbs of substance emission is the QUANTITY attribute (for a more detailed discussion see Fleischhauer 2015).

(70)   λe(high(QUANTITY(EMITTEE(e))))

Russian provides further evidence for the correctness of the paraphrase. In Russian there are two verbs for *bleed*. There is a simplex imperfective verb *krovotočit'* (71) and a complex verb construction *idti krov'* (72) based on the motion verb *idti* 'go.' The imperfective simplex verb cannot be perfectivized, but graded by *očen'*. The interpretation is that the wound is emitting a lot of blood.

(71)   *Rana   krovotočit očen'.*
        wound.NOM bleeds   very
        'The wound is bleeding a lot.'

(72)   *U nego idët krov'.*
        by him goes blood.NOM
        'He is bleeding.'

The verb *krovotočit'* does not license the possessor of the wound as subject argument. To realize the possessor as subject argument, the complex verb construction has to be used (72). In this construction, only the adnominal quantity expression *mnogo* 'much' can be used but not the degree intensifier *očen'* (73). *Mnogo* is used adverbially preceding the verb *idti* but semantically it modifies the nominal head of the complex verb construction.

(73)   *U nego mnogo idët krov'.*
        by him much   goes blood.NOM
        'He is bleeding a lot.'

Polish has a similar construction but overtly indicates that the quantity expression *dużo* 'much' modifies the nominal head of the complex verb

255

7 Verbs of emission

construction (74a) and (b). As is typical for Slavic languages, the combination of a noun with a quantity expression requires gentive case marking on the noun. Hence, *deszcz* 'rain' is in the genitive case in (74b). The interpretation, like in the Russian example, is that a lot of rain has fallen.

(74) a. *Padał deszcz.*
fell rain.NOM
'It rained.'
b. *Padał-o dużo deszcz-u.*
fell-3SG.N much rain-GEN
'It rained a lot.' (lit. 'Much rain has fallen')
c. **Padał-o dużo deszcz.*
fell-3SG.N much rain.NOM

Neither *dużo* in (74b) nor *mnogo* in (73) can be interpreted as extent intensifiers. That *dużo* only functions as a modifier of the nominal head and not of the event predicate (*padać deszcz*) can be seen by the contrast between (74b) and (c). A combination of *dużo* and nominal head in nominative case is ungrammatical; *deszcz* has to be in the genitive if *dużo* is present.

In contrast to Russian, the Polish complex verb construction can be used in the perfective aspect (75). The interpretation of (75) is similar to (74b), in both cases the quantity of emitted rain is indicated as 'large.'

(75) *Spadło dużo deszcz-u.*
fell much rain-gen
'A lot of rain has fallen.'

Grammatical aspect interacts with the degree gradation of verbs of substance emission. With perfective verbs the overall quantity of emitted substance is specified, whereas with progressive verbs it is the rate of emission which is specified (The term 'rate of emission' goes back to Ropertz' (2001) analysis of degree gradation of verbs of substance emission.). This is illustrated in (76) for the German verb *bluten* 'bleed.' In the perfective reading of the perfect construction (a), *sehr* indicates that the overall quantity of emitted blood is 'large.' This is different for (b), since the progressive describes an ongoing event. Therefore, it is not possible to indicate the total quantity of emitted blood. Rather the quantity of emitted blood at a certain stage of the event is specified.

7.5 Degree gradation of verbs of substance emission

(76) a. *Die Wunde hat sehr geblutet.*
the wound has very bled
'The wound bled a lot.'
b. *Die Wunde war sehr am Bluten.*
the wound was very at.the bleeding
'The wound was bleeding a lot.'

In chapter 4, I already mentioned that both readings of degree gradation, the perfective and the progressive one, are related but do not entail each other. If the overall quantity of emitted blood is large, then it is not necessarily the case that at each stage of the event a large quantity of blood has being emitted. Similarly, if at a certain stage of an event someone emits a large quantity of blood, this does not necessarily sum up to the emission of a large overall quantity. At different stages the emitter could emit only a rather small quantity of blood or the bleeding could end before much blood is emitted. Grammatical aspect has a very similar effect on degree gradation of verbs of substance emission as it has on change of state verbs. It is relevant to question what verbs of substance emission and change of state verbs have in common such that grammatical aspect interacts with degree gradation. I will turn to that question in chapter 9, and turn now to some Russian data.[6]

The Russian verb *doždit'* 'rain' is imperfective and can be intensified by *očen'*. Russian imperfective aspect shows a range of possible interpretations, as discussed in chapter 4. Sentence (77a) therefore is ambiguous between two readings, either the total amount of fallen rain is large, or at some time yesterday it rained hard. The first interpretation is related to the denotative use of the imperfective aspect, the second one to the progressive reading. According to my informants, the first reading – specifying the total quantity of rain – is (without any specific context) preferred. Example (b) only has the interpretation that it rains hard, meaning that a large quantity of rain falls at a certain stage of the event. Due to present tense and probably the time adverbial *sejčas* 'now' only a progressive reading is possible.

---

[6] In chapter 4, it was shown that grammatical aspect also interacts with degree gradation of verbs of substance emission in French. The crucial data will not be repeated in this chapter.

7 Verbs of emission

(77) a. *Segondja očen' doždil.*
yesterday very rained
'Yesterday, it rained a lot.'
b. *Sejčas očen' doždit.*
now very rains
'It is raining hard.'

The verb *doždit'* can also be perfectivized by, for example, the prefix *za-*, which adds an inceptive meaning component. Sentence (78) can be used to describe a situation in which it suddenly started to rain hard or in which it already rained but then increased in intensity. We do not get a total quantity interpretation due to the added meaning component of inceptivity.

(78) *Očen' za-doždilo.*
very ZA-rained
'It started to rain a lot.'

As already mentioned in chapter 4, Russian prefixes often add further meaning components to the verb. This surely has an effect on the possible outcome of degree gradation, as demonstrated with (78), and therefore makes it hard to really investigate the influence of grammatical aspect on degree gradation by using Slavic data.

So far, the discussion has shown that degree gradation of verbs of substance emission is the same irrespective whether the emitted substance is semantically incorporated in the verb or overtly realized in a complex verb construction. But as the Russian examples have shown, the device used for degree gradation may differ depending on whether we use a simplex verb – in which case we use *očen'* in Russian – or a complex verb construction – which requires *mnogo*.

Persian also provides some interesting data on the degree gradation of complex verb constructions. The distribution of Persian degree expressions, which was already mentioned in chapter 2, is illustrated below with help of the relevant data. As (79) shows, *kheyli* 'very' is used for verbal degree gradation, whereas *ziad* 'much' is used for extent gradation. *Kheyli* is also used with adjectives, irrespective of whether they are in the positive (80a) or comparative form (b). *Ziad* functions as an adnominal quantity expression, as shown in (81).

7.5 Degree gradation of verbs of substance emission

(79) a. *Oura kheyli dustdarad.*
      3SG.ACC very like.3SG
      'S/he likes him/her very much.'
   b. *(Tabestane gozashte) ziad baran barid.*
      summer last much rain rained
      '(Last summer,) it rained a lot.' (= frequency or duration)

(80) a. *Ou kheyli ghadboland ast.*
      3SG very tall is
      'He is very tall.'
   b. *Pesar kheyli bozorg-tar as dushash ast.*
      boy very taller-COMP than his friend is
      'The boy is much taller than his friend.'

(81) a. *Ou ketabhaye ziadi darad.*
      3SG books much has
      'S/he has many books.'
   b. *Dar daryache ab ziad ast.*
      in.the lake water much is
      'There is much water in the lake.'

In complex verb constructions, Persian allows both intensifiers as shown in (82). The construction *khoonrizi dashtan* 'bleed' (literally 'bleeding have') consists of the noun for blood and a verb meaning *have*. Both examples, (82a) and (b), allow for the reading that the quantity of emitted blood is 'large.' The example in (b) also provides the interpretation that the emitter bleeds often or for a long time, hence the extent reading is possible. This reading is not available in (a). Persian is different from the Slavic languages discussed above and licenses degree as well as extent gradation.

(82) a. *Ou kheyli khoonrizi dasht.*
      3SG very bleeding has
      'S/he bled a lot.' (= degree)
   b. *Ou ziad khoonrizi dasht.*
      3SG much bleeding has
      'S/he bled a lot.' (= extent)

The question arises as to why complex verb constructions (and it only seems to be in such constructions) license extent intensifiers for degree

7 Verbs of emission

gradation? A possible answer suggested by the examples discussed above is that the nominal head of these complex verb constructions could be the reason. Polish shows morphosyntactic evidence that the intensifier, which also functions as an adnominal quantity expression, modifies the nominal head of the construction: the degree expression is placed between the verb and the nominal head and the nominal head requires genitive case marking. In Russian, the opposite pattern can be observed: *mnogo* precedes the verb and the nominal head remains in nominative case. Although *mnogo* is used adverbially, semantically it modifies the nominal head.

In German, we find examples that are similar to the Persian ones in (82). *Sehr* specifies the quantity of emitted blood, which is the degree interpretation as shown above. But (83b) is ambiguous between the interpretation that he bled often, bled for a long time or emitted a lot of blood. Hence, *viel bluten* also seems to have a degree interpretation in which the quantity of emitted blood is specified.

(83)   a.   *Er hat sehr geblutet.*
              he has very bled
              'He bled a lot.'
       b.   *Er hat viel geblutet.*
              he has much bled
              'He bled a lot.'

A difference between *sehr bluten* and *viel bluten* is that the latter does not allow for a degree interpretation if the verb is used in a progressive construction. As discussed in chapter 4, *viel* shifts the interpretation of the progressive constructions towards a habitual reading (84b).

(84)   a.   *Er ist sehr am Bluten.*
              he is very at.the bleeding
              'He is bleeding hard.'
       b.   *Er ist viel am Bluten.*
              he is much at.the bleeding
              'He bleeds a lot (frequently).'

An explanation for the fact both German and Persian extent intensifiers induce a degree interpretation can go along the following lines: *viel* as well as *ziad* indicate either a long duration or a high frequency of events of substance emission. The longer the emission of blood continues, the more blood gets emitted. So one can assume that the indication of a large quantity of emitted blood is secondary to and dependent on the specification of the temporal extent. This would also explain why the degree interpretation vanishes in an explicit progressive construction. If this explanation is accepted, *viel* and *ziad* would still remain strict extent intensifiers and a degree reading only arises due to the fact that they specify the extent of the event. Nevertheless, this does not provide an explanation of the Slavic data.

To conclude, irrespective of how an event of substance emission is linguistically realized, the effect of degree gradation is always the same, namely to indicate the quantity of emitted substance. Variance only exists in the choice of the intensifiers for which I could not provide a full explanation.

7.6 Conclusion

Verbs of emission are not homogeneous with regard to degree gradation. There is a split between verbs of smell/sound/light emission on the one hand and verbs of substance emission on the other hand. The first three subclasses mentioned are graded with respect to the intensity of the implicit emittee argument and degree gradation does not interact with grammatical aspect. The last mentioned class is graded with regard to the quantity of the implicit emitee argument and degree gradation interacts with grammatical aspect. The question, "what makes verbs of substance emission different from the other subclasses of verbs of emission?" will be discussed in chapter 9.

The relevant outcome of this chapter is twofold: first, it has been shown that the gradable property is an attribute of an implicit argument of the verb. In a decompositional structure, verbs of emission are usually represented as shown in (85). The implicit emittee argument is not included in this representation but it is crucial for degree gradation as the gradation scale is not lexicalized by the verb but retrieved from the conceptual knowledge associated with the implicit emittee argument. Hence, an appropriate decomposition has to go beyond event structure templates. A richer lexical

7 Verbs of emission

decomposition has partially been presented in this chapter by explicating the attributes that link the gradable property to the eventuality.

(85)   a.   *bleed*: **do'**(x, **bleed'**(x))
          b.   *drone*: **do'**(x, **drone'**(x))

Second, verbs that belong to the same semantic class and also to the same aktionsart class can differ with regard to degree gradation. Two clear examples are the verbs represented in (85). *Bleed* as well as *drone* are verbs of emission and activity predicates. Therefore, the event structural representation is the same for both. With regard to degree gradation there is a crucial difference between both, which does not, and cannot follow from their event structural representation. Also *bleed* shows an interaction of grammatical aspect and degree gradation, *drone* does not. This indicates that there is a crucial, maybe also grammatically relevant, difference between both verbs, which is not captured by their event structural representation.

8 Experiencer verbs

Experiencer verbs are probably the prototypical instances of gradable verbs. If a grammar presents an example of verb gradation, it is typically of experiencer verbs. Li & Thompson (1989) list the examples in (1) in their discussion of the Mandarin Chinese degree intensifier *hěn* 'very.' They write: " Other than adjectival verbs, certain experiential verbs are the only ones that can take the adverbial modifier *hěn*" (Li & Thompson, 1989, 339).

(1)   a.   *Tā hěn xiǎng wǒ.*
           3SG very miss 1SG
           'S/He misses me a lot.'
    b.   *Wǒ hěn pà gǒu.*
           1SG very afraid dog
           'I am very afraid of dogs.'
    c.   *Wǒmen hěn zhùzhòng cáigàn.*
           1PL very emphasize competence
           'We put a lot of emphasis on competence.'
           (Li & Thompson, 1989, 340)

Li & Thompson's claim that *hěn* is restricted to certain experiential verbs is too strong, as shown in (2). But even if Li & Thompson's statement is too strong, it shows that experiencer verbs are conceived as prototypical instances of gradable verbs.

(2)   *ranhou dou hui hen bang ni o.*
       then all will very help you PART
       'Then, they all will help you a lot.' (Chui, 2000, 48)

Experiencer verbs have triggered an extensive discussion on argument linking. Hence, there is a lot of literature dealing mostly with argument realization patterns of these verbs. I will briefly mention this discussion in 8.1, after specifying what I mean by the term 'experiencer verb.' In section

8.2, I will discuss the semantics of two subclasses of experiencer verbs in more detail. This will provide the background for the discussion of verb gradation in section 8.3.

8.1 Experiencer verbs – a general overview

I have chosen the name 'experiencer verbs' for the class of verbs investigated in this chapter. This class of verbs covers Levin's (1993) 'psych verbs' as well as 'verbs of bodily state and damage to the body' (*hurt, itch*). Although psych verbs describe the "experiencing of some emotion" (Levin & Grafmiller, 2013, 21), the verbs of bodily state included in this chapter describe the experiencing of bodily sensations like pain, hunger or coldness. What these verbs have in common is that one of the arguments of the verb has the experiencer role. Dowty (1991, 577) characterizes experiencers as sentient participants who neither act volitionally nor have some causal impact. This notion of experiencer is too narrow since I will also discuss experiencer verbs as admire which require agentive experiencers in some of their uses. One of the subclasses of psych verbs distinguished by Levin is 'admire verbs.' The experiencer of these verbs can act volitionally by actively admiring something, e.g. a painting. What these verbs have in common is that one of the arguments has the experiencer role. Verbs having an experiencer argument are more numerous than those discussed in this chapter. Perception verbs like *hear, see* and *listen* also have an experiencer argument but are excluded from the discussion. I restrict myself to verbs that express a psychological attitude or physical sensation since these verbs behave uniformly with respect to verbal degree gradation.[1]

Psych verbs have been the focus of much attention in linguistic literature as they are assumed to be puzzling with regard to argument realization. The apparent puzzle is based on examples like those in (3). Both verbs – *frighten* and *fear* – describe the same type of psychological attitude, namely having fear. But they differ with regard to argument realization. *Frighten* realizes the experiencer argument as direct object, whereas *fear* realizes

---

[1] I will not dive into a discussion of the nature of emotions and similar notions but assume that these can be characterized, from a linguistic point of view, simply as internal sensations or states. For a more elaborate and philosophical discussion of this topic see, for example, Ben-Ze'ev (2001).

the experiencer as subject argument. The second argument – *dog* in these examples – is often referred to as stimulus argument.

(3) a. *The dog frightens the boy.*
     b. *The boy fears the dog.*

At first sight, both verbs seem to differ only with regard to the expression of their arguments. Verbs like *fear* are often called 'subject-experiencer verbs,' whereas those like *frighten* are named 'object-experiencer verbs' (Pesetsky, 1995, 19). This terminology highlights the differences in the realization of the experiencer argument these verbs show. The non-uniform linking of the verb's arguments causes a problem for approaches which assume that semantic roles are mapped to a unique syntactic position. A prominent approach of this kind is Baker's (1988, 46) 'Uniformity of Theta Assignment Hypothesis.' The data in (3) do not provide a problem if one does not assume that *frighten* and *fear* differ only with regard to argument realization but also with regard to their lexical semantics. Many researchers, such as Grimshaw (1990); van Voorst (1992); Pesetsky (1995); Härtl (2001); Van Valin (2005) among others, assume that *frighten* and *fear* differ with regard to their respective aktionsart classes and therefore *dog* has two different semantic roles in (3a) and (b). Although it seems to be common sense that verbs such as *fear* are states, there is much more heterogeneity in the analysis of *frighten*-type verbs. Grimshaw (1990) assigns them to the accomplishments class, van Voorst (1992) argues in favor of an achievement analysis, Härtl (2001) takes them to be activities and Butler (2003) as well as Rothmayr (2009) favor a (causative) state analysis. There is even a controversy whether these verbs are causative (Grimshaw, Van Valin) or not (Härtl). I opt for the view that subject-experiencer verbs and object-experiencer verbs differ with regard to aktionsart and most importantly that the former are non-causative in contrast to the first mentioned class. But I turn later to a more detailed discussion of their respective aktionsart classes.

Experiencer verbs provide further interesting properties with regard to linking. Cross-linguistically these verbs display quirky case marking. Quirky case means "the marking of subjects and objects with cases other than the expected ones, e.g. dative, genitive, and accusative subjects, and dative and genitive objects" (Van Valin, 1991, 145). This can be illustrated by the German examples in (4) and (5). In (4) we have two experiencer-object verbs. The experiencer is marked with the accusative in (a), which is the canonical direct object case in German, but it is assigned the dative in (b). The examples in (5) are experiencer-subject verbs and the second argument is either accusative (a), dative (b) or genitive (c). The latter pattern is very restricted and it is doubtful whether the verbs in (b) and (c) can really be considered as being experiencer verbs in the sense mentioned above. For an extensive discussion of case marking patterns of German psych verbs see Wegener (1998) and Klein & Kutscher (2005).

(4) a. Er ängstigt mich.
    3SG.NOM frightens 1SG.ACC
    'He frightens me.'
  b. Er gefällt mir.
    3SG.NOM pleases 1SG.DAT
    'He pleases me.'

(5) a. Er mag mich.
    3SG.NOM likes 1SG.ACC
    'He likes me.'
  b. Er vertraut mir.
    3SG.NOM trusts 1SG.DAT
    'He trusts me.'
  c. Er gedenkt meiner.
    3SG.NOM commemorates 1SG.GEN
    'He commemorates me.'

Quirky case marking of experiencer verbs is attested in many languages, such as Italian Belletti & Rizzi (1988); Arad (1998), Navajo Jelinek & Willie (1998), Czech Filip (1996), Polish Rozwadowska (2007), Russian Sonnenhauser (2010), Spanish Whitley (1995); Arad (1998), Hebrew Arad (1998), Finnish Pylkkänen (1997), French Legendre (1989) and Japanese Matsumura (1996).[2]

The issue of argument linking seems to dominate the discussion on psych verbs and the distinction between *frighten* and *fear*, in particular,

---

[2] See also Næss (2007, chapter 8) for a cross-linguistic discussion of case marking of experiencer arguments and Haspelmath (2001) for a discussion of the argument realization of experiencer verbs in Standard Average European.

has triggered much discussion. There is a systematic relationship between *frighten* and *fear*, as can be seen in languages like Khalka Mongolian, in which *frighten* is derived from *fear* by causativation (6).

(6) Khalka Mongolian (Mongolic < Altaic)
   a. *Ene oxin ter   xüü-gees ai-j   bai-na.*
      DEM girl DEM boy-ABL fear-CON aux-npst
      'The girl fears the boy.'
   b. *Ene xüü ter   oxin-iig ai-lga-j   bai-na.*
      DEM boy DEM girl-ACC fear-CAU-CON AUX-NPST
      'The boy frightens the girl.'

The importance of the *fear/frighten* pair is overestimated in the linguistic literature since these verbs are not prototypical for the class of psych verbs but caused much discussion. Levin & Grafmiller (2013, 13) write: "Most experiencer-subject verbs lack experiencer-object counterparts referring to the same emotion and vice versa." Most experiencer verbs do not behave like *frighten* and *fear*, hence one does not have to look for a systematic relationship between subject-experiencer verbs and object-experiencer verbs. The lack of such an apparent relationship makes the linking differences between these two classes of verbs less puzzling.

In the next section, I discuss different types of experiencer verbs in more detail and relate the subclassification of experiencer verbs to an aktionsart classification.

8.2 Types of experiencer verbs

A first broad subclassification of experiencer verbs has already been mentioned: subject-experiencer verbs can be distinguished from object-experiencer verbs. The first class covers verbs like German *fürchten* 'fear,' *lieben* 'love,' *hassen* 'hate,' *bewundern* 'admire' and *bestaunen* 'marvel at.' The second class consists of verbs like German *ängstigen* 'frighten,' *ärgern* 'annoy,' *faszinieren* 'fascinate,' *erschrecken* 'scare' and *verblüffen* 'baffle.' I will discuss these subclasses separately since the verbs in each class are heterogeneous regarding relevant semantic parameters.

8.2.1 Subject-experiencer verbs

Subject-experiencer verbs are typically analyzed as stative predicates (Grimshaw 1990; Van Valin & LaPolla 1997; Härtl 2001 among others). Since there seems to be agreement on the aktionsart classification of subject-experiencer verbs, I will not discuss this in detail but only illustrate it with an example taken from Maienborn (2003). She shows that the eventuality denoted by verbs such as *hassen* 'hate' cannot be picked up anaphorically (7), which – as discussed in chapter 3.2.1 – is a typical property of stative predicates.

(7)   *Catherine hasste Mozart-Arien. *Das geschah/ passierte*
     Catherine hated Mozart-arias this happened occurred
     während...
     while
     'Catherine hated Mozart arias. This happened/occurred while...'
     (Maienborn, 2003, 69)

In their discussion of the differences between subject-experiencer and object-experiencer verbs, Levin & Grafmiller (2013) conclude that *fear* describes the mental state of an experiencer "as a disposition directed toward something" (p. 31) and not as "a direct response to an immediate stimulus" (p. 31). This characterization of *fear* follows from the types of entities which are typically realized as the stimulus argument. The authors write: "[...] the stimuli found with *fear* represent entities at which a particular emotion can be directed, and the authority inherent in many of these stimuli simply reinforces this. Inherently fear-inducing entities, events, or abstract notions need not be present in the immediate context, or even exist at all, making a direct causal connection between the stimulus and experiencer difficult to establish" (Levin & Grafmiller, 2013, 30f.). The central point is that the referent of the stimulus argument is not the cause of the respective emotion rather it is some property of the entity, like its authority, that causes the experiencer to have an emotional response. The emotional state is dispositional-like in the case of object-experiencer verbs. In the case of subject-experiencer verbs, the emotion is a direct reaction towards the stimulus and the attitude is episodic rather than disposition-like (I will come back to this point in the next section).

8.2 Types of experiencer verbs

Subject-experiencer verbs can be paraphrased as indicated in (8). I use 's' as a placeholder for the respective attitude the experiencer has. The exact type of attitude is lexically specified by the verb. In the case of *lieben* 'love' it is 'love' and in the case of *hassen* 'hate' it is the attitude of 'hate.'

(8) Subject-experiencer verbs: Experiencer has attitude 's' with regard to stimulus

Subject-experiencer verbs express that the experiencer x has an attitude s with respect to the stimulus y. This is represented by the function ATTITUDE which takes the experiencer and the stimulus and returns the attitude s the experiencer has. The respective attitude is further specified by a predicate as, for example, 'love(s)' in (9). A semantic representation of this type is given in (9) for the verb *lieben* 'love.'

(9) ⟦lieben⟧ $= \lambda x \lambda y (\text{ATTITUDE}(x,y)=s \wedge \text{love}(s))$

Most subject-experiencer verbs are transitive but some can only be used intransitively. Such intransitive uses are restricted to verbs of bodily state and damage to the body, as shown in (10). These verbs express bodily sensations and do not even have an implicit stimulus argument. *Frieren* 'be cold' only has an experiencer argument, whereas *schmerzen* 'ache, hurt' allows the experiencer to be implicit and the body part in which the pain is felt to be realized as the single argument of the verb. Since nouns denoting body parts are relational, as a body part always belongs to someone, the experiencer can be inferred as being the possessor of the body part. The experiencer is either expressed in an external possessive construction (b) or as a direct possessor of the body part (c).

(10)   a.   *Ich friere.*
            I   be.cold
            'I am cold.'[3]
       b.   *Das Bein schmerzt (mir).*
            the leg hurts   me
            'The leg hurts.' ('My leg hurts').

---

[3] Klein & Kutscher (2005, 3) mention that *frieren* 'be cold' also allows the experiencer realized in accusative rather than nominative case (*Mich friert*). There seems to be no semantic difference between both constructions, but the one with the experiencer in nominative case seems to be slightly more natural to me.

c. *Mein Bein schmerzt.*
   my leg hurts
   'My leg hurts.'

The semantic representation for intransitive subject-experiencer verbs is given in (11) for the example in (10a). The verb *frieren* simply means that the experiencer has a sensation of low temperature.

(11)   ⟦frieren⟧ = $\lambda x(\text{TEMPERATURE-SENSATION}(x)=\text{low}(\text{TEMPERATURE}(x))$

The subject-experiencer verb *bewundern* 'admire' has two different uses. Sentence (12a) expresses that the man feels admiration towards Van Gogh. In (12a) Van Gogh can be understood as being the painter but also in an abstract sense refering to the work of the painter Van Gogh. But there is also a more concrete reading, as in (12b). This sentence is ambiguous between the interpretation that the man feels admiration towards the respective painting or that the man is actively admiring the painting while, for example, standing in front of it. The first interpretation is possible with the painting being absent such that the sentence expresses a disposition of the man. In the second interpretation, the painting has to be present and the man perceives the painting. Although the man perceives the painting, he is admiring the painting too.

(12)   a.   *Der Mann bewundert Van Gogh.*
            the man admires Van Gogh
            'The man admires Van Gogh.'
       b.   *Der Mann bewundert das Gemälde.*
            the man admires the painting
            'The man admires the painting.'

Härtl (2001, 186) mentions that in the latter reading, subject-experiencer verbs are used as activity predicates. Härtl (2001, 187) assumes that *bewundern* denotes an eventuality consisting of two subevents: a dynamic one which is a dynamic event of perceiving and a stative one which is being in an emotional state. The entity in the emotional state is the object of the perception. I assume a similar representation which is shown in (13).

(13)   ⟦bewundern⟧ = $\lambda x \lambda y \lambda e.(\text{perceive}(e) \wedge \text{PERCEIVER}(e)=x \wedge \text{PERCEIVED}(e)=y \wedge \text{ATTITUDE}(x,y)=s \wedge \text{admiration}(s))$

The verb *bestaunen* 'marvel at' is similar to *bewundern* but only has an agentive interpretation. It always requires some active perception of a stimulus and is not possible in a dispositional reading. Since the activity component can be modified, it shows that it is a meaning component of the verb. Härtl argues that an instrumental-PP[4] can be used to modify the perceptional act (14).

(14) *Peter bewundert gerade mit einer 3D-Brille die Konstruktion.*
  Peter admires just with a 3-D glasses the construction
  'Peter is admiring the construction with 3-D glasses.'
  (Härtl, 2001, 188)

There is a further reading of the agentive use of (12b), which is that the man expresses admiration by means of his behavior. This can be done verbally, by his facial expression or by other means. It is not clear to me whether the man has to feel admiration if he is expressing this feeling. Probably it is the default interpretation that if he is expressing admiration, then he also has the corresponding experience. But surely this is not necessary. Nevertheless, I propose the semantic representation in (15) for this reading, which I will call 'emotion expression' reading in the following. The semantic representation in (15) is very similar to the perception reading of (12b). The difference is that the first subevent is not a perceptual one, but one of expressing a content which is that the agent has a certain attitude towards the stimulus y.

(15) $\lambda x \lambda y \lambda e.(\text{express}(e) \wedge \text{AGENT}(e)=x \wedge$
  $\text{CONTENT}(e)=(\text{ATTITUDE}(x,y)=s \wedge \text{admiration}(s))$

8.2.2 Object-experiencer verbs

Object-experiencer verbs are basically transitive. We do not find underived intransitive experiencer verbs in this class, due to the fact that these verbs do not realize the experiencer argument in subject position. The subject argument can either be an effector or a stimulus but in each case, the emotional state of the experiencer is somehow caused by the referent of the subject argument. In chapter 3.2.2, I have shown that *frighten* allows

---

[4] It would be more precise to call it an 'implement-PP' since subject-experiencer verbs are non-causative.

for a causative paraphrase, whereas *fear* does not. The relevant examples are repeated in (16).

(16) a. *The dog frightened the boy.*
      → *The dog caused the boy to feel fear.*
   b. *The boy feared the dog.*
      ↛ *The dog caused the boy to feel fear.*

A further criterion for causativity, also discussed in chapter 3.2.2, is that only causative verbs license instrument-PPs, in the narrow sense of instrument. If a verb licenses an instrument argument, it usually participates in the instrument-subject alternation, which is exemplified for *frighten* in (17).

(17) a. *The dog frightens the boy with his teeth.*
   b. *The teeth (of the dog) frighten the boy.*

In (16a) and (17a) the dog can either actively frighten the boy by baring his teeth or it may simply cause the boy to be frightened by his mere presence, for example. Only if the dog is doing something to cause the frightening of the boy, can we speak of *dog* as an effector argument. If the dog is not actively engaged in causing the feeling, we can only speak of *dog* as a stimulus argument. In both cases, effector and stimulus stand in a different causal relation to the experiencer. This difference in causation is not captured by the causativity tests. Since this difference does not affect degree gradation, I will not discuss it further.

Frighten allows uses in which the emotion is not directed at the effector but at something else. This can be illustrated by the example in (18). In the example, *they* are the subject of *frighten* but the emotion is directed at *grizzlies*. The effector and the 'subject-matter,' as Pesetsky (1995) calls it, are distinct event participants in this example. In other cases, they can coincide.

(18) *They tried to frighten her with talk of grizzlies, but she just looked out the window at the low, treed terrain...*
      (Levin & Grafmiller, 2013, 30)

The effector causes the respective emotion and the emotion can therefore be seen as a direct reaction to the effector. In contrast to subject-experiencer verbs, emotions are not necessarily dispositional but can be episodic. An appropriate paraphrase of object-experiencer verbs looks like in (19). Basically, these verbs express a causation of an attitude the experiencer has. It is left open whether the attitude is directed at the effector – which can be the case, but need not – or at something else.

(19)   Object-experiencer verbs: effector causes experiencer to have attitude 's'

A semantic representation of the object-experiencer verb *ängstigen* 'frighten' is shown in (20). The representation consists of an unspecified causing event *e* which is responsible for bringing about a state of emotion. The state is represented as the attitude of the experiencer *y* towards a stimulus *z*. The stimulus argument is existentially bound as it is not a syntactic argument of the verb and, as discussed above, does not need to be identical with the effector argument.

(20)   ⟦ängstigen⟧ = $\lambda x \lambda y \exists z \lambda e(\text{CAUSE}(e, (\text{ATTITUDE}(y,z)=s \land \text{fear}(s)) \land \text{EFFECTOR}(e)=x))$

Object-experiencer verbs are basically transitive but they allow for an anticausative construction. As in the case of change of state verbs, the anticausative construction is marked by the reflexive pronoun *sich* as shown in (21).[5] The experiencer is realized as the subject of the sentence, whereas the effector argument is not realized anymore. Rather a stimulus argument can be added in a prepositional phrase, as indicated in the examples.[6]

(21)   a.   *Der Junge ängstigt sich vor dem Hund.*
             the boy   frightens REFL from the dog
             'The boy is frightened of the dog.'
        b.   *Der Mann ärgert   sich über den Hund.*
             the man   annoyes REFL about the dog
             'The man is angry about the dog.'

---

[5] The subject-experiencer verb *fürchten* 'fear' can also be marked by a reflexive; in this case it does not have a decausativizing function. I will not discuss such marginal cases in the thesis and leave a systematic investigation of reflexive marking of experiencer verbs for future work.

[6] Also see the discussion of reflexivized experiencer verbs in French in Pesetsky (1995, 97ff.) and Marín & McNally (2005) on Spanish reflexively marked psychological verbs.

8 Experiencer verbs

The anticausative is marked in the same way as with change of state verbs. I assume that it is the same kind of alternation that can be observed with object-experiencer verbs and change of state verbs (see Alexiadou & Iordăchioaia 2014, who make the same point in a discussion of the psych causative alternation in Greek and Romanian). Usually the discussion of anticausatives is restricted to change of state verbs and I already mentioned the existing analyses in chapter 6. Whether object-experiencer verbs provide new data to this discussion must be left open for future investigation.

The anticausative use of object-experiencer verbs does not differ semantically from underived subject-experiencer verbs. This is no surprise given Levin & Grafmiller's (2013, 13) statement that "[m]ost experiencer-subject verbs lack experiencer-object counterparts referring to the same emotion and vice versa." Anticausative formation fills a gap which is only lexically filled in some cases, such as that of *frighten* and *fear*.

Much like subject-experiencer verbs, object-experiencer verbs also show uses in which the first argument has an agentive interpretation (Grimshaw 1990, 23, Levin 1993, 191). Examples are the verbs *amüsieren* 'amuse,' *ärgern* 'annoy' or *erfreuen* 'please.'[7] In (22a), *das schlechte Wetter* 'the bad weather' is a stimulus which stands in a causal relationship to the emotional state of the man. As the bad weather is not actively annoying the man, it is a stimulus and not an effector argument. In (b), *das Kind* 'the child' can either be an agentive effector or a stimulus argument. It could be the mere presence of the child that annoys the man or the child could intentionally do something to annoy the man, such as making noise or abusing the man.[8]

(22) a. *Das schlechte Wetter ärgert den Mann.*
    the bad   weather annoys the man
    'The bad weather is annoying the man.'
  b. *Das Kind ärgert den Mann.*
    the child annoys the man
    'The child is annoying the man.'

---

[7] For further examples of agentive object-experiencer verbs in German see Härtl (2001, 190).

[8] This is in line with the RRG view of agentivity as merely being an implicature Van Valin & Wilkins (1996). Hence, the thematic role 'agent' is a derivative notion from the more basic role 'effector'.

8.2 Types of experiencer verbs

A remark on the German verb *amüsieren* 'amuse' is in order since it also has an agentive anticausative use. In (23a), *das Kind* is either an agentive or non-agentive effector. Hence, it can amuse the man by intentionally doing something or unintentionally – such as by being clumsy. The anticausative use of *amüsieren* (b) also allows for different readings. One is the stative reading that the man is amused, the effector argument is omitted but an oblique stimulus argument can be realized. In addition, there are two agentive readings, one of which is the 'emotion expression' reading discussed at the end of the last section. In this reading, the man is expressing amusement through his behavior, facial expression or some other manner. In the second reading, the man is understood as making fun of the child. The man is not expressing his feelings, i.e., amusement, but rather he is engaged in other activities, such as joking. As an effect of these activities, he is amusing himself. Such agentive readings of anticausative object-experiencer verbs are very restricted, as is also the case for agentive readings of subject-experiencer verbs.

(23)   a.   *Das Kind amüsiert den Mann.*
               the child amuses the man
               'The child is amusing the man.'
       b.   *Der Mann amüsiert sich (über das Kind).*
               the man amuses REFL over the child
               'The man is amused at the child. / The man makes fun of the child.'

A last type of object-experiencer verbs are so-called 'psych achievements.' For German, Härtl (2001, 191) mentions the two verbs *erschrecken* 'scare' and *verblüffen* 'baffle' as instances of this class. These verbs are clearly punctual, as they receive a repetitive interpretation if combined with durative adverbials (24). In (24), it is not a single baffling or scaring that lasts for an hour but the referent of the subject argument baffles or scares her friend repeatedly within hours.

(24)   a.   *Sie verblüffte ihren Freund stundenlang mit ihren*
               she baffled her friend hours.long with her
               Geschichten.
               stories
               'She baffled her friend with her stories for hours.'

b. *Sie erschreckte ihren Freund stundenlang mit ihren*
   she scared   her   friend hours.long with her
   Geschichten.
   stories
   'She scared her friend with her stories for hours.'

Achievements differ from semelfactives in that only the former are telic, whereas the latter are not. It is not easy to distinguish between these aktionsart classes but it does not matter for the following discussion whether the verbs are causative achievements or causative semelfactives. *Erschrecken* can also be used in the anticausative construction (25a), whereas *verblüffen* cannot (b). The anticausative of *erschrecken* is derived by adding the reflexive pronoun *sich*, whereas *verblüffen* does not take this pronoun. Rather it requires the reflexive construction *sich selbst* 'oneself.' In this case, the referent of the subject argument is understood as being the effector hence we get a reflexive and not an anticausative interpretation. Without *sich* the sentence is akward.

(25) a. *Er erschreckte sich vor ihren Geschichten.*
        he scared   REFL of her   stories
        'He was scared by her stories.'
     b. *Er verblüffte sich selbst mit seinem Verhalten.*
        he baffled   himself   with his   behavior
        'He baffled himself with his own behavior.'

8.3 Degree gradation of experiencer verbs

The last section showed that subject- and object-experiencer verbs differ with regard to aktionsart. This difference, as mentioned in 8, accounts for the different linking properties of these verbs. For the following discussion of verbal degree gradation, it is relevant to keep the aktionsart differences in mind. Subject-experiencer verbs are mainly stative and noncausative predicates, whereas object-experiencer verbs are dynamic and causative predicates. Object-experiencer verbs show a more or less systematic anticausative alternation, whereas both types of experiencer verbs also allow for an agentive interpretation of its first argument. The agentive reading is less systematic with subject-experiencer verbs than with object-

8.3 Degree gradation of experiencer verbs

experiencer verbs. As before, I will discuss degree gradation of subject- and object-experiencer verbs separately.

8.3.1 Degree gradation of subject-experiencer verbs

Subject-experiencer verbs are gradable by *sehr* as shown by the examples in (26). The verbs in (a) and (b) express an emotional attitude, whereas the one in (c) expresses a bodily sensation. In all three cases, degree gradation affects the intensity of the attitude or sensation.

(26) a. *Der Junge liebt seine Mutter sehr.*
 the boy loves his mother very
 'The lad loves his mother very much.'
 b. *Er hasst seinen Nachbarn sehr.*
 he hates his neighbor very
 'He hates his neighbor very much.'
 c. *Ihm schmerzt das Bein sehr.*
 him hurts the leg very
 'His leg hurts very much.'

The paraphrase in (27) indicates that degree gradation affects the strength, i.e., intensity, of the attitude. Hence, degree gradation affects a gradable property of the experiencer's attitude. The relevant attribute chain is shown in (28). INTENSITY is linked to the eventuality through the implicit argument. In the context of degree gradation, the intensity scale can be retrieved from the conceptual knowledge associated with the lexically specified attitude.

(27) a. Subject-experiencer verbs: Experiencer has attitude 's' with regard to stimulus
 b. Graded subject-experiencer verbs: Experiencer has strong/intense attitude 's' with regard to stimulus

(28) $\lambda s.(\text{high}(\text{INTENSITY}(\text{ATTITUDE}(s))))$

A semantic representation for the graded subject-experiencer verb *lieben* is shown in (29).

(29) 〚sehr lieben〛 = $\lambda x \lambda y (\text{ATTITUDE}(x,y)=s \land \text{love}(s) \land \text{high}(\text{INTENSITY}(s)))$

8 Experiencer verbs

In (30), four Russian examples are shown which indicate that *očen'* functions as a degree intensifier for subject-experiencer verbs in Russian, too. In all four cases, *očen'* specifies the intensity of the respective attitude. Like in German, there is no difference whether it is a psychological attitude (a, b, c) or physical sensation (d).

(30) a. *Mužčina očen' boit-sja sobak-u.*
       man.NOM very fear-REFL dog-ACC
       'The man fears the dog very much.'
   b. *Mužčina očen' nenavidit svoego sosed-a.*
       man.NOM very hate his.GEN neighbor-GEN
       'The man hates his neighbor very much.'
   c. *Mal'čik očen' lubit mam-u.*
       boy.NOM very loves mom-ACC
       'The boy loves his mother very much.'
   d. *Noga mužčin-y očen' bolit.*
       leg.NOM man.-gen very hurt
       'The man's leg hurts very much.'

The verbs in (30) are imperfective and some allow the derivation of a perfective verb. In this case, an additional meaning component is contributed by the verbal prefix. For example, the imperfective *bolit'* 'hurt' becomes *za-bolit'* 'start to hurt' and *ljubit'* 'love' becomes *po-ljubit'* 'start to love' (31). Adding the prefix *po-* (31) derives a change of state predicate, the result state is the feeling expressed by the base verb. The intensifier further specifies the resulting state. I discussed similar cases for verbs of smell emission (discussed in the last chapter) and change of state verbs.

(31) *Ja očen' po-ljubila delat' krasivye* […] *klassnye i*
      I very PO-loved do beautiful.ACC cool.ACC and
      raznye konverty […].
      different.ACC envelops.ACC […]
      'I strongly fell in love with making different beautiful and cool envelops […].'[R]

In French, degree gradation of subject-experiencer verbs has the same interpretation as in German and Russian. The example in (32) illustrates this point with the verb *aimer* 'love.' *Beaucoup* indicates that the intensity of the experiencer's love is 'high.'

(32) Il aime beaucoup cette langue.
 he loves a lot   this language
 'He loves this language very much.'

As discussed above, some subject-experiencer verbs have not only a purely stative but also an agentive interpretation. *Bewundern* 'admire' is such a case and both of these readings are gradable by *sehr*. In (33a), *sehr* specifies the intensity of admiration the man feels for Van Gogh. Since (b) also allows for the pure stative reading, the same interpretation as for (a) applies.

(33) a. *Der Mann bewundert Van Gogh sehr.*
  the man admires Van Gogh very
  'The man admires Van Gogh very much.'
 b. *Der Mann bewundert das Gemälde sehr.*
  the man admires the painting very
  'The man admires the painting very much.'

For agentively interpreted verbs, there is a different interpretation of degree gradation. In an episodic reading, it can be said that the man is doing something which can be described as 'admiring.' It is expressed that the man is admiring the painting, which is illustrated, for example, by his behavior or facial expression. In the agentive reading of (b), *sehr* specifies the intensity of the expression of admiration. The behavior of the referent of the subject argument expresses strong admiration. It seems that this 'emotion expression' reading is always possible if the experiencer is conceived to be an agent. If one focuses on the agentive reading, *sehr* does not intensify the perceptual process. This is not unexpected since perception verbs such as *sehen* 'see' or *wahrnehmen* 'perceive' cannot be graded by *sehr* at all.

In (34), the paraphrases for the non-graded and graded agentive constructions are shown. The difference to the non-agentive reading is that it is not only stated that the experiencer has a certain experience but also that he is expressing this experience. I called this the 'emotion-expression' reading in section 8.2.1. Gradation applies again to the intensity scale but this time to the intensity of the expression of the feeling. A strong expression of a feeling does not necessarily entail that the experiencer has a corresponding intense feeling. The expectation that someone also has the attitude he expresses arises due to a Gricean implicature, as suggested by Sebastian Löbner (p.c.).

(34) a. Subject-experiencer verbs: Experiencer expresses attitude 's'
b. Graded agentive subject-experiencer verbs: Experiencer strongly expresses attitude 's'

In the agentive cases, gradation applies to a different gradable property than in the case of non-agentive subject-experiencer verbs. With agentive verbs, it is the intensity of the activity that is specified. In section 9.1.4 we will see that a similar interpretation arises with other verbs expressing activities, like *schlagen* 'hit' for example, as well. I assume that INTENSITY is a part of the manner component of gradable activity verbs but to answer the question how INTENSITY is integrated in the manner component, requires a decomposition of this meaning component which goes beyond the limits of this thesis.

8.3.2 Degree gradation of object-experiencer verbs

Object-experiencer verbs differ from subject-experiencer verbs in encoding a causal relation between the effector/stimulus and the feeling of the experiencer. This difference does not affect degree gradation; object-experiencer verbs admit degree gradation by *sehr* and, as in the case of subject-experiencer verbs, *sehr* specifies the intensity of the sensation. This is illustrated by the examples in (35). In (a), the dog not only causes the child to be frightened but also to be so to a high degree. Similarly in (b), the boy does not simply feel anger but the anger he feels has a high intensity.

(35) a. *Der Hund ängstigt das Kind sehr.*
the dog frightens the child very
'The dog frightens the boy very much.'
b. *Seine schlechten Noten ärgern den Jungen sehr.*
his bad marks annoy the boy very
'His bad marks annoy the boy very much.'

The examples in (35) can be paraphrased as shown in (36). Degree gradation specifies the strength of the experience, i.e., its intensity. As in the case of subject-experiencer verbs, the scale represents a property of the sensation. Degree gradation activates the INTENSITY attribute from the conceptual knowledge that we have of the sensation lexicalized by the verb. In (37), the attribute chain that links intensity to the eventuality is shown.

(36) a. causative Object-experiencer verbs: Effector causes the experiencer to have attitude 's'
      b. Graded causative object-experiencer verbs: Effector causes the experiencer to have a strong attitude 's'

(37) λs.(high(INTENSITY(ATTITUDE(s))))

The semantic representation of graded *ängstigen* 'frighten' is shown in (38).

(38) ⟦sehr ängstigen⟧ = λxλy∃zλe(CAUSE(e, (ATTITUDE(y,z)=s ∧ fear(s) ∧ high(INTENSITY(s)) ∧ EFFECTOR(e)=x)

As for subject-experiencer verbs, we find the same pattern of verbal degree gradation of object-experiencer verbs in Russian and in German. This is exemplified by in (39). The verb *pugat'* 'frighten' can be modified by *očen'*, which in this case means that Fedor's vocation caused a high degree of fear in the Catholic circles.

(39) *Prizvanie   Fedor-a   na   pol'sk-ij   prestol   očen'*
      vocation.NOM Fedor-GEN PREP polish-ACC throne.ACC very
      pugalo   katoličesk-ie   krug-i.
      frightened catholic-ACC.PL circle-ACC.PL
      'Fedor's vocation of the Polish throne frightened the Catholic circles very much.'[R]

The verb *pugat'* is imperfective but perfective verbs can be derived by prefixation. By adding *na-* to *pugat'*, we derive the verb *napugat'* 'scare.' As (40) shows, the verb can be graded by *očen'*, resulting in a specification of the intensity of the experiencer's fear.

(40) *Tak-ie   novost-i   očen' na-pugali   Meri.*
      such-NOM news-NOM very NA-frightened Mary.ACC
      'Such news scared Mary very much.'[R]

Also the affix *iz-* can prefixed to *pugat'* to derive a perfective verb meaning 'scare.' According to my informants, *napugat'* and *izpugat'* differ only in that the former is an unintentional scaring, whereas in the latter case it

8 Experiencer verbs

happens intentionally. *Izpugat'* is also gradable by *očen'* (41) and the interpretation is the same as for *napugat'*. It is the intensity of the feeling that is indicated as 'high.' Example (39) contrasts with (40) and (41) in aspect, the first one is imperfective and the latter two perfective, but there is no difference in the interpretation of degree gradation. Grammatical aspect does not affect degree gradation of eventive experiencer verbs.

(41)   *Vasja   vy-pryg-nu-l   iz   škaf-a   i   očen'*
       Vasja.NOM VY-jump-SEML-PST from closet-GEN and very
       iz-pugal   Vit-ju.
       IZ-frightened Vitja-*acc*
       'Vasja jumped out of the closet and scared Vitja very much.'[R]

This short discussion of the prefixed variants of *pugat'* also leads to a discussion of punctual object-experiencer verbs. German punctual object-experiencer verbs like *erschrecken* 'scare' and *verblüffen* 'baffle' are gradable, too. As for the durative object-experiencer verbs, degree gradation affects the intensity of the experience (42). There is no difference in degree gradation of durative and punctual object-experiencer verbs. Interestingly, degree gradation does not lead to an iterative interpretation of the eventuality, which is what happens with semelfactive verbs of sound and light emission. This is probably due to the fact that *erschrecken* and *verblüffen* are really achievements and not semelfactives and are therefore restricted to the denotation of single events (as discussed in section 7.4).

(42)   a.   *Das Geräusch erschreckte ihn sehr.*
            the sound   scared   him very
            'The sound scared him a lot.'
       b.   *Seine Noten verblüfften ihn sehr.*
            his   marks baffled   him very
            'His marks baffled him very much.'

German examples of graded anticausative object-experiencer verbs are shown in (43). The sentences in (43) are the anticausative correspondences of the ones in (35). As in the latter cases, *sehr* specifies the intensity of the experience.

8.3 Degree gradation of experiencer verbs

(43) a. *Das Kind ängstigt sich sehr (vor dem Hund).*
the child frightens REFL very for the dog
'The child is very frightened of the dog.'
b. *Der Junge ärgert sich sehr (über seine Noten).*
the boy annoys REFL very over his marks
'The boy is very annoyed about his marks.'

Degree gradation affects the same component of the causative as well as anticausative object-experiencer verbs. This can be seen by comparing the paraphrase for the graded anticausative object-experiencer verb in (44) with the paraphrase of the graded causative object-experiencer verb in (36). In both cases, it is the intensity of the experiencer's sensation that is graded. The link of the INTENSITY attribute to the eventuality is shown in (45).

(44) a. Anticausative Object-experiencer verbs: Experiencer has attitude 's'
b. Graded anticausative Object-experiencer verbs: Experiencer has a strong attitude 's'

(45) $\lambda s.(\text{high}(\text{INTENSITY}(\text{ATTITUDE}(s))))$

The semantic representation of a graded anticausative object-experiencer verb is illustrated by using the example of *sich sehr ängstigen* in (46).

(46) ⟦sich sehr ängstigen⟧ = $\lambda y \exists z (\text{ATTITUDE}(y,z)=s \land \text{fear}(s) \land \text{high}(\text{INTENSITY}(s)))$

It is not surprising that degree gradation of the causative and anticausative object-experiencer verbs is the same since the constant part is the state of having a sensation. Since the gradation scale is a property of the felt experience, it is part of the verb's meaning in both the causative and anticausative use. The same can be observed in Russian, which also marks the anticausative with a reflexive marker (47). Degree gradation applies to the INTENSITY attribute of the experiencer's sensation, too.

(47) *Ja často očen' pugal-sja ot neožidann-ogo šum-a.*
I often very frightened-REFL PREP unexpected-gen noise-gen
'I was often very frightened by unexpected noises.'[R]

8 Experiencer verbs

Finally, I turn to the question as to whether agentivity interacts with degree gradation of object-experiencer verbs. In (48), the effector argument can be conceived as intentionally and actively annoying the man. This is in contrast to (35b), in which case the effector argument *seine schlechten Noten* 'his bad marks' is inanimate and therefore does not give rise to an agentive interpretation. The agentivity of the effector argument does not affect degree gradation and the only admissible gradation scale, in this case, is given by the sensation's INTENSITY attribute.

(48)   *Das Kind ärgert den Mann sehr.*
        the child annoys the man very
        'The child is annoying the man very much.'

Somewhat more complicated is the case of *amüsieren*, which licenses the agentive reading if the effector argument is animate. But the verb also licenses an agentive reading in its anticausative use. For the sake of illustration, I will discuss degree gradation of causative and anticausative *amüsieren* in parallel. In (49), we have the basic causative use of *amüsieren*, with an inanimate (a) and an animate effector (b). In the latter case, the effector also allows for an agentive interpretation. Irrespective whether the effector is interpreted agentively or not, *sehr* specifies the intensity of the amusement of the experiencer. So far, there is no difference to the data discussed above.

(49)   a.   *Der Film amüsiert den Mann sehr.*
             the film amuses the man very
             'The film is amusing the man very much.'
        b.   *Das Kind amüsiert den Mann sehr.*
             the child amuses the man very
             'The child is amusing the man very much.'

In (50a), we have the plain anticausative use of *amüsieren*, which simply means that the man is very amused. This interpretation goes parallel to the one of the examples in (49). The example in (b) also allows for an agentive interpretation of *der Mann*. This gives rise to two different readings of the sentence. The first one is the 'expression' reading which has already been discussed in connection to agentively used subject-experiencer verbs. Degree gradation is interpreted in the same way as the corresponding uses of subject-experiencer verbs, it is the intensity of the expression of the respective sensation that is indicated by *sehr*. The second agentive reading of (50b) is that the man makes fun of the child. It could be, for example, that the man is making jokes about the child. The activity is neither directed at the child nor is the child the object of the action. The child is more like the topic of the amusement and sehr indicates the intensity of the amusement of *der Mann*.

(50)   a.   *Der Mann amüsiert sich sehr.*
              the man amuses REFL very
              'The man is very amused.'
      b.   *Der Mann amüsiert sich sehr (über das Kind).*
              the man amuses REFL very over the child
              'The man is very amused at the child./The man is making much fun of the child.'

8.4 Conclusion

In this section, I demonstrated that experiencer verbs do not form a homogeneous class of verbs. On the one hand, there are differences with respect to argument realization and on the other, there are different readings that are licensed by different subsets of experiencer verbs. It turned out that gradation is very homogeneous and always related to an intensity scale. The scale measures the intensity of the feeling of the experiencer. Degree gradation only has a different interpretation for some subject-experiencers if the subject referent has an agentive interpretation. In this case, the intensifier specifies the intensity of the activity of expressing a sensation rather than the intensity of the sensation itself.

Degree gradation of experiencer verbs neither interacts with grammatical nor lexical aspect. The Russian data have shown that the perfective/imperfective contrast is not relevant for the interpretation of verbal degree gradation of experiencer verbs. In (51), it is shown that *ängstigen* 'frighten' is atelic (a) and remains atelic if graded by *sehr* (b). Neither sentence means that after ten minutes the boy was (very much) frightened, rather the interpretation is that the dog starts to frighten the boy after ten minutes. We only get an ingressive interpretation, both in (a) and (b), and therefore the predications are atelic.

8 Experiencer verbs

(51)   a.   *Der Hund ängstigte den Jungen in zehn Minuten.*
the dog frightened the boy in ten minutes
'The dog frightened the boy in ten minutes.'
       b.   *Der Hund ängstigte den Jungen in zehn Minuten sehr.*
the dog frightened the boy in ten minutes very
'The dog frightened the boy in ten minutes a lot.'

Similarly, it has been shown above that degree gradation does not lead to an iterative reading of punctual experiencer verbs such as *erschrecken* 'scare' and *verblüffen* 'buffle.' The fact that degree gradation does not interact with grammatical and lexical aspect as well as the homogeneity of degree gradation beside the heterogeneity of the verb class are two issues which I will discuss in more details in the next chapter.

Agentivity showed up to be relevant in the discussion of experiencer verbs. It was shown that agentivity may affect the reading of certain verbs but only marginally interacts with verbal degree gradation. Agentivity only intervenes with degree gradation if it triggers a meaning shift from a sensational towards an expressive reading of the verb. In all other cases, which do not induce such a meaning shift, agentivity is not an influencing property.

Finally, this chapter has shown the relevance of implicit semantic arguments for verbal degree gradation. As in the case of verbs of emission, experiencer verbs have an implicit semantic argument that licenses the activation of a gradable attribute.

9 Gradation, aspect, and telicity

In the previous chapters, I presented three case studies on verbal degree gradation. In the first part of the current chapter, I want to broaden the general picture and to present a short discussion of further semantic classes of gradable verbs. This discussion will be concluded by a summary of the different subcompositional patterns. In the second section 9.2, the notion of 'subcompositionality' is discussed in detail and I demonstrate why verbal degree gradation is subcompositional. Finally, I will turn in 9.3 to a discussion of the interaction between degree gradation and grammatical aspect as well as telicity.

9.1 Compositional patterns

In chapters 6 to 8, three different semantic verb classes were discussed with respect to verbal degree gradation. In section 9.1.1, I will summarize the different patterns of verb degree gradation found with the semantic verb classes discussed in the foregoing chapters. In the sections 9.1.2 to 9.1.4, I will broaden the view and shortly discuss more patterns of verbal degree gradation that can be found in German and other languages. The aim of section 9.1.5 is to illustrate similarities between the different compositional patterns.

9.1.1 Changes, emissions, and experiences

Change of state verbs express a scalar change in a property of the referent of their theme argument. Degree gradation applies to that scale and either specifies the degree of change, as in the case of degree achievements, or further specifies the degree of the attained result state, which is the case for accomplishments.

Verbs of emission can be classified into in four different subclasses, and three of them show similar patterns regarding verbal degree gradation. In the case of verbs of sound emission, light emission and smell emission, degree gradation affects an intensity scale. The scale represents a gradable property of the implicit emittee argument. Verbs of substance emission differ in that the scale does not measure intensity but quantity. The quantity scale represents a gradable property of the emitted substance as is the case for the scales of the other subtypes of verbs of emission.

Experiencer verbs form a rather heterogeneous verb class consisting of verbs showing different linking patterns as well as belonging to different aktionsart classes (in chapter 8, I showed that these differences go together with differences in the lexical semantics of the verbs). Despite the heterogeneity of experiencer verbs, verbal degree gradation is uniform in specifying a degree on an intensity scale. The scale represents a gradable property of the experiencer's attitude.

The different types of gradation scales found in these three semantic classes of verbs are summarized in table 16. Following Rappaport Hovav (2008) among others, I use the term 'property scale' as a general notion for the different scales lexicalized by change of state verbs. Examples of such property scales are 'size,' 'weight,' 'price,' 'temperature' and so on. Even if different verb classes are related to intensity scales, the exact interpretation of the notion of 'intensity' differs from verb class to verb class. Regarding sound emission, intensity can be understood as 'loudness,' whereas with respect to light emission, intensity is 'brightness.' Interestingly, English employs the synonyms 'sound intensity' and 'light intensity' for 'loudness' and 'lightness' respectively, whereas German does not. For smell emission and sensations 'intensity' is probably the best and only term that can be used. 'Quantity,' in the case of verbs of substance emission, could also be conceived as 'volume'; it measures an amount of substance.

Verb class	Type of scale
Change of state verbs	Property scale
Verbs of sound/smell/light emission	Intensity scale
Verbs of substance emission	Quantity scale
Experiencer verbs	Intensity scale

Table 16: Classes of verbs and their associated types of scales.

In addition to the different scales, we also observe differences in the kind of verbal degree gradation. There is a difference between indicating a differential degree, as is the case for change of state verbs, and a non-differential one, as for verbs of emission and experiencer verbs. In the case of a differential degree, the intensifier specifies the difference between two degrees. For change of state verbs, this is a difference between an initial degree and a final degree at the end of a change of state event. Roughly speaking, a differential degree indicates a difference between two arbitrary degrees on a scale and the intensifier further specifies the extent of the difference between these degrees. The notion of a 'differential degree' is not restricted to scalar changes and I will present examples in the next subsection.

In the case of verbs of emission and experiencer verbs, the intensifier does not specify a difference between two degrees. If one takes *frighten* as an example, then it is not the case that the intensifier specifies the divergence between the initial degree of frightening and a final one. This does not mean that grading experiencer verbs, for example, can never lead to a specification of a difference degree. In fact, we have seen such cases, as provided by certain prefixed verbs in Russian and Polish. In chapter 8, the Russian prefixed verb *po-ljubit'* meaning 'to fall in love' has been mentioned. Prefixation derives a perfective change of state predication of the imperfective state verb *ljubit'* 'love.' Although, in the latter case, degree gradation affects the intensity of love, in the former case it specifies the resulting change. But this is a derived interpretation; the change of state component is induced by the verbal prefix. I will turn to similar examples in section 9.1.3 below.

9.1.2 Verbs expressing divergence & similarity

In his discussion of verb gradation, Löbner (2012b) mentions two classes of verbs which are of interest in the current section. He calls these classes 'verbs of comparison' and 'verbs of marked behavior.' What is interesting about these verbs is that they express a difference between degrees without denoting a change of state.

Starting with verbs of comparison: this class consists of verbs like *sich ähneln* 'be similar' and *sich unterscheiden* 'differ.' These verbs are quite general and express some similarity or difference regarding an unspecified property. In (1a), one has to infer the respective property with respect

9 Gradation, aspect, and telicity

to which the two books are similar; this could be the content, the way the book looks or whatever other properties the books have. But, as also indicated in the example, the respective dimension of comparison can be made explicit. Verbs of comparison are similar to such change of state verbs like *steigen* 'rise' with respect to scalar underspecification (cf. the discussion in section 6.3). As (1b) shows, verbs of comparison can be graded and it is the degree of similarity that is specified by *sehr*.

(1) a. Die beiden Bücher ähneln sich (im Aussehen).
   the both books be.similar REFL in.the appearance
   'The two books are similar in appearance./The two books look similar.'
   b. Die beiden Bücher ähneln sich sehr.
   the both books be.similar REFL very
   'The two books are very similar.'

Regarding verbs of comparison, the intensifier specifies a difference value. For *sich ähneln*, it is expressed that the difference between the two degrees which are the degrees the compared objects have in the respective dimension is small. For a verb such as *sich unterscheiden* 'differ,' *sehr* indicates that this difference is very large. The attribute chain which links the scale of *sich ähneln* to the eventuality is shown in (2). As the representation indicates, SIMILARITY is a comparison between properties of the verb's syntactic arguments and it is not an attribute of an implicit argument of the verb. The scale is lexically encoded in the verb as *sich ähneln* always expresses a comparison and not just in the context of degree gradation. Hence, the scale is not retrieved from the conceptual knowledge.

(2) ⟦sich sehr ähneln⟧ = $\lambda x \lambda y \lambda v.(\text{high}(\text{SIMILARITY}(\text{APPEARANCE}(\text{THEME}(x)), \text{APPEARANCE}(\text{COMPARANDUM}(y))(v))))$

The same holds for the Russian example in (3). The verb *otličat'sja* 'differ' is derived from *otličat'* 'distinguish.' Only the base verb shows an aspectual opposition but not the derived stative predicate, which is imperfective. In (4), a French example is shown which indicates that *beaucoup* can also be used for grading verbs of comparison.

(3)　　Nov-aja　glav-a　　　očen' otličaet-sja ot　star-oj　glav-y.
　　　　new-*nom* chapter-*nom* very　differs-*refl* PREP　old.ACC chapter-ACC
　　　　'The new chapter differs very much from the old one.'

(4)　　Elle se　différencie beaucoup de sa　sœur.
　　　　she REFL differs　　a lot　　　of her sister
　　　　'She differs a lot from her sister.'

Verbs of comparison express a static predication since the values of two objects in a certain, maybe unspecified, dimension are compared. These verbs do not denote an increase or decrease in similarity, which shows that difference values are also found with stative verbs. This is also indicated by the paraphrase of example (1a) in (5).

(5)　　Die beiden Bücher sind sich　sehr　ähnlich (im　　Aussehen).
　　　　the both　books　are　REFL very　similar　in.the appearance
　　　　'The two books are very similar in appearance.'

The German paraphrase, similar to the English translation of the example, makes use of an adjective. This is not surprising as many languages express comparative constructions by using verbs, as they lack a distinct category of adjectives (cf. Stassen 1984, 1985). In contrast to comparative constructions, verbs of comparison are less specific in German. Most adjectival comparatives in German express a comparison in a concrete dimension, as the adjective itself is related to such a dimension. Exceptions to this are the adjectives *anders* (*als*) 'different (to/than),' *verschieden* (*von*) 'different from' and *ähnlich* (*zu*) 'similar to' which are unspecific regarding the dimension.

The second class of verbs mentioned above – verbs of marked behavior – is represented by verbs like *stottern* 'stutter,' *lispeln* 'lisp,' *hinken* 'limp' or *schielen* 'squint.' These verbs express that the referent of the subject argument diverges from some norm. In the case of *stottern* and *lispeln*, it is expressed that the way the subject referent is speaking diverges from the normal way of speaking. Both verbs denote different types of divergences from the normal manner of speaking.

In (6) it is shown that these verbs can be graded by *sehr*. Löbner (2012b, 238) states that "[i]ntensification concerns the extent of deviation from the unmarked." If there is a 'normal,' unmarked manner of speaking, *stottern* 'stutter' denotes a divergence from this manner of speaking with regard to the flow of words. Degree gradation has the effect of further indication of the deviation of the behavior of the subject referent from the normal manner of carrying out the respective action.

(6)   a.   *Der Junge stottert sehr.*
            the boy   stutters very
            'The boy stutters very much.'
    b.   *Der Junge lispelt sehr.*
            the boy   lisps   very
            'The boy lisps very much.'

The same examples can be found in Russian (7) and French (8), too. The Russian imperfective verb *zaikat'sja* 'stutter' has a habitual interpretation in (7) and if graded by *očen'* it expresses that Fëdor is not only stuttering but does so to a high degree. The interpretation for the French example is the same.

(7)   *Fëdor očen' zaikal-sja   v   detstv-e.*
        Fëdor very stuttered-REFL PREP childhood-LOC
        'Fëdor stuttered very much in his childhood.'

(8)   *Le pauvre garçon bégaye beaucoup.*
        the poor boy   stutters a lot
        'The poor boy stutters a lot.'

As stated above, the verbs compare the actual manner of behavior with an unmarked manner and thereby indicate a divergence between the actual and the unmarked behavior. Hence, both classes of verbs discussed in this section indicate some divergence between two degrees – which are either the degree of two different objects or of an object and some norm – and do not denote a change of state.

    Degree gradation of these two classes of verbs neither interacts with lexical nor grammatical aspect. Stative verbs of comparison do not display aspectual contrasts and degree gradation does not render the predication telic (9). If the time-span adverbial is acceptable, it forces a change of state reading, meaning that in ten minutes the books begin to equal each other. In this shifted reading, *ähneln* denotes the attained result state and *sehr* specifies the degree of the resulting state.

(9) #*Die beiden Bücher ähneln   sich in zehn Minuten sehr.*
     the both books be.similar REFL in ten minutes very
     'The two books are very similar in ten minutes.'

At least, the German stative verb of comparison *gleichen* 'to equal' allows the derivation of a change of state predicate by the prefix *an-*. *Angleichen* 'to align' can be graded by *sehr* and is given the same interpretation as change of state predicates.

Verbs of marked behavior show an aspectual opposition, as illustrated in (10). In the perfect (a) as well as progressive (b) example, *sehr* indicates the degree of divergence from normal speech. There is no difference in the interpretation of degree gradation for these sentences. There is also no effect on telicity as these verbs stay atelic even if graded by *sehr* (11).

(10) a. *Der Junge hat sehr gestottert.*
          the boy   has very stuttered
          'The boy stuttered very much.'
      b. *Der Junge ist sehr am   Stottern.*
          the boy   is very at.the stuttering
          'The boy is stuttering very much.'

(11) #*Der Junge hat in zehn Minuten sehr gestottert.*
      the boy   has in ten   minutes very stuttered
      'The boy stuttered very much in ten minutes.'

9.1.3 Erratic verbs

Ropertz (2001) uses the term 'erratische Verben' (erratic verbs) for verbs which express a divergence between the actual result and the intended result of an activity. In German, erratic verbs are derived from simplex verbs by the prefix *ver-* and the reflexive pronoun *sich*.[1] Examples are *sich verschreiben* 'miswrite' derived from *schreiben* 'write,' *sich verlaufen* 'get lost' derived from *laufen* 'go, run' or *sich verfahren* 'to lose one's way' derived from *fahren* 'drive.' The derived verbs are marked by a reflexive pronoun, in contrast to their base verbs. Degree gradation (12) specifies the diver-

---

[1] The prefix *ver-* is multifunctional and does not always derive a complex verb with erratic meaning from some base verb e.g. *verbrauchen* 'consume' derived from *brauchen* 'need'.

gence between the intended result and the actual result. In (12a), it is not only expressed that the boy got lost and missed his goal but that he missed the goal a lot, so the difference between his intended goal and the place where he actually arrives is large.

(12) a. *Der Junge hat sich sehr verlaufen.*
the boy has REFL very got.lost
'The boy got totally lost.'
b. *Das Mädchen hat sich sehr verschrieben.*
the girl has REFL very miswrote
'The girl totally miswrote.'

The relevant gradation scale is one that measures divergence between the intended and the actual result. The scale introduced by the derivational prefix measures some divergence or difference on a scale. Both (12a) and (b) are related to the same kind of scale, as the scale is neither particularly related to going/running in (a) or writing in (b). The link between the gradation scale and the eventuality argument is shown in (13). DIFFERENCE measures the difference between the intended result of the eventuality and its actual result. Stiebels (1996, 151) discusses whether intentionality is really a relevant component in the semantic analysis of these verbs. I will not discuss this topic further but make use of the notion of 'intended result' in (13).

(13) $\lambda v.\text{high}(\text{DIFFERENCE}(\text{INTENDED-RESULT}(v), \text{ACTUAL-RESULT}(v)))$

In (12a), the base verb *laufen* is a manner of motion verb and is a plain activity predicate. The verb does not lexicalize a path scale (cf. the discussion in chapter 3.3 on result verbs) but seems to be associated with a velocity scale, as examples like (14) suggest.

(14) *Er musste sehr laufen um den Bus zu bekommen.*
he had very ran to the bus to get
'He had to run very fast in order to catch the bus.'

Some manner of motion verbs, such as *laufen* or *rennen* 'run,' admit degree gradation. In this case, the intensifier specifies the velocity of movement. But if prefixed by *ver-*, the velocity scale is not available anymore for degree gradation. Examples like (12a) and (14) indicate again that certain constructions can introduce a new scale and block the access to either a lexicalized or conceptually retrieved scale (cf. the discussion in chapter 7.2).

Erratic verbs can be used in the progressive aspect, but degree gradation of this construction is only marginally acceptable (15). If one accepts examples like (15), the intensifier specifies the divergence between the intended and the attained result state, like in the case of the perfect sentence in (12a). There is also a prospective reading of the progressive sentence in (15), meaning that if the boy continues his movement, there will be a large divergence between his received and his intended position. This does not entail that there actually is such a divergence but that his movement will lead to one. The prospective reading is not dependent on the degree context but also results for ungraded erratic verbs in the progressive aspect. Note that in difference to the German sentence, the Enlish translation of (15) is totally acceptable.

(15) ??*Der Junge ist sich sehr am Verlaufen.*
     the boy is REFL very at.the got.lost
     'The boy is getting totally lost.'

Neither ungraded nor graded erratic verbs seem to be telic, as the examples in (16) indicate. With regard to aktionsart, erratic verbs behave like degree achievements as they express the attainment of a result state but are atelic. In contrast to degree achievements, degree gradation does not affect telicity of erratic verbs.

(16)   a. #*Der Junge hat sich in einer Stunde verlaufen.*
          the boy has REFL in one hour got.lost
          'The boy got lost in an hour.'
    b. #*Der Junge hat sich in einer Stunde sehr verlaufen.*
          the boy has REFL in one hour very got.lost
          'The boy got totally lost in an hour.'

9.1.4 Gradable action verbs

Action verbs (the term is taken from Löbner (2012b)) belong to rather different semantic verb classes. I have already discussed verbs of substance emission as well as verbs of sound emission; both classes consist of activity predicates. Both classes of verbs are related to different gradation scales, as discussed above. Further gradable activities belong to the classes of verbs of marked behavior and erratic verbs. But above, I also mentioned that some manner of motion verbs can be graded. This indicates the huge diversity of scales associated with activity predicates. Of particular interest are the verbs of the hit class, like German *schlagen* 'hit, beat' and *treten* 'kick.' Löbner (2012b) briefly discusses the German verb *schlagen* 'hit, beat' and mentions that this verb licenses at least two different readings of verbal degree gradation. He writes: "Intensification may apply to the effort the agent invests into the beating, resulting in a high number of or heavy strokes; it may as well relate to the effect it has on the victim, in terms of pain and harm" (Löbner, 2012b, 238). Taking a sentence like (17) as an example, *sehr* either specifies the intensity of the beating or the intensity of the effect. That someone puts a great deal of effort into his punch does not entail that the victim is hit hard and that the victim is hit hard does not necessarily entail that a lot of effort was put into the beating. Hence, both readings do not necessarily entail each other.

(17)   Der Boxer hat seinen Gegner   sehr geschlagen.
       the boxer has his   opponent very hit
       'The boxer hit his opponent intensively/hard.'

In (18), the attribute chains which link the gradable properties to the eventuality are presented. INTENSITY is either an attribute of the respective action executed in the eventuality and belongs to the manner component of the verb or it is an attribute of the action. Whether INTENSITY is lexicalized in the manner component or inferred from the conceptual knowledge of manners of action is a question that has already been raised in chapter 8. I will leave this question open but assume that the second INTENSITY attribute that belongs to the EFFECT of the action is inferred from the conceptual knowledge of the respective effect. Action verbs which are not related to gradable effects should therefore reject degree gradation. This is clearly true for Levin's (1993) verbs of contact such as German *berühren* 'touch, contact' and *tasten* 'touch' but also for other verb classes like verbs of cutting as *schneiden* 'cut'.

(18) a. λv.(high(INTENSITY(ACTION(v))))
 b. λv.(high(INTENSITY(EFFECT(ACTION(v)))))

Löbner mentions that *sehr schlagen* could also mean to make many strokes. This interpretation arises due to the fact that it is a semelfactive predicate and the same effect as observed for semelfactive verbs of light and sound emission arises. The extent reading is merely an implicature as discussed in the chapters 7.3 and 7.4. There is also a reading of *schlagen* meaning 'to defeat someone.' In this reading, the verb is not gradable by *sehr*.

Grammatical aspect does not interact with degree gradation of *schlagen*. For the graded progressive sentence in (19), the same interpretation obtains as for the graded perfect sentence in (17).

(19) *Der Boxer ist seinen Gegner sehr am Schlagen.*
 the boxer is his enemy very at.the beat
 'The boxer is beating his enemy intensively/hard.'

Since *schlagen* is an activity, it is atelic. It also remains atelic if graded by *sehr*. The time-span adverbial does not license the relevant egressive interpretation in (20).

(20) #*Der Boxer hat seinen Gegner in zehn Minuten sehr geschlagen.*
 the boxer has his enemy in ten minutes very beat
 'The boxer hit his enemy intensely/hard in ten minutes.'

9.1.5 Similarities in the compositional patterns

The discussion above focuses on three essential parameters, namely: (i) the type of scale, (ii) interaction of degree gradation with grammatical aspect and (iii) interaction of degree gradation with telicity. It emerged that four types of scales are of crucial relevance: intensity scales, property scales, divergence scales and quantity scales. Based on the three parameters, the following classification of different types of verbal degree gradation can be derived:

(i) Degree gradation on an intensity scale: This pattern can be found with verbs of smell/sound/light emission, experiencer verbs as well as gradable activity predicates. Gradation is related to an intensity scale on which a non-differential degree is indicated. Neither lexical nor grammatical aspect is affected by degree gradation.

(ii) Degree gradation on a quantity scale: This pattern is found with verbs of substance emission. Gradation is related to a quantity scale on which a non-differential degree is indicated. Degree gradation interacts with grammatical aspect but not with lexical aspect.

(iii) Degree gradation on a divergence scale: This pattern is found with verbs of comparison, verbs of marked behavior and erratic verbs. Gradation is related to a scale measuring a divergence from some norm or comparison degree. The intensifier indicates a differential degree but does not interact with grammatical or lexical aspect.

(iv) Degree gradation on a property scale: This pattern is found with change of state verbs. Gradation is related to a property scale on which a scalar change is measured. The intensifier indicates a differential degree and interacts with grammatical as well as lexical aspect.

The aim of the classification is not to argue for a uniform compositional pattern for each of these classes. Instead of having a compositional rule for the classes listed above, each semantic verb class requires its own rule of composition for verbal degree gradation. Degree gradation of verbs of smell emission and hit verbs, which both belong to the first class, can be described by a single compositional rule. This is what Löbner (2012b) calls 'subcompositionality' and to which I turn in the next section.

Before I end this section, a short note on the contrast between divergence and property scales on the one hand and intensity and quantity scales on the other hand is required. In the first case, degree gradation leads to the specification of a differential degree, whereas in the second case it is a non-differential degree specified by *sehr*. Divergence and quantity scales seem to be always overtly encoded, meaning they are either lexicalized in the verb, as in the case of change of state verbs and verbs of comparison, or they are introduced by a morphological construction like the prefix *ver-* in the case of erratic verbs or the resultative prefix in case of strong resultative constructions. Such scales never seem to be retrieved from conceptual knowledge. This contrast between differential and non-differential degree gradation requires further analysis; in particular a larger cross-linguistic comparison would be interesting.

9.2 Subcompositionality of verbal degree gradation

The last subsections summarized different degree gradational patterns identified in the foregoing chapters and identified further ones. The aim of this subsection is to demonstrate that the different patterns are really distinct and that verbal degree gradation cannot be reduced to a single semantic rule of composition. This leads to a problem with the principle of compositionality, which makes up the foundation of semantics. A general formulation of the principle is shown in (21) and taken from Löbner (2012b, 220); one finds very similar formulations in all works concerned with the notion of 'compositionality' e.g. Partee (1984); Partee et al. (1990).

(21) Principle of compositionality: The meaning of a complex expression is a function of the meanings of its components and the syntactic structure of the whole.

I follow Löbner's exposition of the principle of compositionality. He states that the principle presupposes that the semantic operations employed in composition follow rules which he formulates as the assumption of 'regularity of semantic composition' (22).

(22) Regularity of semantic composition: The meaning of a syntactically regular expression derives from the meaning of its components in a regular way.
(Löbner, 2012b, 220)

Regularity of semantic composition means that (i) syntactic expressions are formed by rules and (ii) there are rules which derive the meaning of regularly formed complex expressions from their components. Hence, the rules apply generally which means they apply to types of expressions and not to individual expressions. As Löbner states: "Types of expressions subsume different individual cases, and they represent general categories" (Löbner, 2012b, 221), therefore regularity of semantic composition means that "[f]or all complex expressions of a given type, the same semantic operation yields its meaning out of the meaning of their components" (Löbner, 2012b, 221). All that means is that if two individual complex expressions E1 and E2 are of the same type γ, then the same semantic rule derives the meaning of these complex expressions from the meaning of their components. By 'type' Löbner means syntactically as well as semantically defined types in the sense of Carpenter (1992). For illustration he uses the German verb *bluten* which belongs to, at least, the following types: 'lexical expression,' 'predicate term,' '1-place predicate term,' '1-place verb,' 'gradable 1-place verb,' 'verb of emission,' 'bluten' (cf. Löbner 2012b, 222). The types are ordered regarding specificity, the first-mentioned types are less specific than those mentioned subsequently. The most specific type is that of the minimal type 'bluten,' which is a subtype of 'verb of emission' and so on.

The resulting question is which types are relevant for semantic composition. Löbner states that two type systems are of importance for compositionality, which are defined by morphosyntactic rules on the one hand and by semantic rules on the other hand. The definition of 'morphosyntactic type' is given in (23) and an example of such a type is 'verb' since verbal inflectional rules have verbs as their (maximal) range of application.

(23)   Morphosyntactic types: t is a morphosyntactic type iff there is a morphosyntactic rule that has t as its (maximum) range of application. (Löbner, 2012b, 222)

Löbner (2012b, 222) defines semantic types as presented in (24). Usually, '1-place predicate term' is taken to be a semantic type since such terms provide a uniform domain of application for a rule of argument saturation.[2]

(24)   Semantic types: t is a semantic type iff there is a semantic composition rule that has t as its (maximum) range of application.

---

[2] Löbner (2012b, 228f.) rejects '1-place predicate term' as a uniform semantic type.

9.2 Subcompositionality of verbal degree gradation

It is a question whether semantic and syntactic types coincide such that there is a direct corresponding syntactic type for each semantic type. In the classical scheme (model-theoretic semantics), as Löbner calls it, it is assumed that both systems match (cf. Montague 1970, 1973 among others). This is expressed by the postulate of 'homomorphy of syntactic and semantic composition' in (25).

(25) Homomorphy of syntactic and semantic composition: For every complex expression of a particular syntactic composition, the same rule of semantic composition applies. (Löbner, 2012b, 225)

What this means is that the way complex expressions are syntactically formed determines their semantic composition. For example, there may be a general rule for the syntactic combination of a verb and its subject argument and it is assumed that there is a single semantic rule corresponding to the syntactic one. But a look at examples such as those in (26) reveals that there is no uniformity regarding the subject arguments of particular verbs. We have a personal name in (a), a definite noun phrase consisting of the definite article and a common noun in (b) and a quantified NP consisting of a quantifier and a common noun in (c).

(26) a. *John is sleeping.*
      b. *The child is sleeping.*
      c. *All the children are sleeping.*

For all three cases, we have the same rule of syntactic composition, although the three different subject arguments are of different logical types. Such a mismatch between the logical types of subject arguments led to a generalization to the worst case and gave rise to Generalized Quantifier Theory (Barwise & Cooper 1981) which takes all subject arguments to be generalized quantifiers. A mismatch between syntactic and semantic composition is avoided by postulating a common type for all noun phrases, irrespective whether they are plain personal names, determined nouns or quantified nouns. This preserves the homomorphism between syntactic and semantic composition.

Löbner argues that there are clear cases of a genuine mismatch between syntactic and semantic composition for which he coins the term 'subcompositionality.' His definition of subcompositionality is presented in (27)

9 Gradation, aspect, and telicity

and what is meant is that for a certain regular syntactic construction not a single rule of semantic composition but different rules are required. Subcompositionality contradicts the assumption that semantic composition is regular (22) – which underlies the principle of compositionality. Hence, subcompositionality provides an attack on the paradigm of formal semantics which builds on the notion of compositionality.

(27) [A] syntactic construction is subcompositional if there is no uniform rule of semantic composition for it.
(Löbner, 2012b, 224)

Löbner's primary example of 'subcompositionality' is verbal degree gradation. The examples in (28) can be used for illustration. All the sentences are basically of the same construction type, which is 'sehr + intransitive verb.' As was shown in detail in the chapters 6 to 8, change of state verbs, experiencer verbs and verbs of substance emission differ regarding verbal degree gradation and the different semantic patterns that can be observed are not reducible to a single, uniform pattern. Since we get a different pattern of verbal degree gradation for these examples, we need to postulate a different semantic rule of composition for each. Hence, we have the same syntactic construction but different semantic rules for its interpretation.

(28) a. *Das Kind ist sehr gewachsen.*
          the child is very grown
          'The child has grown a lot.'
      b. *Sein Kopf schmerzt sehr.*
          his head hurts   very
          'His head hurts very much.'
      c. *Die Wunde blutet sehr.*
          the wound bleeds very
          'The wound is bleeding a lot.'

Löbner (2012b, 239) states: "Although the resulting picture of semantic composition is diverse and complex, there appear to be sub-rules that apply homogeneously for each type of gradable verb." The reasons for the subcompositionality of verbal degree gradation are (i) the verbs are related to different scales and (ii) the scales are differently anchored in the verb meanings. In (28a), the scale measures the change in a property of the ref-

9.2 Subcompositionality of verbal degree gradation

erent of the theme argument; in (b), it is the intensity of the feeling and in (c) it is the quantity of the emitted blood. Also *wachsen* 'grow' is lexically scalar, as discussed in the last section, whereas in (b) and (c) the gradable property is an attribute of an implicit argument of the verb. But in both cases, it is a different kind of implicit argument.

The different compositional patterns correspond to different logical equivalences as Löbner (2012b, 238) mentions. This is illustrated by the paraphrases of verbal degree gradation for verbs of different semantic classes in (29). The paraphrases in (29a) to (d) illustrate the main patterns discussed in chapters 6 to 8 for change of state verbs (a), verbs of smell emission (b), verbs of substance emission (c) and experiencer verbs (d). The paraphrases in (d) for verbs of comparison, (e) for verbs of marked behavior and (f) for erratic verbs are taken from Löbner (2012b, 239).

(29)   a.   *sehr wachsen* ↔ viel größer werden
              very grow   'get much taller'
    b.   *sehr riechen* ↔ starken Geruch absondern
              very smell   'emit strong smell'
    c.   *sehr bluten* ↔ viel Blut absondern
              very bleed   'emit much blood'
    d.   *sehr lieben* ↔ starke Liebe empfinden
              very love   'feel strong love'
    e.   *sehr ähneln*   ↔ sehr ähnlich sein
              very be.similar   'be very similar'
    f.   *sehr stottern* ↔ sehr stockend sprechen
              very stutter   'speak very haltingly'
    g.   *sehr sich verlaufen* ↔ sehr falsch laufen
              very be.lost   'go completely the wrong way'
    h.   *sehr schlagen* ↔ stark schlagen
              very hit   'hit hard'

The reason for the different paraphrases in (29) is the fact that the attribute representing the gradable property differs from verb class to verb class. This can best be illustrated by using attribute chains connecting the gradable property to the eventuality. (30) shows the attribute chains for graded verbs of smell/sound/light emission in (a) and for graded action verbs in (b).

(30) a. λv(high(INTENSITY(EMITTEE(v))))
   b. λe(high(INTENSITY(EFFECT(ACTION(e)))))

The common core of the two cases in (30) is that *sehr* applies to an INTENSITY attribute but the attribute is related via different functions to the eventuality. In (a) INTENSITY is an attribute of EMITTEE which is the implicit semantic argument of the verb, whereas in (b) it is an attribute of the EFFECT of the ACTION. One could abstract over these functions by saying that we need an appropriate function F which relates INTENSITY to the eventuality (31). But F is dependent on the semantic class of verbs and cannot be generalized. This means that there is no general rule that allows us to infer the function that relates the gradable property to the eventuality.

(31)   λvλF(high(INTENSITY(F(v))))

Löbner (2012b, 239) basically argues that the fact that the different equivalences cannot be unified in a single pattern, provides evidence for the subcompositionality of verbal degree gradation. This is even more revealing if we do not only compare verbs which are related to degree gradation on an intensity scale. Examples of degree gradation on a divergence scale have been presented above and it seems that indicating a differential degree cannot be reduced to the indication of a non-differential degree and vice versa. This further supports the irreducibility of the different subcompositional patterns to a single one.

As argued in section 5.4, what distinguishes adjectival degree gradation from verbal degree gradation is that the former is not subcompositional. The semantic composition of *sehr* plus adjective can be accounted for by a single rule. After illustrating subcompositionality in more detail, I finally turn to the interaction of verbal degree gradation with grammatical aspect and also telicity in the next section.

9.3 Event-dependent degree gradation

The discussion of different semantic verb classes revealed that degree gradation interacts with grammatical aspect only in case of (atelic) change of state verbs and verbs of substance emission. In Fleischhauer (2013), I coined the term 'event-dependent degree gradation' for cases in which grammatical aspect affects degree gradation, whereas those cases in which it does not, I called 'event-independent degree gradation.' For change of state verbs and verbs of substance emission, it seems obvious that there is a relationship between the progression of the event and the degree on the associated scale. Starting with change of state verbs, the verb *verbreitern* 'broaden, widen' in example (32) can be taken for illustration. As long as the event of widening takes place, the width of the crack has to increase. If the width of the crack is not increasing anymore, it cannot truthfully be said that the crack is still widening. What definitely is excluded is that the event is progressing and either no change in width obtains or that the width is even decreasing. That changes happen continuously is not a necessary condition, a change could also occur in a single sudden jump from the initial to the final degree. But such a case would exclude the application of the progressive aspect, as it would happen instantaneously. In the remainder, I am only concerned with durative changes that do not happen instantaneously.

(32)   Der Riss   verbreitert sich.
       the crack   widens   REFL
       'The crack is widening.'

Continuity of the change does not entail that the change obtains at each single moment of the event. This is definitely the case for a sentence like *The girl has grown a lot in two years*. The time-adverbial picks out a temporal interval of two years and it is not to be the case that at each single moment the girl increased in size. We have different granularities of relevant instances in which the respective change needs to obtain to speak of a single event of changing. We easily arrive at a discussion of event identity and the question when do we speak of a single event and when do we have to speak of two or more events of the same type. I will not go into the details of that discussion, but what is most relevant for the current discussion is not the exact granularity of the change but that it can be described as being a monotonic increase on the respective scale.

For verbs of substance emission, a similar picture obtains. *Bluten* normally denotes a continuous emission of blood. As in the case of change of state predications, the longer the event of bleeding proceeds, the more blood is emitted. Since *bleed* describes a continuous emission

9 Gradation, aspect, and telicity

of blood, the quantity of emitted blood increases as the event unfolds. There is a monotonic increase of the degrees on the quantity scale. In the case of event-dependent degree gradation, a relationship between the event and the degree on the respective scale holds, this can be informally summarized as in (33). It states that there is a dependency of the degree on the scale and the event such that the progression of the event leads to increasing degrees.[3]

(33) The more the event progresses, the more the degree on the scale increases.

The constraint in (33) does not hold for verbs such as *dröhnen* 'drone' or *ängstigen* 'frighten.' If an engine is droning, the intensity of the emitted sound does not (necessarily) increase – or decrease – if the event progresses. Surely, it may be the case that the intensity increases/decreases but this is merely incidental, whereas it is necessarily the case that the quantity of emitted blood increases as the bleeding event unfolds. This does not entail that *bluten* is a lexically scalar verb, as I only claim that the constraint holds if the quantity scale is activated. In other words: if the scale is activated, the constraint must hold.

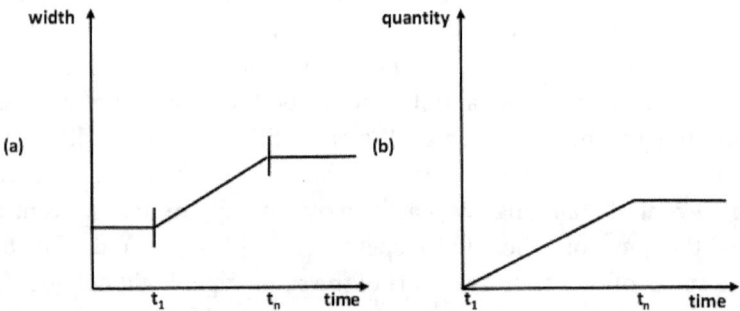

Figure 13: Graphical representation of the relationship between unfolding events (temporal progression) and increasing degrees.

---

[3] To be accurate, the constraint also holds for verbs expressing a decrease of degrees as in *The temperature is falling*.

9.3 Event-dependent degree gradation

Figure 13 is a graphical representation of the relationship between the progression of the event and the increase on the respective scale. In (a), we have the case of a change of state verb like *widen*. The referent of the theme argument has an initial degree of width and during the event, the width increases. t_1 and t_n indicate the initial moment and the final moment of the widening event respectively. In (b), the increase of the quantity of emitted substance is shown for verbs like *rain* or *bleed*. There is an idealization in figure 13, as the change and the emission are represented as constant before and after the respective event. This need not to be the case and is only done for the sake of illustration.

The constraint in (33) requires a homomorphic mapping between the event and the scale which guarantees that the degree increases of the event progresses. Such a kind of homomorphism has been proposed by Krifka (1986, 1998) for explicating the notion of 'incremental change.' Based on Krifka's and related work (e.g., Caudal & Nicolas 2005; Kardos 2012), a homomorphic mapping between the part structure of events and the degrees of an associated scale can be defined as in (34) and (35). The formulas in (34) and (35) presuppose structured domains of events and degrees. Events can be decomposed into subevents and the subevents can be brought into a temporal order (see Krifka 1998, 206 on the temporal trace function that maps events onto their running time). Degrees are inherently linearly ordered. (34) ensures that if a function f maps an event onto a scale and returns some degree d, then for each subevent e' of e, there is a degree d' which is smaller than d and is returned for mapping e' onto the scale.[4] It is not assumed that f directly maps the eventuality and a scale but rather that it relates the eventuality and the scale via some attribute chain as discussed above.

(34) Mapping to degrees: $\forall e \forall e' \forall d[f(e)=d \land e' \subseteq e \rightarrow \exists d'[d'<d \land f(e')=d']]$

In (35), it is expressed that if a function f maps an event e onto a scale and returns a degree d and if there is some d' smaller than d, there exists some subevent e' for which d' is the value of the function.

---

[4] See Krifka (1998) for a formal explication of event mereology. Subevents, i.e., parts of events, are ordered with respect to temporal precedence.

9 Gradation, aspect, and telicity

(35) Mapping to subevents: $\forall e \forall d \forall d'[f(e)=d \land d'\leq d \rightarrow \exists e'[e' \subseteq e \land f(e')=d']]$

The two conditions in (34) and (35) do not hold in case of non-incremental changes. Take *stink* as an example. There is a function that relates the eventuality to an intensity scale and returns (in the case of degree gradation) an intensity degree. The function can return the same degree of any subeventuality.

There are two further conditions which ensure uniqueness of degrees (36) and events (37). (36) states that each subevent e' is mapped onto a unique d', whereas (37) expresses that each degree is mapped onto a unique subevent.

(36) Uniqueness of degrees: $\forall e \forall e' \forall d[f(e)=d \land e' \subseteq e \rightarrow \exists! d'[d'\leq d \land f(e')=d']]$

(37) Uniqueness of events: $\forall e \forall d \forall d'[f(e)=d \land d'\leq d \rightarrow \exists! e'[e' \subseteq e \land f(e')=d']]$

The conditions defined in (34) to (37) guarantee that there is a unique degree associated with each subevent and that each subevent is associated with a unique degree. Mapping to degrees and mapping to subevents defines the notion of an 'incremental (scalar) change.' By adding the uniqueness conditions in (36) and (37) the stricter notion of 'strictly incremental (scalar) changes' results. For the following analysis, it is not crucial whether one assumes the stronger or just the weaker notion of incrementality; all that is required is incrementality.

Following Filip's (1999; 2005) analysis of grammatical aspect, perfective aspect restricts the denotation of verbs to total events, whereas imperfective aspect restricts it to partial events. Total events do not make reference to their various phases but are taken as a single and atomic whole (for a formal definition of the totality inducing perfective operator see Filip 2005, 133f.). Progressive aspect, as a subtype of the general imperfective, restricts the denotation of the event to a subevent (for a semantic definition of progressive aspect see chapter 6.5.1). We derive the difference between the two interpretations in (38a) and (b) due to restricting the denotation of the verb to the total event in (a) but to a subevent in (b). In (a), *sehr* indicates the total amount of change as it provides a specifation of the difference

9.3 Event-dependent degree gradation

obtained in the total event. In (b), *sehr* indicates the amount of change at a certain stage of the event since the denotation is restricted to a subevent.

(38) a. Der Riss hat sich sehr verbreitert.
 the crack has REFL very widened
 'The crack widened a lot.'
 b. Der Riss war sich sehr am Verbreitern.
 the crack was REFL very at.the widening
 'The crack was widening a lot.'

In (a) as well as (b), *sehr* only indicates the difference between the degree at the beginning of the total, respectively the subevent, and the degree at the end of the total, respectively the subevent. Since grammatical aspect has scope over degree gradation (cf. the discussion in chapter 4) first *sehr* applies to the verb and specifies the resulting change. After that the aspectual operator applies to the construction of '*sehr* + verb' and restricts the denotation the verb.

The same analysis can be applied to examples like (39). In (a), *sehr* specifies the total quantity of blood emitted in the event, whereas in (b) it is the quantity of blood emitted at a certain stage of the event. These different readings result from restricting the denotation of the verb to total events in (a) but to a proper part of the bleeding event in (b).

(39) a. Die Wunde hat sehr geblutet.
 the wound has very bled
 'The wound bled a lot.'
 b. Die Wunde war sehr am Bluten.
 the wound was very at.the bleeding
 'The wound was bleeding a lot.'

The next question is why degree gradation affects telicity of change of state verbs but not of verbs of substance emission or other classes of gradable verbs. In chapter 6, I presented Hay et al.'s (1999) analysis of degree achievements. According to their view, telicity arises by inducing a lower bound on the change. Such a lower bound can either be a natural endpoint, a telos indicated by the verb, or introduced by a monotone-increasing intensifier such as English *slightly* or German *sehr*. Specifying a lower bound for the incremental change results in a telic predication. Degree gradation

9 Gradation, aspect, and telicity

can only affect telicity if the verb expresses an incremental change along a scale. This is not the case with verbs of smell/light/sound emission and experiencer verbs, therefore gradation cannot lead to a telic predication in these cases. But if the proposal presented above is right, verbs of substance emission also express an incremental change (see Harley 2005 for a similar view). The question is: why does degree gradation not affect telicity of these verbs? In contrast to change of state verbs, verbs of substance emission do not just express a change in a property of the referent of the theme argument but it is the quantity of the referent of the theme argument that is affected. The same holds for incremental theme verbs like *eat, drink* or *read* (the term 'incremental theme' goes back to Dowty 1991). What is special about incremental theme verbs is that the telicity of the predication is dependent on the referential properties of the theme argument. This is usually captured by the notion of 'aspectual composition' (40).

(40) Aspectual composition of incremental theme predications:
An incremental theme verb combined with a quantized incremental theme argument yields a telic predication, whereas if it combines with a cumulative incremental theme argument it yields an atelic predication (e.g., Krifka 1986, 1998; Filip 1999, 2000).

The notions of quantization and cumulativity are defined in (41) and (42) respectively. Singular count nouns like *apple* have quantized reference, whereas mass nouns and bare plurals refer cumulatively. Quantization is tantamount to saying that no proper part of, for example an apple, falls under the predicate *apple* again, and cumulativity means that you can add apples to apples and denote the sum by the predicate *apples* again. This property does not hold for quantized predicates as you cannot denote the sum of two individual apples by the predicate *apple*; rather you have to use the plural *apples*. Similarly, the property of quantization does not hold for bare plurals and mass nouns as a proper part of apples or soup can be apples or soup again.

(41) Quantization: A predicate P is quantized iff
$\forall x,y[P(x) \wedge P(y) \rightarrow \neg(y<x)]$
(A predicate P is quantized iff it applies to two individuals x and y, and none of them is a proper part of the other.)

(42) Cumulativity: A predicate P is cumulative iff
 $\forall x,y[P(x) \wedge P(y) \rightarrow P(x \oplus y)]$
 (A predicate P is cumulative iff it applies to two individuals x and y, then it also applies to the sum of both.)

If *eat* combines with a quantized incremental theme argument as in (43a), the predication is telic. If the incremental theme argument has cumulative reference (b), the predication is atelic. The event-degrees homomorphism also accounts for incremental theme verbs as these verbs describe a change along a quantity scale. Quantization involves specifying the quantity of the incremental theme argument and thereby inducing a lower bound on the existential change (see Czardybon & Fleischhauer 2014 and the literature cited therein for different strategies of realizing telic incremental theme predications).

(43) a. *Peter hat den Apfel in zehn Minuten gegessen.*
 Peter has the apple in ten minutes eaten
 'Peter ate the apple in ten minutes.'
 b. #*Peter hat Äpfel in zehn Minuten gegessen.*
 Peter has apples in ten minutes eaten
 'Peter ate apples in ten minutes.'

An incremental theme argument is more and more affected as the event progresses. In this regard, the implicit emittee argument of verbs of substance emission can be considered to be an incremental theme argument since the degree of its affectedness increases as the event unfolds. The implicit incremental theme argument of verbs of substance emission denotes the substance emitted during the event and such substances are usually mass terms. As mass nouns refer cumulatively, the predication is atelic (the same argumentation is given by Harley 2005, 47f.). This presupposes a homomorphic mapping between the event and the scale measuring the quantity of emitted substance.

If the emittee argument is an implicit incremental theme argument, quantization of the argument should result in a telic predication. The addition of adnominal quantity expressions like *much* and *a lot* leads to quantization of inherently cumulative nouns. This is shown in (44). The bare mass noun *wine* is not able to delimit the event in (44a) but by adding *a lot*, a telic sentence results (for similar examples see Bach 1986). *A lot* quantizes the incremental theme argument, as it is not (necessarily) the case that a proper part of 'a lot of wine' can be denoted by *a lot of wine* again. The lower bound induced by *a lot* in (44b) is a contextually dependent large quantity of wine.

(44) a. #*I drank wine in ten minutes.*
       b. *I drank a lot of wine in ten minutes.*

Grading a verb of substance emission like *eitern* 'fester' by the addition of *sehr* does not result in telicity (45); also, *sehr* specifies the quantity of emitted stuff. But this is different if we paraphrase the verb *eitern* either by *Eiter verlieren* 'lose pus' or *Eiter abgeben* 'emit pus' like in (46). In the paraphrase, the emittee is not any more implicit but it is the direct object of the verb and *sehr* is replaced by the adnominal quantity expression *viel*. The sentence is telic, irrespective whether the verb *verlieren* 'lose' or *abgeben* 'emit' is used.

(45) #*Die Wunde hat in zehn Minuten sehr geeitert.*
      the wound has in ten   minutes very festered
      'The wound festered a lot in ten minutes.'

(46) *Die Wunde hat in zehn Minuten viel   Eiter verloren/abgegeben.*
      the wound has in ten   minutes much pus   lost/emitted
      'The wound emited a lot of pus in ten minutes.'

The contrast between (45) and (46) allows for, at least, two different explanations. Either *sehr* is not able to quantize an (implicit) nominal argument by specifying its quantity or an implicit semantic argument is not able to measure out an event. The second option is in accordance with Tenny's (1992; 1994) claim that only direct internal arguments can measure out, whereas Harley (2005) claims that implicit, i.e., incorporated arguments can do, too. The example in (47) supports Harley's view as the addition of the measure phrase *zehn Liter* 'ten liters' results in a telic predication due to quantization of the implicit incremental theme argument. Hence, the implicit argument can be quantized and quantization leads to a telic predication but it seems that degree expressions and measure phrases function differently with respect to verbs of substance emission.

(47) Es hat in einer Stunde zehn Liter geregnet.
     it has in one hour ten liters rained
     'It rained ten liters in an hour.'

A further way of quantizing the implicit incremental theme argument is by using the verbal particle *aus-* (48). Prefixation derives the verb *ausbluten* 'bleed out' which can be paraphrased as 'emitting all of the blood' (for a semantic analysis of the German verbal particle *aus-* see Stiebels 1996; McIntyre 2003).

(48) Das Schwein war in zehn Minuten ausgeblutet.
     the pig   was in ten minutes out.bled
     'The pig bled out in ten minutes.'

There is ample evidence that the inherent incremental theme argument can get quantized and that its quantization affects the telicity of the predication. This results in the question as to why *sehr* cannot quantize the inherent incremental theme argument and therefore degree gradation by *sehr* does not result in a telic predication. As I do not have a conclusive answer to this question, it has to be left open for future research.

9.4 Conclusion

This chapter dealt with two general topics. First, it was shown that verbal degree gradation is subcompositional as the different compositional patterns summarized in the first section cannot be unified in a single compositional rule. Second, the interaction between degree gradation and both grammatical aspect and telicity has been discussed. Grammatical aspect affects degree gradation if there is a homomorphic mapping between the event and a scale such that the degree on the scale increases if the event progresses. Such a constraint holds for change of state verbs and verbs of substance emission but not for other classes of gradable verbs. The interaction of telicity with degree gradation is also dependent on this homomorphism as the specification of a lower bound on that scale results in a telic predication. *Sehr* is able to induce a lower bound in the case of (atelic) change of state verbs but not in the case of verbs of substance emission. As demonstrated in the last section, the reason is not that the implicit incremental theme argument cannot be quantized, rather that *sehr* is not able to quantize the emittee argument. Why this is the case is still an open question and requires further research.

10 General conclusions

In the previous chapters, I analyzed the phenomenon of verbal degree gradation. The thesis has both a semantic and a comparative perspective due to its comparisons of degree gradation in German, Russian and French. It builds on the work of Bolinger (1972); Ropertz (2001) and Löbner (2012b) but extends these works by taking more data and, more importantly, a wider range of languages into account. Furthermore, the current thesis contains different case studies that are inspired by the work of Ropertz (2001) but go into greater detail. Verbal degree gradation is a less studied but central semantic topic, as it raises questions concerning the notion of compositionality, telicity and the interaction between lexical semantics and conceptual knowledge. In this last chapter, I like to summarize the central results of the thesis and to indicate open questions which arise from the analyses presented in the various chapters.

As a first general result of the thesis, I demonstrated that the same picture of verbal degree gradation can be observed in the three above-mentioned languages, although the languages do, in fact, show some differences in the formal realization of degree gradation (using a 'd'-adverbial in German and Russian but a 'd/e'-adverbial in French) or grammatical aspect.

The starting point of the analysis is the observation, which goes back to Bolinger (1972), that verb gradation is not a uniform process; rather it can be separated into verbal degree gradation and verbal extent gradation. Degree gradation involves specifying a degree on a scale associated with the verbal predication, whereas extent gradation entails specifying a gradable property of the event such as its temporal duration or frequency. In chapter 4, I demonstrated that both types of verbal degree gradation are related to different syntactic configurations. Degree gradation is expressed by a nuclear adverbial which modifies the predicate of the sentence. Extent gradation is expressed by core adverbials which modify the event description consisting of the predicate and its arguments. In languages like

10 General conclusions

French that use the same expression for extent and degree gradation the adverbial is syntactically ambiguous. In German and Russian on the other hand, which use different expressions for extent and degree gradation, no such syntactic ambiguity exists.

One question that is not addressed in the thesis is how verbal constructions like the resultative construction or a verbal comparison construction fit into the presented syntactic analysis. In an example like (1), *sehr* is used for verbal degree gradation which would require *nach Blumen riechen* 'smell of flowers' to be a nuclear juncture. Independent evidence for this assumption is required to maintain the analysis. If such evidence can be found, verbal degree gradation can be used as an indicator for the syntactic layer of a certain construction.

(1) Die Katze riecht sehr nach Blumen.
     the cat   smells very of   flowers
     'The cat smells very much of flowers.'

The comparison of verbal degree gradation with adjectival degree gradation revealed two essential differences. First, whereas gradable adjectives encode a measure function and therefore lexically express a scalar predication, this is different for verbs. There are some clear cases of lexically scalar verbs, such as change of state verbs and some stative dimensional verbs such as *cost* or *weigh*. But most gradable verbs are not lexically scalar, which means that they do not encode a scale in their lexical semantics. Non-scalarity of these verbs is demonstrated by the fact that in most of their uses they do not express a comparison between degrees, whereas scalar verbs do. *Wachsen* 'grow' (2) expresses such a comparison in each context of use as it means 'become taller than before.' But verbs such as *bluten* 'bleed,' *stinken* 'stink' or *lieben* 'love' do not express a comparison in (3). In (3a), it is not expressed that the wound bled more than it normally does or than another wound has bled. Similarly in (b), it is not said that the dog smells more than normally or some other dog or dogs in general or more unpleasant than usual and in (c) it is not expressed that the boy loves his mother more than someone else or than before. Hence, the ungraded sentences in (3) do not express a comparison and therefore cannot be conceived as being scalar.

(2) Das Kind ist gewachsen.
 the child is grown
 'The child has grown.'

(3) a. Die Wunde hat geblutet.
  the wound has bled
  'The wound bled.'
 b. Der Hund stinkt.
  the dog stinks
  'The dog stinks.'
 c. Der Junge liebt seine Mutter.
  the boy loves his mother
  'The boy loves his mother.'

Verbal degree gradation is regular for semantic classes of verbs such as verbs of smell/sound/light emission, verbs of substance emission, experiencer verbs or action verbs. In each case, the gradation scale is the same for the verbs of the respective semantic class. Most classes of verbs also provide a single scale for verbal degree gradation. Only gradable action verbs seem to license two different gradation scales; one related to the manner component of the verb, the other measuring the effect of the action described by the verb. The gradation scale is constrained by the lexical semantics of the verb. I argued in chapter 5 that if the scale is not lexically encoded in the verb it is retrieved from the conceptual knowledge associated with it. But this process of retrieval (or attribute activation) is not arbitrary, since only meaning components lexically specified in the verb give access to conceptual knowledge. One crucial question, not raised in the thesis, is why these meaning components give, at least in most cases, only access to a single scale. A more detailed investigation of this topic is left open for the future.

The semantic representation of *bluten* 'bleed' is given in (4). It consists of four conjuncts which specify the event, the emitter and the implicit emittee of the emission. Only the implicit emittee argument is lexically specified as being blood and therefore it is only this argument that gives access to conceptual knowledge. The conceptual knowledge here is encyclopedic information about the object 'blood.' This includes, among other things, the knowledge that blood comes in a certain quantity and therefore licenses the retrieving of the quantity attribute (cf. Fleischhauer 2015 for a frame-

10 General conclusions

based representation of verbs of substance emission and the conceptual knowledge given excess to by these verbs).

(4)   ⟦bluten⟧= λxλv(emit(v) ∧ EMITTER(v)=x ∧ THEME(v)=s ∧ blood(s))

As the emitter argument is not lexically specified, it does not give access (at least at the level of the predicate) to conceptual knowledge. Therefore *sehr* cannot modify a gradable property of the emitter but only of the emittee.

The fact that most gradable verbs do not lexicalize a scale gives rise to the assumption that we can enrich the lexical meaning of the verb by relying on conceptual knowledge. As argued above, this process is not unconstrained and therefore the enriched concept cannot include just any arbitrary attribute but rather only attributes licensed by a meaning component specified in the lexical meaning of the verb. A suitable format for representing this process of attribute activation is frame theory as described by Löbner (2014) as well as Petersen (2007). The advantage of the frame approach is that it easily allows the combining of semantic representations of verbs with the conceptual knowledge associated with one of the meaning components. Hence, there is no strict demarcation of lexical and conceptual knowledge in this approach. A next step in the semantic analysis would be an explicit frame analysis of verbal degree gradation (see Fleischhauer et al. 2014 for a first step towards such an analysis).

The second crucial difference between verbal degree gradation and adjectival degree gradation is the fact that degree gradation of verbs is a subcompositional phenomenon. This claim goes back to Löbner (2012b) who states that a morphosyntactic construction is subcompositional if it requires different rules of semantic composition. This is the case for verbal degree gradation, as the different compositional patterns summarized in chapter 9 cannot be reduced to a single one. Rather, each semantic class of verbs requires its own rule of composition. This is due to the fact that the respective gradation scale is differently linked to the eventuality for each semantic class of verbs. Moreover, different classes of verbs are related to different types of scales, some measuring intensity, others a divergence. A different picture emerges for adjectival degree gradation, as the different cases can be accounted for by a single rule of semantic composition. The fact that verbal degree gradation is a subcompositional phenomenon shows that the assumption of the homomorphism of semantic and syntactic composition does not hold. This means that the same rule of semantic composition does not apply for every complex expression of a particular syntactic composition. It is an open question as to which further constructions qualify as subcompositional, but adverbial modification in general seems to have a subcompositional flavor. In (5a), the adverbially used adjective *schnell* 'fast, quick' expresses that it took a short time till Peter responded but it is the manner of the responding that is fast, meaning Peter is speaking fast. In (b), *schnell* indicates the speed of running and not that it took Peter a short time till he ran.[1]

(5)   a.   *Peter antwortete schnell.*
             Peter responded quick
             'Peter responded quickly.'
    b.   *Peter lief schnell.*
             Peter ran fast
             'Peter ran fast.'

Note that this is a different analysis to the one proposed by, for example, Dowty (1979) for the different readings of English *almost* with activity predicates and accomplishment predicates (see the discussion in chapter 3.2.1). Dowty is merely speaking of a scope ambiguity but does not account for the different readings by different rules of composition. In the tradition of generative semantics, the different readings of *almost* have been taken as an argument in favor of lexical decomposition (e.g. Morgan 1969). The same is true for the ambiguity of *again*. The subcompositionality analysis does not simply assume that a scope ambiguity arises due to different decompositional structures but that the different interpretations of the sentences in (5) as well as of verbal degree gradation arises due to different rules of composition. This has not, as far as I know, been claimed so far in the discussion of the ambiguity of *almost* and *again*.

Different compositional patterns of verbal degree gradation have been demonstrated in detail for three semantic classes of verbs: change of state verbs, verbs of emission and experiencer verbs. It has also been demonstrated – in less detail – for some other classes of verbs in chapter 9; namely,

---

[1] The reading that it took Peter a short while till he started running is possible but without further context, the reading that *schnell* indicates the speed of running is preferred.

10 General conclusions

verbs of comparison, erratic verbs, verbs of marked behavior and action verbs. A large class of verbs neglected in this thesis is communication verbs. Examples are the verbs *versprechen* 'promise' or *prahlen* 'boast.' This class is rather heterogeneous with respect to argument realization as well as the lexical semantics of the verbs and it is connected to the expression of speech acts. Hence, in some of their uses they take sentential complements: ample of examples of these verbs, showing that it is a very productive verb class regarding verbal degree gradation, are contained in the German database.

A deeper analysis of German erratic verbs would also be of interest, as in this case the scale is introduced by a verbal particle. Deriving erratic verbs is rather productive in German and would provide an interesting case study on the interaction between degree gradation and verbal prefxiation. This would be of relevance as the scale induced by the prefix blocks the access to a scale associated with the verb (as discussed in chapters 7 and 9).

To get the full picture of verbal degree gradation, a broader corpus-based study would be required with the aim of showing which verbs actually license degree gradation and which not. A first step towards such an analysis has already been undertaken by Sebastian Löbner and resulted in a database containing several thousand examples of gradable verbs.[2] However, to gain a broader view on verbal degree gradation would also require a comparative (corpus-based) study of different intensifiers, as the thesis only focusses on *sehr* and its correspondents in other languages. Other intensifiers might show different restrictions from *sehr* and therefore reveal interesting insights into verbal degree gradation from a more general perspective.

A central issue in the analysis of verbal degree gradation has been the interaction with grammatical as well as lexical aspect. It emerged that grammatical aspect affects the interpretation of verbal degree gradation but only in case of (atelic) change of state verbs and verbs of substance emission. In case of a perfective interpretation, the intensifier indicates the total amount of change, or the total quantity of emitted substance. Progressive aspect restricts the denotation to a subevent, and the intensifier specifies the change

---

[2] The database contains examples collected in the project 'Verb gradation' headed by Sebastian Löbner and financed by the Deutsche Forschungsgemeinschaft 'German Research Foundation' (DFG grand LO 454/1).

or emitted quantity at a stage of the event. This phenomenon has been called 'event-dependent degree gradation,' and it arises if the degree on the scale is coupled with the progression of the event such that the degree increases if the event unfolds. An analysis in terms of a homomorphic mapping between the ordered set of degrees and the part structure of the event has been presented. Change of state verbs as well as verbs of substance emission express an incremental change on their respective scales. In case of atelic change of state verbs, degree gradation by *sehr* results in a telic predication as the intensifier indicates a lower bound that has to be reached in the event. Regarding verbs of substance emission degree gradation does not have an effect on telicity, although the implicit emittee argument is really an implicit incremental theme argument. This has been demonstrated by the fact that quantization of the argument results in a telic predication. Examples like those in (6) illustrate that *sehr* is not able to quantize the implicit incremental theme argument and therefore the graded predication remains atelic.

(6) a. #Die Wunde hat sehr geblutet in zehn Minuten.
        the wound has very bled   in ten minutes
        'The wound bled a lot in ten minutes.'
     b. #Die Wunde hat sehr geeitert in zehn Minuten.
        the wound has very festered in ten minutes
        'The wound festered a lot in ten minutes.'
     c. #Es hat sehr geregnet in zehn Minuten.
        it has very rained   in ten minutes
        'It rained a lot in ten minutes.'

A conclusive explanation of why *sehr* is not able to render verbs of substance emission telic is still missing. Further work on degree gradation and implicit incremental theme arguments is required as it sheds light onto the central notion of telicity.

A further connection between degree gradation and telicity exists in the case of graded accomplishment predicates. Since some accomplishment change of state predications like *stabilisieren* 'stabilize' or *normalisieren* 'normalize' are gradable, a telos cannot necessarily be equated with a maximum scale value. Rather it has been demonstrated that two types of telos need to be distinguished: a maximum telos which is equal to the maxi-

10 General conclusions

mum scale value and a standard telos which represents the onset of an extended result scale. The cross-linguistic discussion revealed that accomplishment change of state predicates are gradable if they are related to a standard telos but that they reject degree gradation by *sehr*, *očen'* or *beaucoup* if they are only related to a maximum telos. It would be interesting to see whether these observations easily connect with the phenomenon of so-called 'non-culminating accomplishments' (see Koenig & Muansuwan 2000; Chief 2007; Koenig & Chief 2008; Tatevosov 2008 among others). Examples from Mandarin Chinese are shown in (7).

(7) a. *Zhangsan sha le Lisi liang ci, Lisi dou mei si.*
 Zhangsan kill PF Lisi two time Lisi all not die
 'Zhangsan killed Lisi twice, but Lisi didn't die. (intended reading)'
 b. *wo kai le men (danshi men mai kai).*
 I open PF door but door not open
 'I opened the door, (but the door was not opened).'
 (Chief, 2007, 32)

The verbs *sha* 'kill' and *kai* 'open' are telic but nevertheless the attainment of a maximal degree can be negated without contradiction. A question would be whether this incompleteness effect, as Chief calls it, can also be accounted for by a distinction between standard and maximum telos. This would probably allow unifying different telicity related phenomena under a single analysis and to find parallels between different and seemingly unrelated phenomena.

A topic connected to verb gradation is verbal scalarity. Three different sources of verbal scales have been mentioned in chapter 5. They can either be lexicalized by a verb, retrieved from conceptual knowledge or introduced by a morphosyntactic construction. The focus of the thesis has been on the first two options: the third one has only been investigated superficially. It was mentioned that the resultative construction and certain types of verbal comparison constructions introduce scales but also verbal prefixes and particles.

Prefixes and particles are either able to introduce a new scale like in the Polish examples in (8) or to modify a scale associated with the verb (9). Whereas in (8b) the prefix shifts the stative verb of smell emission towards an eventive change of state predication, in (9) the prefix introduces an endpoint to a non-lexicalized scale.[3]

(8) a. *Jan bardzo śmierdział.*
Jan very stank
'Jan stank very much.'
b. *Jan bardzo za-śmierdział.*
Jan very ZA-stank
'Jan began to stink very much.'

(9) *Das Schwein war in zehn Minuten ausgeblutet.*
the pig was in ten minutes out.bled
'The pig bled out in ten minutes.'

A typology of scalar constructions, i.e. morphosyntactic constructions that introduce a verbal scale, is still missing and it is an open question which types of further constructions count as scalar. An additional question is how scale components are distributed within a sentence. (9) shows an example in which the verbal particle adds information to the scalar predication, the incremental change on the quantity scale is bounded. Another case of distributed scalar information has been seen with regard to scalar underspecification discussed in chapter 6. In examples like those in (10) the scale parameters (dimension, set of degree and linear ordering relation) is specified by the scale-denoting nouns. It would be interesting to broaden the perspective and to investigate how scales and their components are morphosyntactically encoded in different languages.

(10) a. *Der Druck steigt.*
the pressure rises
'The pressure is rising.'
b. *Der Preis steigt.*
the price rises
'The price is rising.'
c. *Die Temperatur steigt.*
the temperature rises
'The temperature is rising.'

---

[3] See Kagan (2015) for a recent scalar analysis of verbal prefixes in Russian.

10 General conclusions

The thesis investigates an empirical domain which has not received much attention so far. It has been shown that verbal degree gradation is not a marginal phenomenon as many verbs are gradable. It has been shown that the topic of verbal degree gradation is related to other topics independently discussed in syntax and semantics as, for example, scalarity, telicity and compositionality. But it also followed that there are hugh differences between adjectival and verbal degree gradation. The current work is just a first step into the analysis of verbal degree gradation but it indicates many open questions for further research. A central issue is deeper lexical decomposition which is required by verbal degree gradation and probably by adverbial modification in general. Attempts towards such a deeper lexical decomposition have been undertaken but many open questions still need to be investigated.

Appendix: Language data

The appendix presents a summary of data on the cross-linguistic distribution of degree expressions which were discussed in chapter 2.4.2. For all languages, the data are organized as follows: first the adverbial uses of degree expression (degree and extent gradation) are listed, then adadjectival uses (gradation of positive and comparative forms) follows and finally adnominal uses (quantity expressions with mass and count nouns) can be found. If there is nothing special to say on the data, no further comments are added. The relevant discussion of the data can be found in chapter 2.4.2. A note on the translation of degree expressions: if a language distinguishes between a verbal degree and extent intensifier, I gloss the degree intensifier as *very* throughout all its uses and the extent intensifier as *much*. If a language has a general 'de-intensifier', I gloss it as *a lot*.

The appendix lists all the data not presented in chapter 2.4.2 except the Finnish data, which were taken from Karttunen (1975).[4] A short note on the sources of the other data: I collected or at least checked all language data with native speaker consultants, if there is no other source indicated. See the introduction for the list of informants.

Arabian (Morrocan) (Semitic <Afro-Asiatic)

(11) adverbial

   a. *Axa:fa   al-adad-u   al-walad-a   kaθir-an.*
       frightened DET-lion-NOM DET-boy-ACC a lot-ADV
       'The lion frightened the loy a lot.'

---

[4] Karttunen does not discuss the use of Finnish *hyvin* 'very' with the positive form of adjectives. An example of this missing type of data is the following:
   i.   *Talo   on hyvin suuri.*
        house is very tall
        'The house is very tall.'

Appendix: Language data

    b.   *Al-walad-u na:ma kaθir-an fi l-lajlat-i*
        DET-boy-NOM slept a lot-ADV at DET-night-GEN
        l-madˤiyat-i.
        DET-last-GEN
        'The boy slept a lot last night.'
    c.   *ðahaba kaθir-an ila s-si:nima.*
        went a lot-ADV to DET-cinema
        'He went to the cinema a lot.'

(12)   adadjectival
    a.   *Al-walad-u tˤawi:l-um dʒidd-an.*
        DET-boy-NOM tall-NOM very-ADV
        'The boy is very tall.'
    b.   *Al-walad-u atˤwal-u kaθir-an min*
        DET-boy-NOM tall.COMP-NOM a lot-ADV from
        axi-h-i.
        brother-POSS.3SG-GEN
        'The boy is much taller than his brother.'

(13)   adnominal
    a.   *Akala l-kaθir-a mina l-mawz-i.*
        ate DET-a lot-ACC from DET-banana.PL-GEN
        'He ate many bananas.'
    b.   *Akala l-kaθir-a mina ʃ-ʃurbat-i.*
        ate DET-a lot-ACC from DET-soup.SG-GEN
        'He ate a lot of soup.'

Bulgarian (Slavic <Indo-European)

(14)   adverbial
    a.   *Momče-to običa mnogo majka si.*
        boy-DEF loves a lot mother POSS
        'The boy loves his mother very much.'
    b.   *Toj hodi mnogo na kino.*
        he goes a lot PREP cinema
        'He goes to the cinema a lot.'

    c.   *Snošti spah mnogo.*
        last.night sleep.AOR a lot
        'Last night, I slept a lot.' (= long duration)

(15)   adadjectival

    a.   *Momče-to e mnogo visoko.*
        boy-DET AUX a lot tall
        'The boy is very tall.'

    b.   *Momče-to e mnogo po-visoko ot prijatel-ja si.*
        boy-DEF AUX a lot COMP-tall PREP friend-DEF POSS
        'The boy is much taller than his friend.'

(16)   adnominal

    a.   *Toj ima mnogo knigi.*
        he has a lot book.PL
        'He has many books.'

    b.   *V kofa-ta ima mnogo voda.*
        PREP bucket-DEF has a lot water
        'There is a lot of water in the bucket.'

Croatian (Slavic <Indo-European)

(17)   adverbial

    a.   *Pas je dječaka jako prestrašio.*
        dog is boy.ACC very frightened
        'The dog frightened the boy a lot.'

    b.   *Dječak mnogo ide u kino.*
        boy much goes PREP cinema
        'The boy goes to the cinema a lot.'

    c.   *Dječak je mnogo spavao prošle noći.*
        boy is much slept last night
        'The boy slept a lot last night.'

(18)   adadjectival

    a.   *Dječak je jako visko.*
        boy is very tall
        'The boy is very tall.'

Appendix: Language data

       b.   *Dječak je mnogo viši svoje sestre.*
            boy is much tall.COMP REFL sister
            'The boy is much taller than his sister.'

(19)   adnominal

       a.   *Pojeo je mnogo jabuka.*
            eaten is much apple
            'He ate many apples.'
       b.   *Pojeo je mnogo juhe.*
            eaten is much soup
            'He ate much soup.'

Dutch (Germanic <Indo-European)

(20)   adverbial

       a.   *De jongen houdt erg/veel van zijn moeder.*
            the boy loves very/much PART his mother
            'The boy loves his mother very much.'
       b.   *Hij gaat veel naar de cinema.*
            he goes much to the cinema
            'He goes to the cinema a lot.'
       c.   *Voorbije nacht hab ik veel geslapen.*
            last night have I much slept
            'Last night, I slept a lot.'

(21)   adadjectival

       a.   *De jongen is erg/zeer groot.*
            the boy is very/very tall
            'The boy is very tall.'
       b.   *De jongen is veel grot-er dan zijn vriend.*
            the boy is much tall-COMP than his friend
            'The boy is much taller than his friend.'

(22)   adnominal

       a.   *Hij bezit veel boeken.*
            he owns much books
            'He owns many books.'

b. *Er is veel water in de emmer.*
　　it is much water in the bucket
　　'There is a lot of water in the bucket.'

Estonian (Finno-Ugric)

(23)　adverbial
　　a.　*Poiss väga armastab oma ema.*
　　　　boy very loves POSS.SG mother.GEN
　　　　'The boy loves his mother very much.'
　　b.　*Ta käib palju Kino-sse.*
　　　　he goes much cinema-ILL.SG
　　　　'He goes to the cinema l lot.'
　　c.　*Viima-sel öö-sel olen ma plaju maga-nud.*
　　　　last-ADE.SG night-ADE.SG be.1SG I much sleep-PST.PRF
　　　　'Last night, I slept a lot.'

(24)　adadjectival
　　a.　*Poiss on väga suur.*
　　　　boy be.3SG very tall
　　　　'The boy is very tall.'
　　b.　*Poiss on palju suur-em kui tema sõber.*
　　　　boy be.3SG much tall-COMP.SG than 3SG.GEN friend
　　　　'The boy is much taller than his friend.'

(25)　adnominal
　　a.　*Tal on palju raamatu-id.*
　　　　3SG.ADE be.3SG much book-PAR.PL
　　　　'He owns many books.'
　　b.　*Ämbr-is on palju vett.*
　　　　bucket-INE.SG 3SG much water.PAR.SG
　　　　'There is a lot of water in the bucket.'

Appendix: Language data

Georgian (Kartvelian)

(26) adverbial
    a. *bič'-s žalian uq'vars tavis-i deda-∅.*
       boy-DAT very loves his-NOM mother-NOM
       'The boy loves his mother very much.'
    b. *bič'-s c'uxel bevr-i edzina.*
       boy-DAT last.night much-NOM slepp.AOR
       'The boy slept a lot last night.'
    c. *bič'-i bevr-s dadis.*
       boy-NOM much-DAT goes
       'The boy goes a lot.' (= 'he often walks')

(27) adadjectival
    a. *bič'-i žalian didi-a.*
       boy-NOM very be-tall
       'The boy is very tall.'
    b. *bič'-i tavis megobar-ze bevr-da didi-a.*
       boy-NOM is friend-over much-ADV be-tall
       'The boy is much taller than his friend.'

(28) adnominal
    a. *bič'-ma sup-i bevr-i č'ama.*
       boy-ERG soup-NOM much-NOM eat.aor
       'The boy ate a lot of soup.'
    b. *man bevr-i vašl-i č'ama.*
       3SG.ERG much-NOM apple-NOM eat.AOR
       'He ate many apples.'

Hebrew (Semitic <Afro-Asiatic)

(29) adverbial
    a. *Ha-ʔarje meʔod hifxid et ha-jeled.*
       DEF-lion very frightened ACC DEF-boy
       'The lion frightened the boy.'
    b. *Ha-jeled jaΣan harbe ba-lajla (Σeavar).*
       DEF-boy slept much in.DEF-night (previous)
       'The boy slept a lot last night.'

c. *Hu halax harbe ka-kolnoa.*
   he went much to.DEF-cinema
   'He went to the cinema a lot.'

(30) adadjectival

a. *Ha-jeled meʔod gavoa.*
   THE-boy very tall
   'The boy is very tall.'
b. *Ha-jeled harbe joter gavoa me-axiv.*
   DEF-boy much moore tall than-brother.POSS.3SG.MASC
   'The boy is much taller than his brother.'

(31) adnominal

a. *Hu axal harbe bananot.*
   he ate much bananas
   'He ate many bananas.'
b. *Hu axal harbe marak.*
   he ate much soup
   'He ate a lot of soup.'

For more data see Glinert (1989, chapter 20).

Italian (Romance <Indo-European)

(32) adverbial

a. *Mi diverto molto.*
   myself amuse a lot
   'I amuse myself very much.'
b. *Vado molto al cinema.*
   go a lot to.the cinema
   'I go to the cinema a lot.'
c. *Molto lavorato.*
   a lot worked
   'I worked a lot.' (= long duration or frequency)

(33) adadjectival

a. *E'una torre molto alta.*
   is one tower a lot high
   'This is a very high tower.'

b. *Sei molto più   alto di   Luigi.*
    are a lot more tall than Luigi
    'You are much taller than Luigi.'

(34) adnominal
   a. *molti libri*
       a lot books
       'many books'
   b. *molta acqua*
       a lot water
       'a lot of water'

Japanese (isolate)

(35) adverbial
   a. *Sono shōnen wa shinchou ga   totemo nobi-ta.*
       DEM boy   SUB body.size NOM very   grow-PST
       'The boy has grown a lot.'
   b. *Sakuya,   watashi wa takusan suimin o   to-tta.*
       last.night I   SUB much   sleep ACC take-PST
       'I slept a lot last night.' (= long duration)
   c. *Saikin no   kodomo takusan telebi o   mi-ru.*
       newly GEN child   much   TV   ACC watch-PRES
       'Today's children watch TV a lot.' (= often)

(36) adadjectival
   a. *Sono shōnen wa totemo ookii.*
       DEM boy   SUB very   tall
       'The boy is very tall.'
   b. *Sono shōnen wa kare   no tomodachi yori totemo ookii.*
       DEM boy   SUB 3SG.MASC GEN friend   than very   tall
       'The boy is much taller than his friend.'

(37) adnominal
   a. *Baketto ni wa takusan no   mizu ga   haitteiru.*
       bucket in TOP much   GEN water NOM enter.PRES
       'There is a lot of water in the bucket.'

b. *Kare wa takusan no hon o mo-tte*
3SG.MASC SUB much GEN book ACC have-CON
i-ru.
be.there-PRES
'He has many books.'

Khalka Mongolian (Mongolia <Altaic)

(38) adverbial
   a. *Ene xüü eej-iig-ee ix sana-san.*
      DEM boy mother-ACC-REFL.POSS a lot miss-PF
      'The boy misses his mother a lot.'
   b. *Ter kino-(n)d ix yav-dag.*
      3SG kino-DAT a lot go-HAB
      'He goes to the cinema a lot.'
   c. *Öčigdör šönö bi ix unt-san.*
      yesterday night 1SG a lot sleep-PF
      'Last night, I slept a lot.' (= long duration)

(39) adadjectival
   a. *Ene xüü ix öndör/tom.*
      DEM boy a lot high/tall
      'The boy is very tall.'
   b. *Ene xüü naiz-aas-aa iluu ix öndör/tom.*
      DEM boy friend-ABS-REFL.POSS more a lot high/tall
      'The boy is much taller than his friend.'

(40) adnominal
   a. *Xuvin-d ix us bai-na.*
      bucket-DAT a lot water be-NPST
      'There is a lot of water in the bucket.'
   b. *Ter olon nom-toi.*
      3SG much book-COM
      'He owns many books.'

Appendix: Language data

Kikuyu (Bantu <Niger-Congo>)

(41) adverbial

    a. *Ka-hee k-ɛ-ɛne-ɛɛtɛ nyina monɔ.*
       NC12-boy NC12-PRS-love-ASP his.brother a lot
       'The boy loves his mother very much.'

    b. *Ka-hee ka-ra-ko-irɛ monɔ hwae.*
       NC12-boy NC12-PST-sleep-ASP a lot last.night
       'The boy slept a lot last night.'

    c. *Ne a-a-thi-aga monɔ thinɛma.*
       AM 3SG-PST-go-HAB a lot cinema
       'He went to the cinema a lot.'

(42) adadjectival

    a. *Ka-hee ne ka-raihu monɔ.*
       NC12-boy COP NC12-be.tall a lot
       'The boy is very tall.'

    b. *Ka-hee ne ka-raihu makeria ma mo-oro wa nyina.*
       NC12-boy COP NC12-be.tall excessive of CL1-son of his.brother
       'The boy is much taller than his brother.'

It is not clear whether *raihu* is an adjective or a verb; it is translated as a verb but requires the copula, much like predicative adjectives in other languages, e.g. the Bantu language Swahili.

(43) adnominal

    a. *A-a-re-irɛ ma-rigo ma-inge.*
       3SG-PST-eat-ASP NC6-banana NC6-much
       'He ate many bananas.'

    b. *A-a-nyu-irɛ thuβo mo-inge.*
       3SG-PST-drink-ASP soup[NC9] NC9-much
       'He ate a lot of soup.'

Korean (isolate)

(44) adverbial

    a. *ku sonyen-un emeni-lul acwu salangha-nta.*
       DEM boy-TOP mother-ACC very love-DEC
       'The boy loves his mother very much.'

    b. *ku sonyen-un manhi ca-ss-ta.*
       DEM boy-TOP much sleep-PST-DEC
       'The boy slept a lot.'

    c. *ku-nun yenghwakwan-ey manhi ka-nta.*
       he-TOP cinema-to much go-DEC
       'He goes to the cinema a lot.'

(45) adadjectival

    a. *ku namca-nun acwu khu-ta.*
       DEM man-TOP very tall-DEC
       'The man is very tall.'

    b. *ku sonyen-un ne-uy hyeng-pota manhi khu-ta.*
       DEM boy-TOP you-GEN older.brother-than much tall-DEC
       'The boy is much taller than his older brother.'

(46) adnominal

    a. *ku-nun sakwa-lul manhi mek-ess-ta.*
       he-TOP apple-ACC much eat-PST-DEC
       'He ate many apples.'

    b. *ku-nun kwuk-ul manhi mek-ess-ta.*
       he-TOP soup-ACC much eat-PST-DEC
       'He ate a lot of soup.'

Mandarin Chinese (Sinitic <Sino-Tibetian)

(47) adverbial

    a. *nà gè nǚhái hěn xǐhūan nà tiá gǒu.*
       DEM CLA girl very like DEM CLA dog
       'The girl likes the dog very much.'

    b. *tā qiù diànyǐngyùan hěn dūo.*
       3SG go cinema much
       '(S)he goes to the cinema a lot.'

c. *tā zuotian shui le hěn dūo.*
   3SG yesterday sleep PF much
   'Yesterday, he slept a lot.' (= long duration)

(48) adadjectival
   a. *nà gè nánhái hěn gāo.*
      DEM CLA boy very tall
      'The boy is very tall.'
   b. *nà gè nánhái bǐ tā péngyou gāo hěn dūo.*
      DEM CLA boy COMP 3SG friend tall much
      'The boy is much taller than his friend.'

(49) adnominal
   a. *nà gè nánrén yǒu hěn dūo shū.*
      DEM CLA man have much book
      'The man has many books.'
   b. *tā lǐ shuǐ hěn dūo.*
      3SG CLA water much
      'There is a lot of water.'

Nepali (Indo-Aryan <Indo-European)

(50) adverbial
   a. *Tyo singha-le tyo keto-lāi dherai darāyo.*
      that lion-ERG that boy-ACC a lot frightened
      'The lion frightened the boy.'
   b. *Tyo keto hijo rati dherai sutyo.*
      that boy last night a lot slept
      'The boy slept a lot last night.'
   c. *U cinema dherai jānthyo.*
      3SG.MASC cinema a lot went
      'He went to the cinema a lot.'

(51) adadjectival
   a. *Tyo keto dherai aglo chha.*
      that boy a lot tall is
      'The boy is very tall.'

    b.   *Tyo keto usko bhāi   bhandā dherai aglo chaa.*
        that boy his younger.brother than   a lot   tall is
        'The boy is much taller than his younger brother.'

(52) adnominal
    a.   *U-sle   dherai syāu-haru khāyo.*
        3SG.MASC-ERG a lot   apple-PL   ate
        'He ate many apples.'
    b.   *U-sle   dherai jhol khāyo.*
        3SG.MASC-ERG a lot   soup ate
        'He ate a lot of soup.'

Polish (Slavic <Indo-European)

(53) adverbial
    a.   *Ta   dziewczyna bardzo lubi tego psa.*
        DEM girl   very   likes DEM dog
        'The girl likes the dog very much.'
    b.   *Ona chodzi dużo do   kin-a.*
        she goes   much PREP cinema-GEN
        'She goes to the cinema a lot.'
    c.   *On dużo spał.*
        he   much slept
        'He slept a lot.' (= long duration or frequency)

(54) adadjectival
    a.   *Ten chłopiec jest bardzo wysoki.*
        DEM boy   is   very   tall
        'The boy is very tall.'
    b.   *Ten chłopiec jest dużo wyższy niż   swój przyjaciel.*
        DEM boy   is   much tall.COMP than his   friend
        'The boy is much taller than his friend.'

(55) adnominal
    a.   *Ten mężczyzna ma dużo książek.*
        DEM man   has much books
        'The man has many books.'

b. W   jeziorze jest dużo   wody.
PREP sea   is   much water
'There is a lot of water in the sea.'

Romanian (Romance <Indo-European)

(56) adverbial
   a. Băiat-ul o   iubesšte mult pe   mama sa.
      boy-DEF she.ACC loves   a lot PREP mother his
      'The boy loves his mother very much.'
   b. Noapte-a trecută am   dormit mult.
      night-DEF passed have slept   a lot
      'Last night, I slept a lot.'
   c. El merge mult cu   bicileta.
      he goes a lot with bike
      'He rides his bike a lot.'

(57) adadjectival
   a. Băiat-ul este foarte înalt.
      boy-DEF is   very   tall
      'The boy is very tall.'
   b. Băiat-ul este mult mai înalt decât prient-ul   său.
      boy-DEF is   a lot more tall than friend-DEF his
      'The boy is much taller than his friend.'

(58) adnominal
   a. Are mult cărți.
      has a lot books
      'He has many books.'
   b. Este multă apă   în găleată.
      is   much water in bucket
      'There is a lot of water in the bucket.'

Spanish (Romance <Indo-European)

(59) adverbial
    a. *Me gusta mucho el libro.*
        me like a lot the book
        'I like the book a lot.'
    b. *Juan va mucho en tren.*
        Juan goes a lot in train
        'Juan takes the train a lot.'
    c. *Es esa oficina te hacen esperar mucho.*
        in that office CL.you make wait a lot
        'In that office they make you wait for a long time.'

(60) adadjectival (Moriena & Genschow, 2005, 537)
    a. *El camino fue muy pesado.*
        the track was very hard
        'The track was very difficult.'
    b. *Ella es mucho menos estricta de lo que parece.*
        she is a lot less severe PREP it than seems
        'She is much less severe than she seems.'

(61) adnominal
    a. *mucha leche*
        a lot milk
        'much milk'
    b. *muchos amigos*
        a lot friends
        'many friends'

Swahili (Bantu <Niger-Congo)

(62) adverbial
    a. *Simba a-li-m-shtua m-vulana sana*
        lion[NC1] NC1-PST-3SG.OBJ-frighten NC1-boy very
        'The lion frightened the boy a lot.'
    b. *M-vulana a-li-lala sana jana usiku.*
        NC1-boy 3SG-PST-sleep very yesterday night
        'Last night, the boy slept much a lot.'

Appendix: Language data

    c.   A-li-kuwa   yu-a-enda sana kwa sinema.
        3SG-PST-COP 3SG-PST-go very to   cinema
        'He went to the cinema a lot.'

(63)   adadjectival
    a.   *M-vulana ni   m-refu sana.*
        NC1-boy   COP NC1-tall very
        'The boy is very tall.'
    b.   *M-vulana ni   m-refu sana ku-m-liko   ndugu*
        NC1-boy   COP NC1-tall very INF-3SG.OBJ-surpassing brother
        yake.
        his
        'The boy is much taller than his brother.'

(64)   adnominal
    a.   *A-li-kula   ndizi   ny-ingi.*
        3SG-PST-eat bananas NC9/10-much
        'He ate many bananas.'
    b.   *A-li-kunyua supu   ny-ingi.*
        3SG-PST-drink soup[CL9] NC9-much
        'He ate much soup.'

Swedish (Germanic <Indo-European)

Swedish uses *mycket* in all contexts but a different intensifier is used with the positive form of adjectives in negated contexts. In this context, Swedish uses *inte särskilt* 'not very' (68a), whereas in the other contexts – if negated – *inte mycket* 'not much' is used (68b). The same is true for Danish (Allan et al., 1995, 316f.), Finnish and Latvian (Bernard Wälichli p.c.).
Unfortunately, I do not have data for the durative subtype of extent gradation.

(65)   adverbial
    a.   *Eleverna   tyckte mycket om henne.*
        pupils.DET liked a lot   of   her
        'The pupils liked her a lot.' (Holmes & Hinchliff, 2008, 145)

b. *Han sjöng mycket på den tiden.*
   he sang a lot in this time
   'He sang a lot in those days.' (Holmes & Hinchliff, 2008, 197)

(66) adadjectival
   a. *Han var mycket lång.*
      he was a lot tall
      'He was very tall.'
   b. *Han var mycket längre än si bror.*
      he was a lot tall.COMP than his brother
      'He was much taller than his brother.'

(67) adnominal
   a. *mycket mygg i fjällen*
      a lot mosquitoes in mountains
      'a lot of mosquitoes in the mountains' (Holmes & Hinchliff, 2008, 44)
   b. *mycket vatten*
      a lot water
      'a lot of water'

(68) Negation (Holmes & Hinchliff, 2008, 146)
   a. *Han är inte särskilt rik.*
      he is not very rich
      'He is not very rich.'
   b. *Han är inte mycket rikare än sin bror.*
      he is not a lot richer than his brother
      'He is not much richer than his brother.'

Tatar (Turkic <Altaic)

(69) adverbial
   a. *kyčyk bik kurk-yt-ty marat-ny*
      dog very fear-CAUS-PST.3SG Marat-ACC
      'The dog frightened Marat a lot.'
   b. *marat küp jer-i kino-ga.*
      Marat much go-IMPF cinema-DAT
      'Marat goes to the cinema a lot.'

341

Appendix: Language data

    c.   *marat küp jɣkladɣ kicäge ten-ne.*
        Marat much sleep-PST last   night-ACC
        'Marat slept a lot last night.'

(70)   adadjectival

    a.   *marat bik bijek.*
        Marat very tall
        'Marat is very tall.'

    b.   *marat küp-kä alsu-dan bijek-räk.*
        Marat much-DAT Alsu-ABL tall-COMP
        'Marat is much taller than Alsu.'

(71)   adnominal

    a.   *marat küp alma aša-dɣ.*
        Marat much apple eat-PST
        'Marat ate many apples.'

    b.   *marat küp šurba aša-dɣ.*
        Marat much soup eat-PST
        'Marat ate much soup.'

Turkish (Turkic <Altaic)

(72)   adverbial (Güven, 2010, 3)

    a.   *Sibel pembe elbisesini çok beğeniyor.*
        Sibel pink   dress.ACC a lot likes
        'Sibel likes her pink dress a lot.'

    b.   *Sibel o odada çok oynuyor.*
        Sibel that room.LOC a lot plays
        'Sibel plays in that room a lot.'

(73)   adadjectival

    a.   *Brezilya çok büyüktür.*
        Brasil   a lot large.COP
        'Brasil is very large.' (Güven, 2010, 3)

    b.   *Ferrari Ford'dan çok daha hıtlı.*
        Ferrari Ford.ABL a lot more fast
        'Ferrari is faster than Ford.' (Mine Güven, p.c.)

(74) adnominal (Güven, 2010, 5)
 a. *Çok kitap okurum.*
 a lot book read
 'I read a lot of books.'
 b. *Çok su içerim.*
 a lot water drink
 'I drink a lot of water.'

References

Abeillé, Anne, Jenny Doetjes, Adrie Molendijk & Henriëtte de Swart. 2004. Adverbs and quantification. In Francis Corblin & Henriëtte de Swart (eds.), *Handbook of French Semantics*, 185–209. Stanford: CSLI Publications.

Abeillé, Anne & Danièle Godard. 2003. The Syntactic Flexibility of French Degree Adverbs. In Stefan Müller (ed.), *Proceedings of the HPSG03 Conference Michigan State University, East Lansing*, CSLI Publications. http://csli-publications.stanford.edu/.

Alba-Salas, Josep. 2004. Lexically Selected Expletives: Evidence from Basque and Romance. *SKY Journal of Linguistics* 17. 35–100.

Alexiadou, Artemis & Gianina Iordăchioaia. 2014. The psych causative alternation. *Lingua* 148. 53–79.

Allan, Robin, Philip Holmes & Tom Lundskaer-Nielsen. 1995. *Danish: A Comprehensive Grammar*. London: Routledge.

Anderson, Curt & Marcin Morzycki. 2015. Degrees as kinds. *Natural Language and Linguistic Theory* 33. 791–828.

Andersson, Sven-Gunnar. 1989. On the Generalization of Progressive Constructions. *Ich bin das Buch am Lesen* - status and usage in three Varieties of German. In Lars-Gunnar Larsson (ed.), *Proceedings of the Second Scandinavian Symposium on Aspectology*, 95–106. Uppsala: Almqvist & Winkel.

Arad, Maya. 1998. Psych-notes. *UCL Working Paper in Linguistics* 10. 1–22.

Armoskaite, Solveiga. 2012. Effects of pluractional suffixes: Evidence from Lithuanian. In Diane Massam (ed.), *Mass-Count Across Languages*, 129–145. Oxford: Oxford University Press.

REFERENCES

Atkins, Beryl T., Judy Kegl & Beth Levin. 1988. Anatomy of a Verb Entry: from Linguistic Theory to Lexicographic Practice. *International Journal of Lexicography* 1(2). 84–126.

Atkins, Beryl T. & Beth Levin. 1991. Admitting Impediments. In Zernik Uri (ed.), *Lexical Acquisiton: Exploiting On-Line Resources to Build a Lexicon*, 233–262. Hillsdale, NJ: Lawrence Erlbaum.

Bach, Emmon. 1986. The Algebra of Events. *Linguistics and Philosophy* 9. 5–16.

Baker, Mark C. 1988. *Incorporation: A Theory of Grammatical Function Changing*. Chicago: The University of Chicago Press.

Barsalou, Lawrence. 1992a. *Cognitive Psychology. An overview for cognitive scientists*. Hillsdale, NJ: Lawrence Erlbaum.

Barsalou, Lawrence. 1992b. Frames, concepts, and fields. In Adrienne Lehrer & Eva F. Kittay (eds.), *Frames, fields, and contrasts*, 21–74. Hillsdale, NJ: Lawrence Erlbaum.

Barwise, Jon & Robin Cooper. 1981. Generalized Quantifiers and Natural Language. *Linguistics and Philosophy* 4. 159–219.

Beavers, John. 2006. *Argument/Oblique Alternations and the Structure of Lexical Meaning*. Stanford: Stanford University dissertation.

Beavers, John. 2008. Scalar complexity and the structure of events. In Johannes Dölling, Tatjana Heyde-Zybatow & Martin Schäfer (eds.), *Event Structures in Linguistic Form and Interpretation*, 245–265. Berlin/New York: de Gruyter.

Beavers, John. 2012. Lexical Aspect and Multiple Incremental Themes. In Violeta Demonte & Louise McNally (eds.), *Telicity, Change, and State: A Cross-Categorial View of Event Structure*, 23–59. Oxford: Oxford University Press.

Beavers, John. 2013. Aspectual classes and scales of change. *Linguistics* 51(4). 681–706.

Beavers, John & Andrew Koontz-Garboden. 2012. Manner and Result in the Roots of Verbal Meaning. *Linguistic Inquiry* 43(3). 331–369.

Beavers, John & Andrew Koontz-Garboden. 2013. Complications in dignosing lexical meaning: A rejoinder to Horvath and Siloni. *Lingua* 134. 210–218.

Beavers, John & Cala Zubair. 2013. Anticausatives in Sinhala - involitivity and causer suppression. *Natural Language and Linguistic Theory* 31. 1–46.

Beck, Sigrid. 2005. There and Back Again: A Semantic Analysis. *Journal of Semantics* 22. 3–51.

Belletti, Adriana & Luigi Rizzi. 1988. Psych-Verbs and θ-Theory. *Natural Language and Linguistic Theory* 6(3). 291–352.

Beltrama, Andrea & Ryan Bochnak. 2015. Intensification without degrees cross-linguistically. *Natural Language and Linguistic Theory* 33(3). 843–879.

Ben-Ze'ev, Aaron. 2001. *The Subtlety of Emotions*. Cambridge, Mass.: MIT Press.

Bennett, Michael & Barbara Partee. 1972. *Towards the logic of tense and aspect in English*. Bloomington: iULC.

Berghäll, Liisa. 2010. *Mauwake reference grammar*. Helsinki: University of Helsinki dissertation.

Bhat, D.N.S. & Regina Pustet. 2000. Adjectives. In Geert Booji, Christian Lehmann & Joachim Mugdan (eds.), *Morphologie. Ein internationales Handbuch zur Flexion und Wortbildung*, 757–769. Berlin/New York: de Gruyter.

Bhatt, Rajesh & Roumyana Pancheva. 2004. Late merger of degree clauses. *Linguistic Inquiry* 35(1). 1–45.

Bhatt, Rajesh & Roumyana Pancheva. 2006. Implicit Arguments. In Martin Everaert & Henk van Riemsdijk (eds.), *The Blackwell Companion to Syntax*, 554–584. Malden: Blackwell.

REFERENCES

Biedermann, Reinhard. 1969. *Die deutschen Gradadverbien*. Heidelberg: University of Heidelberg dissertation.

Bierwisch, Manfred. 1989. The Semantics of Gradation. In Manfred Bierwisch & Ewald Lang (eds.), *Dimensional Adjectives*, 71–261. Berlin: Springer.

Bobalijk, Jonathan David. 2012. *Universals in Comparative Morphology*. Cambridge, Mass.: The MIT Press.

Bochnak, Ryan. 2013a. *Cross-linguistic Variation in the Semantics of Comparatives*. Chicago: The University of Chicago dissertation.

Bochnak, Ryan. 2013b. Two Sources of Scalarity within the Verb Phrase. In Boban Arsenijecvić, Berit Gehrke & Rafael Marín (eds.), *Studies in the Composition and Decomposition of Event Predicates*, 99–124. Dordrecht: Springer.

Bochnak, Ryan. 2015. The Degree Semantics Parameter and Cross-linguistic Variation. *Semantics and Pragmatics* 8. 1–48.

Bohnemeyer, Jürgen & Robert D. Van Valin. 2013. The Macro-Event Property and the Layered Structure of the Clause. Manuscirpt: The State University of New York at Buffalo & Heinrich-Heine University Düesseldorf.

Bolinger, Dwight. 1967. Adjective comparison: a Semantic Scale. *Journal of English Linguistics* 1(2). 2–10.

Bolinger, Dwight. 1972. *Degree words*. The Hague: Mouton.

Borik, Olga. 2006. *Aspect and Reference Time*. Oxford: Oxford University Press.

Bosque, Ignacio & Pascual Masullo. 1998. On Verbal Quantification in Spanish. In Olga Fullana & Francesc Roca (eds.), *Studies on the Syntax of Central Romance Languages*, 9–63. Girona: Universitat de Girona.

Bouchard, David-Étienne & Heather Burnett. 2007. Quantification at a distance across varieties of French: a critical review of the literature. In Dans M. Radisic (ed.), *Proceedings of the 2007 annual conference of the Canadian Linguistics Association*, http://homes.chass.utoronto.ca/ ~cla-acl/actes2007/Couchard_Burnett.pdf.

Broadwell, George Aaron. 2006. *A Choctaw Reference Grammar.* London: Lincoln.

Butler, Christopher S. 2003. *Structure and Function. A Guide to Three Major Structural Functional Theories. Part 1: Approaches to the simplex clause.* Amsterdam/Philadelphia: John Benjamins.

Carlson, Gregory. 1977. *Reference to kinds in English.* Amherst, MA: University of Massachusetts dissertation.

Carpenter, Bob. 1992. *The Logic of Typed Feature Structures.* Cambridge: Cambridge University Press.

Carstensen, Kai-Uwe. 2013. A cognitivist semantics of gradation. *Zeitschrift für Sprachwissenschaft* 32(2). 181–219.

Caudal, Patrick. 2005. Degree scales and aspect. In Bart Hollebrandse, Angeliek van Hout & Co Vet (eds.), *Crosslinguistic views on Tense, Aspect and Modality. Cahiers Chronos 13*, 103–118. Amsterdam/Paris/New York: Rodopi.

Caudal, Patrick & David Nicolas. 2005. Types of degrees and types of event structure. In Claudia Maienborn & Angelika Wöllstein (eds.), *Event Arguments: Foundations and Applications*, 277–299. Tübingen: Niemeyer.

Chief, Liangcheng. 2007. *Scalarity and Incomplete Event Descriptions in Mandarin Chinese.* Buffalo: State University of New York at Buffalo dissertation.

Chierchia, Gennaro. 2004. A semantics for unaccusatives and its syntactic consequences. In Artemis Alexiadou, Elena Anagnostopoulou & Martin Everaert (eds.), *The Unaccusativity Puzzle*, 22–59. Oxford: Oxford University Press.

Chomsky, Noam. 1995. *The Minimalist Program.* Cambridge, Mass.: The MIT Press.

REFERENCES

Chui, Kawai. 2000. Morphologization of the Degree Adverb *hen*. *Language and Linguistics* 1(1). 45–49.

Chung, Sandra & William Ladusaw. 2004. *Restriction and Saturation*. Cambridge, Mass.: The MIT Press.

Cinque, Guglielmo. 1999. *Adverbs and Functional Heads*. Oxford: Oxford University Press.

Cinque, Guglielmo & Luigi Rizzi. 2008. The Cartography of Syntactic Structures. *STiL - Studies in Linguistics* 2. 42–58.

Comrie, Bernard. 1976. *Aspect*. Cambridge: Cambridge University Press.

Cresswell, Max J. 1976. The Semantics of Degree. In Barbara Partee (ed.), *Montague Grammar*, 261–292. New York: Academic Press.

Croft, William. 1991. *Syntactic Categories and Grammatical Relations: The Cognitive Organization of Information*. Chicago: University of Chicago Press.

Croft, William. 2012. *Verbs – Aspect and Causal Structure*. Oxford: Oxford University Press.

Czardybon, Adrian & Jens Fleischhauer. 2014. Definiteness and Perfectivity in Telic Incremental Theme Predications. In Doris Gerland, Christian Horn, Anja Latrouite & Albert Ortmann (eds.), *Meaning and Grammar of Nouns and Verbs*, 373–400. Düsseldorf: Düsseldorf University Press.

Deo, Ashwini, Itamat Francez & Andrew Koontz-Garboden. 2013. From change to value difference in degree achievements. In *Proceedings of SALT*, vol. 23, 97–115.

Doetjes, Jenny. 1997. *Quantifiers and Selection*. Dordrecht: Holland Institute of Generative Linguistics.

Doetjes, Jenny. 2007. Adverbs and quantification: Degree versus frequency. *Lingua* 117. 685–720.

Doetjes, Jenny. 2008. Adjectives and degree modification. In Louise McNally & Christopher Kennedy (eds.), *Adjectives and Adverbs - Syntax, Semantics and Discourse*, 123–155. Oxford: Oxford University Press.

Doetjes, Jenny. 2012. Count/mass distinctions across languages. In Claudia Maienborn, Klaus von Heusinger & Paul Portner (eds.), *Semantics: An Iinternational Handbook of Natural Language Meaning, Part iii*, 2559–2580. Berlin: De Gruyter.

Dowty, David. 1979. *Word Meaning and Montague Grammar*. Dordrecht: Reidel.

Dowty, David. 1991. Thematic Proto-Roles and Argument Selection. *Language* 67. 547–619.

Ebert, Karen. 2000. Progressive markers in Germanic languages. In Östen Dahl (ed.), *Tense and Aspect in the Languages of Europe*, 605–653. Berlin: Mouton de Gruyter.

Edel, Karen. 1992. Russische und bulgarische Ausdrucksmittel für Intensität auf wortbildender, lexikalischer und Phrasemebene. *Zeitschrift für Slawistik* 37. 601–609.

Engelberg, Stefan. 1994. Ereignisstrukturen: Zur Syntax und Semantik von Verben. Tech. rep. Theorie des Lexikons, Arbeitens des Sonderforschungsbereichs 282 Universität Wuppertal.

Eriksen, Pål, Seppo Kittilä & Leena Kolehmainen. 2010. The linguistics of weather – Crosslinguistic patterns of mereological expressions. *Studies in Language* 34(3). 565–601.

Ernst, Thomas. 2002. *The Syntax of Adjuncts*. Cambridge: Cambridge University Press.

Esau, Helmut. 1973. Form and Function of German Adjective Endings. *Folia Linguistica* 6. 136–145.

Eschenbach, Carola. 1995. *Zählangaben – Maßangaben: Bedeutung und konzeptuelle Interpretation von Numeralia*. Wiesbaden: Deutscher Universitätsverlag.

Faraclas, Nicholas. 1984. *A Grammar of Obolo*. Indiana University, Bloomington: Studies in African Grammatical Systems.

REFERENCES

Filip, Hana. 1996. Psychological Predicates and the Syntax-Semantics Interface. In Adele Goldberg (ed.), *Conceptual Structure, Discourse and Language*, 131–147. Stanford: CSLI Publications.

Filip, Hana. 1999. *Aspect, Eventuality Types and Noun Phrase Semantics*. New York/London: Garland.

Filip, Hana. 2000. The Quantization Puzzle. In Carol Tenny & James Pustejovsky (eds.), *Events as Grammatical Objects*, 39–93. Stanford: CSLI Publications.

Filip, Hana. 2005. On Accumulating and Having it All: Perfectivity, Prefixes and Bare Arguments. In Henk Verkuyl, Henriette de Swart & Angeliek van Hout (eds.), *Perspectives on Aspect*, 125–148. Dordrecht: Springer.

Filip, Hana & Gregory Carlson. 1997. Sui Generis Genericity. In *Penn Working Papers in Linguistics. vol. 4.*, 91–110. Philadelphia: The University of Pennsylvania.

Fillmore, Charles J. 1968. The case of case. In Emond Bach & Robert T. Harms (eds.), *Universals in Linguistic Theory*, 1–88. New York: Holt, Rinehart and Winston.

Fleischhauer, Jens. 2013. Interaction of telicity and degree gradation in change of state verbs. In Boban Arsenijević, Berit Gehrke & Rafael Marín (eds.), *Studies in the Composition and Decomposition of Event Predicates*, 125–152. Dordrecht: Springer.

Fleischhauer, Jens. 2015. Activation of attributes in frames. In V. Pirrelli, C. Marzi & M. Ferro (eds.), *Word structure and word usage*, 58–62. http://ceur-ws.org.

Fleischhauer, Jens & Thomas Gamerschlag. 2014. We are going through changes: How change of state verbs and arguments combine in scale composition. *Lingua* 141. 30–47.

Fleischhauer, Jens, Thomas Gamerschlag & Wiebke Petersen. 2014. Bleeding, droning and yowling in(to) frames. Talk at the' 4th Conference on Concept Types and Frames in Language, Cognition, and Science'. Heinrich-Heine University, Düsseldorf.

Foley, William & R. D. Van Valin. 1984. *Functional Syntax and Universal Grammar*. Cambridge: Cambridge University Press.

Fortuin, Egbert. 2008. Frequency, iteration and quantity: the semantics of expressions of frequent repetition in Russian and their relationship to aspect. *Russian Linguistics* 32. 203–243.

Frense, J. & P. Bennett. 1996. Verb Alternations and Semantic Classes in English and German. *Language Science* 18(1-2). 205–217.

Gabbay, Dov M. & Julius M. Moravcsik. 1980. Verbs, events, and the flow of time. In Christian Rohrer (ed.), *Time, Tense, and Quantifiers*, 59–83. Tübingen: Niemeyer.

Gallego, Ángel J. & Aritz Irurtzun. 2010. Verbal Quantification in Romance. Handout of a talk at the 'Workshop on Verb meaning, Event Semantics, and Argument Structure'. Universitat Autònoma de Barcelona, Barcelona.

Gamerschlag, Thomas. 2014. Stative Dimensional Verbs in German. *Studies in Language* 8(2). 275–334.

Gamerschlag, Thomas, Wilhelm Geuder & Wiebke Petersen. 2014. Glück auf, der Steiger kommt: a frame account of extensional and intensional *steigen*. In Doris Gerland, Chirstian Horn, Anja Latrouite & Albert Ortmann (eds.), *Meaning and Grammar of Nouns and Verbs*, 115–144. Düsseldorf: Düsseldorf University Press.

Gamerschlag, Thomas & Wiebke Petersen. 2012. An analysis of the evidential use of German perception verbs. In Christopher Hart (ed.), *Selected papers from UK-CLA Meetings*, vol. 1, 1–18.

Gärdenfors, Peter. 2000. *Conceptual Spaces*. Cambridge, MA: MIT Press.

Garey, Howard. 1957. Verbal Aspect in French. *Language* 33(2). 91–110.

Gary, Edward Norman. 1979. *Extent in English – A Unified Account of Degree and Quantity*. Los Angeles: University of California dissertation.

REFERENCES

Gawron, Mark. 2009. The Lexical Semantics of Extent Verbs. Manuscript: San Diego State University. http://www-rohan.sdsu.edu/gawron/submitted_sparial_aspect.pdf.

Gehrke, Berit. 2008. *Ps in motion: On the semantics and syntax of P elements and motion events.* Nederlands Graduate School of Linguistics: LOT Dissertation Series.

Gerling, Martin & Norbert Orthen. 1979. *Deutsche Zustands- und Bewegungsverben. Eine Untersuchung zu ihrer semantischen Struktur und Valenz.* Tübingen: Narr.

Gisborne, Nikolas. 2010. *The event structure of perception verbs.* Oxford: Oxford University Press.

Glinert, Lewis. 1989. *The Grammar of Modern Hebrew.* Cambridge: Cambridge University Press.

Gnutzmann, Claus. 1975. Some Aspects of Grading. *English Studies* 56. 421–433.

Goldberg, Adele. 2005. Argument realization: The role of constructions, lexical semantics and discourse factors. In Jan-Ola Ostman & Mirjam Fried (eds.), *Construction Grammars: Cognitive Grounding and Theoretical Extensions,* 17–43. Amsterdam: John Benjamins.

Gonzáles-Díaz, Victorina. 2008. Recent developments in English intensifiers: the case of *very much.* *English Language and Linguistics* 12(2). 221–243.

Gordon, Lynn. 1986. *Maricopa Morphology and Syntax.* Berkeley: University of California Press.

Grano, Thomas. 2012. Mandarin *hen* and Universal Markedness in gradable adjectives. *Natural Language and Linguistic Theory* 30. 513–565.

Grano, Thomas & Christopher Kennedy. 2012. Mandarin Transitive Comparatives and the Grammar of Measurement. *Journal of East Asian Linguistics* 21. 219–266.

Grimshaw, Jane. 1990. *Argument Structure.* Cambridge, Mass.: MIT Press.

Güven, Mine. 2010. Underspecification in a degree modifier: The case of *çok* 'very much, well' in Turkish. Manuscript: Beykent University.

Hale, Kenneth. 2000. A Uto-Aztecan (O'odham) reflection of a general limit on predicate argument structure. In Eugene Casad & Thomas Willett (eds.), *Uto-Aztecan – structural, temporal, and geographic perspectives*, 155–169. Hermosillo, Sonora: Univ. de Sonora.

Hale, Kenneth & Samuel Jay Keyser. 1993. On argument structure and the lexical expression of syntactic relations. In Kenneth Hale & Samuel Jay Keyser (eds.), *The View from Building 20: A Festschrift for Sylvain Bromberger*, 53–108. Cambridge, Mass.: MIT Press.

Harley, Heidi. 2005. How Do Verbs Get Their Name? Denominal verbs, Manner incorporation, and the Ontology of Verb Roots in English. In Nomi Erteschik-Shir & Tova Rapoport (eds.), *The Syntax of Aspect*, 42–64. Oxford: Oxford University Press.

Härtl, Holden. 2001. *CAUSE und CHANGE. Thematische Relationen und Ereignisstrukturen in Konzeptualisierung und Grammatikalisierung.* Berlin: Akademie.

Haspelmath, Martin. 1993. More on the typology of inchoative/causative verb alternations. In Bernard Comrie & Maria Polinsky (eds.), *Causatives and transitivity*, 87–120. Amsterdam: Benjamins.

Haspelmath, Martin. 2001. Non-canonical marking of core arguments in European languages. In Alexandra Aikhenvald, Robert M. W. Dixon & Masayuki Onishi (eds.), *Non-canonical Marking of Subjects and Objects*, 53–83. Amsterdam: John Benjamins.

Hay, Jennifer, Christopher Kennedy & Beth Levin. 1999. Scalar structure underlies telicity in "degree achievements". In Tanya Mathews & Devon Strolovitch (eds.), *Salt IX*, 127–144. Ithaca: CLC Publications.

Heidinger, Steffen. 2012. Frequenz und die Kodierung der Kausativ-Antikausativ-Alternation im Französischen. *Romanistisches Jahrbuch* 62. 31–58.

REFERENCES

Hoeksema, Jack. 1983. Plurality and Conjunction. In Alice ter Meulen (ed.), *Studies in Model-theoretic Semantics*, 63–83. Dordrecht: Foris.

Holmes, Philip & Ian Hinchliff. 2008. *Swedish: A Comprehensive Grammar*. New York: Routledge.

Horn, Lawrence. 1969. A presuppositional analysis of *only* and *even*. CLS 5. 98–107.

Horn, Lawrence. 1989. *A Natural History of Negation*. Chicago: University of Chicago Press.

Horn, Lawrence. 1998. Towards a New Taxonomy for Pragmatic Inference – Q-Based and R-Based Implicatures. In Asa Kasher (ed.), *Pragmatics - Critical Concepts*, vol. 4, 383–418. London: Routledge.

Horvath, Julia & Tal Siloni. 2011. Anticausatives: Against reflexivization. *Lingua* 121. 2176–2186.

Jackendoff, Ray. 1972. *Semantic Interpretation in Generative Grammar*. Cambridge, Mass.: MIT Press.

Jackendoff, Ray. 1983. *Semantics and Cognition*. Cambridge, Mass.: MIT Press.

Jelinek, Eloise & Maryann Willie. 1998. "Psych" Verbs in Navajo. In Eloise Jelinek, Sally Midgette, Karen Rice & Leslie Saxon (eds.), *Athabaskan Language Studies. Essays in Honor of Robert W. Young*, 15–34. Albuquerque: University of New Mexico Press.

Kagan, Olga. 2015. *Scalarity in the Verbal Domain: The Case of Verbal Prefixation in Russian*. Cambridge: Cambridge University Press.

Kallmeyer, Laura & Rainer Osswald. 2013. Syntax-driven semantic frame composition in Lexicalized Tree Adjoining Grammars. *Journal of Language Modelling* 1(2). 267–330.

Kardos, Éva. 2012. *Towards a scalar analysis of telicity in Hungarian*. Debrecen: University of Debrecen dissertation.

Karttunen, Lauri. 1975. On the Syntax of the word *paljon* in Finnish. In Paul Hallap (ed.), *Congressus tertinus internationalis fenno-ugristarum, I: Acta linguistica*, 227–235. Tallinn: Valgus.

Katz, E. Graham. 1995. *Stativity, Genericity, and Temporal Reference*. Rochester, NY: University of Rochester, New York dissertation.

Kaufmann, Ingrid & Dieter Wunderlich. 1998. Cross-linguistic patterns of resultatives. Tech. Rep. 109 Theorie des Lexikons, Arbeiten des Sonderforschungsbereichs 282, Heinrich-Heine Universität Düsseldorf.

Kawaletz, Lea & Ingo Plag. 2015. Predicting the Semantics of English Nominalizations: A Frame-Based Analysis of *-ment* Suffixation. In Laurie Bauer, Lívia Körtvélyessy & Pavol Stekauer (eds.), *Semantics of Complex Words*, 289–319. Heidelberg/New York: Springer.

Kearns, Kate. 2007. Telic senses of deadjectival verbs. *Lingua* 117. 26–66.

Kennedy, Christopher. 1999a. Gradable adjectives denote measure functions, not partial functions. *Studies in Linguistic Sciences* 29(1). 65–80.

Kennedy, Christopher. 1999b. *Projecting the Adjective – The Syntax and Semantics of Gradability and Comparison*. New York: Garland.

Kennedy, Christopher. 2001. Polar Opposition and the Ontology of 'Degrees'. *Linguistics and Philosophy* 24. 33–70.

Kennedy, Christopher. 2007. Vagueness and grammar: the semantics of relative and absolute gradable adjectives. *Linguistics and Philosophy* 30(1). 1–45.

Kennedy, Christopher. 2012. The Composition of Incremental Changes. In Violeta Demonte & Louise McNally (eds.), *Telicity, Change, State: A Cross-linguistic View of Event Structure*, 103–138. Oxford: Oxford University Press.

Kennedy, Christopher & Beth Levin. 2008. The adjectival core of degree achievements. In Louise McNally & Christopher Kennedy (eds.), *Adjectives and Adverbs: Syntax, Semantics and Discourse*, 156–182. Oxford: Oxford University Press.

REFERENCES

Kennedy, Christopher & Louise McNally. 1999. From Event Structure to Scale Structure: Degree Modification in Deverbal Adjectives. In Tanya Matthews & Devon Strolovitch (eds.), *Proceedings of Semantics and Linguistics Theory 9*, 163–180. Ithaca: CLC Publications.

Kennedy, Christopher & Louise McNally. 2005a. Scale Structure, Degree Modification, and the Semantics of Gradable Predicates. *Language* 81(2). 345–381.

Kennedy, Christopher & Louise McNally. 2005b. The Syntax and Semantics of Multiple Degree Modification in English. In Stefan Müller (ed.), *The Proceedings of the 12th International Conference on Head-Driven Phrase Structure Grammar*, 178–191. Stanford, CA: CSLI Publications.

Kirschbaum, Ilja. 2002. *Schrecklich nett und voll verrückt – Muster der Adjektivintensivierung im Deutschen*. Düsseldorf: Heinrich-Heine Universität Düsseldorf dissertation.

Klein, Ewan. 1980. A Semantics for Positive and Comparative Adjectives. *Linguistics and Philosophy* 4. 1–45.

Klein, Ewan. 1982. The interpretation of adjectival comparatives. *Journal of Linguistics* 18. 113–136.

Klein, Katharina & Silvia Kutscher. 2005. Lexical Economy and Case Selection of Psych-Verbs in German. Manuscript: University of Bochum. http://www.linguistics.ruhr-uni-bochum.de/~klein/papers/LexEconPsych.pdf.

Koenig, Jean-Pierre & Liangcheng Chief. 2008. Scalarity and state-changes in Mandarin, Hindi, Tamil, and Thai. In Oliver Bonami & Patricia Cabredo Hofherr (eds.), *Empirical Issues in Syntax and Semantics 7*, 241–262. http://www.cssp.cnrs.fr/eiss7/index_en.html.

Koenig, Jean-Pierre & Nuttanart Muansuwan. 2000. How to end without ever finishing: Thai semi-perfective markers. *Journal of Semantics* 17. 147–184.

Koontz-Garboden, Andrew. 2009. Anticausativization. *Natural Language and Linguistic Theory* 27. 77–138.

Koontz-Garboden, Andrew. 2012. The monotonicity hypothesis. In Violeta Demonte & Louise McNally (eds.), *Telicity, Change, and State: A Cross-Categorial View of Event Structure*, 139–161. Oxford: Oxford University Press.

Krifka, Manfred. 1986. *Nominalreferenz und Zeitkonstitution*. München: Fink.

Krifka, Manfred. 1990. Four Thousand Ships Passed Through the Lock – Object-Induced Measure Functions on Events. *Linguistic and Philosophy* 13. 487–520.

Krifka, Manfred. 1991. Massennomina. In Dieter von Stechow, Arnim und Wunderlich (ed.), *Semantik - Ein internationales Handbuch zeitgenössischer Forschung*, 399–417. Berlin: de Gruyter.

Krifka, Manfred. 1998. The Origins of Telicity. In Susan Rothstein (ed.), *Events and Grammar*, 197–235. Dordrecht: Kluwer.

Krifka, Manfred & Sabine Zerbian. 2008. Quantification Across Bantu Languages. In Lisa Matthewson (ed.), *Quantification: A cross-linguistic perspective*, 383–414. Bingley: Emerald.

Kriz, Manuel. 2011. Issues in the Semantics of Degree Achievements. Diploma-Thesis, University of Vienna.

Landman, Fred. 1992. The progressive. *Natural Language Semantics* 1. 1–32.

Lang, Ewald. 1990. Primary Perceptual Space and Inherent Proportion Schema: Two Interacting Categorization Grids Underlying the Conceptualization of Spatial Objects. *Journal of Semantics* 7. 121–141.

Legendre, Géraldine. 1989. Inversion with certain French experiencer verbs. *Language* 65(4). 752–782.

Leisi, Ernst. 1971. *Der Wortinhalt*. Heidelberg: UTB.

Levin, Beth. 1991. Building a Lexicon: The Contribution of Linguistics. *International Journal of Lexicography* 4(3). 205–226.

REFERENCES

Levin, Beth. 1993. *English verb classes and alternations.* Chicago: Chicago University Press.

Levin, Beth. 1999. Objecthood: An event structure perspective. *CLS* 35(1). 223–247.

Levin, Beth & Jason Grafmiller. 2013. Do you always fear what frightens you? In Tracy Holloway King & Annie de Paiva (eds.), *From Quirky Case to Representing Space: Papers in Honor of Annie Zaenen*, 21–32. Stanford, CA: CSLI Online Publications.

Levin, Beth & Malka Rappaport Hovav. 1995. *Unaccusativity.* Cambridge, Mass.: MIT Press.

Levin, Beth & Malka Rappaport Hovav. 2005. *Argument Realization.* Cambridge: Cambridge University Press.

Levin, Beth & Malka Rappaport Hovav. 2011. Lexical Conceptual Structure. In Claudia Maienborn, Klaus von Heusinger & Paul Portner (eds.), *Semantics: An International Handbook of Natural Language Meaning*, vol. 1 (HSK), 420–440. Berlin/New York: de Gruyter.

Levin, Beth & Malka Rappaport Hovav. 2013. Lexicalized Meaning and Manner/Result Complementarity. In Boban Arsenijević, Berit Gehrke & Rafael Marín (eds.), *Studies in the Composition and Decomposition of Event Predicates*, 49–70. Dordrecht: Springer.

Levin, Beth, Grace Song & Beryl Atkins. 1997. Making Sense of Corpus Data: A Case Study of Verbs of Sound. *International Journal of Corpus Linguistics* 2. 23–64.

Lewis, David. 1975. Adverbs of quantification. In Edward Keenan (ed.), *Formal Semantics of Natural Language*, 3–15. Cambridge: Cambridge University Press.

Li, Charles & Sandra Thompson. 1989. *Mandarin Chinese: A functional reference grammar.* Berkeley: University of California Press.

Liu, Chen-Sheng Luther. 2010. The positive morpheme in Chinese and adjectival structure. *Lingua* 120. 1010–1056.

Löbner, Sebastian. 1979. *Intensionale Verben und Funktionalbegriffe.* Tübingen: Niemeyer.

Löbner, Sebastian. 1981. Intensional verbs and functional concepts: more on the "rising temperature" problem. *Linguistic Inquiry* 12(3). 471–477.

Löbner, Sebastian. 1985. Definites. *Journal of Semantics* 4. 279–326.

Löbner, Sebastian. 1987a. Natural Language and Generalized Quantifier Theory. In Peter Gärdenfors (ed.), *Generalized Quantifiers*, 181–201. Dordrecht: Reidel.

Löbner, Sebastian. 1987b. Quantification as a Major Module of Natural Language Semantics. In Jeroen Groenendijk, Dick de Jongh & Martin Stokhof (eds.), *Studies in Discourse Representation Theory and the Theory of Generalized Quantifiers*, 53–85. Dordrecht: Foris.

Löbner, Sebastian. 1990. *Wahr neben Falsch.* Tübingen: Niemeyer.

Löbner, Sebastian. 2002. Is the German Perfekt a perfect Perfect? In Ingrid Kaufmann & Barbara Stiebels (eds.), *More than Words*, 369–391. Berlin: Akademie-Verlag.

Löbner, Sebastian. 2011a. Concept Types and Determination. *Journal of Semantics* 28(3). 279–333.

Löbner, Sebastian. 2011b. Dual oppositions in lexical meaning. In Claudia Maienborn, Klaus von Heusinger & Paul Portner (eds.), *Semantics: An International Handbook of Natural Language Meaning*, vol. 1 (HSK), 479–506. Berlin/New York: de Gruyter.

Löbner, Sebastian. 2012a. Functional concepts and frames. Manuscript: Heinrich-Heine University Düsseldorf. http://semanticsarchive.net/Archive/jl1NGEwO/Loebner_Functional_Concepts_and_Frames.pdf.

Löbner, Sebastian. 2012b. Sub-compositionality. In Markus Werning, Wolfram Hinzen & Edouard Machery (eds.), *The Oxford Handbook of Compositionality*, 220–241. Oxford: Oxford University Press.

Löbner, Sebastian. 2013. *Understanding Semantics.* Albington: Routledge 2nd edn.

REFERENCES

Löbner, Sebastian. 2014. Evidence for frames from human language. In Thomas Gamerschlag, Doris Gerland, Rainer Osswald & Wiebke Petersen (eds.), *Frames and Concept Types: Applications in Language and Philosophy*, 23–68. Heidelberg/New York: Springer.

Löbner, Sebastian. to appear. The semantics of nominals. In Nick Riemer (ed.), *The Routledge Handbook of Semantics*, London/ New York: Routledge.

Lüpke, Friederike. 2005. *A grammar of Jalonke argument structure*. Mijmegen: Radboud Universiteit Nijmegen dissertation.

Maienborn, Claudia. 1996. *Situation und Lokation. Die Bedeutung lokaler Adjunkte von Verbalprojektionen*. Tübingen: Stauffenburg.

Maienborn, Claudia. 2003. *Die logische Form von Kopula-Sätzen*. Berlin: Akademie.

Marín, Rafael & Louise McNally. 2005. The Aktionsart of Spanish Reflexive Psychological Verbs. In Emar Maier, Corien Bary & Janneke Huitink (eds.), *Proceedings of SuB 9*, 212–225. http://ru.nl/ncs/sub9.

Matsumura, Hiromi. 1996. On Japanese psych-verbs. *Toronto Working Papers in Linguistics* 15. 123–140.

Matthews, Stephen & Virginia Yip. 1994. *Cantonese: A Comprehensive Grammar*. London/New York: Routledge.

McConnell-Ginet, Sally. 1982. Adverbs and Logical Form: A Linguistically Realistic Theory. *Language* 58(1). 144–184.

McIntyre, Andrew. 2003. Preverbs, argument linking and verb semantics. *Yearbook of Morphology* 2003. 119–144.

McKoon, Gail & Talke MacFarland. 2000. Externally and Internally Caused Change of State Verbs. *Language* 76(4). 833–858.

McNally, Louise. to appear. Modification. In Maria Alonim & Paul Dekker (eds.), *Cambridge Handbook of Semantics*, Cambridge: Cambridge University Press.

Mittwoch, Anita. 2013. On the Criteria for Distinguishing Accomplishments from Activities and Two Types of Aspectual Misfits. In Boban Arsenijević, Berit Gehrke & Rafael Marín (eds.), *Studies in the Composition and Decomposition of Event Predicates*, 27–48. Dordrecht: Springer.

Moltmann, Friederike. 1997. *Parts and Wholes in Semantics*. Oxford: Oxford University Press.

Montague, Richard. 1970. Universal Grammar. *Theoria* 36. 373–398.

Montague, Richard. 1973. The proper treatment of quantification in ordinary English. In Jaako Hintikka, J. M. E. Moravcsik & Patrick Suppes (eds.), *Approaches to Natural Language. Proceedings of the 1970 Stanford Workshop on Grammar and Semantics*, 221–242. Dordrecht: Reidel.

Moravcsik, Edith A. 1978. Reduplicative Constructions. In Joseph A. Greenberg (ed.), *Universals of Human Language. Vol. 3 Word Structure*, 297–334. Stanford: Stanford University Press.

Moravcsik, Edith A. 2013. *Introducing Language Typology*. Cambridge: Cambridge University Press.

Morgan, Jerry. 1969. On Arguing About Semantics. *Papers in Linguistics* 1. 49–70.

Mori, Yoshiki, Sebastian Löbner & Katharina Micha. 1992. Aspektuelle Verbklassen im Japanischen. *Zeitschrift für Sprachwissenschaft* 11. 189–215.

Moriena, Claudia & Karen Genschow. 2005. *Große Lerngrammatik Spanisch*. Ismaning: Hueber.

Morzycki, Marcin. 2009. Degree modification of gradable nouns: size adjectives and adnominal degree morphemes. *Natural Language Semantics* 17. 175–203.

Morzycki, Marcin. 2013. Modification. Manuscript: Michigan State University. http://www.msu.edu/~morzycki/work/book/.

Mourelatos, Alexander. 1978. Events, Processes, and States. *Linguistics and Philosophy* 2. 415–434.

REFERENCES

Muroi, Yoshiyuki. 2010. Dimensionsausdrücke: Deutsch/Japanisch kontrastiv. *Linguistische Berichte* 223. 297–329.

Næss, Aashild. 2007. *Prototypical transitivity*. Amsterdam: John Benjamins.

Naumann, Ralf. 2014. Phase Quantification and Frame Theory. In Doris Gerland, Christian Horn, Anja Latrouite & Albert Ortmann (eds.), *Meaning and Grammar of Nouns and Verbs*, 237–265. Düsseldorf: Düsseldorf University Press.

Neeleman, Ad, Hans van de Koot & Jenny Doetjes. 2004. Degree Expressions. *The Linguistic Review* 21. 1–66.

Nicolay, Nathalie. 2007. *Aktionsarten im Deutschen: Prozessualität und Stativität*. Tübingen: Niemeyer.

Obenauer, Hans-Georg. 1984. On the Identification of Empty Categories. *The Linguistic Review* 4. 153–202.

van Os, Charles. 1989. *Aspekte der Intensivierung im Deutschen*. Tübingen: Narr.

Partee, Barbara. 1984. Compositionality. In Fred Landman & Frank Veltman (eds.), *Varieties of Formal Semantics: Proceedings of the 4th Amsterdam Colloquium, Sept. 1982*, 281–312. Dordrecht: Foris.

Partee, Barbara. 1988. Many Quantifiers. In Joyce Powers & Kenneth de Jongh (eds.), *Proceedings of the Fifth Eastern States Conference on Linguistics*, 383–402. Columbus: Ohio State University Press.

Partee, Barbara, Alice ter Meulen & Robert E. Wall. 1990. *Mathematical Methods in Linguistics*. Dordrecht: Kluwer.

Perlmutter, David M. 1978. Impersonal Passives and the Unaccusativity Hypothesis. In *Proceedings of the 4th Annual Meeting of the Berkeley Linguistics Society*, 157–190.

Perlmutter, David M. 1980. Relational grammar. In Edith Moravcsik & Jessica Wirth (eds.), *Syntax and Semantics: Current Approaches to Syntax*, vol. 13, 195–229. New York: Academic Press.

Pesetsky, David. 1995. *Zero Syntax: Experiencer and Cascades.* Cambridge, Mass.: MIT Press.

Petersen, Wiebke. 2007. Representation of Concepts as Frames. In Jurgis Skilters, Fiorenza Toccafondi & Gerhard Stemberger (eds.), *Complex Cognition and Qualitative Science. The Baltic International Yearbook of Cognition, Logic and Communication*, vol. 2, 151–170. Riga: University of Latvia.

Petersen, Wiebke & Thomas Gamerschlag. 2014. Why chocolate eggs can taste old but not oval: A frame.theoretic analysis of inferential evidentials. In Thoms Gamerschlag, Doris Gerland, Rainer Osswald & Wiebke Petersen (eds.), *Frames and concept types: Applications in language and philosophy*, 199–220. Dordrecht: Springer.

Piñón, Christopher. 2005. Adverbs of Completion in an Event Semantics. In Henk Verkuyl, Henriette de Swart & Angeliek van Hout (eds.), *Perspectives on Aspect*, 146–166. Dordrecht: Springer.

Piñón, Christopher. 2008. Aspectual composition with degrees. In Louise McNally & Christopher Kennedy (eds.), *Adjectives and Adverbs*, 183–219. Oxford: Oxford University Press.

Potashnik, Joseph. 2012. Emission Verbs. In Martin Everaert, Marijana Marelj & Tal Siloni (eds.), *The Theta System*, 251–278. Oxford: Oxford University Press.

Pylkkänen, Liina. 1997. The Linking of Event Structure and Grammatical Functions in Finnish. In Miriam Butt & Tracy Holloway KIng (eds.), *Proceedings of the LFG97 Conference*, Stanford: CSLI Publications. http://web.stanford.edu/group/cslipublications/cslipublications/LFG/2/lfg97-toc.html.

Quirk, Randolph, Sidney Greenbaum, Geoffrey Leech & Jan Svartvik. 1985. *A Comprehensive Grammar of the English Language.* London/New York: Erlbaum.

Rapp, Irene. 1997. *Partizipien und semantische Struktur. Zu passivischen Konstruktionen mit dem 3. Status.* Tübingen: Stauffenburg.

REFERENCES

Rappaport Hovav, Malka. 2008. Lexicalized meaning and the internal temporal structure of events. In Susan Rothstein (ed.), *Theoretical and Crosslinguistic Approaches to the Semantics of Aspect*, 13–42. Amsterdam/Philadelphia: John Benjamins.

Rappaport Hovav, Malka & Beth Levin. 1998. Building Verb Meanings. In Miriam Butt & Wilhelm Geuder (eds.), *The Projection of Arguments: Lexical and Compositional Factors*, 97–134. Stanford: CSLI Publications.

Rappaport Hovav, Malka & Beth Levin. 2000. Classifying Single Argument Verbs. In Peter Coopmans, Martin Everaert & Jane Grimshaw (eds.), *Lexical Specification and Insertion*, 269–304. Amsterdam/Philadelphia: John Benjamins.

Rappaport Hovav, Malka & Beth Levin. 2005. Change-of-State Verbs: Implications for Theories of Argument Projection. In Nomi Erteschik-Shir & Tova Rapoport (eds.), *The Syntax of Aspect. Deriving Thematic and Aspectual Interpretation*, 274–286. Oxford: Oxford University Press.

Rappaport Hovav, Malka & Beth Levin. 2010. Reflections on Manner/Result Complementarity. In Malka Rappaport Hovav, Edit Doron & Ivy Sichel (eds.), *Lexical Semantics, Syntax and Event Structure*, 21–38. Oxford: Oxford University Press.

Rappaport Hovav, Malka & Beth Levin. 2012. Lexical Uniformity and the Causative Alternation. In Martin Everaert, Marijana Marelj & Tal Siloni (eds.), *The Theta system*, 150–176. Oxford: Oxford University Press.

Rett, Jessica. 2007. Antonymy and Evaluativity. In T. Friedman & M. Gibson (eds.), *Salt xvii*, 210–227. Ithaca, NY: Cornell University.

Rett, Jessica. 2013. Similatives and the argument structure of verbs. *Natural Language and Linguistic Theory* 32. 1101–1137.

Rice, Karen. 1989. *A Grammar of Slave*. Berlin: Mouton de Gruyter.

Rice, Karen. 2000. *Morpheme Order and Semantic Scope*. Cambridge: Cambridge University Press.

Roberts, John. 1987. *Amele*. London: Croon Holmes.

Ropertz, Ruth. 2001. *Das Wort sehr als Modifikator deutscher Adjektive und Verben.* Heinrich-Heine Universität Düsseldorf MA thesis.

Rosen, Sara Thomas. 1996. Events and verb classification. *Linguistics* 34. 191–223.

Rothmayr, Antonia. 2009. *The Structure of Stative Verbs.* Amsterdam: John Benjamins.

Rothstein, Susan. 2004. *Structuring Events - A Study in the Semantics of Lexical Aspect.* Malden, MA/Oxford: Blackwell.

Rotstein, Carmen & Yoad Winter. 2004. Total adjectives vs. partial adjectives: Scale structure and higher-order modifiers. *Natural Language Semantics* 12(3). 259–288.

Rozwadowska, Bożena. 2007. Various faces of the psych-phenomenon in Polish. In Peter Kosta & Lilia Schürcks (eds.), *Investigations into Formal Slavic Linguistics*, 557–575. Berlin: Peter Lang.

Rullmann, Hotze. 1995. *Maximality in the Semantics of Wh-Constructions.* Amherst, MA: University of Massachusetts at Amherst dissertation.

Sapir, Edward. 1944. Grading: A Study in Semantics. *Philosophy of Science* 11(2). 93–116.

Sassoon, Galit Weidmann. 2010. Measurement theory in linguistics. *Synthese* 174. 151–180.

Schachter, P. 1976. The subject in Philippine languages. In Charles Li (ed.), *Subject and Topic*, 491–518. New York: Academic Press.

Schwarzschild, Roger. 2006. The Role of Dimensions in the Syntax of Noun Phrases. *Syntax* 9(1). 67–110.

Smith, Carlota. 1997. *The Parameter of Aspect.* Dordrecht: Kluwer.

Solt, Stephanie. 2009. *The Semantics of Adjectives of Quantity.* New York: The City University of New York dissertation.

REFERENCES

Solt, Stephanie. 2011. Vagueness in quantity: two case studies from a linguistic perspective. In Petr Cintula, Christian G. Fermueller, Lluis Godo & Petr Hajek (eds.), *Understanding Vagueness. Logical, Philosophical and Linguistic Perspectives*, 157–174. London: College Publicatons.

Sonnenhauser, Barbara. 2010. The event structure of verbs of emotion in Russian. *Russian Linguistics* 34. 331–353.

Stassen, Leon. 1984. The Comparative compared. *Journal of Semantics* 3. 142–182.

Stassen, Leon. 1985. *Comparison and Universal Grammar*. Oxford: Blackwell.

von Stechow, Arnim. 1984. My reaction to Cresswell's, Hellan's, Hoeksema's, and Seuren's comments. *Journal of Semantics* 3. 183–199.

von Stechow, Arnim. 1996. The Different Readings of *Wieder* 'Again': A Structural Account. *Journal of Semantics* 13(2). 87–138.

von Stechow, Arnim. 2008. Topics in Degree Semantics: 4 Lectures. Handout 1: Degrees. Handout. http://www.sfs.uni-tuebingen.de/~astechow/.

Stevens, S. S. 1946. On the Theory of Scales of Measurement. *Science* 103. 677–680.

Stiebels, Barbara. 1996. *Lexikalische Argumente und Adjunkte: Zum semantischen Beitrag von verbalen Präfixen und Partikeln*. Berlin: Akademie-Verlag.

de Swart, Henriëtte. 1993. *Adverbs of quantification: A generalized quantifier approach*. New York: Garland.

de Swart, Henriëtte. 1998. *Introduction to Natural Language Semantics*. Stanford: CSLI Publications.

Sybesma, Rint P. E. 1999. *The Mandarin VP*. Dordrecht: Kluwer.

Talmy, Leonard. 2000. *Towards a cognitive semantics. Vol. 2*. Cambridge, MA: MIT Press.

Tatevosov, Sergej. 2008. Subevental structure and non-culmination. In Oliver Bonami & Patricia Cabredo (eds.), *Empirical Issues in Syntax and Semantics 7*, 393–423. http://www.cssp.cnrs.fr/eiss7.

Tenny, Carol. 1992. The Aspectual Interface Hypothesis. In Ivan Sag & Anna Szabolcsi (eds.), *Lexical Matters*, 1–27. Stanford: CSLI Publications.

Tenny, Carol. 1994. *Aspectual Roles and the Syntax-Semantics Interface*. Dordrecht: Kluwer.

Tenny, Carol. 2000. Core events and adverbial modification. In Carol Tenny & James Pustejovsky (eds.), *Events as Grammatical Objects*, 285–334. Stanford: CSLI Publications.

Travis, Lisa. 2000. Event Structure in Syntax. In Carol Tenny & James Pustejovsky (eds.), *Events as Grammatical Objects*, 145–185. Stanford: CSLI Publications.

Tsujimura, Natsuko. 2001. Degree Words and Scalar Structure in Japanese. *Lingua* 111. 29–52.

Van Valin, Robert D. 1977. *Aspects of Lakhota Syntax*. Berkeley: University of California, Berkeley dissertation.

Van Valin, Robert D. 1980. On the Distribution of Passive and Antipassive Constructions in Universal Grammar. *Lingua* 50. 303–321.

Van Valin, Robert D. 1991. Another Look at Icelandic Case Marking and Grammatical Relations. *Natural Language and Linguistic Theory* 9(1). 145–194.

Van Valin, Robert D. 2005. *Exploring the Syntax-Semantics Interface*. Cambridge: Cambridge University Press.

Van Valin, Robert D. 2008. RPs and the nature of lexical and syntactic categories in Role & Reference Grammar. In Robert D. Jr. Van Valin (ed.), *Investigations of the Syntax-Semantics-Pragmatics Interface*, 161–178. Amsterdam: John Benjamins.

Van Valin, Robert D. & Randy LaPolla. 1997. *Syntax. Structure, meaning & function*. Cambridge: Cambridge University Press.

REFERENCES

Van Valin, Robert D. & David Wilkins. 1996. The case of 'effector': case roles, agents and agency revisited. In Masayoshi Shibatani & Sarah Thompson (eds.), *Grammatical constructions*, 289–322. Oxford: Oxford University Press.

Vecchiato, S. 1999. On the relative order of *beaucoup, guère, peu* and *trop* in french. *University of Venice Working Papers in Linguistics* 9. 255–296.

Vendler, Zeno. 1957. Verbs and Times. *The Philosophical Review* 66(2). 143–160.

Vendler, Zeno. 1967. Verbs and Times. In Zeno Vendler (ed.), *Linguistics in philosophy*, 97–121. Ithaca/NY: Cornell University Press.

Verkuyl, Henk. 1972. *On the compositional nature of the aspects*. Dordrecht: Reidel.

Viberg, Åke. 1984. The verbs of perception: A typological study. In Brian Butterworth (ed.), *Explanations for language universals*, 123–162. Berlin: Mouton.

Viberg, Åke. 2001. Verbs of Perception. In Martin Haspelmath, Ekkehard König, W. Österreicher & W. Raible (eds.), *Language Typology and Language Universals – An International Handbook*, 1295–1309. Berlin: de Gruyter.

Vinet, Marie-Thérèse. 1996. On certain adverbs of quantification in Quebec French. *Probus* 8. 207–221.

van Voorst, Jan. 1992. The Aspectual Semantics of Psychological Verbs. *Linguistics and Philosophy* 15. 65–92.

Schulte im Walde, Sabine. 2006. Experiments on the Automatic Induction of German Semantic Verb Classes. *Computational Linguistics* 32(2). 159–194.

Washio, Ryuichi. 1997. Resultatives, compositionality and language variation. *Journal of East Asian Linguistics* 6. 1–49.

Watters, James. 2009. Tepehua verb morphology, operator scope, and the encoding of arguments. In Lilián Guerrero, Sergio Ibanez Cerda & Valeria A. Belloro (eds.), *Studies in Role & Reference Grammar*, 247–267. Mexico: Universidas Nacional Autónoma de Mexico.

Wegener, Heike. 1998. Die Kasus des EXP. In Marcel Vuillaume (ed.), *Die Kasus im Deutschen*, 71–84. Tübingen: Stauffenburg.

Wellwood, Alexis, Valentine Hacquard & Poumyana Pancheva. 2012. Measuring and Comparing Individuals and Events. *Journal of Semantics* 29. 207–228.

Westney, Paul. 1986. Notes on Scales. *Lingua* 69. 333–354.

Whitley, M. Stanley. 1995. *Gustar* and other Psych Verbs: A Problem in Transitivity. *Hispania* 78(3). 573–585.

Whitt, Richard J. 2009. Auditory evidentiality in English and German: The case of perception verbs. *Lingua* 119. 1083–1095.

Wiese, Heike. 1997. *Zahl und Numerale*. Berlin: Akademie-Verlag.

Wilkins, David P. 1989. *Mparnte Arrernte (Aranda): Studies in the structure and semantics of grammar*. Canberra: Australian National University dissertation.

Wunderlich, Dieter. 1997. Cause and the Structure of Verbs. *Linguistic Inquiry* 28(1). 27–68.

Yoon, Youngeun. 1996. Total an partial predicates and the weak and strong interpretations. *Natural Language Semantics* 4(3). 217–236.

Yu, Alan. 2003. Pluractionality in Chechen. *Natural Language Semantics* 11. 289–321.

Zhang, Niina Ning. 2015. Functional head properties of the degree word *hen* in Mandarin Chinese. *Lingua* 153. 14–41.

Index

adjective
    absolute, 34, 168–170
    closed-scale, 30–34
    gradable, 1, 13, 16–17, 26, 27, 147, 178
    nongradable, 13, 17
    open-scale, 30–34
    relative, 33
adverbial
    degree, 53
    degree/extent, 53
    extent, 53
agentivity, 80, 274, 286
aktionsart, 66–76
alternation, 62
    anticausative, 62–63, 187–189, 273–275
    body-part possessor ascension, 252
    middle, 62–63, 94, 95
aspect, 124, 125, 128, 129
    imperfective, 124, 126, 127, 257, 308
    perfect, 125, 128, 129
    perfective, 124, 308
    progressive, 127, 128, 214, 308
aspectual composition, 310
attribute, 175
    activation, 174–176, 237, 250, 255, 317, 318
    chain, 237, 303

causality, 80–81, 186, 272
change, 86
    direction of, 197
    incremental, 7, 307–309
    non-incremental, 308
    non-scalar, 85
    scalar, 84, 85, 87, 90, 199, 202, 209, 217
comparative, 12–14, 36, 162
comparison, 16
comparison class, 16, 32, 33
compositionality
    homomorphy, 301
    pattern, 298, 303
    principle of, 299
    subcompositionality, 177, 298, 302, 319
cumulativity, 311

degree, 29–30, 146
    differential, 289
    equivalence class, 146
    non-differential, 289
degree achievement, 89, 182–184, 207
degree argument, 150, 160, 162, 164, 166, 170, 172, 178, 202

degree expression, 36, 38–40, 64, 160, 161
    classification, 40–44, 161
    template, 151
degree morphology, 13, 15, 36–38, 147, 149, 150, 170
degree operator, 25–26, 38
degree-event-homomorphism, 307–308
dimension, 27, 28, 193, 198
    non-scalar, 28, 171
    scalar, 28, 171
durativity, 67
dynamicity, 67

end range, 32, 34, 170
endpoint, 32–34, 67, 68, 86, 98, 170, 201, 204, 221, 223
equative, 12
event structure, 66, 83

frame theory, 175, 318

Generalized Quantifier Theory, 24, 156
gradability, 12, 13, 92
gradable property, 17, 18, 26, 175
gradation, 12, 16, 36
    degree, 19–21, 64, 176–178, 247, 289, 297
        extent implicature, 249, 297
        event-dependent, 304, 306
        event-independent, 305
    extent, 19–21, 247

implicit argument, 174, 176, 234–235, 311, 312, 317
incommensurability, 28–29

intensification, *see* gradation
intensifier, 162
    monotone-increasing, 206, 219, 223, 309

measure construction, 12, 13, 151
measure function, 26–27, 147, 150, 170, 190, 199
    extensive, 26
    non-extensive, 26–27
modification, 156–157
modifier
    endpoint, 30, 151
    proportional, 30

norm, *see* standard
noun
    functional, 190–191, 199, 211
    scale-denoting, 190–193, 198, 199, 211, 323

operator, 116, 118
    aspectual, 121
    clausal, 119
    core, 119, 138, 141
    degree, 120, 122
    event quantification, 120–122
    NP, 138
    nucleus, 119, 138
    number, 141

phase quantification, 151–154
positive
    form, 14–16
    null morpheme, 25, 148–172
predicate
    accomplishment, 68, 69, 73–75, 79, 206

INDEX

achievement, 68, 69, 79
activity, 68, 73–75, 78
closed-scale, 30
durative, 75–76
dynamic, 69–84
gradable, 26
open-scale, 30
punctual, 75–76
scalar, 177
semelfactive, 79, 246–247, 249
stative, 68–73, 78

quantification, 19, 23–25, 156–157, 159
    at a distance, 104
quantization, 310

reduplication, 37
root, 82–83

scalarity, 28, 83, 87, 91, 102, 178, 180, 316, 322
scale, 27–30
    activation, 176–177, 237, 242, 255, 299
    closed, 29
    interval, 35
    lexicalization, 39, 64, 90, 174, 177, 192, 196
    multivalue, 86–87, 182
    nominal, 35
    open, 29
    ordinal, 35
    path, 91
    property, 91, 288
    ratio, 35
    source, 176, 295, 298, 322–323

two-point, 86–87, 182
underspecification, 196, 198, 211, 290, 323
volume/extent, 91
scope, 123
    aspect, 133
    degree expression, 133
    operator, 134
standard, 32–35, 149–151, 168
    absolute, 33, 34, 149–150
    context-dependent, 33
    relative, 33, 34
superlative, 12, 14

telicity, 67, 68, 183, 201, 205, 223, 309
telos, 224
    maximum telos, 221, 223–225, 322
    standard telos, 221, 223–225

unselective binder, 22–23

verb
    change of state, 63, 64, 87, 89–91, 93, 94, 112, 170, 174, 179–186, 192, 196, 198, 200, 201, 205, 214, 219, 223, 226, 287, 304, 309, 313, 316, 321
    degree, 61, 92, 97
    emission, 227–235, 261, 287, 289, 310
      light, 229, 242, 243
      smell, 233, 235, 236, 238, 322
      sound, 229, 232, 234, 245, 246, 249, 250
      substance, 64, 173, 234, 251–253, 255, 257, 304, 305, 309, 310, 312, 313, 317, 321

experiencer, 64, 65, 263–271, 273–276, 279, 280, 282, 288, 289, 310
extensional, 180–182, 191, 211
gradable, 2, 5, 27, 45, 46, 61, 173, 176–178, 263, 287, 316, 318
incremental, 90, 93, 94, 183, 311
intensional, 182, 189–190, 192, 193, 195, 199, 211
manner, 84
motion, 65, 90, 91, 93, 94, 100, 193, 294, 296
non-scalar change, 85–90
result, 83, 84, 87
scalar, 61, 83, 85–91, 174, 179, 194, 196
stative dimensional, 171–173, 180, 316